Anglophone Students Abroad

Anglophone students abroad: Identity, social relationships and language learning presents the findings of a major study of British students of French and Spanish undertaking residence abroad. The new dataset presented here provides both quantitative and qualitative information on language learning, social networking and integration and identity development during residence abroad.

The book tracks in detail the language development of participants and relates this systematically to individual participants' social and linguistic experiences and evolving relationship. It shows that language learning is increasingly dependent on students' own agency and skill and the negotiation of identity in multilingual and lingua franca environments.

Rosamond Mitchell is Emeritus Professor of Applied Linguistics in the Department of Modern Languages at the University of Southampton.

Nicole Tracy-Ventura is Assistant Professor of Applied Linguistics in the Department of World Languages at the University of South Florida.

Kevin McManus is Assistant Professor in the Department of Applied Linguistics at Pennsylvania State University.

Anglophone Students Abroad
Identity, social relationships and language learning

Rosamond Mitchell,
Nicole Tracy-Ventura, and
Kevin McManus

LONDON AND NEW YORK

First published 2017
by Routledge

2 Park Square, Milton Park, Abingdon, Oxfordshire OX14 4RN
52 Vanderbilt Avenue, New York, NY 10017

Routledge is an imprint of the Taylor & Francis Group, an informa business

First issued in paperback 2019

Copyright © 2017 Rosamond Mitchell, Nicole Tracy-Ventura, and Kevin McManus

The right of Rosamond Mitchell, Nicole Tracy-Ventura, and Kevin McManus to be identified as the authors of this work has been asserted by them in accordance with sections 77 and 78 of the Copyright, Designs and Patents Act 1988.

All rights reserved. No part of this book may be reprinted or reproduced or utilised in any form or by any electronic, mechanical, or other means, now known or hereafter invented, including photocopying and recording, or in any information storage or retrieval system, without permission in writing from the publishers.

Notice:
Product or corporate names may be trademarks or registered trademarks, and are used only for identification and explanation without intent to infringe.

Library of Congress Cataloging-in-Publication Data
Names: Mitchell, Rosamond, author. | Tracy-Ventura, Nicole, author. | McManus, Kevin (Linguist) author.
Title: Anglophone students abroad : identity, social relationships and language learning / authored by Rosamond Mitchell, Nicole Tracy-Ventura, and Kevin McManus.
Description: New York : Routledge/Taylor & Francis Group, [2017] | Includes bibliographical references.
Identifiers: LCCN 2016046590 | ISBN 9781138940406 (hardback)
Subjects: LCSH: English language—Study and teaching—Foreign countries—Languages. | English language—Social aspects—Foreign speaking countries. | Language and languages—Study and teaching—English speakers. | Intercultural communication—English speaking countries. | Foreign study—Social aspects. | Student mobility. | Sociolinguistics. | Education and globalization.
Classification: LCC PE1128.A2 M5538 2017 | DDC 428.0071—dc23
LC record available at https://lccn.loc.gov/2016046590

ISBN: 978-1-138-94040-6 (hbk)
ISBN: 978-0-367-87436-0 (pbk)

Typeset in Goudy
by Apex CoVantage, LLC

For Paul, Max and Evie Harsch
and
For Ellen and George McManus

Contents

List of figures xii
List of tables xv
Acknowledgements xvii

1 **Introduction** 1
   1.1 Sojourning abroad in an age of global English 1
   1.2 Anglophone traditions in the language-learning sojourn 4
   1.3 Researching the Anglophone language-learning sojourn 7
      1.3.1 An SLA research tradition 7
      1.3.2 Studying the context for L2 development 8
      1.3.3 An emergent sociocultural tradition 9
   1.4 The LANGSNAP project 10
   1.5 Outline of the book 11

2 **Language learning during residence abroad: Key constructs** 18
   2.1 Introduction 18
   2.2 Language 18
      2.2.1 The target language construct and the goals of language education 18
      2.2.2 The ideal of "immersion" 19
      2.2.3 Language variation and plurilingualism in everyday practice 20
      2.2.4 Sojourner perspectives on target language variation and multilingualism 21
      2.2.5 Empirical studies of sojourners' language practices 23
      2.2.6 Language learning and development during the sojourn abroad 24
      2.2.7 The CAF framework 25
   2.3 Identity 28
      2.3.1 Views of identity in SLA 28
      2.3.2 Identity in study abroad research 30
      2.3.3 Identity: A summing up 36

viii   Contents

    2.4 Culture 37
        2.4.1 Conceptualizations of culture in language education 37
        2.4.2 Intercultural learning in study abroad 37
    2.5 Communities and social networks 38
        2.5.1 Student communities and social relations 38
        2.5.2 Role-related settings and practices for the sojourn abroad 39
        2.5.3 Domestic settings during the sojourn 40
        2.5.4 Leisure practices during the sojourn 41
        2.5.5 Social networking during the sojourn 41
        2.5.6 Home contacts and communication practices 43
    2.6 Conclusion 44

3 **The LANGSNAP project: Design and methodology** 52
    3.1 Introduction 52
    3.2 Project aims and design 52
    3.3 Participants 52
    3.4 Procedure for data collection 55
    3.5 Project instruments 57
        3.5.1 Elicited Imitation Test (EIT) 57
        3.5.2 Oral interview 58
        3.5.3 Oral picture-based narratives 59
        3.5.4 Argumentative essay 60
        3.5.5 The X-Lex test 61
        3.5.6 The Language Engagement Questionnaire (LEQ) 61
        3.5.7 The Social Networks Questionnaire (SNQ) 62
        3.5.8 The Multicultural Personality Questionnaire (MPQ) 64
        3.5.9 Reflective interview 64
        3.5.10 Additional data sources 64
    3.6 Creation of learner corpus 65
    3.7 Analysis of complexity, accuracy and fluency (CAF) 66
        3.7.1 Syntactic complexity 66
        3.7.2 Lexical complexity 66
        3.7.3 Accuracy 67
        3.7.4 Fluency 67
    3.8 Analyses of social data 68
    3.9 Conclusion 69

4 **Linguistic development in French** 72
    4.1 Introduction 72
    4.2 L2 French development during study abroad 72
        4.2.1 Sociolinguistic development 73
        4.2.2 General proficiency in L2 French 74

Contents   ix

    4.2.3 Fluency in L2 French 74
    4.2.4 Accuracy in L2 French 75
    4.2.5 Syntactic complexity in L2 French 76
    4.2.6 Lexical development in L2 French 77
    4.2.7 Summary of the literature 78
  4.3 French language development in the LANGSNAP project 78
    4.3.1 Measurement of overall proficiency: The French Elicited Imitation Test 79
    4.3.2 Fluency development: French group 80
    4.3.3 Accuracy development in speech: French group 84
    4.3.4 Accuracy development in writing: French group 89
    4.3.5 Development of syntactic complexity: French group 91
    4.3.6 Development of lexical complexity: French group 96
    4.3.7 Receptive lexical development: French group 97
  4.4 Conclusion 98

5 Linguistic development in Spanish   105
  5.1 Introduction 105
  5.2 Background 105
    5.2.1 General proficiency in L2 Spanish 106
    5.2.2 Fluency in L2 Spanish (oral and written) 106
    5.2.3 Accuracy in L2 Spanish (oral and written) 107
    5.2.4 Syntactic complexity in L2 Spanish 108
    5.2.5 Lexical complexity in L2 Spanish 108
    5.2.6 Summary 109
  5.3 Spanish language development in the LANGSNAP project 110
    5.3.1 Measurement of overall proficiency: The Spanish Elicited Imitation Test 110
    5.3.2 Fluency development in speech: Spanish group 111
    5.3.3 Fluency development in writing: Spanish group 113
    5.3.4 Accuracy development in speech: Spanish group 115
    5.3.5 Accuracy development in writing: Spanish group 119
    5.3.6 Development of syntactic complexity: Spanish group 121
    5.3.7 Development of lexical complexity: Spanish group 123
    5.3.8 Receptive lexical development: Spanish group 125
  5.4 Comparing linguistic development in the French and Spanish groups 127

6 Social networks and social relationships during the sojourn   134
  6.1 Introduction 134
  6.2 Social networking: The quantitative findings 134
    6.2.1 Size of sojourners' social networks 134
    6.2.2 Strength of network ties 137

6.2.3 Intensity of social networks: The "Top 5" 137
6.2.4 Two Social Networking Indices 139
6.3 Making and sustaining social relationships during the sojourn 142
6.3.1 Presojourn hopes 142
6.3.2 Potential for early social contacts: The domestic and leisure domains 144
6.3.3 Friendships with international peers 146
6.3.4 Friendships with local peers 150
6.3.5 Informal social relations with other age groups 156
6.3.6 Gender and romantic partnerships 159
6.3.7 Sustaining relationships with home friends and family 162
6.4 Conclusion 163

7 Language practices insojourn 165
7.1 Introduction 165
7.2 Language engagement: The quantitative survey 165
7.2.1 French and English use in France 165
7.2.2 Spanish and English use in Spain 167
7.2.3 Spanish and English use in Mexico 169
7.2.4 Other languages used in France, Spain and Mexico 170
7.3 Qualitative accounts of language practices 171
7.3.1 Introduction: Structure and agency in language choice 171
7.3.2 Negotiating the use of French and Spanish 171
7.3.3 Using English 189
7.3.4 Using additional languages 192
7.4 Conclusion 194

8 L2 identity and the ideal L2 self 196
8.1 Introduction: The foundations of L2 identity 196
8.2 Traditional demographic factors: Gender, nationality, culture and social class 197
8.2.1 Gender 197
8.2.2 Nationality and culture 199
8.2.3 Social class and ethnicity 203
8.2.4 Traditional demographic factors: Conclusion 205
8.3 The sojourner identity 205
8.3.1 The temporary sojourner 205
8.3.2 The student identity downshifted 206
8.3.3 Coming of age 209
8.4 The L2 self 210
8.4.1 Identity-related L2 proficiency 210
8.4.2 An interim ideal L2 self 214

Contents xi

    8.5 *The return to study* 215
        8.5.1 *Foregrounding of student identity* 215
        8.5.2 *Transnational futures* 216
    8.6 *Conclusion* 219

9 The L2 impact of the sojourn experience   222
    9.1 *Introduction* 222
    9.2 *Relations among social networking, language engagement and L2 development: The quantitative evidence* 222
        9.2.1 *Relations between SNI, LEQ and L2 performance measures* 222
    9.3 *Examining learning gains* 223
        9.3.1 *Defining learning gain scores* 225
        9.3.2 *Relations between SNI, LEQ and learning gain scores* 225
    9.4 *Explaining learning gains: A case study approach* 226
        9.4.1 *Identifying the fastest-progressing sojourners* 226
        9.4.2 *Case studies of "high gain" sojourners* 228
    9.5 *Discussion and conclusion* 244
        9.5.1 *Overview of high gainer characteristics* 244
        9.5.2 *Relationships as drivers of L2 development* 245

10 Advising and supporting Anglophone sojourners: Key issues   249
    The world is multilingual 249
    The sojourner is plurilingual 249
    Sojourner identity is many stranded 250
    Sojourners must be problem-solvers 250
    Short-term and long-term ideal L2 selves 251
    Intercultural learning 251
    Engaging in the placement 251
    Touristic travel 252
    Conclusion 252

Names Index   255
Subject Index   260

Figures

2.1	Potential second language outcomes of study abroad (after Benson et al., 2013)	35
3.1	Locations of sojourners in France	53
3.2	Locations of sojourners in Spain	54
3.3	Locations of sojourners in Mexico	54
3.4	Sample pages from the Sisters Story	60
3.5	Extract from Language Engagement Questionnaire (LEQ)	62
3.6	Extract from Social Networks Questionnaire (SNQ)	63
4.1	EIT scores for individual L2 French participants at Presojourn, Insojourn 2 and Postsojourn 1	80
4.2	Mean Speech Rate (syllables per second) and Mean Length of Run (syllables between silent pauses) for L2 French group (over time) and L1 French group	81
4.3	Speech Rate scores for individual L2 French participants, oral narrative	82
4.4	Mean Length of Run for individual L2 French participants, oral narrative (n=26; heritage and bilingual speakers omitted)	83
4.5	Mean writing fluency scores for L2 French group (over time) and L1 French group	83
4.6	Writing fluency scores for individual L2 French participants	84
4.7	Mean percentage of error-free clauses and error-free ASUs for L2 French group, oral narrative	85
4.8	Percentage of error-free clauses for individual L2 French participants, oral narrative	86
4.9	Percentage of error-free ASUs for individual L2 French participants, oral narrative	86
4.10	Mean percentage of accurate *Passé Composé* and *Imparfait* use for L2 French group, oral narrative	87
4.11	Percentage of appropriate *Imparfait* use for individual L2 French participants	87
4.12	Percentage of appropriate *Passé Composé* use for individual L2 French participants	88

4.13	Mean percentage of error-free clauses and error-free T-units for L2 French group, argumentative essay	89
4.14	Percentage of error-free clauses for individual L2 French participants, argumentative essay	90
4.15	Percentage of error-free T-units for individual L2 French participants, argumentative essay	91
4.16	Mean ratio of clauses to T-units and mean length of T-unit for L2 French group (over time) argumentative essay	92
4.17	Complexity in French writing: Ratio of clauses to T-units by prompt, L2 French group and L1 French group	93
4.18	Ratio of clauses to T-units for individual L2 French participants, argumentative essay	93
4.19	Complexity in French writing: Mean length of T-unit by prompt, L2 French group and L1 French group	94
4.20	Mean length of T-unit for individual L2 French participants	94
4.21	Mean ratio of finite clauses to all clauses for L2 French group and L1 French group, argumentative essay	95
4.22	Ratio of finite clauses to all clauses for individual L2 French participants, argumentative essay	95
4.23	Mean lexical diversity scores (*D*) for L2 French group (over time) and L1 French group, oral interview	96
4.24	Lexical diversity scores (*D*) for individual L2 French participants, oral interview	97
4.25	X-Lex test scores for individual L2 French participants at Presojourn (n=29) and at Insojourn 3 (n=24)	98
5.1	EIT scores for individual L2 Spanish participants at Presojourn, Insojourn 2 and Postsojourn 1	111
5.2	Mean Speech Rate (syllables per second) and Mean Length of Run (syllables between silent pauses) for L2 Spanish group (over time) and L1 Spanish group	112
5.3	Speech Rate scores for individual L2 Spanish participants, oral narrative (n=24, three participants excluded for technical reasons)	112
5.4	Mean Length of Run for individual L2 Spanish participants, oral narrative (n=24)	113
5.5	Mean writing fluency scores for L2 Spanish group (over time) and L1 Spanish group	114
5.6	Writing fluency scores for individual L2 Spanish participants	115
5.7	Mean percentage of error-free clauses and error-free ASUs for L2 Spanish group, oral narrative	116
5.8	Percentage of error-free clauses for individual L2 Spanish participants, oral narrative	116
5.9	Percentage of error-free ASUs for individual L2 Spanish participants, oral narrative	117

xiv *Figures*

5.10	Mean percentage of accurate preterit and imperfect use for L2 Spanish group, oral narrative	117
5.11	Percentage of appropriate preterit use for individual L2 Spanish participants	118
5.12	Percentage of appropriate imperfect use for individual L2 Spanish participants	118
5.13	Mean percentage of error-free clauses and error-free T-units for L2 Spanish group, argumentative essay	119
5.14	Percentage of error-free clauses for individual L2 Spanish participants, argumentative essay	120
5.15	Percentage of error-free T-units for individual L2 Spanish participants, argumentative essay	120
5.16	Mean ratio of clauses to T-unit and mean length of T-unit over time, L2 Spanish group, argumentative essay	121
5.17	Complexity in Spanish writing: Ratio of clauses to T-units by prompt, L2 Spanish group and L1 Spanish group	122
5.18	Complexity in Spanish writing: Mean length of T-unit by prompt, L2 Spanish group and L1 Spanish group	123
5.19	Ratio of clauses to T-units for individual L2 Spanish participants, argumentative essay	123
5.20	Mean length of T-unit for individual L2 Spanish participants, argumentative essay	124
5.21	Mean lexical diversity (*D*) scores for L2 Spanish group (over time) and L1 Spanish group, oral interview	125
5.22	Lexical diversity scores (*D*) for individual L2 Spanish participants, oral interview	125
5.23	X-Lex test scores for individual L2 Spanish participants at Presojourn and at Insojourn 3	127

Tables

3.1	Overview of LANGSNAP data collection	56
3.2	LANGSNAP corpus composition (number of words)	65
3.3	Average words per task per participant, French groups	65
3.4	Average words per task per participant, Spanish groups	66
4.1	Summary results of the French Elicited Imitation Test	80
4.2	Summary results of the French X-Lex test	98
5.1	Summary results of the Spanish Elicited Imitation Test	110
5.2	Summary results of the Spanish X-Lex test	126
6.1	Network size by language and context (% and number of reported contacts): France group (n=29)	135
6.2	Network size by language and context (% and number of reported contacts): Spain group (n=18)	136
6.3	Network size by language and context (% and number of reported contacts): Mexico group (n=9)	136
6.4	Strength of network ties, by language: Strong, medium and weak (% of total Top 5 contacts per group, mean numbers of Top 5 contacts per individual)	138
6.5	Mean Top 5 contacts, by language (standard deviations)	139
6.6	Group scores for L2 Social Network Index (SNIL2)	141
6.7	Group scores for L1 Social Network Index (SNIL1)	141
7.1	France group language use: Mean frequencies for L2 and L1 activities, Insojourn 1–3	166
7.2	Spain group language use: Mean frequencies for L2 and L1 activities, Insojourn 1–3	167
7.3	Mexico group language use: Mean frequencies for L2 and L1 activities, Insojourn 1–3	169
7.4	LEQ responses for use of various languages in France, Spain and Mexico	170
9.1	Correlations between selected linguistic and social measures, Presojourn and end sojourn (Spearman's rho)	224
9.2	Overview of linguistic gain scores, Presojourn to end sojourn (all sojourners)	226

9.3	Relationships among selected linguistic gain scores, SNI mean scores (L2 and L1), and LEQ mean scores (L2 and L1)	227
9.4	Top 10 gainers at end sojourn (in rank order): French	228
9.5	Top 10 gainers at end sojourn (in rank order): Spanish	228

Acknowledgements

First of all we wish to express our gratitude to the 57 participants in the LANGSNAP project who shared their thoughts and experiences with us very generously and patiently over the lifetime of the project.

The project was funded by the Economic and Social Research Council (award no. RES-062-23-2996), and it received significant academic and administrative support from the Department of Modern Languages, University of Southampton.

The project was successfully completed because of the commitment and hard work of a large number of people, and first mention must go to the project co-investigators, Laurence Richard and Patricia Romero de Mills. They were stalwart colleagues throughout and contributed to all aspects of the project. In particular, they brought educational and linguistic expertise and in-country knowledge to the team. Karen Ruebens was an effective project administrator. Fieldwork was facilitated by our international advisory group: Cristobal Lozano (University of Granada, Spain); Pat Grounds (Polytechnic University of San Luis Potosí, Mexico); and Henry Tyne (University of Perpignan, France). Jean-Marc Dewaele (Birkbeck College) advised on the use of the Multicultural Personality Questionnaire, and Amanda Huensch (University of South Florida) made a special contribution to the analysis of fluency. A number of University of Southampton colleagues and part-time research assistants also contributed to fieldwork, data preparation and data analysis; these include Oriane Boulay, Susana Sabin Fernández, Sylvie Goodlow, Christine Guilfoyle, Andrea Martin Muñoz, Sonia Morán Panero, Lidia Montero Micharet, Alison Porter, Martina Schneider Forroova and Juliet Solheim. A group of student assistants at the University of South Florida also helped with data analysis, including Crystal Bonano, Judith Bridges, Jhon Cuesta, Salvio Illiano, Wendy Timirau and Cedric Torres.

Finally, following the recent UK referendum vote to leave the European Union, we wish to acknowledge the historical opportunities offered by the Union for British student mobility through the Erasmus scheme, and express the hope that UK students will be supported to participate fully in European mobility schemes into the future.

1 Introduction

1.1 Sojourning abroad in an age of global English

The worldwide expansion of higher education today has been accompanied by greatly increased student mobility. Without including exchange students in the count, around 4 million altogether, just under 2% of the world student population, went to study for a degree abroad in 2012 (UNESCO, 2014). Much of this mobility involves students with sufficient personal resources leaving their home educational setting to study for a first degree or a higher degree in a country where higher education institutions are seen as having better academic/scientific resources (i.e., what Teichler (2015) calls "vertical" mobility). And much of this international student traffic is targeting the university systems of the developed Anglophone world more specifically. In 2012, just five countries hosted almost half of the world total of mobile students (UNESCO, 2014): the United States (18%), the United Kingdom (11%), France (7%), Australia (6%) and Germany (5%). Increasingly, also, in addition to this flow of students toward traditionally Anglophone institutions, the push toward internationalization and recruitment of international students is promoting the use of English as medium of instruction (EMI) in non-Anglophone higher education settings (Dimova, Hultgren, & Jensen, 2015; Kirkpatrick, 2014; Wächter & Maiworm, 2014). English is widely encountered as a lingua franca for informal as well as professional communication in higher education, in EMI settings and beyond (Byram & Dervin, 2008; Haberland, Lonsmann, & Preisler, 2013; Kalocsai, 2011), and English is the leading language of concern in discussions about student mobility, internationalization and intercultural learning (Sharifian, 2012).

This book deals with the new world of internationalizing higher education, but not as it directly affects students moving to Anglophone contexts. Instead, our focus is on the more uncommon case (in modern times at least) of students moving in the opposite direction – that is, students from a traditionally Anglophone institution (a British university) undertaking an extended sojourn abroad, and doing so with L2 learning as a major objective.

Our participants have inherited a long-standing tradition of language learning abroad, yet they are acting counter to broad international trends. De Swaan (2001) has proposed his so-called "world language system" to account for contemporary patterns of multilingualism and second language acquisition. For him, the languages of the world are hierarchically arranged in terms of status, which can be peripheral, central or supercentral. L2 learning is accordingly asymmetrical, with learners most predisposed to acquire a relevant language which is superordinate to the language(s) they know already. Thus for example, Quechua speakers in Peru will be motivated and expected to learn Spanish in addition (but not the reverse); Cantonese speakers in southern China are expected to learn Mandarin; Arabic speakers in southern France or the Paris *banlieue* are expected to learn French. In all these cases, speakers of a (locally) peripheral language are learning a more central one. In this system, of course, English has the status of hypercentral language, with hundreds of millions of learners worldwide, including speakers of the 100 or so central languages in De Swaan's system. It is unsurprising that in contemporary discussions of multilingualism, lingua franca usage, and translanguaging (Breidbach, 2003; Canagarajah, 2013; Garcia & Wei, 2014; Jenkins, 2015), English is the central case.

Given the status of the English language today, in this world language system, it is also unsurprising that Anglophone young people are reluctant language learners (Lanvers, 2016). For the United States, Kinginger (2009) describes language teaching as a "marginalised pursuit" (p. 12). While federal efforts since the 1970s have tried to promote language learning in support of both economic competitiveness and national security (Kolb, 2009), the number of US citizens reporting that they speak a language other than English remains relatively unchanged at around a quarter of the population, and around 8% of college students enroll for any foreign language course (Rivers & Robinson, 2012). In the UK, only a minority of secondary school students continue with foreign language learning up to age 16 (48% in 2015: Tinsley & Board, 2016). Levels of proficiency achieved among British schoolchildren in school-taught languages are generally low (European Commission, 2012). In higher education, a very small minority of students undertake degrees in languages (3% in 2010–2011: British Academy, 2013), though more than twice that number follow language programmes alongside other degrees, perhaps compensating for perceived deficiencies in their earlier schooling (British Academy, 2014). British students persisting with languages are predominantly white, female and middle class (Lanvers, 2016).

Along with their relative reluctance to pursue language learning, British students are also reluctant sojourners abroad (King, Findlay, & Ahrens, 2010). For example, in 2013–2014, around 15,500 British students in total took part in all branches of the European Erasmus student mobility scheme (which targets students in all disciplines). This was less than half the number of participants from other large-sized European countries (Germany, France and Spain: data from www.go.international.ac.uk). Male UK students seem particularly reluctant to participate; they consistently comprise only one-third of the participants. The numbers of participants are currently rising, though this is from a persistently low base; according to Go International, in 2013–2014 just 1.2% of all UK-domiciled students spent time abroad, and three Anglophone countries (the United States,

Australia and Canada) are among the top 10 destinations. Around 30% of all mobile UK students are languages majors.

American students have also shown somewhat increased numbers sojourning abroad in recent decades. However, the absolute proportion remains low (less than 3% of full-time students); additionally, most of these programmes involve "shorter timeframes and students majoring in social sciences, business or management" (Kinginger, 2009, p. 15). A significant percentage head for other Anglophone destinations, and language learning is not expressly prioritized in many cases. Again, participants are predominantly female and Caucasian (Kinginger, 2009).

Nonetheless, despite a long relative decline in popularity compared with other school and university subjects, languages retain the loyalty and interest of a minority of young Anglophones. With contemporary globalization and related waves of migration, including postcolonial influxes following World War II and the free movement historically facilitated through membership of the European Union, British society is also increasingly diverse, linguistically as well as ethnically and culturally. With one in six children attending school in England now bilingual or multilingual, according to official statistics (current figures available from www.naldic.org.uk), multilingualism and accompanying practices such as translanguaging are increasingly familiar in urban Britain. The supposed attractiveness to employers in a global economy, not only of multilingual proficiency but also of the intercultural awareness which accompanies it, is increasingly promoted among both educational professionals and their students (British Academy, 2014).

Recent research shows clearly that languages majors in UK universities have typically made a very positive choice, and have come to terms with their exceptionality. Studies by Busse and Williams (2010) and by Stolte (2015) explore in some detail the language-learning biographies of university students of German. These researchers conclude that enjoyment of the language-learning opportunity available while at school, plus perceived personal success and aptitude for languages, create intrinsic motivation and play a key role in British students' pursuit of languages beyond the compulsory stages. Additionally, early opportunities to visit Germany and to meet German people, either through school exchanges or through family holidays and contacts, had provided participants in both of these studies with influential tasters of the communicative possibilities which arise from language-learning effort. Instrumental motivation had some influence, but to a lesser degree, and students in neither study showed classic integrative motivation (despite pleasant impressions of Germany gained through short visits). These researchers also consider the relevance to their participants of the L2 motivational self-system proposed by Dörnyei (2009); they find little evidence for an ought-to self among British students, unsurprisingly (i.e., societal expectations and pressures for language learning success are weak). However, they agree in interpreting their participants as possessing a distinctive ideal L2 self which values multilingual proficiency in general and oral proficiency in particular. That is, these languages students now see themselves as prospective bilingual/

multilingual speakers, with associated characteristics such as aptitude for mobility and intercultural awareness.

When Anglophone university students do venture abroad, with positive motivation and commitment to L2 learning, they are likely to target one of de Swaan's "supercentral" languages – French, German, Spanish or perhaps Chinese, Arabic or Japanese. Their sojourns are most often spent in countries where these languages have historical status as national standard languages (for current figures see www.gointernational.ac.uk). However, whatever their desired linguistic target, sojourners abroad are now increasingly likely to enter a linguistically complex environment, with English embedded and available to many as a socially valued L2/lingua franca. (On the availability of English across Europe, see, e.g., the annual English Proficiency Index published by Education First: http://www.ef.co.uk/epi/regions/europe/; on linguistic superdiversity see, e.g., Blommaert and Rampton, 2011). A further complication is the transformation of contemporary students' immediate social and linguistic context, due to the constant availability of the internet and social media. These offer the potential to sustain existing social networks with a quite new immediacy and facility (Coleman, 2013; Coleman & Chafer, 2010; Kinginger, 2010). The isolation from home reported in older qualitative accounts of study abroad, such as Hawkins' description of his stay in Germany in the 1930s (Hawkins, 1999), is now a thing of the past, with corresponding implications for continuing access to English among modern Anglophone sojourners.

1.2 Anglophone traditions in the language-learning sojourn

Study abroad has a long social history in Europe, with mobility among early medieval scholars very evident, and the earliest European universities (such as Bologna or Paris) attracting students from across the continent, who organized themselves to live and socialize together as diverse "nations" (de Ridder-Symoens, 1992). From the Renaissance onward, the education of a European aristocrat might also include a sojourn abroad, to learn a range of gentlemanly arts, including languages (Gallagher, 2014).

The modern European university tradition is, however, grounded in 19th-century nationalism, and (re)conceived to serve the growing economic and social needs of the nation state for educated personnel (de Wit & Merkx, 2012). German universities led modernizing trends, and when modern languages appeared on the British university curriculum in the later 19th century, they were much influenced by the German tradition of philological study (Rüegg, 2004). Thus, universities were ambivalent about the teaching of practical language skills, and these were often left to lower-status language tutors. However, periods of study and residence abroad appeared as part of the modern languages higher education curriculum in England from the early 20th century, initially as a voluntary extra supporting the development of practical skills (as for Eric Hawkins in the 1930s: 1999), but increasingly as a compulsory element of the course. For example, Britain and France have exchanged students as language teaching assistants since

1904, and similar exchanges with Germany followed soon afterward (Rowles & Rowles, 2005).

Following World War II, a period abroad, embedded within the programme, became compulsory for languages students at most UK universities (Evans, 1988; Nott, 1996). Thus, a guide for prospective students of languages published by the Modern Language Association in 1961 advises the interested that a languages degree will involve

> willingness on your part to spend some time – ranging from one month to a full year – in the country concerned
>
> (Stern, 1961).

The goal of this stay abroad is described in another 1960s guide as

> a general finishing device for oral proficiency, as well as for the acquisition of first-hand knowledge of the foreign culture
>
> (Healey, 1967, p. 7).

Practice was inconsistent however, so that Healey could describe the stay abroad as

> a very variable quantity, ranging from stipulations that certain amounts of vacation time must be spent in a country speaking the language, to the requirement that a whole year be spent in that country
>
> (Healey, 1967, p. 7).

The extent of supervision, and academic tasks required, on the part of the home university also varied widely. Healey could assume that any student spending a full year abroad would "normally" do so as a teaching assistant in a school (p. 86), and by the late 1970s, the language assistantship scheme was attracting around 2,000 participants annually (Dyson, 1984). However, others might spend their sojourn as an exchange student, or on a work placement (Willis, Doble, Sankarayya, & Smithers, 1977).

Following British accession to the European Economic Community, and the subsequent creation of the Erasmus student exchange programme in the 1980s, UK students have benefited from much more systematic institutional links and financial support offered by the scheme, which supports large numbers of student exchanges across Europe, including those targeting languages majors (Ballatore, 2015; Byram & Dervin, 2008; Teichler, 1997; Teichler & Ferencz, 2011). Correspondingly, the balance between sojourn types has shifted, with the student exchange becoming the most popular type among British students by the 1990s (Coleman, 1995, 1996). At this point, the goals of the sojourn became elaborated, as further potential benefits were recognized in terms of personal development ("greater maturity, independence, self-reliance, self-awareness and confidence": Coleman, 1996, p. 66), and also intercultural awareness. In the 1990s, this last was a particular focus, with specific collaborative projects involving a number of British universities in schemes preparing students to experience the sojourn abroad as an ethnographic encounter, such as the LARA project (Roberts, Byram, Barro, Jordan, & Street, 2001). However, across the British system, considerable diversity of preparation and expectations of sojourners remains, on the part of the home institutions (see Johnston, Mitchell, Myles, & Ford, 2011, Chapter 5).

The development of US study abroad is reviewed by Hoffa (2007) and by Hoffa and DePaul (2010a). In the 19th century, considerable numbers of students left a growing home university system for postgraduate studies in Germany, while others made less systematic extracurricular trips; however, with the growth of indigenous postgraduate studies, plus of course the disruption of World War I, such students increasingly stayed at home. In the 1920s, student travel revived, and a small number of liberal arts institutions introduced the "Junior Year Abroad" (JYA) for languages majors (who were mostly women). This was typically a carefully designed credit-bearing programme including homestays, language instruction and courses in culture, literature, and so on, devised by institutions abroad to meet the needs of visiting students, but also including one or more courses alongside local students. Paris was the most popular JYA destination; however, before World War II, all educational programmes abroad involved only "a truly marginal number" of the total student population (Hoffa, 2007, p. 101). Following World War II and the much greater subsequent international engagement of the United States, including the perceived need for Cold War cultural competition, diverse types of study abroad programme grew rapidly (though these were still mostly non-credit-bearing), with perhaps 20,000 students participating annually by the early 1960s (Hoffa, 2007, pp. 227–235). The JYA-style programme with a strong focus on language learning continued, alongside one-semester variants, but student numbers on other types of programme strongly outpaced these (Hoffa & DePaul, 2010b). Debates in the 1960s on future directions for study abroad revealed tensions between academics "who were chiefly concerned with academic standards and course quality", including language learning standards, and those who prioritized the "experiential and crosscultural opportunities distinctive to study abroad" (Comp & Merritt, 2010, p. 456). Commitment and participation fluctuated during the 1970s period of the Vietnam War (Keller & Frain, 2010), but rose again following the collapse of the Soviet Union and in tune with the increasing impact since the 1990s of internationalization and globalization philosophies within higher education.

By the mid-2000s, over 200,000 US students were taking part in some form of study abroad annually, around 5% of the total cohort (Keller & Frain, 2010, pp. 41–42); ambitions were expressed at this time by a Congress-commissioned report for "one million Americans studying abroad" (Commission on the Abraham Lincoln Study Abroad Program, 2005). However, given the rise of English as a lingua franca and as an increasingly important medium of instruction in international higher education, the place of language learning in US study abroad programmes is of declining importance; by the mid-2000s also, around 25% of participants were located in English-speaking countries (the UK, Australia, etc.), and a majority of all study abroad programmes did not have a language prerequisite (De Winter & Rumbley, 2010). Kinginger (2010) notes a fall in the proportion of languages majors making a stay abroad, to below 10%. Contemporary American students also typically make a relatively short stay abroad (95% do so for a semester or less: Wolcott, 2013, p. 131). Many follow "island" programmes, with American-designed curricula and methodologies which ensure continuity with American academic culture, rather than experiencing at first hand the educational traditions of the host country (Wolcott, 2013, p. 132). This evolution is viewed critically by some commentators, such as Kinginger (2010), who argues that the opportunity is restricted for American sojourners to experience "negotiation of difference" leading to intercultural awareness and global civic engagement.

1.3 Researching the Anglophone language-learning sojourn

1.3.1 An SLA research tradition

The increasing promotion of the sojourn abroad among British and American students of languages, from the 1960s onward, led in due course to concern about learning outcomes. Freed (1995a) reviewed early empirical studies of language development among sojourners. She identified as the earliest substantial American study a report by J.B. Carroll on the language proficiency of almost 3,000 college seniors in French, German, Italian and Russian (Carroll, 1967). This study showed that experience of study abroad was a strong predictor of greater target language proficiency, which could, for example, compensate for lower levels of language aptitude. The first notable British study is that by Willis, Doble, Sankarayya and Smithers, who administered pre- and posttests in the target language to 88 students spending a year in France or Germany, and documented significant improvement (Willis et al., 1977). Freed's (1995a) review comprised the introduction to an edited volume (Freed, 1995b), which brought together for the first time a range of studies dealing with different aspects of language learning by Anglophones during a sojourn abroad, and was clearly influenced by the emergence of SLA as a discipline in the previous two decades (Mitchell, Myles, & Marsden, 2013, Chapter 2). Freed's volume included explorations of presojourn experience which may influence linguistic gains insojourn; comparisons between the language gains of students at home and abroad; and identification of different dimensions of L2 proficiency which seem to benefit from time abroad, including L2 communicative strategies, fluency, pragmatic behaviours (politeness) and sociolinguistic variation. However, this group of studies showed inconsistent results, and considerable individual variation, in the development of some of these dimensions, and more particularly in the domain of morphosyntax. The collection also acknowledged aspects of students' sociocultural experiences abroad, which may be mediating factors affecting the extent to which language learning opportunities are available and availed of; for example, the collection included a report by Polanyi (1995) on the perceived "sexual harassment" experienced by American female students in Russia, which "not only inhibit[s] their language learning opportunities but their ultimate performance on tests" (Freed, 1995a, p. 25).

The Freed (1995b) volume thus set out a multidimensional research agenda focusing on second language development among student sojourners, which has been pursued up to the present, as evidenced in successive state-of-the-art reviews (Collentine, 2009; DeKeyser, 2014; Llanes, 2011; Regan, Howard, & Lemée, 2009; Sanz, 2014). Much of this work continues to deal with Anglophone sojourners learning "supercentral" languages such as French, German or Japanese, though other European student sojourners learning L2 English have increasingly been studied in this same tradition (Pérez-Vidal, 2014).

The 2011 review of Llanes shows considerable continuity with the research agenda set out by Freed (1995a, 1995b). She shows that there has been a decline in popularity of global measures of L2 proficiency in study abroad research, which have been largely replaced by study of the development of distinct dimensions of proficiency, including (oral) fluency, lexis, morphosyntax, pragmatics and sociolinguistic variation. According to Llanes, more recent research confirms the findings summarized by Freed (1995a) in showing clear impact of a period of time spent abroad for fluency, lexis and pragmatics, but more conflicting results for morphosyntactic development, and also for the skill of writing (insofar as this has been studied). Research on linguistic development among sojourners has continued to note considerable variability in learning outcomes, and some researchers have sought to explore/explain this variability with reference to individual differences such as initial L2 proficiency level, working memory and other cognitive factors, though without clear success (DeKeyser, 2014, pp. 320–321; Llanes, 2011, pp. 205–206). DeKeyser (2010, for grammar) and Schauer (2009, for pragmatics) view metalinguistic awareness as an important mediating factor in individual L2 development. Length of stay has generally been seen as a positive influence on L2 development (i.e., the longer the stay, the better: Llanes, 2011). However, with longer stays (over six months), this is not necessarily the case (Rees & Klapper, 2007; Yang, 2016).

1.3.2 Studying the context for L2 development

Researchers in the essentially psycholinguistic SLA research tradition described so far have been aware, of course, that the supposed L2 immersion environment of a sojourn abroad needs to be problematized and investigated; that is, extensive availability of "input" cannot be taken for granted, far less its conversion into "intake". Comparison studies of learners abroad and at home have often but not always confirmed an advantage for the former (Freed, Segalowitz, & Dewey, 2004). From within the SLA tradition, different approaches to the study of the L2 setting have been explored; the contribution of different placement types, instructional settings, homestays and service encounters to L2 development when abroad have all been investigated (see Kinginger, 2009, Chapter 4, for a critical survey). From a methodological perspective, Freed and colleagues have proposed documenting sojourners' language practices while abroad through questionnaire surveys and offer the Language Contact Profile as a suitable instrument (Freed, Dewey, Segalowitz, & Halter, 2004). Others have used learner journals and interviews for similar purposes; some have turned to social network theory to model sojourners' social relationships and degree of integration with the host community (Dewey, Bown, Baker, Martinsen, Gold, & Eggett, 2014; Dewey, Bown, & Eggett, 2012; Dewey, Ring, Gardner, & Belnap, 2013; Gautier & Chevrot, 2015; Isabelli-García, 2006), so as to relate these in turn to L2 use and development during the sojourn. However, the findings of such research have proved complex, with few clear demonstrations of, for example, increased hours of L2 use leading directly to higher L2 gains.

1.3.3 An emergent sociocultural tradition

> In second-language research, interest in identity and socialization is an inevitable outcome of listening to learners' stories.
> – (Kinginger, 2009, p. 155)

Since the mid-1990s, sociocultural themes of identity and language socialization have become increasingly prominent in debates on second language acquisition. This "social turn" (Block, 2003) is also reflected in research on L2 sojourners abroad, alongside the continuing tradition of outcomes-focused research briefly introduced above. Kinginger has reviewed this tradition more than once (Kinginger, 2009, Chapter 5; 2012, 2013). She argues (2009) that the context of language acquisition cannot be reduced to a number of external factors with positive or negative effects on L2 development, any more than learner identity can be reduced to a set of individual differences. Focusing on processes rather than outcomes, this tradition is interested in the evolving identity of the sojourner, dealing with dimensions such as gender, national identity, sociolinguistic competence and intercultural awareness. It is understood that the learner contributes to the construction of the language acquisition context, and in turn is changed by it, so that identity and language socialization are not given characteristics of the learner and the setting, which interact on each other as distinct factors, but follow dynamic trajectories and are to some degree jointly constructed by the sojourner and his or her interlocutors.

Methods adopted in this process-oriented tradition include ethnographic interviews and observations, narrative enquiry, and conversational analysis of recorded interactions between hosts and sojourners (e.g., dinner table talk), or among sojourners themselves. The language socialization studies reviewed by Kinginger (2009, Chapter 5) mainly deal with Anglophone sojourners, but this tradition has also attracted researchers studying non-Anglophones who are sojourning in Anglophone and other settings – for example, the work of Jackson with Hong Kong students sojourning in the UK (Jackson, 2008, 2010) or that of Patron with French students in Australia (Patron, 2007). Mixed-group studies are also found in this tradition: for example, the study by Behrent of language practices among international students in the *Cité Internationale Universitaire* in

10 *Introduction*

Paris (Behrent, 2007), or Taguchi's study of the interactional competence in L2 Japanese of diverse student sojourners in Tokyo (Taguchi, 2015).

There are further important studies of the identity and intercultural adaptation of student sojourners which do not discuss language practices in much detail (other than acknowledging the role of lingua franca English) and pay limited or no attention to language learning outcomes (Byram & Dervin, 2008; Dervin & Machart, 2014; Ehrenreich, 2006; Messelink & ten Thije, 2012). Some of this work is nonetheless very helpful in trying to explore the relationship between sojourner identity, learning context, intercultural adaptation and language development. Here, the work of Murphy-Lejeune on "the travelling European student" is a key example (2002) which will be discussed further in Chapter 2.

Looking more closely at the language socialization tradition, including Kinginger's own work (2008, 2015), we find considerable insights and evidence concerning the dynamically constructed language learning opportunities available to sojourners, and the language practices in which they engage. These are shown to be influenced by the "stances of learners and hosts and the framing of language learning at broader societal and ideological levels" (Kinginger, 2009, p. 203); some examples of this work are discussed more fully in Chapter 2. But work of this type is limited, and we are far from a situation where the combined study of "learners' interactive positioning in language socialization, the stances they adopt, the nature of their interactions *and* the qualities of their evolving communicative repertoires" (Kinginger, 2009, p. 204: emphasis in original) has become routine.

1.4 The LANGSNAP project

Against the background just painted of recent traditions in researching language learning by sojourners abroad, we now turn to introduce the empirical study of Anglophone sojourners abroad, which is the main focus of this book.

The project's official title was "Social networks, target language interaction and second language acquisition during the year abroad: a longitudinal study"; however, this was generally abbreviated to the "Language and Social Networks Abroad Project", or LANGSNAP for short. Funded by the UK Economic and Social Research Council (ESRC), the project ran from May 2011 until October 2013 (30 months). The overall aim of the study was to explore L2 development before, during and after a temporary sojourn abroad, and its relationship with sojourners' personal development, social experiences and language practices while abroad. The project tracked 57 British undergraduate students, majoring in languages at a single research-intensive university, over a period of 21 months, including an academic year spent either as an exchange student, a language assistant or a workplace intern in France, Spain or Mexico. Using mixed methods, data concerning participants' L2 development and also their social engagement were collected on six occasions during this time. It was hoped the project could make a theoretical contribution to the better understanding of informal language learning by previously instructed adults over an extended period, and in particular to a better understanding of the complex triangular relationship between sojourners' identity and personal development, their social experiences abroad and their L2 development.

1.5 Outline of the book

In Chapter 2 we present a series of theoretical concepts which have underpinned our research. We analyse the ideologies which have traditionally underpinned study abroad for Anglophone language learners, including notions of linguistic and cultural immersion and intercultural competence. We acknowledge the centrality of multilingualism in contemporary understandings of language and language development, and discuss its relationship to language practices and language ideologies espoused during the sojourn abroad. We argue for a conceptualization of identity relevant to the temporary student sojourner (Murphy-Lejeune, 2002; Pellegrino Aveni, 2005; Plews, 2015) and to the second language learner (Benson, Barkhuizen, Bodycott, & Brown, 2013; Block, 2007). We explore dynamic conceptualizations of culture, learning context, social networks and community, acknowledging the virtual dimensions attaching to these today. And we present the approach adopted in the study to the conceptualization of linguistic development, in terms of complexity, accuracy and fluency (Housen, Kuiken, & Vedder, 2012; Norris & Ortega, 2009).

In Chapter 3, we present in detail the design and methodology of the LANGSNAP project. We introduce the participants and the range of tasks used over time to document their linguistic and personal development and their social engagement.

In Chapters 4 (French) and 5 (Spanish), we provide detailed descriptions of the linguistic development of the participants. Based on quantitative analysis of learners' oral and written production on the range of linguistic tasks described in Chapter 3, group developmental trends and individual results are presented, for overall proficiency, fluency, accuracy, and syntactic and lexical complexity.

Chapter 6 explores the social networks into which the sojourners entered while abroad, paying attention to domestic life, to leisure activities and to travel. The maintenance of home networks (with parents and friends in England) through virtual media and through reciprocal visiting is described, as are the new international and local networks being constructed by sojourners. Chapter 7 explores in detail the patterns of language use engaged in by sojourners during their time abroad. Overall the chapter documents the multilingual nature of the sojourn, and how participants navigate this multilingual environment to achieve personal learning goals.

Chapter 8 examines the evolution of sojourners' identity and personality while abroad. Qualitative data are drawn upon to explore sojourners' changing sense of self as students, as young independent adults, and as language learners, including their sociolinguistic understandings and immediate target language goals, as well as any longer-term ideal L2 self.

Chapter 9 presents the overall conclusions of the project regarding relationships among L2 identity, the experiences of the sojourn, and L2 development.

This is achieved through a combination of statistical analyses and case studies of individual "high gain" sojourners, bringing together all strands of analysis discussed in earlier chapters. Chapter 10 presents a brief discussion of the implications of the LANGSNAP findings for the successful management of study and residence abroad programmes, including student preparation presojourn and follow-up activities.

References

Ballatore, M. (2015). The Erasmus programme: Achievements, inequalities and prospects – an overall approach. In F. Dervin & R. Machart (Eds.), *The new politics of global academic mobility and migration* (pp. 41–60). Frankfurt am Main: Peter Lang.

Behrent, S. (2007). *La communication interalloglotte*. Paris: L'Harmattan.

Benson, P., Barkhuizen, G., Bodycott, P., & Brown, J. (2013). *Second language identity in narratives of study abroad*. Basingstoke: Palgrave Macmillan.

Block, D. (2003). *The social turn in second language acquisition*. Edinburgh: Edinburgh University Press.

Block, D. (2007). *Second language identities*. London: Continuum.

Blommaert, J., & Rampton, B. (2011). Language and superdiversity. *Diversities, 13*(2), 1–22.

Breidbach, S. (2003). *Plurilingualism, democratic citizenship in Europe and the role of English*. Strasbourg: Council of Europe.

British Academy. (2013). *Languages: The state of the nation*. London: British Academy.

British Academy. (2014). *Born global: Summary of interim findings*. London: British Academy.

Busse, V., & Williams, M. (2010). Why German? Motivation of students studying German at English universities. *The Language Learning Journal, 38*(1), 67–85.

Byram, M., & Dervin, F. (Eds.). (2008). *Students, staff and academic mobility in higher education*. Newcastle: Cambridge Scholars Publishing.

Canagarajah, S. (2013). *Translingual practice*. Abingdon: Routledge.

Carroll, J. B. (1967). Foreign language proficiency levels attained by language majors near graduation from college. *Foreign Language Annals, 1*(2), 131–151.

Coleman, J. A. (1995). The current state of knowledge concerning student residence abroad. In G. Parker & A. Rouxeville (Eds.), *The year abroad: Preparation, monitoring, evaluation* (pp. 17–42). London: Association for French Language Studies in association with the Centre for Information on Language Teaching and Research.

Coleman, J. A. (1996). Residence abroad and its impact. In J. A. Coleman (Ed.), *Studying languages: A survey of British and European students* (pp. 59–90). London: Centre for Information on Language Teaching and Research.

Coleman, J. A. (2013). Researching whole people and whole lives. In C. Kinginger (Ed.), *Social and cultural aspects of language learning in study abroad* (pp. 17–46). Amsterdam: John Benjamins.

Coleman, J. A., & Chafer, T. (2010). Study abroad and the internet: Physical and virtual context in an era of expanding telecommunications. *Frontiers: The Interdisciplinary Journal of Study Abroad, 19*, 151–167.

Collentine, J. (2009). Study abroad research: Findings, implications and future directions. In M. H. Long & C. J. Doughty (Eds.), *The handbook of language teaching* (pp. 218–233). Chichester: Wiley-Blackwell.

Commission on the Abraham Lincoln Study Abroad Program. (2005). *Global competence and national needs: One million Americans studying abroad.* Washington, DC: NAFSA.

Comp, D., & Merritt, M. (2010). The development of qualitative standards and learning outcomes for study abroad. In W.W. Hoffa & S.C. DePaul (Eds.), *A history of US study abroad: 1965–present* (pp. 451–490). Carlisle, PA: Frontiers Journal.

DeKeyser, R. (2010). Monitoring processes in Spanish as a second language during a study abroad program. *Foreign Language Annals, 43*(1), 80–92.

DeKeyser, R. (2014). Research on language development during study abroad: Methodological considerations and future perspectives. In C. Pérez-Vidal (Ed.), *Language acquisition in study abroad and formal acquisition contexts* (pp. 313–326). Amsterdam: John Benjamins.

de Ridder-Symoens, H. (1992). Mobility. In H. de Ridder-Symoens (Ed.), *A history of the university in Europe. Volume 1: Universities in the middle ages* (pp. 280–304). Cambridge: Cambridge University Press.

de Swaan, A. (2001). *Words of the world: The global language system.* Cambridge: Polity.

De Winter, U. J., & Rumbley, L. E. (2010). The diversification of education abroad across the curriculum. In W.W. Hoffa & S.C. DePaul (Eds.), *A history of US study abroad: 1965–present* (pp. 55–114). Carlisle, PA: Frontiers.

de Wit, H., & Merkx, G. (2012). The history of internationalisation of higher education. In D.K. Deardorff, H. de Wit, J. Heyl, & T. Adams (Eds.), *The Sage handbook of international education* (pp. 43–60). Thousand Oaks/London: Sage.

Dervin, F., & Machart, R. (Eds.). (2014). *The new politics of global academic mobility and migration.* Frankfurt am Main: Peter Lang.

Dewey, D. P., Bown, J., Baker, W., Martinsen, R. A., Gold, C., & Eggett, D. (2014). Language use in six study abroad programs: An exploratory analysis of possible predictors. *Language Learning, 64*(1), 36–71.

Dewey, D. P., Bown, J., & Eggett, D. (2012). Japanese language proficiency, social networking, and language use during study abroad: Learners' perspectives. *Canadian Modern Language Review, 68*(2), 111–137.

Dewey, D. P., Ring, S., Gardner, D., & Belnap, R. K. (2013). Social network formation and development during study abroad in the Middle East. *System, 41*(2), 269–282.

Dimova, S., Hultgren, A. K., & Jensen, C. (Eds.). (2015). *English-medium instruction in European higher education. English in Europe, Volume 3.* Berlin: De Gruyter Mouton.

Dörnyei, Z. (2009). The L2 motivational self system. In Z. Dörnyei & E. Ushioda (Eds.), *Motivation, language identity and the L2 self* (pp. 9–42). Clevedon: Multilingual Matters.

Dyson, P. (1984). The assistantship evaluation project: An interim report. In G. Doble & B. Griffiths (Eds.), *Oral skills in the modern languages degree* (pp. 204–207). London: Centre for Information on Teaching and Research.

Ehrenreich, S. (2006). The assistant experience in retrospect and its educational and professional significance in teachers' biographies. In M. Byram & A. Feng (Eds.), *Living and studying abroad: Research and practice* (pp. 186–210). Clevedon: Multilingual Matters.

European Commission. (2012). *First European survey on language competences: Final report.* Brussels: European Commission.

Evans, C. (1988). *Language people: The experience of teaching and learning modern languages in British universities.* Milton Keynes: Open University Press.

Freed, B. F. (1995a). Language learning and study abroad. In B.F. Freed (Ed.), *Second language acquisition in a study abroad context* (pp. 3–34). Amsterdam: John Benjamins.

Freed, B. F. (Ed.). (1995b). *Second language acquisition in a study abroad context.* Amsterdam: John Benjamins.

Freed, B. F., Dewey, D. P., Segalowitz, N., & Halter, R. (2004). The language contact profile. *Studies in Second Language Acquisition, 26*(2), 349–356.

Freed, B. F., Segalowitz, N., & Dewey, D. P. (2004). Context of learning and second language fluency in French: Comparing regular classroom, study abroad, and intensive domestic immersion programs. *Studies in Second Language Acquisition, 26*(2), 275–301.

Gallagher, J. (2014). *The linguistic encounters of English speakers in the early modern world, c. 1483–1730*. (PhD), University of Cambridge.

Garcia, O., & Wei, L. (2014). *Translanguaging: Language, bilingualism and education*. Basingstoke: Palgrave Macmillan.

Gautier, R., & Chevrot, J.-P. (2015). Social networks and acquisition of sociolinguistic variation in a study abroad context: A preliminary study. In R. Mitchell, N. Tracy-Ventura, & K. McManus (Eds.), *Social interaction, identity and language learning during residence abroad. EUROSLA Monographs 4* (pp. 169–184). Amsterdam: European Second Language Association.

Haberland, H., Lonsmann, D., & Preisler, B. (Eds.). (2013). *Language alternation, language choice and language encounter in international tertiary education*. Dordrecht: Springer.

Hawkins, E. (1999). *Listening to Lorca: A journey into language*. London: Centre for Information on Language Teaching and Research.

Healey, F. G. (1967). *Foreign language teaching in the universities*. Manchester: Manchester University Press.

Hoffa, W. W. (2007). *A History of US study abroad: Beginnings to 1965*. Carlisle, PA: Forum on Education Abroad.

Hoffa, W. W., & DePaul, S. C. (Eds.). (2010a). *A history of US study abroad: 1965–present*. Carlisle PA: Frontiers Journal.

Hoffa, W. W., & DePaul, S. C. (2010b). Introduction. In W. W. Hoffa & S. C. DePaul (Eds.), *A history of US study abroad: 1965–present* (pp. 1–14). Carlisle PA: Frontiers Journal.

Housen, A., Kuiken, F., & Vedder, I. (Eds.). (2012). *Dimensions of L2 performance and proficiency: Complexity, accuracy and fluency in SLA*. Amsterdam: John Benjamins.

Isabelli-García, C. (2006). Study abroad, social networks, motivation and attitudes: Implications for second language acquisition. In M. A. DuFon & E. Churchill (Eds.), *Language learners in study abroad contexts* (pp. 231–258). Clevedon: Multilingual Matters.

Jackson, J. (2008). *Language, identity and study abroad*. London: Equinox.

Jackson, J. (2010). *Intercultural journeys: From study to residence abroad*. Basingstoke: Palgrave Macmillan.

Jenkins, J. (2015). Repositioning English and multilingualism in English as a Lingua Franca. *Englishes in Practice, 2*(3), 49–85.

Johnston, B., Mitchell, R., Myles, F. & Ford, P. (2011). *Developing student criticality in higher education*. London: Continuum.

Kalocsai, K. (2011). The show of interpersonal involvement and the building of rapport in an ELF community of practice. In A. Archibald, A. Cogo, & J. Jenkins (Eds.), *Latest trends in English as a Lingua Franca research* (pp. 113–138). Newcastle Upon Tyne: Cambridge Scholars Publishing.

Keller, J. M., & Frain, M. (2010). The impact of geo-political events, globalization and national policies on study abroad programming and participation. In W. W. Hoffa & S. C. DePaul (Eds.), *A history of US study abroad: 1965–present* (pp. 15–54). Carlisle, PA: Frontiers Journal.

King, R., Findlay, A., & Ahrens, J. (2010). *International student mobility literature review: Report to HEFCE, and co-funded by the British Council, UK National Agency for*

Erasmus. Retrieved 29 December 2016 from http://www.hefce.ac.uk/media/hefce/content/pubs/2010/rd2010/rd20_10.pdf

Kinginger, C. (2008). Language learning in study abroad: Case studies of Americans in France. *The Modern Language Journal, 92*(Special issue), 1–124.

Kinginger, C. (2009). *Language learning and study abroad: A critical reading of research.* Basingstoke: Palgrave Macmillan.

Kinginger, C. (2010). American students abroad: Negotiation of difference? *Language Teaching, 43*(2), 216–227.

Kinginger, C. (2012). Language socialization in study abroad. In C. A. Chapelle (Ed.), *The encyclopedia of applied linguistics.* Chichester: Wiley-Blackwell. doi: 10.1002/9781405198431.wbeal1121

Kinginger, C. (2013). Introduction. In C. Kinginger (Ed.), *Social and cultural aspects of language learning in study abroad* (pp. 3–16). Amsterdam: John Benjamins.

Kinginger, C. (2015). Language socialization in the homestay: American high school students in China. In R. Mitchell, N. Tracy-Ventura, & K. McManus (Eds.), *Social interaction, identity and language learning during residence abroad.* EUROSLA Monographs 4 (pp. 53–74). Amsterdam: European Second Language Association.

Kirkpatrick, A. (2014). English as a medium of instruction in east and southeast Asian universities. In N. Murray & A. Scarino (Eds.), *Dynamic ecologies: A relational perspective on languages education in the Asia-Pacific region* (pp. 15–30). Dordrecht: Springer Science.

Kolb, C. (2009). International studies and foreign languages: A critical American priority. In R. Lewin (Ed.), *The handbook of practice and research in study abroad: Higher education and the quest for global citizenship* (pp. 49–60). New York: Routledge.

Lanvers, U. (2016). On the predicaments of the English L1 language learner: A conceptual article. *International Journal of Applied Linguistics, 26*(2), 147–167.

Llanes, À. (2011). The many faces of study abroad: An update on the research on L2 gains emerged during a study abroad experience. *International Journal of Multilingualism, 8*(3), 189–215.

Messelink, A., & ten Thije, J. D. (2012). European capacity and intercultural inquisitiveness of the Erasmus generation 2.0. *Dutch Journal of Applied Linguistics, 1*(1), 80–101.

Mitchell, R., Myles, F., & Marsden, E. (2013). *Second language learning theories.* Abingdon: Routledge.

Murphy-Lejeune, E. (2002). *Student mobility and narrative in Europe: The new strangers.* New York: Routledge.

Norris, J. M., & Ortega, L. (2009). Towards an organic approach to investigating CAF in instructed SLA: The case of complexity. *Applied Linguistics, 30*(4), 555–578.

Nott, D. (1996). University degree courses. In E. Hawkins (Ed.), *Thirty years of language teaching* (pp. 61–69). London: Centre for Information on Language Teaching and Research.

Patron, M.-C. (2007). *Culture and identity in study abroad contexts: After Australia, French without France.* Oxford: Peter Lang.

Pellegrino Aveni, V. (2005). *Study abroad and second language use.* Cambridge: Cambridge University Press.

Pérez-Vidal, C. (Ed.). (2014). *Language acquisition in study abroad and formal instruction contexts.* Amsterdam: John Benjamins.

Plews, J. (2015). Intercultural identity-alignment in second language study abroad, or the more-or-less Canadians. In R. Mitchell, N. Tracy-Ventura, & K. McManus (Eds.), *Social*

interaction, identity and language learning during residence abroad. EUROSLA Monographs 4 (pp. 281–304). Amsterdam: European Second Language Association.
Polanyi, L. (1995). Language learning and living abroad: Stories from the field. In B. F. Freed (Ed.), *Second language acquisition in a study abroad context* (pp. 271–292). Amsterdam: John Benjamins.
Rees, J., & Klapper, J. (2007). Analysing and evaluating the linguistic benefit of residence abroad for UK foreign language students. *Assessment & Evaluation in Higher Education, 32*(3), 331–353.
Regan, V., Howard, M., & Lemée, I. (2009). *The acquisition of sociolinguistic competence in a study abroad context*. Bristol: Multilingual Matters.
Rivers, W. P., & Robinson, J. P. (2012). The unchanging American capacity in languages other than English: Speaking and learning languages other than English, 2000–2008. *The Modern Language Journal, 96*(3), 369–379.
Roberts, C., Byram, M., Barro, A., Jordan, S., & Street, B. (2001). *Language learners as ethnographers*. Clevedon: Multilingual Matters.
Rowles, D., & Rowles, V. (2005). *Breaking the barriers: 100 years of the language assistants programme 1905–2005*. London: British Council.
Rüegg, W. (2004). Theology and the arts. In W. Rüegg (Ed.), *A history of the university in Europe. Volume 3: Universities in the nineteenth and early twentieth centuries (1800–1945)* (pp. 393–459). Cambridge: Cambridge University Press.
Sanz, C. (2014). Contributions of study abroad to our understanding of SLA processes and outcomes. In C. Pérez-Vidal (Ed.), *Language acquisition in study abroad and formal instruction contexts* (pp. 1–16). Amsterdam: John Benjamins.
Schauer, G. A. (2009). *Interlanguage pragmatic development: The study abroad context*. London: Continuum.
Sharifian, F. (2012). World Englishes, intercultural communication and requisite competences. In J. Jackson (Ed.), *The Routledge handbook of language and intercultural communication* (pp. 310–322). Abingdon: Routledge.
Stern, H. H. (Ed.). (1961). *Modern languages in the universities*. London: Modern Language Association.
Stolte, R. (2015). *German language learning in England: Understanding the enthusiasts*. (PhD), University of Southampton.
Taguchi, N. (2015). *Developing interactional competence in a Japanese study abroad context*. Bristol: Multilingual Matters.
Teichler, U. (1997). The British involvement in European higher education programmes: Findings of evaluation studies on Erasmus, Human Capital and Mobility and Tempus. In Society for Research in Higher Education (Ed.), *The Thirtieth Anniversary Seminars* (pp. 39–64). London: Society for Research into Higher Education.
Teichler, U. (2015). The impact of temporary study abroad. In R. Mitchell, N. Tracy-Ventura, & K. McManus (Eds.), *Social interaction, identity and language learning during residence abroad. EUROSLA Monographs 4* (pp. 15–32). Amsterdam: European Second Language Association.
Teichler, U., & Ferencz, I. (2011). Student mobility data: Recent achievements, current issues and future prospects. In U. Teichler, I. Ferencz, & B. Wächter (Eds.), *Mapping Mobility in Higher Education in Europe. Volume I: Overview and trends* (pp. 151–177). Bonn: Deutscher Akademischer Austauschdienst.
Tinsley, T., & Board, K. (2016). *Language Trends 2015/16: The state of language learning in primary and secondary schools in England*. London: British Council/ Education Development Trust.

UNESCO. (2014). *Global flow of tertiary level students*. Retrieved June 19, 2016, from http://www.uis.unesco.org/Education/Pages/international-student-flow-viz.aspx
Wächter, B., & Maiworm, F. (Eds.). (2014). *English-taught programmes in European higher education: The state of play in 2014*. Bonn: Lemmens.
Willis, F., Doble, G., Sankarayya, U., & Smithers, A. (1977). *Residence abroad and the student of modern languages: A preliminary survey*. Bradford: Modern Languages Centre, University of Bradford.
Wolcott, T. (2013). An American in Paris: Myth, desire, and subjectivity in one student's account of study abroad in France. In C. Kinginger (Ed.), *Social and cultural aspects of language learning in study abroad* (pp. 127–154). Amsterdam: John Benjamins.
Yang, J.-S. (2016). The effectiveness of study abroad on second language learning: A metaanalysis. *Canadian Modern Language Review, 72*(1), 66–94.

2 Language learning during residence abroad
Key constructs

2.1 Introduction

This chapter discusses a number of underlying concepts which are central to understanding the sojourn abroad as both a social and a language learning experience, from an interdisciplinary perspective. In Section 2.2, we begin by discussing interpretations of the nature of language, language use and language learning, relevant to the sojourner abroad. In Section 2.3, we review different conceptualizations of sojourner identity and L2 identity, together with their potential for interpreting sojourner behaviour and L2 learning. Section 2.4 briefly reviews current concerns with intercultural competence and the "intercultural speaker" as L2 educational goals, and considers their relevance for the sojourn abroad. In Section 2.5, we review previous research on a range of social factors which have been argued to influence L2 learning during study abroad: student and young adult lifestyle preferences, placement roles, domestic settings, leisure practices and social networking. These concepts, and relationships among them, form points of reference throughout the book.

2.2 Language

2.2.1 The target language construct and the goals of language education

As a first step in understanding the language learning goals of the Anglophone sojourners who are the subject of this book, it is necessary to examine the view of language to which they have been exposed in their presojourn language education.

The participants were already advanced learners of French or Spanish (and often of other languages), before they went abroad. As instructed learners, they had typically undertaken a systematic study of French/Spanish grammar, and regularly practised both speech and writing, encountering teaching materials which present a "standard" version of the target language as the learning goal.

For example, two commonly used university reference grammars of this type are *French Grammar and Usage* by Hawkins and Towell (2015), and *New Reference Grammar of Modern Spanish* (Butt & Benjamin, 2013). These French and Spanish texts differ in the number of language norms identified (one for French, several for Spanish, reflecting the national role of the language in a range of Latin American countries as well as Spain: Paffey, 2012). However, they each present quite restricted accounts of linguistic variation. Both volumes distinguish spoken and written modalities, and both talk about the existence of more and less formal "registers" within French and Spanish. The informal register recognized by Hawkins and Towell is described as "the relaxed register used by educated speakers of standard European French" (p. x). Butt and Benjamin similarly use the term "colloquial" to describe "forms that are acceptable in spontaneous educated speech but are usually avoided in formal speech or writing" (p. ix). Both these volumes pay little attention to other types of informal speech ("dialect", "slang" for H&T, "familiar", "popular" for B&B), and B&B warn the learner not to use them. Both volumes say almost nothing about regional-, class- or age-based variation within national varieties of the languages, and H&T say nothing about French beyond metropolitan France.

Overall then, these reference materials convey similar messages to students about the status of the language they are learning: that there are one or more discrete national varieties in each case, which are appropriate targets for L2 learners, and which show internal variation primarily in terms of the distinctions between speech and writing, and more/less formal usage. During their university studies, languages majors may gain some understanding of wider sociolinguistic variation; however, the instructional target for their own performance remains largely determined by standard language ideology. Studies by van Compernolle and Williams (2011, 2012) suggest that against this background, classroom learners of French, for example, struggle to adopt variable features as appropriate personal targets. Kinginger (2008) investigated the development of sojourners' awareness of colloquial and vernacular expressions in French, which overcame to some extent learners' "caution and reluctance" about using vernacular language (Kinginger, 2009, p. 103). However, overall, Kinginger (2009) noted an absence of studies investigating learners' awareness of how language use "may be marked for gender, age, region, or social class" (p. 101).

2.2.2 The ideal of "immersion"

> Because it can provide large amounts of input and interaction with native speakers, immersion in the target country has been considered the ideal context for language learning.
> – (Magnan & Lafford, 2012, p. 525)

The metaphor of linguistic and cultural "immersion" is a powerful driver in historical thinking about the sojourn abroad, which continues to be reflected in current advice manuals for Anglophone sojourners (Doerr, 2013). This metaphor survives despite long-standing problematizations of the extent and feasibility of immersion during study abroad by scholars such as S. Wilkinson (1998).

Some study abroad programmes continue to manage students' experience in the interests of immersion: for example, by discouraging contact with international peers or family members, by promoting local interactions through homestays, buddy schemes and tandem language exchanges, and/or through the device of the "language pledge", where participants commit themselves to monolingual target language use (Connor-Linton, 2015). These controls are most feasible, however, on short-term intensive study abroad programmes where participants are accompanied by mentors/instructors from the home institution and follow tailor-made courses in language and culture. They do not apply to those young adult sojourners who join regular courses in a local institution, or who become employed as language teaching assistants or workplace interns and must negotiate their own living accommodation and social networks. How far the concept of immersion remains relevant to such sojourners is very much a focus of the present study.

2.2.3 Language variation and plurilingualism in everyday practice

As just discussed, L2 education traditionally presents Anglophone learners with a standardized L2 target and measures their achievements against this yardstick. However, a standard language focus abstracts strongly away from the complex and dynamic reality of everyday language practices, which sojourners will encounter during any substantial stay abroad.

Long-standing sociolinguistic research on both French and Spanish has documented extensive social and regional variation, crosslinguistic influences, and dynamic evolution, well beyond the formal/informal register distinctions acknowledged in standard grammars: see for example Beeching, Armstrong, and Gadet (2009); Gadet (2003); and Gadet and Ludwig (2015) for French, and Mar-Molinero (1997) and Mar-Molinero and Stewart (2006) for Spanish. More broadly, contemporary societies are widely characterized by multilingual diversity and individual plurilingualism (Rindler Schjerve & Vetter, 2012). These may involve interactions between regional languages such as Basque, Catalan, Galician or Valenciano in Spain, and peninsular Spanish (Lasagabaster & Huguet, 2007). They will also involve newer immigrant languages, such as Arabic, Urdu, Chinese or Polish, now established in many European cities, where they also interact with national or regional languages (Blackledge & Creese, 2010; Extra & Yağmur, 2004). Finally, of course, English as a global language is entrenched in many educational, professional and leisure settings internationally (Crystal, 2003), including an increasing presence in international higher education (Dimova, Hultgren, & Jensen, 2015; Wächter & Maiworm, 2014). Language practices in such complex linguistic environments are well known to draw variably on the language resources available to the participants, including the mixed practices of codeswitching or translanguaging, and lingua franca usage. (For examples from the international workplace and contemporary higher education, see Berthoud, Grin, & Lüdi, 2013.)

Codeswitching has traditionally been defined as spoken interaction including elements drawn from more than one language or language variety, and is a phenomenon well studied by sociolinguists (Gardner-Chloros, 2008). More recently, *translanguaging* has been defined as

> an approach to the use of language, bilingualism and the education of bilinguals that considers the language practices of bilinguals not as two autonomous language systems [. . .] but as one linguistic repertoire with features that have been societally constructed as belonging to two separate languages
> (Garcia & Wei, 2014).

In this view, plurilingual individuals are to be understood as drawing freely on all elements of their personal linguistic repertoire to achieve successful communication and perform acts of identification, regardless of the origins of individual language elements. Similarly, the term *lingua franca* traditionally refers to "the communicative medium of choice among speakers of different first languages" (Hülmbauer & Seidlhofer, 2013, p. 388). However, scholars of today's pre-eminent lingua franca – English as a lingua franca (ELF) – argue that ELF is best understood also as a set of flexible interlingual practices, rather than a distinct language variety:

> ELF cannot be pinned down to a specific set of formal features [. . .] It is neither restricted to particular fields of use, nor does it generally lack linguistic resources. On the contrary, the communicative potential in ELF is grounded in the fact that [. . .] conventional structures can be, and are, appropriated and expanded in line with speakers' communicative purposes and pragmatic motives [. . .] there is in principle, room for integration of plurilingual elements [and] ELF thus clearly has to be viewed as a multilingual mode
> (Hülmbauer & Seidlhofer, 2013, p. 390).

Given the broader context just described, it is clear that even the temporary sojourner must expect to encounter and accommodate to a great diversity of language resources and practices in their chosen location abroad, even while pursuing a particular L2 learning goal.

2.2.4 Sojourner perspectives on target language variation and multilingualism

As noted by Kinginger (2009), we have only limited evidence on sojourners' responses to the actuality of socially and regionally indexed language variation and plurilingual practice. In this section, we draw together some available evidence regarding Anglophone sojourners' attitudes toward target language variability.

The research programme on sociolinguistic variation in L2 French summarized by Regan, Howard, and Lemée (2009) suggests that sojourners are generally interested in using less formal registers of language. Studies of Anglophones sojourning in Japan also describe some learners who are motivated to master variations in speech style (Cook, 2008; Taguchi, 2015). Some direct studies of interactions between sojourners and host families provide positive evidence of socialization into local linguistic and cultural norms, such as the practice of teasing (Kinginger, 2015), or dietary preferences and belief systems (Cook, 2006; DuFon, 2006). However, interaction studies also show that host-sojourner linguistic practices may construct a special identity for the sojourner (as a pupil: Wilkinson, 2002; Pellegrino Aveni, 2005; or as a "family pet": Iino, 2006). The studies of Iino (2006) and of Brown (2013) both documented cases of sojourners being constructed through the language practices of their local interlocutors as "cute" foreigners, who could not be expected to follow local norms of politeness. Some sojourners saw advantage in accepting this kind of outsider position:

> If I speak good Japanese, I thought they would not think me *kawaii* [amiable], and expect me to use all the *keigo* rules and manners. I don't know much about *keigo* and I have no intention to be like a Japanese businessman
> (MBA student, in Iino, 2006, p. 160).

Others, however, find such expectations demeaning. One of the sojourners studied by Brown (2013) strongly objected to any suggestion that the honorific categories of Korean (such as those relating to age) might not apply to him:

> I mean if somebody doesn't use the appropriate like – appropriate – you know – honorifics to me, if they are younger than me then I actually sometimes do get upset. [. . .] There was a situation here, a girl who was three years younger than me, she always kept talking to me using *panmal* [intimate speech style], almost from the start. But if the person thinks they don't need to use honorifics to me because I'm a foreigner, then that's rude
> (Sojourner Patrick, in Brown, 2013, p. 291).

However, sojourners may also resist aspects of socially indexed target language variation, where this conflicts with their sense of self; thus, for example, Siegal (1996) documents the conflicted reactions of American women to the prospect of acquiring gendered language behaviours in Japanese, which they associated with subordinate social positioning.

Regarding international sojourners' attitudes toward regional varieties of their chosen target language, and/or to regional minority languages, there are only limited findings. The previously mentioned study of Iino (2006) examined relations between American sojourners and their host families in Kyoto, Japan. Iino notes the sojourners' negativity about the Kyoto dialect of Japanese. A study by Garrett and Gallego Balsà (2014) reports some negativity toward the academic use of Catalan among international students at the University of Lleida, Catalonia, and their preference for Spanish and/or English. However, the study of Shiri (2013) found generally positive attitudes to regional dialects of Arabic among American sojourners in varied settings, who had previously been studying Modern Standard Arabic (MSA). These few examples show responses influenced by the particularities of different sociolinguistic settings, and clearly the field of sojourner attitudes and expectations regarding target language variation requires further investigation, linked to explorations of their sense of self as multilingual individuals (as in the work of van Compernolle and Williams with classroom learners: 2012).

2.2.5 Empirical studies of sojourners' language practices

It is evident that even under the strongest available conditions of immersion, sojourners will not forget their home language(s). The review by Dewey, Bown, Baker, Martinsen, Gold, and Eggett (2014) makes it overwhelmingly clear that sojourners will normally operate plurilingually, including ongoing regular use of their own home language(s) for certain purposes, throughout the sojourn. Despite language pledges which may lead to some exceptions, most sojourners use L1 within national friendship groups abroad, and when sustaining links with family and friends from home, or pursuing personal leisure/media interests.

There is also considerable evidence for the use of lingua francas among sojourners. The use of ELF is widely reported, for example, among international students in Finland (Dervin, 2013), in France (Kinginger, 2008) or in Hungary (Kalocsai, 2011; Peckham, Kalocsai, Kovàcs, & Sherman, 2012). Dervin describes complex attitudes toward ELF among sojourners:

> On the one hand, it allows the students to communicate with each other and the locals but, on the other, it limits the learning of the local languages, constrains encounters with the locals, and in some cases, transforms the students' English language skills "for the worse"
>
> (Dervin, 2013, p. 114).

Sojourners' use of French as a lingua franca (FLF) has also been studied (Behrent, 2007; Dervin, 2013). Behrent (2007) reports on a substantial corpus of interactions directly recorded among international Erasmus students in the *Cité Internationale Universitaire* in Paris. These students largely sustained the use of FLF, though with side sequences in their home languages, and also using English, in order to seek help/negotiate meanings/carry out conversational repair. In the following FLF example, a Latin American student (AL) is trying to describe the changing nature of Spanish to a mixed-language group, but seeks help from another Spanish speaker (FR) to fill a lexical gap. The assistance is offered in English, which opens up the possibility that others might contribute to the repair, yet the main line of the conversation continues in French:

AL: mais c'est très drôle parce que l'espagnol change bEAUcoup pour euh pour region et aussi nous avons des::/ par exemple les::/ comment s'écrit/ que s'appelle en anglais par exemple *la novela*?
FR: *novela*?

AL: *si*
FR: en anglais? *Telenovela . . . soap opera*
AL: *soap opera* . . . est-ce que tu connais qu'est-ce que c'est un *soap opera?* . . . je sais pas comment s'appelle ça en français . . . oui. et *soap opera(s)* de venezuela et de colombie (Behrent, 2007, p. 197: emphasis added).

Behrent describes her multilingual participants as making positive and sustained choices to speak French, despite the general availability of ELF. She also describes them as aspiring not only to use French but to gain better control of standard French, with frequent error checking and side sequences discussing language issues.

2.2.6 Language learning and development during the sojourn abroad

In Chapter 1, we summarized past research on the language development of sojourners, which shows the most consistent gains being made in the domains of fluency and of lexis, with more inconsistency in the areas of grammar/morphosyntax and of sociopragmatics. There is general agreement among study abroad researchers on this broad picture, but the theoretical explanations offered differ considerably: Generativist, functionalist, interactionist, sociocognitivist, skills-based and sociocultural accounts can all be found.

Dewey et al. (2014) probably reflect the most common position, when they relate L2 learning insojourn to Long's Interaction Hypothesis (1996): that is, learning of new grammar or lexis is most likely to take place when L2 input and/or output are interactionally modified as a result of meaning-focused negotiation and repair in discourse. From this point of view, sojourners' inconsistency in learning L2 morphosyntax can be attributed to variable opportunities for this type of interaction, and/or to troubles in this interaction process. However, DeKeyser (2010) offers a different theoretical explanation, in line with skill acquisition theory. For him, on the one hand, fluency gains quickly arise from the proceduralization of declarative L2 knowledge previously established in the language classroom (including explicit knowledge). On the other hand, in DeKeyser's view, the inefficient learning of morphosyntax among lower proficiency sojourners is due to their lack of previously acquired declarative knowledge – that is, they flounder when interacting insojourn, because they have nothing to proceduralize.

Regan et al. (2009, pp. 54–57) follow the general ideas of Bartning (1997) concerning the "advanced learner variety", which they view as applicable to the sojourners they have studied. According to this functionalist perspective (Klein & Perdue, 1992), learners lack grammatical morphology in the early stages, and their L2 use at that point is "based on pragmatic means". By the advanced stage, L2 morphology has generally been acquired and made available for use by a process of "grammaticalization". However, its use in "fragile zones" such as verb morphology may still be variable, and proceduralization of this knowledge is still required, once again through real-time practice. Generativist theorists provide more specific explanations for persistent "fragility"/variability at certain key points in L2 morphosyntax. Thus, they appeal to concepts such as parameter resetting and feature reassembly to explain the challenges for Anglophones of acquiring particular domains of Romance morphosyntax, such as the pronoun system and tense/aspect morphology, which apply equally for sojourners as for other adult L2 learners (Rothman & Pascual y Cabo, 2014). Another group of SA researchers argue for the relevance of language socialization theory, for the acquisition of L2 sociopragmatic competence in particular (Cook, 2008; Kinginger, 2012, 2015; Shively, 2011).

From our own perspective, we believe that the development of instructed L2 learners to an advanced level involves a coalition of learning processes. Generative theory is helpful in explaining the persistent difficulties of advanced learners with particular points in L2 morphosyntax where the L1 works differently. The varied opportunities for L2 input and meaning-focused interaction afforded during the sojourn should provide rich opportunities for matching meaning to new forms, as well as for the proceduralization of existing L2 knowledge. Language socialization theory is especially useful in understanding the development of sociopragmatic knowledge, though we also need to account for sojourners' resistance to some L2 norms of behaviour, and the influence of desired L2 identities in the evolution, for example, of sojourners' politeness behaviour (Kaltschuetz, 2014).

2.2.7 The CAF framework

In terms of a framework appropriate to capture major aspects of L2 development during the sojourn, we have found it helpful to adopt the widely used CAF framework (complexity, accuracy, fluency). The CAF framework originated in discussions in the 1970s on how best to characterize L2 proficiency (Skehan, 1996, 1998). There is a consensus among many SLA researchers that L2 proficiency has multiple components, seen for example in "four skills" models, or models of "communicative competence". CAF has recently emerged as a leading framework, which can be justified in terms of psycholinguistic theory (Skehan, 2009), and which has also found considerable empirical support (Norris & Ortega, 2009).

The components of CAF are introduced in a recent authoritative review in the following way:

> Complexity is commonly characterised as the ability to use a wide and varied range of sophisticated structures and vocabulary in the L2, accuracy as the ability to produce target-like and error-free language, and fluency as the ability to produce the L2 with native-like rapidity, pausing, hesitation, or reformulation
>
> (Housen, Kuiken, & Vedder, 2012, p. 2).

Given growing acknowledgement of the complexity of L2 development in sojourn (Llanes, 2011), the relevance of CAF to study abroad L2 research is clear, and

SA researchers increasingly orient their work toward aspects of the framework, notably fluency and accuracy (see, e.g., chapters in Pérez-Vidal, 2014; Godfrey, Treacy, & Tarone, 2014). In Chapters 4 and 5, we review this work in respect of French and Spanish, the languages in focus in this volume. Here, we briefly review the main components of the CAF framework itself, as used in our study.

2.2.7.1 Structural complexity

Pallotti (2009, 2015) notes that complexity can refer to a number of different, but related, phenomena, such as the structural properties of words, sentences, and utterances, or design features of communicative tasks, as well as the relative ease with which learners acquire particular language features. He defines these different types of complexity as follows:

> 1. Structural complexity, a formal property of texts and linguistic systems having to do with the number of their elements and their relational patterns; 2. Cognitive complexity, having to do with the processing costs associated with linguistic structures; 3. Developmental complexity, i.e. the order in which linguistic structures emerge and are mastered in second (and, possibly, first) language acquisition
>
> (Pallotti, 2015, p. 118).

Similarly, Crystal (1997) suggests that "[i]n linguistics, complexity refers to both the [. . .] internal structuring of linguistic units and to the psychological difficulty in using or learning them" (p. 76). By internal structuring, Crystal refers to the combinations of different linguistic constituents that a speaker may use, situated at the heart of many quantitative approaches to measuring complexity, using clauses, T-units (Wolfe-Quintero, Inagaki, & Kim,1998) and Analysis of Speech Units (ASUs: Foster, Tonkyn, & Wigglesworth, 2000) as basic structural units. In this study, our focus is linguistic complexity understood in terms of this "internal structuring of linguistic units" (Crystal, 1997).

Following Housen et al. (2012), we further distinguish between syntactic and lexical complexity. Syntactic complexity refers to the sentential, clausal and phrasal characteristics of linguistic utterances. It is can be measured in a variety of ways (Bulté & Housen, 2012), with the most commonly employed measures being based on length (e.g., number of words per T-unit), or on ratios between different syntactic elements (e.g., number of clauses per T-unit).

2.2.7.2 Lexical complexity

Lexical complexity has recently been reviewed by De Clercq (2015). This construct has to do with the size and depth of the L2 lexicon, as reflected in language use. De Clercq distinguishes between three components of lexical complexity: lexical diversity, lexical sophistication and lexical density.

Lexical diversity is related to the size of the mental lexicon, and "is taken to be reflected by the proportion of unique words in a text, and the language user's ability to introduce new lexical items" (De Clercq, 2015, pp. 71–72). It is measured by exploring the proportion of unique words (types) relative to the total length of a text (measured in word tokens). Different ways of calculating this ratio while taking account of bias due to text length have been proposed; a commonly used lexical diversity measure is D, popularized by Malvern and colleagues (Malvern, Richards, Chipere, & Duran, 2004). In the LANGSNAP project, we operationalized lexical complexity as lexical diversity, measured with D.

Lexical sophistication involves the learner's knowledge and use of less common words. It is typically operationalized as word frequency; "the assumption is that less frequent words are more advanced and difficult, and that their appearance in texts will correlate with proficiency" (De Clercq, 2015, p. 72). Lexical density refers to the information packaging of a text, and this has been measured, for example, through the ratio of content words to function words, or by examining the proportions of nouns or verbs in a text (De Clercq, 2015, p. 72).

2.2.7.3 Accuracy

Distinctions between accurate and non-accurate production are often made through comparisons with L1 speakers:

> Accuracy (or *correctness*) in essence refers to the extent to which an L2 learner's performance (and the L2 system that underlies this performance) deviates from the norm (i.e. usually the native speaker)
> (Housen et al., 2012, p. 4).

As noted by Lambert and Kormos (2014), there are two common approaches to operationalizing accuracy in the CAF framework: "(i) calculating the ratio of errors in a text to some unit of production (e.g. words, clauses, sentential units) and (ii) calculating the proportion of these units that are error free" (p. 609). Such broad operationalizations have been criticized because all errors are treated as equivalent, though we know that not all grammatical features develop at the same rate, and many researchers draw on more focused measures of accuracy development, such as past tense use (Kihlstedt, 2002; Labeau, 2005; McManus, 2013, 2015). Such studies measure accuracy in terms of suppliance in obligatory contexts and/or target-like use of a specific grammatical feature (e.g., the *Imparfait* in French). In the present study, we operationalize accuracy in both ways: as a global measure (all errors) and with reference to specific language features (see Chapter 3). We understand accuracy to refer to use of the L2 that L1 speakers would judge as acceptable/typical usage. For example, accurate gender attribution (*la table* and not *le table*) and verb-subject agreement (*elles finissent* and not *elles finit*).

2.2.7.4 Fluency

Lennon (1990) distinguishes between broad and narrow fluency. Fluency in its broad sense is a general descriptor of a person's language and/or speech ability (or general language proficiency), which can refer to a strong command of the language in terms of grammar, vocabulary, pronunciation and ease with which someone speaks (Bosker, Pinget, Quené, Sanders, & De Jong, 2013; Chambers, 1997). Fluency in its narrow sense, however, is defined in terms of temporal aspects of production, including total speaking time, pauses, hesitations and repairs, which can be objectively measured from a speech sample. Segalowitz (2010) describes this as "utterance fluency"; Tavakoli and Skehan (2005) distinguish between breakdown fluency (number and length of pauses, length of run between pauses, etc.), speed fluency (how many words or syllables are produced during a given time unit), and repair fluency (numbers of hesitations and repairs) (see also De Jong, Steinel, Florij, Schoonen, & Hulstijn, 2012).

In this study, we understand fluency in terms of the temporal aspects of language production, and focus on measures of speed fluency. Although fluency is perhaps most often understood to refer to speech, this study also examines written fluency, operationalized as speed fluency (words written per minute).

2.3 Identity

2.3.1 Views of identity in SLA

Kramsch (2009) has described the language learner as (potentially) a multilingual subject, defined by possession of what she calls "symbolic competence". This consists in an understanding of the symbolic value of language, and the "different cultural memories evoked by different symbolic systems", as well as the capacity to use these different systems "to reframe ways of seeing familiar events, create alternative realities, and find an appropriate subject position between languages" (p. 201).

Discussions of identity in the applied linguistics and SLA literature have increasingly adopted similarly dynamic and subjective perspectives (Block, 2007; Dervin, 2013; Norton, 2000, 2014), influenced by broader arguments in social science by theorists such as Chris Weedon and Judith Butler. Briefly, from this point of view, identity is seen as "multiple, changing and a site of struggle" (Norton, 2014, p. 61).

Block provides an extended definition, relating the individual "performance" of identity to the wider social context. For him, identities comprise:

> Socially constructed, self-conscious, ongoing narratives that individuals perform, interpret and project in dress, bodily movements, actions and language. Identity work occurs in the company of others – either face-to-face or in an electronically mediated mode – with whom to varying degrees individuals share beliefs, motives, values and practices. Identities are about negotiating new subject positions at the crossroads of the past, present and future. Individuals are shaped by their sociohistories but they also shape their sociohistories as life goes on. The entire process is conflictive as opposed to harmonious and individuals often feel ambivalent. There are unequal power

relations to deal with, around the different capitals – economic, cultural and social – that both facilitate and constrain interactions with others in the different communities of practice with which individuals engage in their lifetimes. Finally, identities are related to different traditionally demographic categories such as ethnicity, race, nationality, migration, gender, social class and language

(Block, 2007, p. 27).

Here, Block stresses the social construction of identity ("identity work" occurs in the company of others). However, elsewhere, Block, Kramsch and others acknowledge the need to distinguish a more internal and psychological dimension to identity, and Kramsch returns to Weedon's original term "subjectivity" for this (Block, 2013a; Kramsch, 2015). Similarly, Taylor (2014) makes a distinction between the public selves displayed in social interaction, and a so-called private self, which together make up an individual person's identity. To explain this distinction Taylor quotes Baumeister (1986):

> The public self is the self that is manifested in the presence of others, that is formed when other people attribute traits and qualities to the individual, and that is communicated to other people in the process of self-presentation. The private self is the way the person understands himself or herself and is the way the person really is
>
> (Baumeister, 1986, p. v).

For Taylor, dissonance between these private and public selves can be a dynamic force for change; she cites the example of an anxious L2 learner (private self) who manages to display the public self of a confident L2 speaker, and so creates the possibility of eventually internalizing this alternative self (p. 97).

Taylor also introduces the self-discrepancy theory of Higgins (1987), according to which the private self comprises three "domains": the *actual self*, the *ideal self*, and the *ought self*.

> The actual self is defined as a person's beliefs of what s/he is as an individual in the present, the ideal self represents what they would like to become in the future, and the ought self is defined as what individuals feel they should become
>
> (Taylor, 2014, p. 98).

Such imagined "possible selves" are important for second language learners (Pavlenko, 2005; Ryan & Irie, 2014), and the ideal self and the ought-to self have become familiar in the SLA field through the L2 Motivational Self System proposed by Zoltan Dörnyei (2009). Researchers who have studied the motivation of Anglophone learners of other languages in particular have found that an ideal L2 self plays an important role, though an ought-to self is harder to pin down (Busse & Williams, 2010).

30 *Key constructs*

Block (2013b) has more recently criticized applied linguistics discussions of identity, which he sees as over-privileging agency; that is, focusing attention primarily on the voluntary choices and performances of individuals, rather than on the broader social (and linguistic) structures which constrain these choices. That is, for Block, insufficient attention has been paid to the "structure/agency dynamic" (2013b, p. 142). He joins Macdonald and O'Regan (2012) in proposing the critical realism of Bhaskar (1998, 2008) as the basis for a more balanced view:

> Society must be regarded as an ensemble of structures, practices and conventions which individuals reproduce or transform, but which would not exist unless they did so. Society does not exist independently of human activity (the error of reification). But it is not the product of it (the error of voluntarism) [. . .] Society, then, provides necessary conditions for intentional human action, and intentional human action is a necessary condition for it. Society is only present in human action, but human action always expresses and utilizes some or other social form. Neither can, however, be identified with, reduced to, explained in terms of, or reconstructed from the other. There is an ontological hiatus between society and people, as well as a model of connection (viz transformation)
>
> (Bhaskar, 1998, pp. 36–37 in Block, 2013b, pp. 137–138).

This brief review shows how identity has been conceptualized and debated in the fields of applied linguistics and SLA, including acknowledgement of tensions between social performances and internal states, as well as the implications for conceptualizations of identity deriving from different views on the relations between structure and agency. In the next section we examine more specifically the dimensions of identity which have so far attracted the most attention in study abroad research.

2.3.2 Identity in study abroad research

Students contemplating study abroad have high expectations of the experience. A recent survey of more than 1,500 British undergraduates identified the following motivations:

- To have an interesting and enjoyable experience;
- To broaden horizons;
- To enhance employability and employment prospects;
- To develop intercultural awareness and a range of interpersonal skills, particularly independence and self-confidence;
- To improve the prospects of working abroad in the long term;
- To develop or heighten language skills, mainly for languages students;
- To support or enhance their degree outcome

(Mellors-Bourne, Jones, Lawton, & Woodfield, 2015).

Very similar beliefs are documented among other groups (Härkonen & Dervin, 2015; Van Mol, 2015). It is therefore unsurprising that researchers have been interested in the actual evolution of sojourner identity when abroad. Useful reviews, with a prime but not exclusive focus on Anglophone sojourners, have been published by Block (2007, Chapter 6), by Kinginger (2009, Chapter 5); and by Plews (2015). These writers agree on a number of central themes: the influence of some "traditionally demographic" factors on the sojourn experience (gender and nationality); the positioning of sojourners as outsiders or socially less competent persons; "coming of age" narratives, that is, sojourners' progression over time to greater personal autonomy and resilience; and intercultural learning.

2.3.2 1 *Sojourners as new strangers*

Several of these themes are brought together in the research on student sojourners of the anthropologist Elizabeth Murphy-Lejeune (2002), who proposes an overarching identity for the temporary student sojourner, in European contexts: that of the "new stranger".

In the anthropological literature, the concept of the "stranger" was originally developed to address the cases of "the traditional migrant and the marginal" (p. 33); such strangers are understood to experience multiple dislocations, in terms of space, time, social and symbolic positions, and identity (p. 34). Murphy-Lejeune investigates how far these ideas are applicable to her group of "new strangers": student sojourners. She studied groups of European students on different types of mobility placement: Erasmus university exchanges, language teaching assistantships, and an international business school programme. In her study, only the teaching assistants were specialist language learners; the rest were following business studies or other non-language programmes. She highlights that even before departure, her participants are not typical of the student majority but rather come from a "migratory elite" (p. 73); that is, they have considerable previous experience of travel in various forms, and good support from their families (who may also be well travelled). Murphy-Lejeune then describes her participants' trajectory through their sojourn abroad, documenting their arrival and associated culture shock, their entry into new physical and social settings and their creation of a new social fabric. She describes adaptation processes, such as getting to feel comfortable and at ease in the new setting, or acquiring a personal history there. Important for successful adaptation are personal attitude, social participation and the development of local interpersonal relations (p. 213); necessary qualities for good adaptors include openness, tolerance and flexibility (p. 216). A major general outcome is that of the "opening of social space" and personal self-discovery:

> One of the main benefits derived from an experience which perturbs them is that the learning gained contributes to their overall capacity to adapt to other difficult passages in life. Individuals who have gone through this emerge stronger, asserting their individuality. During this new socialization which students manage on their own, they become emancipated. Most students

mention this kind of elation, of enlargement of their world and of personal opening, as "growing up". Then the stay is truly vested with the value of a rite of passage and a "life lesson"

(p. 226).

Toward the end of their stay, Murphy-Lejeune invited her participants to rate their "final position" in the host culture, choosing from among five possibilities: *tourist, survivor, resident, near citizen,* and *citizen*. Most positioned themselves as *residents* on this scale, and explained that this meant that they had a professional or student role in the country and had contacts and friends in that milieu. But the resident would not, for example, "master the complexities of local history . . . the 'resident' denotes above all a person whose stay will be temporary" (p. 224). However, most of the language specialists found the *near citizen* label most appropriate; for example, this was the group that most typically expressed enthusiasm for considerably extending the stay abroad (and who thus might eventually become first-generation permanent migrants). Overall, Murphy-Lejeune concludes that her participants "extend their range of possible memberships and sometimes acquire the freedom of the potential wanderer [. . .] their world is an expanding, open, wider world" (p. 227).

2.3.2.2 The gender factor

Murphy-Lejeune does not discuss gender as making any strong contribution to the shaping of "new stranger" identity. However, gender is the most commonly discussed "traditional" demographic factor in the L2 study abroad literature. Several researchers working with data collected mostly in the 1990s reported discomfort on the part of American female sojourners who felt themselves to be sexually harassed, or at risk of being so, both on the street and also by male acquaintances; these discomforts have been reported in studies in Russia (Pellegrino Aveni, 2005; Polanyi, 1995), in Costa Rica (Twombly, 1995), and in Spain (Goldoni, 2013; Talburt & Stewart, 1999), and resulted in some alienation and reluctance to socialize with locals. Kinginger (2009) notes that this issue does not arise in most studies of non-American sojourners, and argues that American sojourners' perceptions may have been reported too uncritically. For her, such perceptions need to be interpreted in light of sojourners' own prior socialization in their society of origin, as well as in local and intercultural context (p. 196). In her own empirical work with sojourners in France (Kinginger, 2008), she shows how participants' immediate perceptions of gendered relations were shaped by long-standing stereotypes learned at home. Work by Trentman (2015) records how some American female sojourners in the more culturally distant setting of Egypt learned to negotiate a range of gendered subject positions/identities, including *traditional good girls, loose foreign women, targets of sexual harassment, female interlocutors, guests of the family,* and *romantic partners*. She concludes that although

the general consensus supported the narrative of sexual harassment and fear of interactions with local males, difficulty making female friends, and subsequent refuge in the study abroad peer group, there were also gendered experiences that resisted this pattern, which offered varied routes to improved social integration

(Trentman, 2015, p. 267).

The positive contribution of the "romantic partner" role for both intercultural learning and L2 development is further discussed by Goldoni (2013).

2.3.2.3 The nationality factor

Both Block (2007) and Kinginger (2009) review research on American sojourners in respect of perceived changes in national identity during the sojourn abroad. The studies they discuss show varied outcomes, with many sojourners tending toward greater ethnocentrism as they encounter unfamiliar forms of social organization, but also more especially, encounter perhaps for the first time negative views of aspects of American lifestyle and foreign policy. This tendency is documented in the previously mentioned studies by Polanyi (1995), Twombly (1995), Talburt and Stewart (1999), Pellegrino Aveni (2005), and Kinginger and Farrell Whitworth (2005), and also by Wilkinson (1998), Isabelli-García (2006) and Goldoni (2013). Kinginger herself was collecting data from her case study participants in France during the 2003 US-led invasion of Iraq, and she documented their reactions to vocal anti-Americanism, encountered both on the streets and in homestay interactions (2008). In several cases these sojourners retreated into "the superiority of American culture" (Kinginger, 2009, p. 199), associated more exclusively with fellow nationals, and returned with a heightened sense of national identity. Both Isabelli-García (2006) and Kinginger (2004) offer counterexamples of US sojourners who achieve a degree of ethnorelativism in the course of longer stays abroad, but acknowledge that this outcome is by no means assured.

Both Block and Kinginger suggest that increasing ethnocentricity may be a distinctive trait of American sojourners. They see a contrasting example in the European participants in the study of Murphy-Lejeune, for example, to whom they attribute an "emergent pan European identity" (Kinginger, 2009, p. 199). Murphy-Lejeune collected her data in the mid-1990s, arguably a time of relative harmony among nation states within the European Union, and thus a moment when ethnocentrism was less likely to be provoked by immediate events. Nonetheless, Murphy-Lejeune herself comments quite extensively (pp. 184–188) on the tendency of her participants to cluster in "ethnic groups", that is, the Irish with the Irish and the Germans with the Germans, which suggests that ethnocentrism was not absent in this study either. She quotes Amin, an Irish student, who makes a considered choice over time to associate mostly with fellow nationals:

> "I found I really . . . I didn't have much in common with the Belgians. I mean, I spoke to them, we went out sometimes together for a few drinks . . . but what they enjoyed I didn't enjoy and vice versa [. . .] I ended up . . . well, I, I, I ended up really going out with my Irish . . . with Irish friends who came

over in the second term because it . . . in some ways, it was because we all had wanted to do the same thing, we wanted to travel, we wanted to go . . . we wanted to visit different places"

(Murphy-Lejeune, 2002, p. 184).

It is hard to interpret data of this kind as evidence of an emergent pan-European identity, and in fact Murphy-Lejeune herself does not make such claims.

Plews (2015) reviews earlier work on the nationality factor, and argues that this work may lead to some over-simple assumptions, i.e. that:

> Negative orientations and interactional experiences in SL study abroad may cause participants to reject others' viewpoints and values and to assert a more steadfastly national self. Correspondingly, positive orientations and interactions may lead participants to take on others' viewpoints and values and position themselves as more intercultural and less definitively associated with a given monocultural identity. This might lead to a simplistic equation in which less intercultural is equated with more national and more intercultural equals less national
>
> (pp. 285–286).

From his own empirical research, Plews presents several case studies of Canadian students undertaking a short language-learning sojourn in Germany. While a minority adopt strong ethnocentric positions, most adopt a relativist, intercultural position, though this may still be combined with a positive sense of being Canadian. A female sojourner, Frida, comments on this combination:

> Well, I still feel very Canadian. Um but I wasn't born in Canada. [. . .] And it's always a puzzle. And they[my local German contacts] are like, "Oh, so you're not actually Canadian," and I'm like, "Actually, I am REALLY Canadian" because that's what Canada is, it's a mix of so many people from so many places. Um, so I think, um, yeah I think I'll feel more Canadian and more okay to be from so many different places in a way. [. . .] You know, I am very Canadian, but it doesn't mean that [. . .] you know, this is who I am because I can adapt to other cultures and [. . .] What I like to do is to go unnoticed in other places, not to be pinpointed as the foreigner
>
> (Plews, 2015, p. 295).

Plews comments that his participants' ability to adopt a relativist, intercultural position may be eased by the "multicultural" ideology which forms part of Canadian national rhetoric, and this is illustrated in Frida's comments quoted above. From these various cases, it can be seen that particular national origins and ready-made discourses on national characteristics may make sojourners more or less open to adopting intercultural positions, but such interpretations clearly need fuller testing in additional research.

2.3.2.4 Bringing language into focus

Of those researchers who have discussed sojourner identity, Benson, Barkhuizen, Bodycott, and Brown (2013) are among those who bring language clearly into focus. They follow other theorists discussed here in viewing identity as both subjective and socially constructed:

> We begin from a social view of identity as a dialectical relationship between the "inner" and "outer" aspects of the self, involving our own sense of who we are, the ways in which we represent ourselves, and how we are represented and positioned by others
>
> (p. 2).

These writers view the development of second language identity as "largely a matter of incorporating experiences of second language learning and use into an ongoing sense of who we are" (p. 2). Thus, they believe that "language proficiency outcomes can often be interpreted in terms of identity development, while personal competence outcomes can be interpreted in terms of language development" (p. 42). Figure 2.1 shows their view of the relationship between second language identity, and a continuum of possible second language outcomes from study abroad.

By *identity-related L2 proficiency*, Benson et al. refer to the L2 abilities needed to project desired dimensions of identity. Here they primarily have sociopragmatic competence in mind; thus, for example, sojourners in France may make choices among more or less formal sociolinguistic variants in French (Regan et al., 2009), or prioritize the mastery of young people's informal speech style, in order to project a variety of identities. Sojourners may choose to assimilate to native speaker norms of politeness, or to produce intermediate styles signalling a distinct sojourner identity, as has been noted in studies of sojourners accommodating to "plain" and "polite" styles in Japanese (Iwasaki, 2010; Siegal, 1996; Taguchi, 2015), and also in some studies of sociopragmatic development in European languages (Barron, 2006).

By *linguistic self-concept*, Benson et al. refer to sojourners' affiliations to the languages that they know (and to different varieties of these), to beliefs about language learning and self-assessments of proficiency, and to perceptions of the self as a language learner and a language user: "the self-beliefs that a learner holds

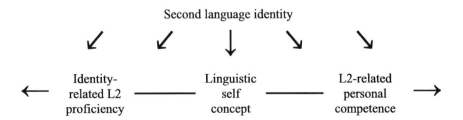

Figure 2.1 Potential second language outcomes of study abroad (after Benson et al., 2013)

and takes with them into any encounter, not just in respect to one specific context" (Mercer, 2011, in Benson et al., 2013, p. 46). They illustrate this concept with reference to the study of Allen (2010), who describes the varied motivations of US sojourners undertaking a short study programme in France, from an activity theory perspective. Allen's participants included a philosophy student, Eric, who wanted to add a reading knowledge of French to his existing repertoire of relevant languages (Latin, German, etc.); and Elise, who planned a career in the foreign service, and saw herself using French to assist American tourists in difficulties. Others, however, saw the programme as a means of enhancing their professional credentials in general terms. Allen claims that "enhanced language learning motivation and persistence" emerged primarily for sojourners such as Eric and Elise, but not for those with less clear motivations; that is, sojourners' initial goals influenced their language learning behaviours and activities. The study abroad context does not of itself generate transformative learning; instead, context itself "can be understood as emergent from students' motives, goals and resultant actions" (Allen, 2010, p. 46).

In describing *L2-related personal competence*, Benson et al. refer to constructs already encountered: personal confidence, self-reliance and independence on the one hand, and reflective capacity, ethnorelativism and intercultural competence on the other hand.

2.3.3 Identity: A summing up

This short review shows that researchers studying the Anglophone sojourner abroad have generally accepted the flexible interpretations of identity as performance that are currently prevalent in applied linguistics. The research to date shows certain biases, most notably a concern with the perspective of the sojourner themselves, rather than those of receiving social groups. Nonetheless, broad trends are apparent which will be helpful in approaching the LANGSNAP data (in Chapter 8 in particular). To interpret these data, it will be necessary to take account of the following:

- Participants' presojourn and insojourn language-learning goals and motivations, linguistic self-concept and ideal L2 self;
- Participants' presojourn and postsojourn home identities (positioning as student, as family member, as friend, as romantic partner);
- The temporary nature of the sojourn, and its implications for identity (as a language learner and user? A student? A tourist? A party animal?);
- The possibility of identity dislocation and disruption;
- The "coming of age" dimension;
- The gender dimension;
- The role of national affiliations, but also any possible emergence of transnational subjectivities;
- Social positioning by locals – as outsider? As young professional? As fellow student? As friend? As romantic partner? (Like many other projects, LANGSNAP has to rely on indirect evidence here.)

2.4 Culture

2.4.1 Conceptualizations of culture in language education

As noted in Chapter 1, traditional models of language education have treated culture as a bounded phenomenon, associated with particular languages and nation states (J. Wilkinson, 2012). A related assumption concerning study abroad was that sojourners would gain "first-hand knowledge of the foreign culture" (Healey, 1967), as part of a developmental process which would allow them to approximate increasingly to native speaker norms of language and behaviour.

As for identity, discussed in the last section, more dynamic and flexible concepts of culture have been generally adopted by contemporary social theorists (Holliday, 2012). Accordingly, second language educators have argued for the promotion of "intercultural communicative competence and intercultural citizenship" (Byram, 2012), and for the replacement of the native speaker target in language education by the "intercultural speaker" target; that is, someone who

> has an ability to interact with "others", to accept other perspectives and perceptions of the world, to mediate between different perspectives, to be conscious of their evaluations and differences
> (Byram, Nichols, & Stevens, 2001, p. 5).

Kramsch (1998, in J. Wilkinson, 2012, p. 298) pointed out that language learners today are likely to be operating even in the home classroom in multilingual and multicultural communities, and argued that the intercultural speaker operates at all times "at the border between several languages or language varieties, moving his/her way through the troubled waters of crosscultural misunderstandings" (p. 27).

2.4.2 Intercultural learning in study abroad

In line with these changing perspectives, educators concerned with study abroad have re-evaluated the type of cultural learning they aim to promote, reducing the emphasis on encyclopedic knowledge-gathering concerning one particular culture, and promoting general sensitivity to cultural difference. There have been numerous initiatives to encourage critical reflection on cultural issues among sojourners, such as the UK LARA project (Roberts, Byram, Barro, Jordan, & Street, 2001; Wilkinson, 2012), which trained sojourners to undertake specific ethnographic projects when abroad. Jackson (2012) has argued for consistent attention to intercultural awareness throughout the entire study programme, from pre- to postsojourn; for Phipps (2003), this should lead to a "disposition for action" (p. 11) which supports the learner in shaping a new cultural identity and linguistic practices relevant to that identity.

Empirical research on sojourners has shown, however, that the position of "intercultural speaker" is not necessarily acquired, even by sojourners with advanced L2 proficiency (Jackson, 2012; Papatsiba, 2006). Some researchers have suggested that other strands of sojourner identity may conflict with this position (Kinginger, 2010). Thus, the important "coming of age" dimension may lead to a strong preoccupation with the self and the personal, including myth-making and romanticization of the sojourn setting as an exotic backdrop to personal development (Wolcott, 2013). Sojourners may be most comfortable socially with other international sojourners with whom they share a similar cultural background and/or immediate experiences of cultural dislocation (Murphy-Lejeune, 2002). They are enthusiastic about touristic travel to "heritage" locations, a trait which has also been seen as detrimental to local social integration and deep intercultural learning (Adams, 2006; Kinginger, 2008), though it is treated more sympathetically by Papatsiba (2006), who argues that cultural tourism is an inevitable stage in making sense of the sojourn setting (pp. 111–112).

Overall, the acquisition of intercultural competence is closely connected with the evolution of sojourner identity, where "intercultural speaker" is just one of a range of possible identity positions. Within the LANGSNAP project, these connections are acknowledged and intercultural learning is treated as an aspect of sojourner identity development (see Chapter 8).

2.5 Communities and social networks

2.5.1 Student communities and social relations

Student sojourners are emerging young adults, yet still not fully independent in an economic sense (Arnett, 2014; Blum, 2012, 2016). This has important consequences both for the identity positions they adopt and for the social relations in which they prefer to engage.

At the contemporary home university, students are expected to undertake both structured and independent study, to pass examinations, and to achieve good degree results which can act as a passport to employability. However, home student life also has a strong "coming of age" dimension. Many British undergraduate students are living a largely collective life with same-aged peers, in halls or rented accommodation (Holdsworth, 2006; Holton, 2016). Many are sexually active and establish longer-term romantic partnerships while still students (Finn, 2013; Monto & Carey, 2014), which may endure when undergraduate collective life is over. Leisure activities may involve sport, music, video gaming and other media consumption; "going out" to pubs, clubs and parties is a regular group activity, and stimulants such as alcohol are central to social life (Selwyn, 2008).

It must be expected that student sojourners will seek continuity with many aspects of this lifestyle during their stay abroad, and that this will influence their preferences both when seeking living accommodation and when building friendships and social networks. This continuity connects to the earlier discussion of "coming of age" aspects of sojourner identity (Section 2.3.2).

2.5.2 Role-related settings and practices for the sojourn abroad

The sojourners who are the focus of the LANGSNAP project chose from a number of structured placement options. Each of these settings offered potential integration into some type of local community of practice and social networking with target language speakers. However, each also presented certain challenges for the sojourner.

2.5.2.1 The exchange student setting

For European students, an Erasmus exchange studentship in a different European country is a very common option. However, Murphy-Lejeune (2002, pp. 165–167) points out a range of challenges connected with attempting to integrate into a new higher education setting and educational culture. Institutions vary considerably in the degree of mentoring and personal support offered to students, so that some may be baffled from the start, for example, by unfamiliar procedures of timetabling and course selection. Local curricula may assume domains of knowledge which sojourners lack; teaching and assessment methods may be unfamiliar; local lecturers and students may appear critical and unhelpful. The extent to which local students' social and leisure activities centre on the campus may also vary.

Some North American institutions address these problems by offering "island" programmes (Wolcott, 2013) where curricula and instructors follow North American pedagogical norms, but this approach limits informal contact between sojourners and the local peers they are keen to get to know. Many studies report that whether following "island" or integrated study programmes, student sojourners are similarly likely to socialize extensively with fellow nationals and/or with international student peers (de Federico de la Rúa, 2008; Meier & Daniels, 2011; Murphy-Lejeune, 2002; Papatsiba, 2006).

2.5.3.2 The language assistant setting

Placement as a language teaching assistant in a school or college is an especially popular option with Anglophone sojourners, who are in wide demand internationally for their English language skills. The assistants interviewed by Murphy-Lejeune (2002, pp. 167–175) accepted their professional role within unfamiliar school systems uncritically and quickly adopted "insider" perspectives on educational practices. For these sojourners, the school experience was most significant as a source of social contact with schoolteachers, pupils and their families, and as a site for leisure activities, sports, and so on. Other studies report more varied experiences and attitudes; Alred and Byram (2006) describe assistants who felt marginalized at school and socialized mainly with other fellow assistants, as well as those who found lasting local friendships through school-based networks. In a retrospective interview study, with language teachers who had formerly worked as German language assistants in Anglophone countries, Ehrenreich (2006) reports

40 Key constructs

that positive contact with children during the assistantship year had confirmed their choice of career. However, they had been disappointed with their professional experience, and felt that Anglophone pedagogic culture was not very relevant to teaching in Germany.

2.5.3.3 The workplace internship

The workplace interns studied by Murphy-Lejeune were students following an international MBA, whose programme included a workplace internship. For this group, the internship offered their major opportunity for local social integration, and they were very enthusiastic about socializing with workplace colleagues:

> Always it was integration and what they were interested to talk, what they were interested to eat, how they make business, separated from the [other sojourners], just among the French . . . to get along also, you know, to work is a special relation, you cannot walk out, you cannot say "Ok, I don't work this way". You have to make the effort
> (Intern Thomas, Murphy-Lejeune, 2002, p. 170).

Similarly positive responses concerning the social integration of interns are reported in other studies (Meier & Daniels, 2011; Willis, Doble, Sankarayya, & Smithers, 1977), with only a few individual exceptions.

2.5.3 Domestic settings during the sojourn

The residence arrangements which sojourners enter into are of three main types: placement with a local family (the "homestay"), living in an institutional residence or living independently in a shared apartment or studio.

The homestay has been traditionally viewed as the most desirable arrangement, from the perspective of language and culture learning, and has correspondingly been the most frequently researched (see survey in Kinginger, 2009, pp. 130–139). From the perspective of the "coming of age" sojourner, however, who may have only recently started to live independently of their own family, a return to family living may be unappealing; Murphy-Lejeune reports a number of breakdowns in the sojourner-host family relationship among her relatively mature MBA student interns who tried it (p. 158). Kinginger herself suggests that younger sojourners may be more willing to accept the identity of temporary child within a host family (2015). As we have seen in earlier sections, even when durable, homestay social relations have been shown in practice to involve complex negotiation of identity positions, which may influence language and cultural learning in idiosyncratic ways.

The social implications of other types of residence have been less studied. Through a questionnaire survey, Bracke and Aguerre (2015) compared the communities of practice entered into by sojourners at a French university who were sharing apartments, with those living in more individualized institutional accommodation (*chambres universitaires*). They argue that the sojourners in shared accommodation (whether sharing with French students or other international sojourners) engaged in a greater diversity of communities of practice, and developed somewhat more varied relationships with local French people. Murphy-Lejeune reported that most of the Erasmus exchange students in her study had accepted offers of accommodation in institutional residences, with "the inevitable consequence of getting into a social network made up of other international students" (2002, p. 156). Only those with prior experience of living abroad were sufficiently confident to seek flatshares with local people. On the other hand, where institutional arrangements place sojourners alongside local students in university dormitories, these have been shown to provide valuable entry points to local networks (Trentman, 2015). Klapper and Rees (2012) compared the residence arrangements of "high gain" and "low gain" sojourners, in terms of their development in L2 German. They found that whether by accident or design, the high gainers had mostly lived in shared apartments with German speakers.

2.5.4 Leisure practices during the sojourn

Murphy-Lejeune described her sojourners as taking part in three main types of group leisure activities, all of them resembling practices at home: "casual meetings", including meetings in cafés and pubs, parties and get-togethers in student residences, and visits to nightclubs; regular organized pastimes, such as sports or music groups; and irregular events, such as excursions and travel (2002, p. 171). Under the additional heading of cultural activities, she included reading, use of media, and trips to cinemas, theatres, concerts, and so on. In her cohort, only the language assistants received invitations to meals and other social events in the homes of local residents.

Most of these activities have potential for building local relationships, and the literature includes accounts of sojourners successfully achieving this. For example, Goldoni (2013) reports successful local relationship-building by sojourners in Spain through football, dance and Bible study. Meier and Daniels (2011) report similar outcomes from sport and also from sojourners undertaking voluntary work (in a Latin American context). The "high gainers" of Klapper and Rees (2012) spent much of their leisure time with their German flatmates, as well as using German media extensively, either alone or in groups. However, international networks excluding locals may also be created around leisure activities, including "going out", partying, and in particular, travel and touristic excursions (Adams, 2006; Goldoni, 2013; Murphy-Lejeune, 2002, Chapter 9; Papatsiba, 2006).

2.5.5 Social networking during the sojourn

In Sections 2.5.1–2.5.4, we have explored a range of contextual factors which have been suggested to affect sojourners' social relationships, language practices, interaction opportunities and learning outcomes. In this section we examine the use made by a number of study abroad researchers of Social Network Analysis (SNA), in order to build a more integrated picture.

The use of SNA in linguistic studies was pioneered by Milroy (1987) to document and interpret language use and sociolinguistic change among settled working-class communities in Belfast. It has subsequently been adapted to theorize linguistic innovation in more heterogeneous networks (Fagyal, Swarup, Escobar, Gasser, & Lakkaraju, 2010), and it has been employed in studies of L2 use and the development of L2 communicative competence (de Bot & Stoessel, 2002; Lybeck, 2002; Wiklund, 2002).This line of research typically documents the relative density, frequency, intensity, multiplexity and/or durability of social interactions and how these relate to language use, change and development.

Most investigations of language learning during/after study abroad using SNA are small-scale case studies (Gautier & Chevrot, 2015; Isabelli-García, 2006; Kurata, 2004; Whitworth, 2006). For example, Isabelli-García (2006) used data from interviews, diaries and regularly completed network logs so as to model the social networks built by four Anglophone case study participants undertaking study abroad in Argentina. Two of her case study participants succeeded in moving beyond open, first-order networks with local Spanish speakers, in order to enter denser and more multiplex networks; these sojourners also developed/sustained high integrative motivation and progressed in their overall Spanish proficiency as measured by the Oral Proficiency Interview (OPI: American Council on the Teaching of Foreign Languages, 2012). The networks of the other two sojourners remained simple (uniplex and open; i.e., the sojourners spoke Spanish with a short list of individuals only, and in single transactional roles).

Larger-scale quantitative studies involving SNA have been conducted more recently by Dewey and associates (Baker-Smemoe, Dewey, Bown, & Martinsen, 2014; Dewey et al., 2014; Dewey, Bown, & Eggett, 2012; Dewey, Ring, Gardner, & Belnap, 2013). Dewey et al. (2012) investigated the size, intensity, durability, density and dispersion of the social networks developed by over 200 sojourners in Japan, using a specially developed Study Abroad Social Interaction Questionnaire. Using multiple regression, they related this information to participants' self-reported language learning, along with a number of other social factors (their confidence predeparture, time spent using Japanese insojourn, and time spent using English). In this particular study, the factors which predicted learning gain most strongly were length of sojourn, social network dispersion (i.e., the number of different networks in which sojourners took part), and time spent speaking Japanese. In another study, which compared the influence of social factors across six different study abroad programmes in six countries, the contribution of social networking to learning outcomes was masked by programme effects – that is, some programmes were much more powerful than others in promoting all kinds of engagement with the L2, including the extent of social networking by sojourners (Dewey et al., 2014). However, when the participants in this same cohort were separated in a different study into two groups of "high gainers" and "low gainers", across the different programmes (based on pre and post OPI scores), certain variables emerged which distinguished these two groups (Baker-Smemoe et al., 2014). These were preprogramme proficiency, preprogramme intercultural sensitivity and (the strongest factor) social networking while abroad. The "high gainers" developed "stronger and deeper relationships with fewer speakers", which the authors believe to reflect greater opportunity for "more indepth and sustained personal interactions" (Baker-Smemoe et al., 2014, p. 482).

Although these lines of research have revealed important trends in learners' social network patterns, including how learners' social networks change, what we know about their structure and development is still somewhat limited. Firstly, little is known about longitudinal social network development over the course of the sojourn. Secondly, we have little idea about translanguaging and mixed language use within network interactions, in different social contexts and communities of practice, and how these language preferences change over time. As Dewey et al. (2013) acknowledge, there is a need for qualitative research to investigate more directly the nature of interactions within different types of social networks. All of these issues are of concern to the LANGSNAP research agenda, and will be revisited in later chapters.

2.5.6 Home contacts and communication practices

So far, we have considered the nature of the social networks and relationships formed by sojourners in the new context, whether with co-nationals, locals or international peers, and these relationships are the main focus of study abroad research. However, sojourners also sustain pre-existing social networks involving family, friends and perhaps romantic partners at home, and may derive considerable emotional support from these when abroad.

Murphy-Lejeune describes active home contact on the part of her new strangers in Europe, including home visiting and visits from families to the sojourn location; she describes the visit home at Christmas as an important staging point in the sojourn, emphasizing its temporary nature, but also raising awareness of growth and change, and the increasing importance to the sojourner of new networks (Murphy-Lejeune, 2002, pp. 139–141). Coleman and Chafer (2010) report a survey of past students who had sojourned in Dakar (Senegal), a location where frequent trips home were much less practical, between 1987 and 2009. Over this period of time, telephone and internet communication were transformed, with corresponding changes in sojourners' patterns of contact with home; by the beginning of the 2000s, sojourners were generally reporting weekly contact by internet, and by the end of the period, most of them reported daily contact. Kinginger (2008) describes how intensive internet contact with home can substitute for local linguistic and cultural engagement, for the alienated sojourner. Overall, it is clear from these studies that sojourners now find the active maintenance of home relations a routine matter, further undermining the view of the sojourn as an "immersion" experience, and providing further evidence that language learning opportunity insojourn must be actively constructed by sojourners who are active and strategic.

2.6 Conclusion

This chapter has presented a review of key concepts which will inform the linguistic and sociocultural strands of our investigation into the Anglophone sojourner abroad, set out in later chapters. In the next chapter we describe the LANGSNAP project itself, and show how its longitudinal and interdisciplinary design reflects our concerns to describe and explain the dynamic and evolving relationships between identity development, plurilingual social practices and L2 learning, as these play out over time during the contemporary sojourn abroad.

References

Adams, R. (2006). Language learning strategies in the study abroad context. In M. A. DuFon & E. Churchill (Eds.), *Language learners in study abroad contexts* (pp. 259–292). Clevedon: Multilingual Matters.

Allen, H. W. (2010). Language-learning motivation during short-term study abroad: An activity theory perspective. *Foreign Language Annals, 43*(1), 27–49.

Alred, G., & Byram, M. (2006). British students in France: 10 years on. In M. Byram & A. Feng (Eds.), *Living and studying abroad: Research and practice* (pp. 210–231). Clevedon: Multilingual Matters.

American Council on the Teaching of Foreign Languages (2012). *Oral proficiency interview familiarization manual*. White Plains, NY: ACTFL.

Arnett, J. J. (2014). *Emerging adulthood: The winding road from the late teens through the twenties* (2nd ed.). Oxford: Oxford University Press.

Baker-Smemoe, W., Dewey, D. P., Bown, J., & Martinsen, R. A. (2014). Variables affecting L2 gains during study abroad. *Foreign Language Annals, 47*, 464–486.

Barron, A. (2006). Learning to say "you" in German: The acquisition of sociolinguistic competence in a study abroad context. In M. A. DuFon & E. Churchill (Eds.), *Language learners in study abroad contexts* (pp. 59–88). Clevedon: Multilingual Matters.

Bartning, I. (1997). L'apprenant dit avancé et son acquisition d'une langue étrangère. *Acquisition et Interaction en Langue Etrangère, 9*, 9–50.

Baumeister, R.F. (Ed.). (1986). *Public self and private self*. New York: Springer-Verlag.

Beeching, K., Armstrong, N., & Gadet, F. (Eds.). (2009). *Sociolinguistic variation in contemporary French*. Amsterdam: John Benjamins.

Behrent, S. (2007). *La communication interalloglotte*. Paris: L'Harmattan.

Benson, P., Barkhuizen, G., Bodycott, P., & Brown, J. (2013). *Second language identity in narratives of study abroad*. Basingstoke: Palgrave Macmillan.

Berthoud, A.-C., Grin, F., & Lüdi, G. (2013). *Exploring the dynamics of multilingualism*. Amsterdam: John Benjamins.

Bhaskar, R. (1998). *The possibility of naturalism* (3rd ed.). London: Routledge.

Bhaskar, R. (2008). *Fathoming the depths of reality*. London: Routledge.

Blackledge, A., & Creese, A. (2010). *Multilingualism: A critical perspective*. London: Continuum.

Block, D. (2007). *Second language identities*. London: Continuum.

Block, D. (2013a). Issues in language and identity research in applied linguistics. *Estudios de Lingüística inglesa applicada, 13*, 11–46.

Block, D. (2013b). The structure and agency dilemma in identity and intercultural communication research. *Language and Intercultural Communication, 13*(2), 126–147.

Blum, S. D. (2012). *A strange way of coming of age: Why the higher education conversation needs anthropology*. Paper presented at the conference Learning in and out of school: Education across the globe, University of Notre Dame.

Blum, S. D. (2016). *"I love learning, I hate school": An anthropology of college*. Ithaca, NY: Cornell University Press.

Bosker, H. R., Pinget, A.-F., Quené, H., Sanders, T., & De Jong, N. (2013). What makes speech sound fluent? The contributions of pauses, speed and repairs. *Language Testing*, 30(2), 159–175.

Bracke, A., & Aguerre, S. (2015). Erasmus students: Joining communities of practice to learn French? In R. Mitchell, N. Tracy-Ventura, & K. McManus (Eds.), *Social interaction, identity and language learning during residence abroad. EUROSLA Monographs 4* (pp. 139–168). Amsterdam: European Second Language Association.

Brown, L. (2013). Identity and honorifics use in Korean study abroad. In C. Kinginger (Ed.), *Social and cultural aspects of language learning in study abroad* (pp. 269–298). Amsterdam: John Benjamins.

Bulté, B., & Housen, A. (2012). Defining and operationalising L2 complexity. In A. Housen, F. Kuiken, & I. Vedder (Eds.), *Dimensions of L2 performance and proficiency: Complexity, accuracy and fluency in SLA* (pp. 21–46). Amsterdam: John Benjamins.

Busse, V., & Williams, M. (2010). Why German? Motivation of students studying German at English universities. *The Language Learning Journal*, 38(1), 67–85.

Butt, J., & Benjamin, C. (2013). *A new reference grammar of modern Spanish* (4th ed.). Abingdon/New York: Routledge.

Byram, M. (2012). Conceptualizing intercultural (communicative) competence and intercultural citizenship. In J. Jackson (Ed.), *The Routledge handbook of language and intercultural communication* (pp. 85–98). Abingdon/New York: Routledge.

Byram, M., Nichols, A., & Stevens, D. (Eds.). (2001). *Developing intercultural competence in practice*. Clevedon: Multilingual Matters.

Chambers, F. (1997). What do we mean by oral fluency? *System*, 25(4), 535–544.

Coleman, J. A., & Chafer, T. (2010). Study abroad and the internet: Physical and virtual context in an era of expanding telecommunications. *Frontiers: The Interdisciplinary Journal of Study Abroad*, 19, 151–167.

Connor-Linton, J. (2015). Finding the right combination for Spanish oral proficiency development: Individual learner characteristics and study abroad program features. In C. Sanz, B. Lado, & S. K. Bourns (Eds.), *AAUSC 2013 Volume – Issues in language program direction: Individual differences, L2 development and language program administration: From theory to application* (pp. 108–127). Stamford, CT: Cengage Learning.

Cook, H. M. (2006). Joint construction of folk beliefs by JFL learners and Japanese host families. In M. A. DuFon & E. Churchill (Eds.), *Language learners in study abroad contexts* (pp. 120–150). Clevedon: Multilingual Matters.

Cook, H. M. (2008). *Socialising identities through speech style*. Bristol: Multilingual Matters.

Crystal, D. (1997). *A dictionary of linguistics and phonetics* (4th ed.). Cambridge: Cambridge University Press.

Crystal, D. (2003). *English as a global language*. Cambridge: Cambridge University Press.

de Bot, K., & Stoessel, S. (2002). Introduction: Language change and social networks. *International Journal of the Sociology of Language*, 153, 1–7.

De Clercq, B. (2015). The development of lexical complexity in second language acquisition: A cross-linguistic study of L2 French and English. In L. Roberts, K. McManus, N. Vanek, & D. Trenkic (Eds.), *EUROSLA Yearbook Volume 15* (pp. 69–94). Amsterdam: John Benjamins.

de Federico de la Rúa, A. (2008). How do Erasmus students make friends? In S. Ehrenreich, G. Woodman, & M. Perrefort (Eds.), *Schule und Studium: Bestandesaufnahmen aus Forschung und Praxis* (pp. 89–104). Münster: Waxmann.

De Jong, N., Steinel, M. P., Florij, A., Schoonen, R., & Hulstijn, J. H. (2012). The effect of task complexity on functional adequacy, fluency and lexical diversity in speaking performances of native and non-native speakers. In A. Housen, F. Kuiken, & I. Vedder (Eds.), *Dimensions of L2 performance and proficiency: Complexity, accuracy and fluency in SLA* (pp. 121–142). Amsterdam: John Benjamins.

DeKeyser, R. (2010). Monitoring processes in Spanish as a second language during a study abroad program. *Foreign Language Annals, 43*(1), 80–92.

Dervin, F. (2013). Politics of identification in the use of lingua francas in student mobility to Finland and France. In C. Kinginger (Ed.), *Social and cultural aspects of language learning in study abroad* (pp. 101–126). Amsterdam: John Benjamins.

Dewey, D. P., Bown, J., Baker, W., Martinsen, R. A., Gold, C., & Eggett, D. (2014). Language use in six study abroad programs: An exploratory analysis of possible predictors. *Language Learning, 64*(1), 36–71.

Dewey, D. P., Bown, J., & Eggett, D. (2012). Japanese language proficiency, social networking, and language use during study abroad: Learners' perspectives. *Canadian Modern Language Review, 68*(2), 111–137.

Dewey, D. P., Ring, S., Gardner, D., & Belnap, R. K. (2013). Social network formation and development during study abroad in the Middle East. *System, 41*(2), 269–282.

Dimova, S., Hultgren, A. K., & Jensen, C. (Eds.). (2015). *English-medium instruction in European higher education: English in Europe, Volume 3*. Berlin: De Gruyter Mouton.

Doerr, N. M. (2013). Do 'global citizens' need the parochial cultural other? Discourse of immersion in study abroad and learning-by-doing. *Compare: A Journal of Comparative and International Education, 43*(2), 224–243.

Dörnyei, Z. (2009). The L2 motivational self system. In Z. Dörnyei & E. Ushioda (Eds.), *Motivation, language identity and the L2 self* (pp. 9–42). Clevedon: Multilingual Matters.

DuFon, M. A. (2006). The socialization of taste during study abroad in Indonesia. In M. A. DuFon & E. Churchill (Eds.), *Language learners in study abroad contexts* (pp. 91–119). Clevedon: Multilingual Matters.

Ehrenreich, S. (2006). The assistant experience in retrospect and its educational and professional significance in teachers' biographies. In M. Byram & A. Feng (Eds.), *Living and studying abroad: Research and practice* (pp. 186–210). Clevedon: Multilingual Matters.

Extra, G., & Yağmur, K. (Eds.). (2004). *Urban multilingualism in Europe: Immigrant minority languages at home and school*. Clevedon: Multilingual Matters.

Fagyal, Z., Swarup, S., Escobar, A. M., Gasser, L., & Lakkaraju, K. (2010). Centers and peripheries: Network roles in language change. *Lingua, 120*(8), 2061–2079.

Finn, K. (2013). Young, free and single? Theorising partner relationships during the first year of university. *British Journal of Sociology of Education, 34*(1), 94–111.

Foster, P., Tonkyn, A., & Wigglesworth, G. (2000). Measuring spoken language: A unit for all reasons. *Applied Linguistics, 21*(3), 354–375.

Gadet, F. (2003). *La variation sociale en français*. Paris: Editions Orphrys.

Gadet, F., & Ludwig, R. (2015). *Le français au contact d'autres langues*. Paris: Editions Ophrys.

Garcia, O., & Wei, L. (2014). *Translanguaging: Language, bilingualism and education*. Basingstoke: Palgrave Macmillan.

Gardner-Chloros, P. (2008). *Codeswitching*. Cambridge: Cambridge University Press.

Garrett, P., & Gallego Balsà, L. (2014). International universities and implications of internationalisation for minority languages: Views from university students in Catalonia and Wales. *Journal of Multilingual and Multicultural Development, 35*(4), 361–375.

Gautier, R., & Chevrot, J.-P. (2015). Social networks and acquisition of sociolinguistic variation in a study abroad context: A preliminary study. In R. Mitchell, N. Tracy-Ventura, & K. McManus (Eds.), *Social interaction, identity and language learning during residence abroad. EUROSLA Monographs 4* (pp. 169–184). Amsterdam: European Second Language Association.

Godfrey, L., Treacy, C., & Tarone, E. (2014). Change in French second language writing in study abroad and domestic contexts. *Foreign Language Annals, 47*(1), 48–65.

Goldoni, F. (2013). Students' immersion experiences in study abroad. *Foreign Language Annals, 46*(3), 359–376.

Härkonen, A., & Dervin, F. (2015). "Talking just about learning languages and getting to know cultures is something that's mentioned in very many applications": Student and staff imaginaries about study abroad. In F. Dervin & R. Machart (Eds.), *The new politics of global academic mobility and migration* (pp. 101–118). Frankfurt am Main: Peter Lang.

Hawkins, R. D., & Towell, R. (2015). *French grammar and usage* (4th ed.). New York/Abingdon: Routledge.

Healey, F. G. (1967). *Foreign language teaching in the universities*. Manchester: Manchester University Press.

Higgins, T.E. (1987). Self-discrepancy: A theory relating self and affect. *Psychological Review, 94*(3), 319–340.

Holdsworth, C. (2006). "Don't you think you're missing out, living at home?" Student experiences and residential transitions. *The Sociological Review, 54*(3), 495–519.

Holliday, A. (2012). Culture, communication, context and power. In J. Jackson (Ed.), *The Routledge handbook of language and intercultural communication* (pp. 37–51). New York/Abingdon: Routledge.

Holton, M. (2016). Living together in student accommodation: Performances, boundaries and homemaking. *Area, 48*(1), 57–63.

Housen, A., Kuiken, F., & Vedder, I. (2012). Complexity, accuracy and fluency: Definitions, measurement and research. In A. Housen, F. Kuiken, & I. Vedder (Eds.), *Dimensions of L2 performance and proficiency: Complexity, accuracy and fluency in SLA* (pp. 1–20). Amsterdam: John Benjamins.

Hülmbauer, C., & Seidlhofer, B. (2013). English as a lingua franca in European multilingualism. In A.-C. Berthoud, F. Grin, & G. Lüdi (Eds.), *Exploring the dynamics of multilingualism* (pp. 387–406). Amsterdam: John Benjamins.

Iino, M. (2006). Norms of interaction in a Japanese homestay setting: Toward a two-way flow of linguistic and cultural resources. In M. A. Dufon & E. Churchill (Eds.), *Language learners in study abroad contexts* (pp. 151–173). Clevedon: Multilingual Matters.

Isabelli-García, C. (2006). Study abroad, social networks, motivation and attitudes: Implications for second language acquisition. In M.A. DuFon & E. Churchill (Eds.), *Language learners in study abroad contexts* (pp. 231–258). Clevedon: Multilingual Matters.

Iwasaki, N. (2010). Style shifts among Japanese learners before and after study abroad in Japan: Becoming active social agents in Japanese. *Applied Linguistics, 31*(1), 45–71.

Jackson, J. (2012). Education abroad. In J. Jackson (Ed.), *The Routledge handbook of language and intercultural communication* (pp. 449–463). Abingdon/New York: Routledge.

Kalocsai, K. (2011). The show of interpersonal involvement and the building of rapport in an ELF community of practice. In A. Archibald, A. Cogo, & J. Jenkins (Eds.), *Latest trends in English as a Lingua Franca research* (pp. 113–138). Newcastle upon Tyne: Cambridge Scholars Publishing.

Kaltschuetz, D. (2014). *Study abroad and the development of L2 requests: The development of pragmalinguistic behaviour as operationalized in request realizations of UK based study abroad students in Germany/Austria*. (PhD), University of Southampton.

Kihlstedt, M. (2002). Reference to past events in dialogue: The acquisition of tense and aspect by advanced learners of French. In M.R. Salaberry & Y. Shirai (Eds.), *The L2 acquisition of tense-aspect morphology* (pp. 323–362). Amsterdam: John Benjamins.

Kinginger, C. (2004). "Alice doesn't live here any more": Foreign language learning as identity (re)construction. In A. Pavlenko & A. Blackledge (Eds.), *Negotiation of identities in multilingual contexts* (pp. 219–242). Clevedon: Multilingual Matters.

Kinginger, C. (2008). Language learning in study abroad: Case studies of Americans in France. *The Modern Language Journal*, 92(Special issue), 1–124.

Kinginger, C. (2009). *Language learning and study abroad: A critical reading of research.* Basingstoke: Palgrave Macmillan.

Kinginger, C. (2010). American students abroad: Negotiation of difference? *Language Teaching*, 43(2), 216–227.

Kinginger, C. (2012). Language socialization in study abroad. In C.A. Chapelle (Ed.), *The encyclopedia of applied linguistics*. Chichester: Wiley-Blackwell.

Kinginger, C. (2015). Language socialization in the homestay: American high school students in China. In R. Mitchell, N. Tracy-Ventura, & K. McManus (Eds.), *Social interaction, identity and language learning during residence abroad.* EUROSLA Monographs 4 (pp. 53–74). Amsterdam: European Second Language Association.

Kinginger, C. & Farrell-Whitworth, K. (2005). *Gender and emotional investment in language learning during study abroad.* CALPER Working Papers Series, No. 2. The Pennsylvania State University, Center for Advanced Language Proficiency Education and Research.

Klapper, J., & Rees, J. (2012). University residence abroad for foreign language students: Analysing the linguistic benefits. *Language Learning Journal*, 40(3), 335–358.

Klein, W., & Perdue, C. (1992). *Utterance structure: Developing grammars again.* Amsterdam: John Benjamins.

Kramsch, C. (1998). The privilege of the intercultural speaker. In M Byram & M. Fleming (Eds.), *Language learning in intercultural perspective: Approaches through drama and ethnography* (pp. 16–31). Cambridge: Cambridge University Press.

Kramsch, C. (2009). *The multilingual subject.* Oxford: Oxford University Press.

Kramsch, C. (2015). Identity and subjectivity: Different timescales, different methodologies. In F. Dervin & K. Risager (Eds.), *Researching identity and interculturality* (pp. 211–230). Abingdon: Routledge.

Kurata, N. (2004). Communication networks of Japanese language learners in their home country. *Journal of Asian Pacific Communication*, 14(1), 153–178.

Labeau, E. (2005). *Beyond the aspect hypothesis: Tense-aspect development in advanced L2 French.* Oxford: Peter Lang.

Lambert, C., & Kormos, J. (2014). Complexity, accuracy, and fluency in task-based L2 research: Toward more developmentally based measures of second language acquisition. *Applied Linguistics*, 35(5), 607–614.

Lasagabaster, D., & Huguet, Á. (Eds.). (2007). *Multilingualism in European bilingual contexts: Language use and attitudes.* Clevedon: Multilingual Matters.

Lennon, P. (1990). Investigating fluency in EFL: A quantitative approach. *Language Learning*, 40(3), 387–417.

Llanes, À. (2011). The many faces of study abroad: An update on the research on L2 gains emerged during a study abroad experience. *International Journal of Multilingualism*, 8(3), 189–215.

Lybeck, K. (2002). Cultural identification and second language pronunciation of Americans in Norway. *The Modern Language Journal*, 86(2), 174–191.

Macdonald, M. M., & O'Regan, J. P. (2012). A global agenda for intercultural communication research and practice. In J. Jackson (Ed.), *The Routledge handbook of language and intercultural communication* (pp. 553–567). Abingdon: Routledge.

Magnan, S. S., & Lafford, B. A. (2012). Learning through immersion during study abroad. In S. M. Gass & A. Mackey (Eds.), *The Routledge handbook of second language acquisition* (pp. 525–540). Abingdon/New York: Routledge.

Malvern, D., Richards, B., Chipere, N., & Duran, P. (2004). *Lexical diversity and language development: Quantification and assessment*. Basingstoke: Palgrave Macmillan.

Mar-Molinero, C. (1997). *The Spanish-speaking world: A practical introduction to sociolinguistic issues*. London/New York: Routledge.

Mar-Molinero, C., & Stewart, M. (Eds.). (2006). *Globalization and language in the Spanish-speaking world: Macro and micro perspectives*. Basingstoke: Palgrave Macmillan.

McManus, K. (2013). Prototypical influence in second language acquisition: What now for the aspect hypothesis? *International Review of Applied Linguistics, 51*(3), 299–322.

McManus, K. (2015). L1-L2 differences in the acquisition of form-meaning pairings: A comparison of English and German learners of French. *Canadian Modern Language Review, 71*(2), 155–181.

Meier, G., & Daniels, H. (2011). "Just not being able to make friends": Social interaction during the year abroad in modern language degrees. *Research Papers in Education, 28*(2), 212–238.

Mellors-Bourne, R., Jones, E., Lawton, W., & Woodfield, S. (2015). *Student perspectives on going international*. London: UK HE International Unit.

Mercer, S. (2011). Language learner self-concept: Complexity, continuity and change. *System, 39*(3), 335–346.

Milroy, L. (1987). *Language and social networks* (2nd ed.). Oxford: Blackwell.

Monto, M. A., & Carey, A. G. (2014). A new standard of sexual behavior? Are claims associated with the "hookup culture" supported by general social survey data? *The Journal of Sex Research, 51*(6), 605–615.

Murphy-Lejeune, E. (2002). *Student mobility and narrative in Europe: The new strangers*. New York: Routledge.

Norris, J., & Ortega, L. (2009). Toward an organic approach to investigating CAF in instructed SLA: The case of complexity. *Applied Linguistics, 30*(4), 555–578.

Norton, B. (2000). *Identity and language learning*. London: Longman.

Norton, B. (2014). Identity and poststructuralist theory in SLA. In S. Mercer & M. Williams (Eds.), *Multiple perspectives on the self in SLA* (pp. 59–74). Bristol: Multilingual Matters.

Paffey, D. (2012). *Language ideologies and the globalization of 'standard' Spanish*. London: Bloomsbury Academic.

Pallotti, G. (2009). CAF: Defining, refining and differentiating constructs. *Applied Linguistics, 30*(4), 590–601.

Pallotti, G. (2015). A simple view of linguistic complexity. *Second Language Research, 31*(1), 117–134.

Papatsiba, V. (2006). Study abroad and experiences of cultural distance and proximity: French Erasmus students. In M. Byram & A. Feng (Eds.), *Living and studying abroad: Research and practice* (pp. 108–133). Cleveland: Multilingual Matters.

Pavlenko, A. (2005). *Emotions and multilingualism*. Cambridge: Cambridge University Press.

Peckham, D. J., Kalocsai, K., Kovàcs, E., & Sherman, T. (2012). English and multilingualism, or English only in a multilingual Europe? In P. Studer & I. Werlen (Eds.),

Linguistic diversity in Europe: Current trends and discourses (pp. 179–202). Berlin: Walter de Gruyter.

Pellegrino Aveni, V. (2005). *Study abroad and second language use: Constructing the self.* Cambridge: Cambridge University Press.

Pérez-Vidal, C. (Ed.). (2014). *Language acquisition in study abroad and formal instruction contexts.* Amsterdam: John Benjamins.

Phipps, A. (2003). Languages, identities, agencies: Intercultural lessons from Harry Potter. *Language and Intercultural Communication, 3*(1), 6–19.

Plews, J. (2015). Intercultural identity-alignment in second language study abroad, or the more-or-less Canadians. In R. Mitchell, N. Tracy-Ventura, & K. McManus (Eds.), *Social interaction, identity and language learning during residence abroad* (pp. 281–304). Amsterdam: European Second Language Association.

Polanyi, L. (1995). Language learning and living abroad: Stories from the field. In B.F. Freed (Ed.), *Second language acquisition in a study abroad context* (pp. 271–292). Amsterdam: John Benjamins.

Regan, V., Howard, M., & Lemée, I. (2009). *The acquisition of sociolinguistic competence in a study abroad context.* Bristol: Multilingual Matters.

Rindler Schjerve, R., & Vetter, E. (2012). *European multilingualism: Current perspectives and challenges.* Bristol: Multilingual Matters.

Roberts, C., Byram, M., Barro, A., Jordan, S., & Street, B. (2001). *Language learners as ethnographers.* Clevedon: Multilingual Matters.

Rothman, J., & Pascual y Cabo, D. (2014). Generative approaches to Spanish second language acquisition. In K.L. Geeslin (Ed.), *The handbook of Spanish second language acquisition* (pp. 46–63). Chichester: Wiley Blackwell.

Ryan, S., & Irie, K. (2014). Imagined and possible selves: Stories we tell ourselves about ourselves. In S. Mercer & M. Williams (Eds.), *Multiple perspectives on the self in SLA* (pp. 109–126). Bristol: Multilingual Matters.

Segalowitz, N. (2010). *Cognitive bases of second language fluency.* Abingdon/New York: Routledge.

Selwyn, N. (2008). "High-jinks" and "minor mischief": A study of undergraduate students as perpetrators of crime. *Studies in Higher Education, 33*(1), 1–16.

Shiri, S. (2013). Learners' attitudes toward regional dialects and destination preferences in study abroad. *Foreign Language Annals, 46*(4), 565–587.

Shively, R. L. (2011). L2 pragmatic development in study abroad: A longitudinal study of Spanish service encounters. *Journal of Pragmatics, 43*(6), 1818–1835.

Siegal, M. (1996). The role of learner subjectivity in second language sociolinguistic competency: Western women learning Japanese. *Applied Linguistics, 17*(3), 356–382.

Skehan, P. (1996). Second language acquisition and task-based instruction. In J. Willis & D. Willis (Eds.), *Challenge and change in language teaching* (pp. 17–30). Oxford: Heinemann.

Skehan, P. (1998). *A cognitive approach to language learning.* Oxford: Oxford University Press.

Skehan, P. (2009). Modelling second language performance: Integrating complexity, accuracy, fluency, and lexis. *Applied Linguistics, 30*(4), 510–532.

Taguchi, N. (2015). *Developing interactional competence in a Japanese study abroad context.* Bristol: Multilingual Matters.

Talburt, S., & Stewart, M. (1999). What's the subject of study abroad? Race, gender and "living culture". *The Modern Language Journal, 83*(2), 163–175.

Tavakoli, P., & Skehan, P. (2005). Strategic planning, task structure, and performance testing. In R. Ellis (Ed.), *Planning and task performance* (pp. 239–273). Amsterdam: John Benjamins.

Taylor, F. (2014). Relational view of the self in SLA. In S. Mercer & M. Williams (Eds.), *Multiple perspectives on the self in SLA* (pp. 92–102). Bristol: Multilingual Matters.

Trentman, E. (2015). Negotiating gendered identities and access to social networks during study abroad in Egypt. In R. Mitchell, N. Tracy-Ventura, & K. McManus (Eds.), *Social interaction, identity and language learning during residence abroad. EUROSLA Monographs 4* (pp. 263–280). Amsterdam: European Second Language Association.

Twombly, S. (1995). Piropos and friendships: Gender and culture clash in study abroad. *Frontiers: The Interdisciplinary Journal of Study Abroad, 1*, 1–27.

Van Compernolle, R. A., & Williams, L. (2011). Metalinguistic explanations and self-reports as triangulation data for interpreting second language sociolinguistic performance. *International Journal of Applied Linguistics, 21*(1), 26–50.

Van Compernolle, R. A., & Williams, L. (2012). Reconceptualizing sociolinguistic competence as mediated action: Identity, meaning-making, agency. *The Modern Language Journal, 96*(2), 234–250.

Van Mol, C. (2015). Why do students move? An analysis of mobility determinants among Italian students. In F. Dervin & R. Machart (Eds.), *The new politics of global academic mobility and migration* (pp. 19–40). Frankfurt am Main: Peter Lang.

Wächter, B., & Maiworm, F. (Eds.). (2014). *English-taught programmes in European higher education: The state of play in 2014*. Bonn: Lemmens.

Whitworth, K. F. (2006). *Access to language learning during study abroad: The roles of identity and subject positioning*. (PhD), Pennsylvania State University.

Wiklund, I. (2002). Social networks from a sociolinguistic perspective: The relationship between characteristics of the social networks of bilingual adolescents and their language proficiency. *International Journal of the Sociology of Language, 153*, 53–92.

Wilkinson, J. (2012). The intercultural speaker and the acquisition of intercultural/global competence. In J. Jackson (Ed.), *The Routledge handbook of language and intercultural communication* (pp. 296–309). Abingdon/New York: Routledge.

Wilkinson, S. (1998). Study abroad from the participants' perspective: A challenge to common beliefs. *Foreign Language Annals, 31*(1), 23–39.

Wilkinson, S. (2002). The omnipresent classroom during summer study abroad: American students in conversation with their French hosts. *The Modern Language Journal, 86*(2), 157–173.

Willis, F., Doble, G., Sankarayya, U., & Smithers, A. (1977). *Residence abroad and the student of modern languages: A preliminary survey*. Bradford: Modern Languages Centre, University of Bradford.

Wolcott, T. (2013). An American in Paris: Myth, desire, and subjectivity in one student's account of study abroad in France. In C. Kinginger (Ed.), *Social and cultural aspects of language learning in study abroad* (pp. 127–154). Amsterdam: John Benjamins.

Wolfe-Quintero, K., Inagaki, S., & Kim, H.-Y. (1998). *Second language development in writing: Measures of fluency, accuracy and complexity: Technical Report 17*. Honolulu: Second Language Teaching & Curriculum Center, University of Hawai'i.

3 The LANGSNAP project
Design and methodology

3.1 Introduction

This chapter provides an overview of the LANGSNAP project design, participants, methodology and analysis procedures. The project aims and design are described in Section 3.2, followed by the participants (3.3) and data collection procedures (3.4). Next, the instruments used are presented (3.5), and the resulting learner corpus based on the production data is introduced (3.6). The analysis procedures are outlined in Sections 3.7 (analysis of L2 development) and 3.8 (qualitative analysis).

3.2 Project aims and design

The project was an interdisciplinary one, which drew both on traditions of corpus-based research in second language acquisition (SLA), and also on ethnographic/sociocultural traditions investigating social engagement and identity and their role in L2 development. The project focused on Anglophone university students majoring in languages, and it aimed to document their developing knowledge of either L2 French or L2 Spanish over a 21-month period, including a 9-month sojourn abroad. The project also aimed to investigate a) participants' evolving social networks and language practices while abroad, and b) the evolution of participants' L2 identity during and following the sojourn. Overall, it was hoped to advance our general understanding of the relationships between L2 development and social aspects of residence abroad. A final aim of the project was to build a longitudinal database of advanced L2 French and L2 Spanish that would be made publicly available for use by other researchers and language professionals.

3.3 Participants

The participants were students of French and Spanish at a research-intensive university in England (known here as Home City University). They were volunteers from a larger year group; most were female (as is typical for language programmes in this setting), and all had studied one or more languages in institutional settings for a number of years. The participants joined the project toward the end of their second year of university, at a time of intensive preparation for their third year, to be spent abroad; initially, 60 were recruited (30 for each language). Participant attrition was low, and only four of those originally recruited failed to complete the study. The final data set therefore comes from a total of 29 learners of L2 French and 27 learners of L2 Spanish. On recruitment, a background questionnaire was administered to record participants' previous language-learning biographies.

All of the participants were majoring in either French or Spanish, with some who were majoring in both, or in another two-language or three-language combination (e.g., French and German; French, Spanish and Portuguese). Eleven participants were combining a single language with another subject (history, n=5; management science, n=4; philosophy, n=1; film studies, n=1).

All of the L2 French participants spent the academic year in France (Figure 3.1 shows approximate locations). Of this group, 25 were L1 English speakers, two were heritage French speakers (English + French), one was an L1 Spanish speaker and one was an L1 speaker of a Nordic language. The mean age for the French group was 21 (range 20–24), with 26 females and three males. Their mean length of previous French study was 11 years (range

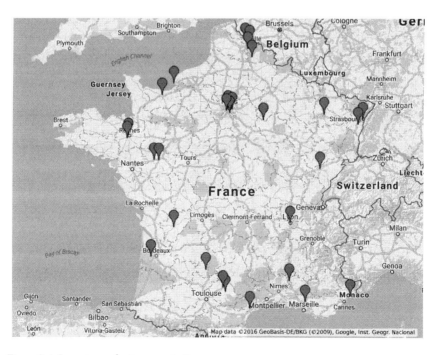

Figure 3.1 Locations of sojourners in France

Figure 3.2 Locations of sojourners in Spain

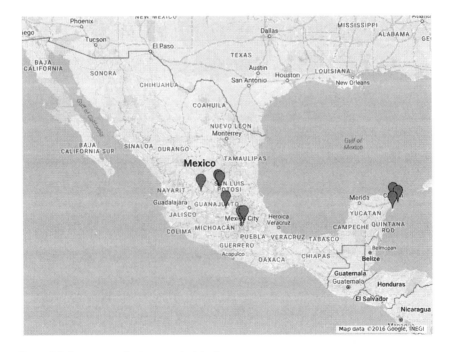

Figure 3.3 Locations of sojourners in Mexico

9–15 years), and the mean age of first exposure was 9.5 years old. Four of the French group were majoring in two languages, and two were majoring in three; nine others were taking another language as a minor component (Italian, German, Spanish or Chinese). Regarding sojourner roles, the group in France included six workplace interns, 15 teaching assistants and eight exchange students.

The L2 Spanish participants sojourned in either Spain (n=18) or Mexico (n=9) (see Figures 3.2 and 3.3). Of this group, 25 were L1 English speakers and two were L1 Polish speakers. Their mean age was 20.5 (range 20–25), with 20 females and 7 males. Their mean length of Spanish study was 5.5 years (range 2–14), and the mean age of first exposure was 15 years old. A group of these participants (n=8) had started Spanish as beginners when they entered university and had followed an accelerated programme during their first two years, including a two-week stay in Mexico organized by the home university. Fourteen of the Spanish participants were majoring in two languages (always Spanish and French), and four participants were majoring in three. Two others were taking another language as a minor component (German, Portuguese). This group included two workplace interns, 16 teaching assistants, and nine exchange students. All of the sojourners in Mexico were teaching assistants.

A group of 10 L1 French speakers and 10 L1 Spanish speakers who were taking part in the Erasmus student exchange programme at Home City University were also recruited as a comparison group. They completed the same language production tasks as the main participants, but on one occasion only. All participants gave informed consent to take part in the project, on condition of anonymity. All were monetarily compensated for their participation and received individual feedback on their progress at the end of the study.

3.4 Procedure for data collection

LANGSNAP was a longitudinal study with six data collection points. An overview of the tasks completed at each of these points is provided in Table 3.1. The order of tasks and tests was counterbalanced at all data collection points for each participant.

Presojourn data collection took place in May 2011. Participants met individually with a member of the research team at the university, and they completed all the Presojourn assessments in one sitting. In September 2011, participants completed the Multicultural Personality Questionnaire online.

The first in-country data collection point (Insojourn 1) occurred in November 2011. All sojourners were visited individually by a member of the research team. They met in a convenient location and all the tasks and questionnaires were completed in one session. This visit was the first time sojourners completed the Social Networking and Language Engagement Questionnaires. The second in-country data collection visits (Insojourn 2) began in February 2012. Insojourn 3 occurred in May 2012, and again, most participants were visited in-country.

Table 3.1 Overview of LANGSNAP data collection

Data Collection Cycle	Location	L2 Oral Production Tasks	L2 Written Task (Argumentative Essay)	Other tests/tasks	Questionnaires
Presojourn: May 2011	Home University	Oral Interview Cat Story	Gay Marriage & Adoption	Elicited Imitation Test X-Lex test	Multicultural Personality (Sept 2011)
Insojourn 1: Oct 2011	Abroad	Oral Interview Sisters Story	Legalization of Marijuana	Grammaticality Judgement Test	Social Networks Language Engagement
Insojourn 2: Feb 2012	Abroad	Oral Interview Brothers Story	Taxes on Junk Food	Elicited Imitation Test	Social Networks Language Engagement
Insojourn 3: May 2012	Abroad	Oral Interview Cat Story	Gay Marriage & Adoption	X-Lex test Grammaticality Judgement Test L1 Reflective Interview	Social Networks Language Engagement
Postsojourn 1: Oct 2012	Home University	Oral Interview Sisters Story	Legalization of Marijuana	Elicited Imitation Test	Multicultural Personality (Sept 2012)
Postsojourn 2: Feb 2013	Home University	Oral Interview Brothers Story	Taxes on Junk Food		

However, a few of the France group had returned to Home City at this point, and they completed the Insojourn 3 tasks and questionnaires there. At Insojourn 3, participants also completed a reflective interview in English.

In September 2012 participants completed the Multicultural Personality Questionnaire again online. In October 2012, the first set of follow-up data (Postsojourn 1) was collected on the home campus. The final survey (Postsojourn 2) took place in February 2013. All participants graduated from the university in July 2013.

3.5 Project instruments

In this section we provide brief introductions to the various instruments listed in Table 3.1 and used throughout the six survey points, to gather data concerning participants' overall L2 proficiency, their L2 development in terms of CAF and their sociocultural engagement.

3.5.1 Elicited Imitation Test (EIT)

Many study abroad researchers have employed oral interviews as their main measure of sojourners' L2 proficiency (Kinginger, 2009, Chapter 2). We also wanted to include a measure of L2 proficiency but decided on an Elicited Imitation Test (EIT), a test which requires participants to listen to test stimuli and orally repeat them as accurately as possible. The idea behind the EIT as a measure of L2 proficiency is that learners can only imitate sentences that they have both parsed and comprehended (Bley-Vroman & Chaudron, 1994). EITs, particularly those with a range of sentence lengths, have been found to be valid and reliable measures of L2 proficiency (Yan, Maeda, Lv, & Ginther, 2015). This form of test was therefore a good complement to the range of language production measures used in LANGSNAP to explore participants' CAF development.

The Spanish EIT used for the LANGSNAP project was initially designed by Ortega, Iwashita, Norris, and Rabie (2002), and has also been used by Ortega (2000) and Bowden (2016). A parallel French EIT was specially created for the LANGSNAP project (Tracy-Ventura, McManus, Norris, & Ortega, 2014).

The EIT was administered by computer and took just over nine minutes to complete. It included 30 test sentences, prerecorded by an L1 speaker of the relevant language. The French items ranged from 7–19 syllables in length, and the Spanish items ranged from 7–17 syllables. These sentence stimuli were presented in order from lowest to highest number of syllables, and the participants' attempted imitations were recorded for later analysis and scoring. Each item was scored using the 5-point rubric (0–4) outlined in Ortega (2000), giving a maximum possible score of 120 points. A score of 4 was given for exact repetition, 3 for repetitions preserving the original meaning of the stimulus but including small changes in grammar, 2 for repetitions departing slightly from the original meaning of the stimulus, 1 for repetitions missing important content, and 0 for repetitions including little to none of the original content. This test was administered on three occasions (Presojourn, Insojourn 2 and Postsojourn 1).

3.5.2 Oral interview

A lengthy semistructured L2 oral interview was administered by a member of the research team at each data collection point. These interviews served a double purpose: a) to provide extended interactive L2 speech samples, relevant to several dimensions of CAF, including lexical development, and b) to provide ongoing accounts of sojourners' experiences, relevant to our interests in social networking, language practices and L2 identity.

On each occasion, the interviewers followed a list of pre-established questions focusing on sojourners' experiences and opinions about the sojourn. For example, at Presojourn they were asked to describe any ideas they had for practising the language and meeting people, and what their goals were for the year. Insojourn, questions centred on sojourners' immediate experiences, the people they were living and spending time with, their plans for the next three months and what they thought they would miss most once back home. At Postsojourn 1 and 2, participants were asked about their ongoing contact with people met abroad, whether they would change anything about their experience if they could repeat the sojourn, and any suggestions they had for students going abroad, as well as about their current studies and future life plans. A sample excerpt from a Postsojourn 1 interview is provided below:

*INT: Y qué consejos les darías a los chicos que están por irse al extranjero ahora?
   [What advice would you give to students who are about to go abroad now?]
156: Que se involucren en todo, todo lo que pueda, en los grupos, en en amigos españoles. O sea, de donde son, de los los mexicanos o los franceses o los españoles. Que hablen tanto como sea posible.
   [That they get involved in everything, everything they can, with groups, with Spanish friends. I mean wherever they're from, Mexicans, French, Spanish. That they talk as much as possible.]

We attempted to include questions in each interview that would encourage discussion of the present, the future and the past, as well as of hypothetical events; this linguistic goal fitted comfortably alongside the parallel sociocultural aims of the interviews. Some questions were repeated at each data collection cycle. Every interview was digitally recorded and later transcribed following the Codes for the Human Analysis of Transcripts (CHAT) conventions (MacWhinney, 2000). (The full CHAT-transcribed set of L2 interviews are available in the project digital repository at https://langsnap.soton.ac.uk; in this book we have simplified and translated all extracts for the sake of readability.)

3.5.3 Oral picture-based narratives

To elicit examples of participants' monologic oral L2 production, relevant in particular to analysing the development of accuracy and fluency, three picture-based narratives were used in sequence throughout the study. Each story was repeated once, approximately a year after the first administration. On each occasion, participants were given a short time to preview the story and ask any clarification questions. They could look at the pictures while retelling the story. Again, every oral narrative was digitally recorded and later transcribed in CHAT (MacWhinney, 2000); all transcripts are available in the project repository.

The first story, the Cat Story, was originally created for research on the acquisition of tense and aspect (the SPLLOC 2 project: Domínguez, Tracy-Ventura, Arche, Mitchell, & Myles, 2013), and is adapted from the children's book *Missing!* (Langley, 2001). This story was designed to elicit a variety of past tense verb forms (both perfective and imperfective), and was thus judged appropriate to the study of accuracy development among the relatively advanced LANGSNAP participants. The story begins with a description of activities that a little girl and her cat would do every morning (the background) before the start of the main storyline, or foreground, in which the little girl and her cat cannot find each other. The second picture-based narrative, the Sisters Story, had also originally been developed for SPLLOC 2, but the storyline was changed slightly for LANGSNAP, so as to begin also with habitual activities before leading into the main events. The main storyline is about two sisters who travel together to Spain. The story begins by describing their different childhood activities, to demonstrate personality differences which affect the main events of their trip. The final story, the Brothers Story, was specially designed for the LANGSNAP project and is based on the children's book *I Very Really Miss You* (Kemp & Walters, 2006). It followed a similar structure, starting with information about the habitual relationship between two brothers, before the main storyline about what happened when the older brother left for university. Sample pictures from the Sisters Story are provided in Figure 3.4 and the excerpt below comes from a retelling of that story by an L2 Spanish participant during Insojourn 1:

*152: Hubo dos gemelas que empezó una vacación a España en dos mil seis.
 [There were two sisters who started a vacation in Spain in 2006.]
*152: Eh en camino a su destino estaban hablando sobre su niñez y sobre cómo estaban y cómo eran y qué hiciera.
 [Eh on the way to their destination they were talking about their childhood and about what they were like and what they used to do.]
*152: Por ejemplo el la niña que se llama Sara era muy traviese era muy traviesa en comparación a Gwen que era muy organizada, muy trabajadora.
 [For example, the girl who is called Sara, was very mischievous in comparison to Gwen, who was very organized, very hard-working.]

60 The LANGSNAP project

Figure 3.4 Sample pages from the Sisters Story
Credit: SPLLOC (http://splloc.soton.ac.uk/splloc2/lhnt.html)

3.5.4 Argumentative essay

It was decided to include an L2 writing task in the LANGSNAP project as a distinctive source of evidence on the development of complexity in L2, as well as additional evidence on accuracy and lexis. The task selected was the argumentative essay, a genre commonly found in L2 corpus research (Lozano & Mendikoetxea, 2013). This choice was felt appropriate for our cohort of intermediate to advanced learners, though it did somewhat limit comparability with the LANGSNAP oral production data (where the tasks captured other genres, i.e., narrative and interview).

As shown in Table 3.1, three argumentative essay prompts were used in sequence, each repeated once. The first prompt focused on gay marriage and adoption and the second on the legalization of marijuana; these were both borrowed from the CEDEL2 corpus (Lozano & Mendikoetxea, 2013). The third prompt focused on the idea of taxing junk food. The essay writing task was designed to run offline, on stand-alone computers, as fieldwork conditions often made this necessary. At the start of the program, participants saw the prompt on the computer screen and were allowed three minutes for planning and note taking. They were then automatically taken to the main writing page, where they were given up to 15 minutes to write approximately 200 words (with the prompt still visible, a running word count, and a facility to insert individual accented characters in the text box). Once the 15 minutes had elapsed, the program closed and the participant could not write anything more; there was also a "submit" button for participants who finished early. Participants' actual writing time was automatically logged in seconds; this meant that written fluency (operationalized as number of words produced per minute) could also be investigated. A sample excerpt from Gay Marriage (Presojourn) is provided below:

*169: En el mundo de hoy, es chocante que ya existe el prejudicio hasta los homosexuales.

[In today's world, it is shocking that there still exists prejudice against homosexuals.]

*169: Esta claro que los parejas gay tienen el derecho de casarse y adoptar niños.
[It is clear that gay couples have the right to get married and adopt children.]

*169: Primeramente, no hay ningún razón de limitar los derechos de estas personas de casarse.
[First, there is no reason to limit the rights of these people to marry.]

*169: Es lamentable que hay países donde estas personas no pueden mostrar amor que se sienten por su pareja con un matrimonio.
[It is appalling that there are countries in which these people cannot demonstrate the love that they feel for their partner through marriage.]

3.5.5 The X-Lex test

To complement analysis of L2 vocabulary in production tasks, sojourners' L2 vocabulary recognition ability was measured via the Swansea Levels X-Lex test (Meara & Milton, 2005) which is available in both French and Spanish. This is a yes/no test where learners see a word and have to decide whether they recognize it as a real word or not. They see 120 words, of which 100 are real and 20 are false. The real words come from different frequency bands based on native speaker corpora. Points are gained for recognizing real words, and lost for recognizing false ones. This test was administered at Presojourn and at Insojourn 3.

3.5.6 The Language Engagement Questionnaire (LEQ)

The LEQ was specially designed to document LANGSNAP participants' language use practices for a range of typical year-abroad activities. The LEQ differs from the commonly used Language Contact Profile (Freed, Dewey, Segalowitz, & Halter, 2004) in two main ways: a) less precise demands were made of participants' retrospective recollections of language use, thus hopefully increasing the reliability of responses; and b) participants were asked to record all aspects of their multilingual practices (not only use of L1 and L2). The LEQ could be completed either online or on paper. Participants began the LEQ by indicating which languages they used on a regular basis (English, French, Spanish, other). If "other" was selected, they were asked to name their additional language(s). For each language listed, participants were provided with a list of 26 activities and asked to indicate how often they were currently doing each activity in that language. They recorded responses on a 5-point scale, choosing from every day (5), several times a week (4), a few times a week (3), a couple of times per month (2), rarely (1), and never (0). (There was thus a theoretical maximum score of 130 per language, if all activities had been undertaken every day.) Participants could also add qualitative comments, such as naming magazines they read or TV programmes they watched. Figure 3.5 is an extract from the LEQ;

3. French Questions

Question 1.

How often do you do the following in FRENCH?

	everyday	several times a week	a few times a week	couple times a month	rarely	never
watch television						
watch films						
browse the internet (eg. read news, etc)						
use social networking sites (eg. Facebook/Twitter)						
read emails						
write emails						
listen to music						
listen to talk radio						
listen to lectures						
participate in seminar/ language classes						
read literature (eg. fiction, poetry, etc)						
read academic texts						
read newspapers						
read magazines						
read text messages						
write text messages						
write reports (eg. work, academic)						
write for leisure (eg. journal)						
use instant messaging						

Figure 3.5 Extract from Language Engagement Questionnaire (LEQ)

Credit: iSurvey (http://isurvey.soton.ac.uk)

this questionnaire was administered at Insojourn 1, 2 and 3. (The full LEQ is available from the IRIS digital repository: https://www.iris-database.org/.)

3.5.7 *The Social Networks Questionnaire (SNQ)*

The SNQ was specially designed to collect information about participants' social networks, in particular their regular L1- and L2-using contacts in five different social contexts (work/university, organized free time, general free time, home, and virtual social activities). For each context, participants listed individuals with whom they had had active contact over the past month. For each person listed, there was a series of follow-up questions:

> How many hours do you spend together?

1. How often do you interact with this person?
   - Every day
   - Several times a week
   - A few times a week
   - A couple of times a month

2. What language(s) do you use when communicating with this person?
   - French
   - English
   - Spanish
   - Other
   - Mixture → specify which and approximate proportions
3. What is your relationship to this person?
4. How did you first meet?

Additional questions were included for organized free time (What is the organized activity you do together, e.g., attend church, gym?) and virtual social activity (What type(s) of virtual social activity do you use, e.g., Facebook, Skype, MSN?). Before completing the SNQ, participants were made aware about the questionnaire's purpose, and reminded that the same person might appear in multiple contexts. After information had been provided for all the contexts, participants were asked to list their "Top 5" (i.e., the five people they interacted with the most across all contexts), and to make any further explanatory comments they wished. Figure 3.6 is an extract from the SNQ; this questionnaire was also administered at Insojourn 1, 2 and 3. The full questionnaire is also available at www.iris-database.org.

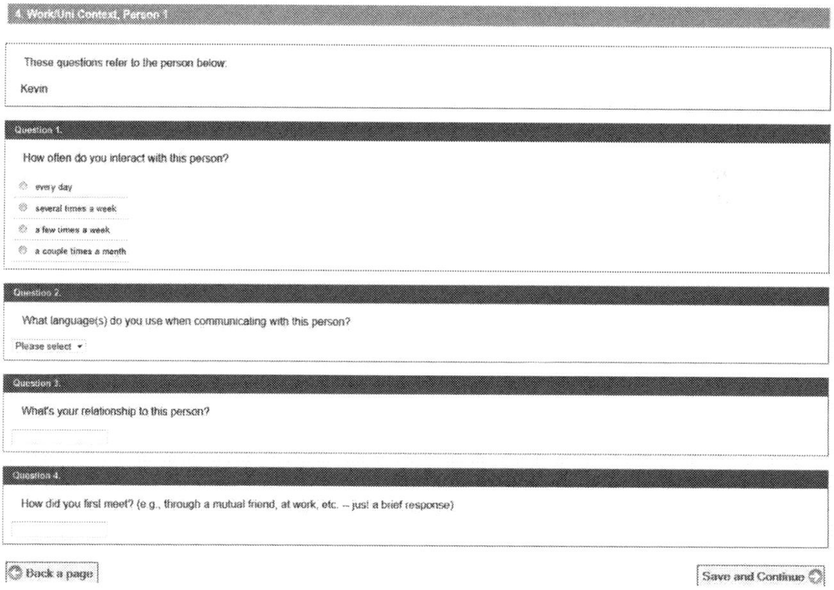

Figure 3.6 Extract from the Social Networks Questionnaire (SNQ)
Credit: iSurvey (http://isurvey.soton.ac.uk)

3.5.8 The Multicultural Personality Questionnaire (MPQ)

It was an important LANGSNAP aim to document development and change in identity and personality during the sojourn. The main data set used for this purpose was the set of semistructured interviews. However, this qualitative evidence was complemented by administration of a personality questionnaire appropriate to young adult multilinguals: the MPQ of Van der Zee and van Oudenhoven (2000). The validity and reliability of the MPQ has already been documented in a number of studies (e.g., Leone, Van der Zee, van Oudenhoven, Perugini, & Ercolani, 2005). In the current study, the Cronbach's alpha was .93, demonstrating very high consistency in responses.

In total the MPQ includes 91 items reflecting five factors: *Cultural Empathy* (18 items, e.g., 8. Understands other people's feelings; 70. Notices when someone is in trouble), *Open mindedness* (18 items, e.g., 35. Finds other religions interesting; 62. Gets involved in other cultures), *Social Initiative* (17 items, e.g., 25. Takes the lead; 34. Easily approaches other people), *Emotional Stability* (20 items, e.g., 36. Considers problems solvable; 65. Is self-confident), and *Flexibility* (18 items, e.g., 12. Changes easily from one activity to another; 88. Seeks challenges). For each item, participants select their answer on a 5-point scale: (1) totally not applicable, (2) hardly applicable, (3) moderately applicable, (4) largely applicable and (5) completely applicable. Most items are scored this way, apart from 32 items which are scored inversely. The questionnaire was made available online, and the order in which the items appeared on the questionnaire was randomized at each administration. The MPQ was administered on two occasions, after Presojourn (September 2011) and before Postsojourn 1 (September 2012). Participants were emailed a unique link and they completed the questionnaire in their own time.

3.5.9 Reflective interview

At Insojourn 3, 53/57 participants were interviewed in English to gather their extended reflections on the sojourn experience. Like the L2 interviews, this was a semistructured interview with a set of starter questions, but with considerable flexibility based on the participants' responses. In these interviews participants were asked to think about the sojourn as a whole and to reflect on their learning of the target language, the challenges they faced living abroad, their most memorable times and whether they felt they had changed as a result of this experience. These interviews were also transcribed in CHAT (MacWhinney, 2000).

3.5.10 Additional data sources

Additional types of data were collected during the project that will not be discussed further in this book beyond a mention here. A timed grammaticality judgement test focusing on the subjunctive was administered at Insojourn 1 and Insojourn 3; results based on the French data are presented in McManus and Mitchell (2015). Additionally, a total of 12 participants volunteered to complete two additional activities: participant observation and self-recording. Participant observation involved agreeing to be shadowed by a member of the research team for a whole day, at Insojourn 2. The researcher accompanied the sojourner to their place of work or study, and to their evening activities, taking detailed notes on the day's events, an exercise which broadly validated the sojourners' accounts of their usual experiences. The same participants also agreed to make two self-recordings of authentic interactions with members of their social networks, as yet unanalysed.

3.6 Creation of learner corpus

From the perspective of SLA, corpus approaches typically assemble a set of spoken and/or written texts produced by language learners, transcribe these according to set conventions, and run a variety of linguistic analyses on the resulting electronic data sets (Granger, 2009; Myles, 2008). The LANGSNAP project set out to make a substantial part of the data collected available to other researchers, including both audio recordings and transcripts, complementing earlier corpus projects at the University of Southampton, UK (see www.flloc.soton.ac.uk, www.splloc.soton.ac.uk).

The LANGSNAP corpus comprises all of the French and Spanish data resulting from the three main L2 production tasks: the L2 oral interviews, the oral narratives and the argumentative essays. Table 3.3 provides the total word counts for each task type. Tables 3.4 and 3.5 present the average number of words per task per participant, by language.

The LANGSNAP corpus is available in the project's public repository at https://langsnap.soton.ac.uk.

Table 3.2 LANGSNAP corpus composition (number of words)

Participants	Oral interview	Oral narrative	Argumentative essay	Total
French L2 (n=29)	222,014	65,905	36,339	324,258
French L1 (n=10)	18,225	11,451	6,695	36,401
Spanish L2 (n=27)	214,364	53,497	36,059	303,920
Spanish L1 (n=10)	12,146	8,789	6,699	27,634
Total	466,779	139,642	85,792	692,213

Table 3.3 Average words per task per participant, French groups

	Oral interview		Oral narrative		Argumentative essay	
	L2	L1*	L2	L1*	L2	L1*
Presojourn	1033	1214	260	307	193	220
Insojourn 1	1685		388	343	197	223
Insojourn 2	1764		285	228	207	225
Insojourn 3	1636		311		218	
Postsojourn 1	938		370		204	
Postsojourn 2	883		237		209	

*Note: The L1 French speakers completed each task once, so that their word count corresponds to the tasks given to the sojourners at Presojourn for oral interview, and at Presojourn, Insojourn 1 and Insojourn 2 for oral narrative and written essay.

Table 3.4 Average words per task per participant, Spanish groups

	Oral interview		Oral narrative		Argumentative essay	
	L2	L1*	L2	L1*	L2	L1*
Presojourn	1033	1214	260	307	193	220
Insojourn 1	1685		388	343	197	223
Insojourn 2	1764		285	228	207	225
Insojourn 3	1636		311		218	
Postsojourn 1	938		370		204	
Postsojourn 2	883		237		209	

*Note: The L1 Spanish speakers completed each task once, so that their word count corresponds to the tasks given to the sojourners at Presojourn for oral interview, and at Presojourn, Insojourn 1 and Insojourn 2 (for oral narrative and written essay).

3.7 Analysis of complexity, accuracy and fluency (CAF)

3.7.1 Syntactic complexity

Syntactic complexity was analysed in the argumentative essays only, as it is generally accepted that written genres offer the greatest scope for complexity development. Measuring syntactic complexity in written data requires the identification of T-units and clauses within each written text (Wolfe-Quintero, Inagaki, & Kim, 1998). This is a complex issue, as definitions of clauses, for example, differ among scholars of French linguistics in particular (Baschung & Desmets, 2000; Rowlett, 2007), and also among CAF researchers (Bulté & Housen, 2012). In our study, a T-unit was defined as a main/independent clause with an explicit subject (or coordinated subjects) and a finite verb (or coordinated finite verbs), plus all associated subordinate elements including finite subordinate clauses, nonfinite VPs, adverbials, and so on. Our definition of a clause was based on Bulté and Housen (2012): "a unit consisting of a subject (visible or implied) plus a predicate, i.e. a construction with a finite or nonfinite predicator or verb as its head" (p. 39). We treated modal verbs (e.g., *devoir, falloir, pouvoir, vouloir* in French; *deber, tener que, poder, haber que* in Spanish) as auxiliaries, and therefore bare nonfinite VPs following these verbs were treated as complement phrases but not as separate clauses.

All T-units were marked in the essays following CHAT conventions. Every new T-unit started on its own line with the participant number (e.g., *100). The symbol [^ c] was manually inserted within the T-unit line where appropriate to mark clause boundaries. Using this coding and the total word count per essay, we operationalized syntactic complexity in two ways for both languages: 1) ratio of clauses to T-units and 2) mean length of T-unit. In the French analysis, the ratio of finite clauses to all clauses was also investigated (the lower the ratio, the more complex the writing).

3.7.2 Lexical complexity

Lexical complexity was operationalized as lexical diversity and analysed in the oral interview (and for Spanish, also in the oral narrative and argumentative essay).

Lexical diversity was computed using the VocD command in the CHILDES linguistic analysis program CLAN (MacWhinney, 2000), resulting in the score D. Although related to type-token ratio (TTR), D has been argued to be less sensitive to text length compared to TTR as it uses random text sampling and a coefficient D formula, which is run three times and then averaged, resulting in a D score for that sample (for more details see Malvern & Richards, 2002). Because D is not based on a single index (in contrast to TTR), but a combination of different indexes plus averaging, validation work has argued that it represents a robust measure of lexical diversity (McCarthy & Jarvis, 2007, 2010). D scores tend to range from 10 to 100; the higher the score, the higher a sample's lexical diversity.

3.7.3 Accuracy

Accuracy was analysed in the oral narratives and the argumentative essays. We operationalized accuracy for the oral narratives using several different measures. Firstly, we used two global measures: 1) percentage of error-free Analysis of Speech Units (ASUs), and 2) percentage of error-free clauses. The ASU has been widely used as an alternative to the T-unit for the analysis of spoken language, following the proposals of Foster, Tonkyn, and Wigglesworth (2000). These authors define it as "a single speaker's utterance consisting of an independent clause or subclausal unit, together with any subordinate clause(s) associated with either" (p. 365). The narrative transcripts were divided into ASUs and clauses following detailed analysis protocols, and adequate reliability was assured through double rating of transcripts and discussion. The identified ASUs and clauses were then judged for overall accuracy by trained raters.

In the oral narrative we also adopted a specific measure of verb tense accuracy, operationalized as the percentage of correct *Passé Composé* (or preterit for Spanish) and *Imparfait* (or imperfect for Spanish). This was calculated by identifying all appropriate contexts in the narratives as told by each participant for using either the preterit or imperfect. The verb form actually used in each context was then judged correct or incorrect, depending on whether it matched the context; errors of person and number were ignored provided forms could be attributed reliably to a particular verb tense. Use of historic present tense was not accepted; again reliability was assured through a process of double coding and discussion of disagreements. For L2 French only, we also examined the use of subjunctive in the oral interviews, following a similar procedure.

Written accuracy was operationalized in terms of two similar global measures: 1) percentage of error-free T-units (Wolfe-Quintero et al., 1998), and 2) percentage of error-free clauses. In judging written accuracy, orthographic errors including those involving silent letters were ignored. For L2 French writing only, again, we examined the use of subjunctive as a focused feature.

3.7.4 Fluency

Fluency was analysed for all performances of two tasks. In the monologic oral narratives we analysed three dimensions of utterance fluency: speed fluency, breakdown fluency, and repair fluency (Bosker, Pinget, Quené, Sanders, & De Jong, 2013; Skehan, 2003; Tavakoli & Skehan, 2005). However, in this book we will report the results for speed fluency only. This was operationalized using two measures: 1) Speech Rate (the number of syllables/total speaking time, including pauses) and 2) Mean Length of Run (the average number of syllables between silent pauses of .25 milliseconds or greater). These two measures have been adopted in a number of SA studies on fluency development (Freed, Segalowitz, & Dewey, 2004; Mora & Valls-Ferrer, 2012; Towell, Hawkins, & Bazergui, 1996). Analysis of audio files was supported using the Praat software package to identify and measure pauses.

In the writing task, fluency was operationalized as the number of words produced per minute (Sasaki, 2007). As the writing task was timed, all participants' time on task was automatically calculated, even if they finished early.

3.8 Analyses of social data

The quantitative data collected using the various questionnaires were analysed with support from a statistical program (SPSS); summary overviews of these findings are presented in Chapters 6 and 7. A key source of qualitative information concerning participants' ongoing experience of the sojourn was the series of interviews conducted individually in L2 at each survey point, plus the reflective interview in English conducted at Insojourn 3. These data have some limitations. Firstly, they involve retrospective self-report, with its attendant biases and complexity of interpretation. Secondly, they reflect the perspective of the sojourners alone – that is, they are not counterbalanced with any data reflecting the perspective of hosts, mentors, local friends or any other members of sojourners' social networks when abroad, as recommended by, for example, Kinginger (2009). And thirdly, the fact that most interviews were conducted in L2 may also have limited somewhat the nature of sojourners' responses. However, the sojourners were usually very eager to share their reflections and personal anecdotes with the research team, and the longitudinal nature of the interview series meant that personal themes were revisited, and narratives developed, as time passed, providing ongoing ecological validation of individual interviews.

The complete set of interviews was imported into the qualitative analysis program NVivo and coded both by individual interview questions and by crosscutting themes. This approach allowed for identification of the range of perspectives adopted by sojourners on particular issues and their relative popularity. It also allowed for longitudinal tracking of individual sojourners' accounts of their evolving social networks and language practices. An important adjunct was the qualitative section of the Social Networks Questionnaire, where participants named and described the individual contacts most important to them; this information frequently helped to triangulate/disambiguate the interview data. Overall, when analysed in this way, the bank of interviews provided rich insights into the evolution of sojourners' L2 identity, at the group and the individual level.

In order to protect participants' identity, throughout the book they are identified by numbers rather than names. The individuals who are the subjects of case studies in Chapter 9 are given new names; any other names (occurring in quotations, etc.) have also been changed. Actual names have been used for major cities (e.g., Paris, Cancún), but smaller cities are identified by a letter code.

3.9 Conclusion

This chapter has presented the overall design and main tools of the LANGSNAP project. In the following chapters, we have set out to present an accessible account of this interdisciplinary project, presenting main quantitative findings in straightforward tables and figures, and relating these consistently to qualitative results. We provide information on the main trends over time in both language learning and social development for the two language groups, as well as information on individual sojourners. Readers seeking more information on the detail of project tasks, as well as on other project publications, are referred to the project website: https://langsnap.soton.ac.uk.

References

Baschung, K., & Desmets, M. (2000). On the phrasal vs. clausal syntactic status of French infinitives: Causative constructions and subject inversion. *Journal of French Language Studies, 10*(02), 205–228.

Bley-Vroman, R., & Chaudron, C. (1994). Elicited imitation as a measure of second-language competence. In E. Tarone, S.M. Gass, & A.D. Cohen (Eds.), *Research methodology in second language acquisition* (pp. 245–261). Hillsdale, NJ: Lawrence Erlbaum.

Bosker, H. R., Pinget, A.-F., Quené, H., Sanders, T., & De Jong, N. (2013). What makes speech sound fluent? The contributions of pauses, speed and repairs. *Language Testing, 30*(2), 159–175.

Bowden, H. W. (2016). Assessing second-language oral proficiency for research. *Studies in Second Language Acquisition, 38*(4), 647–675.

Bulté, B., & Housen, A. (2012). Defining and operationalising L2 complexity. In A. Housen, F. Kuiken, & I. Vedder (Eds.), *Dimensions of L2 performance and proficiency: Complexity, accuracy and fluency in SLA* (pp. 21–46). Amsterdam: John Benjamins.

Domínguez, L., Tracy-Ventura, N., Arche, M., Mitchell, R., & Myles, F. (2013). The role of dynamic contrasts in the L2 acquisition of Spanish past tense morphology. *Bilingualism: Language and Cognition, 16*(3), 558–577.

Foster, P., Tonkyn, A., & Wigglesworth, G. (2000). Measuring spoken language: A unit for all reasons. *Applied Linguistics, 21*(3), 354–375.

Freed, B. F., Dewey, D. P., Segalowitz, N., & Halter, R. (2004). The language contact profile. *Studies in Second Language Acquisition, 26*, 349–356.

Freed, B. F., Segalowitz, N., & Dewey, D. P. (2004). Context of learning and second language fluency in French: Comparing regular classroom, study abroad, and intensive domestic immersion programs. *Studies in Second Language Acquisition, 26*(2), 275–301.

Granger, S. (2009). The contribution of learner corpora to second language acquisition and foreign language teaching: A critical evaluation. In K. Aijmer (Ed.), *Corpora and Language Teaching* (pp. 13–32). Amsterdam: John Benjamins.

Kemp, J., & Walters, J. (2006). *I very really miss you*. London: Frances Lincoln Children's Books.

Kinginger, C. (2009). *Language learning and study abroad: A critical reading of research*. Basingstoke: Palgrave Macmillan.

Langley, J. (2001). *Missing!* London: Frances Lincoln Children's Books.

Leone, L., Van der Zee, K. I., van Oudenhoven, J. P., Perugini, M., & Ercolani, A. P. (2005). The cross-cultural generalizability and validity of the Multicultural Personality Questionnaire. *Personality and Individual Differences*, 38(6), 1449–1462.

Lozano, C., & Mendikoetxea, A. (2013). Learner corpora and second language acquisition: The design and collection of CEDEL2. In A. Diaz-Negrillo, N. Ballier, & P. Thompson (Eds.), *Automatic treatment and analysis of learner corpus data* (pp. 65–100). Amsterdam: John Benjamins.

MacWhinney, B. (2000). *The CHILDES Project: Tools for analyzing talk* (3rd ed.). Mahwah, NJ: Lawrence Erlbaum.

Malvern, D., & Richards, B. (2002). Investigating accommodation in language proficiency interviews using a new measure of lexical diversity. *Language Testing*, 19(1), 85–104.

McCarthy, P., & Jarvis, S. (2007). vocd: A theoretical and empirical evaluation. *Language Testing*, 24(4), 459–488.

McCarthy, P., & Jarvis, S. (2010). MTLD, vocd-D, and HD-D: A validation study of sophisticated approaches to lexical diversity assessment. *Behavior Research Methods*, 42(2), 381–392.

McManus, K., & Mitchell, R. (2015). Subjunctive use and development in L2 French: A longitudinal study. *Language Interaction and Acquisition*, 6(1), 42–73.

Meara, P. M., & Milton, J. (2005). *X-Lex: The Swansea levels test*. Newbury: Express.

Mora, J. C., & Valls-Ferrer, M. (2012). Oral fluency, accuracy, and complexity in formal instruction and study abroad learning contexts. *TESOL Quarterly*, 46(4), 610–641.

Myles, F. (2008). Investigating learner language development with electronic longitudinal corpora: Theoretical and methodological issues. In L. Ortega & H. Byrnes (Eds.), *The longitudinal study of advanced L2 capacities* (pp. 58–72). Abingdon: Routledge.

Ortega, L. (2000). *Understanding syntactic complexity: The measurement of change in the syntax of instructed L2 Spanish learners*. (PhD), University of Hawaii at Manoa.

Ortega, L., Iwashita, N., Norris, J., & Rabie, S. (2002). *An investigation of elicited imitation tasks in crosslinguistic SLA research*. Paper presented at the Second Language Research Forum, Toronto, Canada.

Rowlett, P. (2007). *The syntax of French*. Cambridge: Cambridge University Press.

Sasaki, M. (2007). Effects of study-abroad experiences on EFL writers: A multiple-data analysis. *The Modern Language Journal*, 91(4), 602–620.

Skehan, P. (2003). Task based instruction. *Language Teaching*, 36(1), 1–14.

Tavakoli, P., & Skehan, P. (2005). Strategic planning, task structure, and performance testing. In R. Ellis (Ed.), *Planning and task performance* (pp. 239–273). Amsterdam: John Benjamins.

Towell, R., Hawkins, R., & Bazergui, N. (1996). The development of fluency in advanced learners of French. *Applied Linguistics*, 17(1), 84–119.

Tracy-Ventura, N., McManus, K., Norris, J., & Ortega, L. (2014). "Repeat as much as you can": Elicited imitation as a measure of oral proficiency in L2 French. In P. Leclercq, A. Edmonds, & H. Hilton (Eds.), *Measuring L2 proficiency: Perspectives from SLA* (pp. 143–166). Bristol: Multilingual Matters.

Van der Zee, K. I., & van Oudenhoven, J. P. (2000). The Multicultural Personality Questionnaire: A multidimensional instrument for multicultural effectiveness. *European Journal of Personality*, 14(3), 291–309.

Wolfe-Quintero, K., Inagaki, S., & Kim, H.-Y. (1998). *Second language development in writing: Measures of fluency, accuracy and complexity: Technical Report 17*. Honolulu: Second Language Teaching and Curriculum Center, University of Hawai'i at Manoa.

Yan, X., Maeda, Y., Lv, J., & Ginther, A. (2015). Elicited imitation as a measure of second language proficiency: A narrative review and meta-analysis. *Language Testing, 33*(4), 497–528.

4 Linguistic development in French

4.1 Introduction

This is the first of two companion chapters presenting our main findings for L2 development in terms of global proficiency, fluency, accuracy and complexity. Our aim is to present similar accounts for French and Spanish (see Chapter 5), though in places our analyses differ in detail. In both chapters we provide readers with an overview of development, summarizing group trends using straightforward tables and bar charts, and referring where appropriate to other publications with greater statistical detail. We also provide charts giving an overview of individual performances on all measures, which provide a useful reference point for subsequent qualitative chapters and case studies of individual participants.

In this chapter we present the linguistic development of the subgroup of participants majoring in L2 French. As described in Chapter 3, proficiency was measured using spoken data collected from the French Elicited Imitation Test, and our analyses for fluency, accuracy and complexity draw on participants' spoken and written L2 production and a test of receptive lexical knowledge.

This chapter begins with an overview of previous L2 French study abroad (SA) research (Section 4.2), and in Section 4.3 we present the LANGSNAP main findings for L2 French.

4.2 L2 French development during study abroad

The acquisition of French has been generally well studied from a variety of theoretical perspectives, and in a range of formal and informal settings (Dewaele, 2005; Guijarro-Fuentes, Schmitz, & Muller, 2016; Perdue, Deulofeu, & Trévise, 1992; Prévost, 2009; Véronique, Carlo, Granger, Kim, & Prodeau, 2009). Substantial studies have been undertaken of advanced learners in instructed settings, similar to the participants in LANGSNAP. A programme of work by Bartning and colleagues has conceptualized L2 French development in terms of a series of stages drawing on development sequences for particular language features, including tense and aspect, negation, and subordination (Bartning, 1997, 2009, 2012; Bartning & Schlyter, 2004). This line of research continues, exploring additional dimensions, including the development of discourse and information structure, vocabulary and formulaic language among advanced learners (Bartning, Forsberg Lundell, & Hancock, 2012; Lindqvist & Bardel, 2014), or learning beyond the advanced-high level (Forsberg Lundell & Bartning, 2015; Forsberg Lundell, Bartning, Engel, Gudmundson, Hancock, & Lindqvist, 2014).

By comparison with some other languages, however, L2 French learners' development during SA is comparatively little studied. French figured in some major early studies demonstrating proficiency development during SA, alongside other languages (Carroll, 1967; Coleman, 1996; Dyson, 1988; Willis, Doble, Sankarayya, & Smithers, 1977). However, Yang's (2016) recent meta-analysis of SA research highlighted that of 66 empirical studies published since 1991, which included measures of learning outcomes, only nine examined L2 French, contrasting with 27 for L2 English and 21 for L2 Spanish. In the survey which follows, we concentrate on this more limited set of studies which have researched the development of L2 French in the SA context. We begin with the strongest tradition of SA research in French, concerned with sociolinguistic variation, before moving to examine studies of fluency, accuracy and complexity.

4.2.1 Sociolinguistic development

A distinctive body of L2 French research has examined learners' acquisition of sociolinguistic variation in phonology, lexis and morphosyntax, in both study abroad and L2 immersion contexts (for overviews see Howard, 2012; Mougeon, Nadasdi, & Rehner, 2010; Regan, Howard, & Lemée, 2009). This research has described the informal learning of a range of variable features commonly found in contemporary French, and signalling differing degrees of formality/informality, yet not typically available in instructed contexts. These include the variable use of the negative particle *(ne) . . . pas* (Dewaele & Regan, 2002); variable use of the first-person pronouns *nous* vs. *on* (Lemée, 2003); variable use of composed vs. simple future verb forms (e.g., *il va jouer* vs. *il jouera*) (Howard, 2009); variable /l/ deletion (Howard, 2006b); and formal vs. vernacular lexical forms (Nadasdi, Mougeon, & Rehner, 2008). The work of Howard and others has shown that for advanced learners of L2 French, study abroad is normally central in providing access to these variable features (though van Compernolle and Williams, 2012, show that they are also teachable).

In the LANGSNAP project, we have focused on the CAF model of L2 development and have not systematically investigated our participants' learning of variable features. However, it will be seen later that the LANGSNAP participants were keen to acquire more informal speech styles, and the issue is revisited in Chapter 8 when discussing sojourners' L2 identity. Indeed, a number of other SA researchers working in qualitative traditions on sojourner identity, sociopragmatic development, language learning practices, and engagement with the local environment have also focused all or part of their work on L2 French (Allen, 2010; Cohen & Shively, 2007; Kinginger, 2008; Kinginger & Blattner, 2008; Paige, Cohen, & Shively, 2004; Wilkinson, 1998, 2002).

4.2.2 General proficiency in L2 French

As discussed in Chapter 1, SA research generally shows benefits for global L2 proficiency, and this is also true for L2 French (Coleman, 1996; Kinginger, 2009, 2011; Magnan & Lafford, 2012; Yang, 2016). However, the French SA literature also provides evidence of variable achievement, including instances where individuals' L2 French proficiency scores did not improve (Kinginger, 2008; Magnan & Back, 2007).

Magnan and Back (2007) collected spoken L2 French data through the Oral Proficiency Interview (OPI: ACTFL, 2012) from a group of 20 American students spending a semester in France. They found that 12/20 students made measurable improvement, while eight did not. Contrary to expectation, Magnan and Back failed to find any significant relationship between sojourners' use of French as measured using the Language Contact Profile (Freed, Dewey, Segalowitz, & Halter, 2004), and their improvement in oral proficiency. Kinginger (2008) administered the *Test de français international*, described as a "standardized test of reading and listening comprehension that includes sections directly addressing sentence-level grammatical competence" (p. 34), before and after SA. Comparisons of group test scores showed significant improvement following SA. However, individual results showed that 13/23 participants' overall proficiency rankings had not changed; in particular, following SA, 7/23 participants' reading scores were lower, whereas only one participant received a lower listening score. Learners' self-ratings also reflect this trend for less to no improvement in reading (and writing) during SA. For example, Meara (1994) reported self-ratings from post-SA students of French, German and Spanish, concerning "how much they thought they had improved on a scale from 1 (=not at all) to 5 (=very much)" (p. 34). Participants judged their speaking and listening to have improved very much, but were considerably less confident of improvement for writing and reading (see also Dyson, 1988).

Together, these L2 French studies confirm the more general findings in the literature of a general tendency toward improvement in proficiency combined with considerable individual variability and some imbalance between skills, and also the challenges of relating this variability to particular aspects of the SA experience (Dewey, Belnap, & Hilstrom, 2013).

4.2.3 Fluency in L2 French

There is a widespread belief that oral fluency is a prime candidate for development during study abroad (Freed, 1995), and this is broadly confirmed by empirical research (Mora & Valls-Ferrer, 2012; Segalowitz & Freed, 2004; Valls-Ferrer & Mora, 2014). In an examination of oral fluency development in L2 French, Towell, Hawkins, and Bazergui (1996) analysed a range of temporal and hesitation phenomena and concluded that "a group of advanced learners of French become more fluent in their language production ability as a result of a period of residence abroad" (p. 112). They tested 12 advanced university learners using a film retelling task, before and after a six-month sojourn in France. Their results showed significant increases after study abroad for speech rate, speaking time, and mean length of run, that is, "an increase in the length and complexity of the linguistic units which are uttered between pauses" (p. 112–113). As they see it, learners have improved in how they access knowledge for online use, consistent with the perspective of DeKeyser (2007, 2014) on SA as primarily a site for practice, which consolidates learners' previous classroom-based experience. A limitation of this research was that while Towell et al. believe that opportunities for L2 use play a key role in fluency development, they did not collect information about this.

Freed, Segalowitz, and Dewey (2004), however, measured both fluency gain and L2 French contact and use, and explored the relations between them. Their study included three groups of participants (normal classes at home, intensive immersion at home, and SA), and findings were compared across all three. Participants had studied French for 2–4 years only, and the SA group (n=8) undertook a 12-week sojourn in France including language classes. In this study, the greatest fluency gains were made by the immersion group, though the SA group also made gains compared to the regular at-home group. The fluency data used by Freed et al. were an extract from an OPI-like interview. Fluency was operationalized through speech rate, mean length of run and articulation rate, as well as measures of breakdown and repair. Language use was documented using the Language Contact Profile, and it turned out that the immersion group reported much the greatest number of hours using French outside of classes. In sum, when compared to regular at-home learning, study abroad was more beneficial, but not when compared to intensive learning plus informal L2 use in an immersion context. Thus, Towell et al. and Freed et al. agree that opportunities for L2 use and interaction help promote L2 fluency development, though Freed et al. clearly challenge the assumption made by the earlier researchers that SA will automatically provide this.

In another pioneering study, Freed and colleagues compared the writing development of the same at-home and SA students using a pre-post design (Freed, So, & Lazar, 2003). While the SA students showed no advantage for written accuracy nor for syntactic complexity, their essays were holistically judged "more fluent" by a professional panel, and they wrote longer assignments than the AH group.

4.2.4 Accuracy in L2 French

In general, we know less about L2 grammatical development during study abroad than we do about oral fluency (Llanes, 2011; Magnan & Lafford, 2012; Yang, 2016), especially for L2 French. Researchers looking at a variety of languages have most frequently compared grammatical accuracy of SA and at-home learners, finding few differences between the groups (DeKeyser, 2010; Isabelli-García, 2010; Mora & Valls-Ferrer, 2012; Serrano, Llanes, & Tragant, 2011). These findings lead DeKeyser to the conclusion that "even when clear progress is made, it tends to be in the area of fluency rather than accuracy or complexity" (DeKeyser, 2014, p. 314).

There are however some counterexamples in a range of languages which find positive evidence for morphosyntactic development during SA (Grey, Cox, Serafini, & Sanz, 2015; Guntermann, 1995; Isabelli & Nishida, 2005; Rees & Klapper, 2007; Yager, 1998). One longitudinal study by Serrano, Tragant, and Llanes (2012) found evidence of accuracy improvement in L2 English, for example, but found that this emerged only at the end of a yearlong stay abroad, whereas improvement in fluency and in lexis emerged much sooner.

Turning to L2 French, as we saw earlier, there are substantial programmes of research on the general course of morphosyntactic development, including studies within a CAF framework (see various chapters in Housen Kuiken & Vedder, 2012), but rather few of these have been carried out in an SA context. Early studies by Möhle and Raupach (1983) and Freed (1990) found little evidence of progress in French syntactic accuracy during SA. However, later studies concerning development of specific L2 features, studied separately, have found more positive results. Thus, Duperron (2007) and Howard (2002, 2005a, 2005b) report on the development of past time reference. For example, Howard (2005b) compared learning of *Passé Composé* and *Imparfait* by Irish undergraduates spending a year abroad with those studying for a similar period at home, and found significantly more accurate and appropriate past tense usage among the SA group. Howard's study of the *Plus-que-parfait* found similar results (Howard, 2005c), and a third study of development in L2 French verb morphology (marking of third-person plural), while documenting variable development, concluded: "it is the informal language contact that our [SA] learners have experienced which has overwhelmingly brought about a level of third person plural marking which most approaches native speaker norms" (Howard, 2006a, p. 16). A small-scale study by Godfrey, Treacy, and Tarone (2014) of gender concord in L2 French writing found greater improvement among an SA group than among an AH group. On the other hand, a study of the acquisition of the subjunctive did not show any significant advantage for the SA group (Howard, 2008). The general trend of these studies suggests that a lengthy SA experience, at least, can contribute significantly to the accuracy development of advanced learners of L2 French.

4.2.5 *Syntactic complexity in L2 French*

As mentioned earlier, there are a number of studies involving French in the general CAF literature. Definitions of "complexity" are variable in these studies; thus, for example, Ågren, Granfeldt, and Schlyter (2012) define complexity development as a general increase in control of L2 French morphosyntax, conceptualized in the stages of the Lund French L2 developmental model, whereas Granfeldt (2007), Gunnarsson (2012) and Kuiken and Vedder (2012) define complexity essentially in terms of T-unit length and internal structure, as in Wolfe-Quintero, Inagaki, and Kim (1998) and in the LANGSNAP study. Kuiken and Vedder (2012) report three different studies with university-level

L2 learners, exploring the impact of varying task complexity and L2 proficiency on aspects of CAF including lexical variation, in written L2 French and L2 Italian (and in one study, in L2 speech). Their main findings for complexity were that higher L2 proficiency was associated with greater written complexity in L2 Italian (though not in L2 French: Study 1), and that complexity was lesser in the spoken mode (i.e., fewer dependent clauses were produced: Study 3). Granfeldt (2007) and Gunnarsson (2012) ran studies of L2 French CAF development among Swedish high school students, but both researchers concluded that the age and proficiency level of the participants meant that the complexity findings were of limited interest.

The study by Godfrey et al. (2014) compared the development of complexity (defined as clauses per T-unit) in the L2 French writing of small at-home and SA groups, finding a slight advantage for the at-home group. A similar study by Freed et al. (2003) found no advantage for either an at-home or an SA group. Otherwise, we have been unable to locate any previous studies exploring the development of complexity in the context of L2 French study abroad. However, this brief survey of the general literature suggests that the relatively advanced LANGSNAP participants are at a stage where meaningful complexity development may be expected to appear, at least in certain modalities (notably writing).

4.2.6 Lexical development in L2 French

Despite thorough examination of lexical development in instructed contexts, this area of linguistic development has also been subject to considerably fewer investigations in study abroad contexts (Collentine, 2009; Kinginger, 2011). A small number of studies with other L2s, however, show lexical development during SA (Ife, Vives Boix, & Meara, 2000; Milton & Meara, 1995; Serrano et al., 2012).

In L2 English, Milton and Meara (1995) examined learners' vocabulary knowledge using the Eurocentres Vocabulary Size Test (Meara & Jones, 1990), a yes/no test of vocabulary knowledge. Learners were tested at the beginning of their stay abroad and then six months later, and they showed very large improvements in receptive vocabulary between the two test points. Similar findings are reported by Foster (2009), but using learner productions. She compared a SA group (in London) and an at-home group (in Tehran) on a range of lexical measures based on oral retellings of stories (see also Tavakoli & Foster, 2008). The learner groups performed significantly differently for lexical diversity (*D*), with the SA group (mean *D* score = 38.61) far outperforming the at-home group (mean *D* score = 28.98). Furthermore, whilst the at-home group's *D* scores were significantly different from a comparison group of L1 English speakers, no differences were found between the L1 group and the SA group.

Specific to L2 French, there are a number of studies of the development of lexical diversity using *D* (De Clercq, 2015; Granfeldt, 2007; Marsden & David, 2008; Tidball & Treffers-Daller, 2007). Of these studies, that of Tidball and Treffers-Daller (2007) is most relevant for LANGSNAP, as their participants are British university learners of French, and the study includes both pre–year abroad (year 1) and post–year abroad groups. Lexical diversity was analysed using storytelling L2 production tasks, and the postsojourn group performed significantly more strongly. However, these researchers also documented substantial within-group variability, related to variability in overall proficiency but also (they speculate) to different levels of language engagement when abroad: "While some have been able to expand the range of vocabulary used during their [sojourn] abroad, others may not have used the opportunity to improve their language to the same extent" (2007, p. 148).

Another relevant study of the development of "lexical richness" in L2 French is that of Lindqvist, Bardel, and Gudmundson (2011). Using a linguistic profiling approach to measuring lexical richness, rather than the D measure, they analysed advanced learners' spoken productions in L2 French, in terms of the frequency bands from which their vocabulary was drawn. (Lexical frequency bands for spoken French were first of all established through analysis of a contemporary corpus, *Corpaix*; development in "lexical richness" was defined as growth in use of lower-frequency words.) The learners were drawn from "Low Advanced" and "High Advanced" levels, in terms of the Lund scale; a distinguishing feature was that the "High" group had all spent at least a year in a Francophone country; that is, they were a post-SA group. The lexical richness of this "High" group was significantly different from that of the "Low" group, but not significantly different from that of a comparison group of L1 speakers. Thus, using a somewhat different methodology, Lindqvist et al. also confirmed the important contribution of SA to lexical development.

As with fluency development, the general literature suggests that the SA context mainly benefits lexical development early on in the sojourn (Serrano et al., 2011; Serrano et al., 2012). In this respect, lexical development seems to contrast with accuracy development (Collentine, 2004; DeKeyser, 2014; Howard, 2009). These issues have not yet been explored in relation to L2 French.

4.2.7 *Summary of the literature*

This review has shown that work to date on L2 French development during study abroad is relatively limited. However, available findings support more general results in the field: fluency is understood to develop relatively quickly during SA, whereas accuracy seems slower to develop. Notable gaps in the L2 French SA literature concern the development of syntactic and lexical complexity, and the related issue of the development of writing.

In the next section, the LANGSNAP L2 French linguistic development results are presented. We begin with the larger category of L2 proficiency, before examining more precise areas of L2 development in fluency, accuracy and complexity.

4.3 French language development in the LANGSNAP project

This section is designed to provide an accessible general overview of L2 French development among the LANGSNAP participants, and it is organized by construct. First we provide overall group results for oral proficiency, followed by fluency, accuracy, syntactic complexity, and lexical knowledge. Where appropriate, results are compared with the L1 French speaker group (n=10) on the same set of tasks. More detailed analyses of some of these results have been presented in other places, and we refer to those publications where appropriate. Readers are referred to McManus, Tracy-Ventura, and Mitchell (2016) for fuller statistical treatment of CAF development.

For our analysis, we checked the normality of distribution of the French test scores at each testing phase, which showed the whole data set not to be normally distributed (Shapiro Wilk, p < .05). As a result, we used non-parametric tests throughout. First, Friedman tests were used to compare test score differences over time and across all test phases (Presojourn to Postsojourn 2), followed by Wilcoxon Signed Rank tests (post hocs) if a statistically significant Friedman result was found (with Bonferroni adjustment applied: 15 comparisons/0.05 = p ≤ .003). We used Mann-Whitney U tests when comparing learner and French L1 scores. We report Cohen's *d* effect sizes for all Wilcoxon Signed Rank and Mann-Whitney U tests, calculated using means and standard deviations (see Plonsky, 2015). Effect sizes are interpreted following the field-specific benchmarks proposed by Plonsky and Oswald (2014) for Cohen's *d*: *d* = .60 (small), 1.00 (medium) and 1.40 (large).

4.3.1 Measurement of overall proficiency: The French Elicited Imitation Test

Participants' oral proficiency was measured with the French Elicited Imitation Test (EIT) described in Chapter 3. We administered the French and Spanish EITs three times to the relevant groups, each approximately nine months apart, to limit any practice effects: at Presojourn, at Insojourn 2 and later at Postsojourn 1. The French group's mean performance on the EIT improved steadily over time, scoring 62.9 at Presojourn, 80.1 at Insojourn 2 and 85.6 at Postsojourn 1. The sharpest increase was found between Presojourn and Insojourn 2, with less difference between Insojourn 2 and Postsojourn 1. Table 4.1 summarizes these group results, and individual scores are shown in Figure 4.1.

Group comparisons of learners' EIT scores (Friedman tests) showed all testing phases to be significantly different from each other ($X^2(2) = 44.702$, p < .001). Effect sizes between the different test phases were as follows: medium between Presojourn and Insojourn 2 (p < .001, *d* = .99) and large between Presojourn and Postsojourn 1 (p < .001, *d* = 1.37). A marginal effect size was found for EIT scores between Insojourn 2 and Postsojourn 1 (p = .003, *d* = .34). Mann-Whitney U tests were used to compare performance with the L1 French group (mean EIT score = 118.4) and showed that learners' scores were significantly lower at each testing phase (p < .001, *d* = 2.54).

Figure 4.1 presents the individual scores of the 29 French participants in order of EIT achievement at Presojourn. It can be seen that while almost all sojourners made gains (as indicated by the changes in group mean scores), the highest

80 Linguistic development in French

Table 4.1 Summary results of the French Elicited Imitation Test

	Mean EIT score (k=120)	SD	Range
Presojourn	62.9	17.9	36–97
Insojourn 2	80.1	16.8	51–113
Postsojourn 1	85.6	15.2	54–109

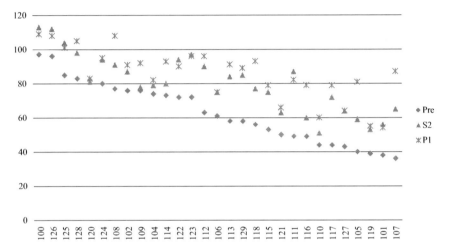

Figure 4.1 EIT scores for individual L2 French participants at Presojourn, Insojourn 2 and Postsojourn 1

attainers early on improved somewhat less than those with middle- or lower-ranked scores, presumably due to ceiling effects.

4.3.2 Fluency development: French group[1]

Oral fluency development was measured at all six data collection points, using the monologic narrative data. Written fluency development was analysed using the timed argumentative essay task.

4.3.2.1 Oral fluency in L2 French

Our oral fluency analysis examined speed fluency via two different measures: Speech Rate (mean number of syllables per second) and Mean Length of Run (average number of syllables produced between silent pauses) in L2 French (see Chapter 3 for more information about these measures). As Figure 4.2 shows, Speech Rate scores indicate a sharp increase early on in the sojourn (Presojourn,

M = 2.00; Insojourn 1, M = 2.65), and that this development is largely maintained during the rest of the sojourn (Insojourn 2, M = 2.44; Insojourn 3, M = 2.62) and on returning back home (Postsojourn 1, M = 2.71; Postsojourn 2, M = 2.48). Individual results can be seen in Figure 4.3, which indicate considerable development for those learners scoring lower at Presojourn (e.g., participants 107, 112 and 118), suggesting unsurprisingly that the slowest speakers have most scope for subsequent L2 fluency development.

Friedman tests showed a significant effect of time on Speech Rate ($X^2(5)$ = 66.488, p = .000). Post hoc comparisons (Wilcoxon Signed Rank tests) showed medium effects only between Presojourn and the other testing phases (p < .001, $d \geq 1.00$). We found a medium effect size for time between Presojourn and Insojourn 1 (p < .001, d = 1.20), but only marginal effects between Insojourn 1 and Insojourn 2 (p = 1.00, d =.39), and Insojourn 2 and Insojourn 3 (p = .017, d = .37), suggesting that learners' rate of speech increased early on in their sojourn (see also Figure 4.2). Mann-Whitney U tests showed that the L1 French speakers' rate of speech (M = 3.79) remained significantly faster than that of the L2 French learners at each survey point (p < .001, $d \geq 1.42$).

For Mean Length of Run (see Figure 4.2), our results show that the average number of syllables produced between silent pauses increases between Presojourn (M = 4.2) and Insojourn 1 (M = 6.5). L2 French learners' MLR scores appear stable for the remaining Insojourn points (Insojourn 2, M = 6.0; Insojourn 3, M = 6.3). A small increase appears at Postsojourn 1 (M = 6.9), which then falls at Postsojourn 2 (M = 6.0). Although variation over time is clear, the L2 developmental trend found here seems similar to Speech Rate.

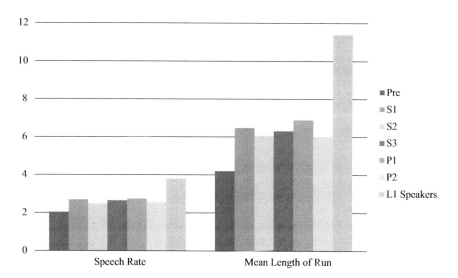

Figure 4.2 Mean Speech Rate (syllables per second) and Mean Length of Run (syllables between silent pauses) for L2 French group (over time) and L1 French group

82 Linguistic development in French

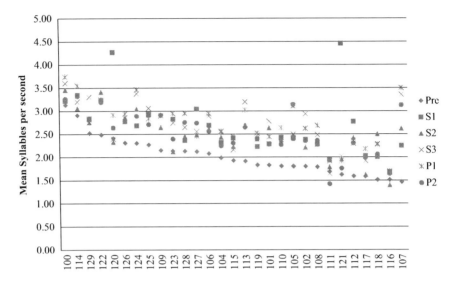

Figure 4.3 Speech Rate scores for individual L2 French participants, oral narrative

Friedman tests showed a significant effect for time on L2 French learners' MLR: ($X^2(5) = 57.012$, p = .000). Post hoc tests (Wilcoxon Signed Rank) showed medium effect sizes between Presojourn and all other survey points (p = .000, $d \geq 1.21$), due to significantly higher MLR scores from Insojourn 1 onwards. Marginal effects were found between the Insojourn points (p > .05, $d \leq .22$), and between the Postsojourn survey points (p < .001, $d = .46$). Altogether, these findings indicate a clear and early benefit of SA for learners' MLR scores. In comparison with L1 French speakers, Mann-Whitney U tests showed that L2 learners' scores were significantly lower, with large effect sizes (p < .001, $d \geq 2.35$).

In terms of the individual results, Figure 4.4 indicates a lot of variation across the group for MLR. Participants with both low and high Presojourn scores might show considerable development (e.g. participants 112, 107, 120, 125). However, there was a small cluster of participants with low Presojourn scores that demonstrated little development over time (e.g. participants 106, 111, 121).

4.3.2.4 Written fluency in L2 French

We operationalized written fluency in L2 French as the number of words produced per minute, dividing the total number of words by the actual time it took individual participants to type their argumentative essay at each data collection point.

For this measure, very few overall changes emerged, although written fluency appeared to increase slightly over time. It is possible that task-specific effects mediated performance. Overall, the results presented in Figure 4.5 indicate improvement over time on performance of the same prompt.

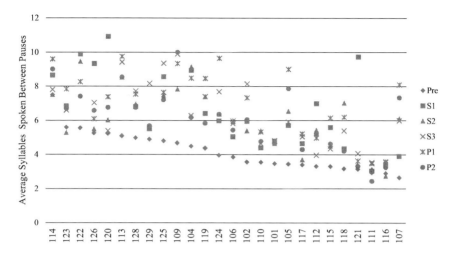

Figure 4.4 Mean Length of Run for individual L2 French participants, oral narrative (n=26; heritage and bilingual speakers omitted)

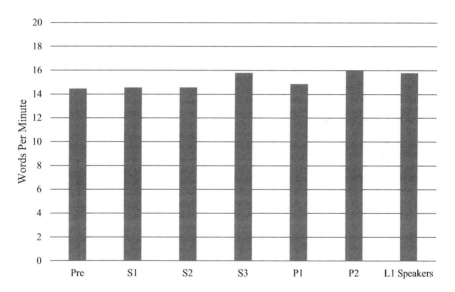

Figure 4.5 Mean writing fluency scores for L2 French group (over time) and L1 French group

Our analysis (Friedman test) showed a significant effect for time ($X^2(5) = 16.184$, p = .006). Post hoc tests (Wilcoxon Signed Rank) showed marginal effect sizes for Gay Marriage (Presojourn–Insojourn 3, p = .043, d = .48), for Junk Food (Insojourn 2–Postsojourn 2, p = .012, d = .46), and for Marijuana (Insojourn 1–Postsojourn 1, p = 1.00, d = .08). Our comparisons

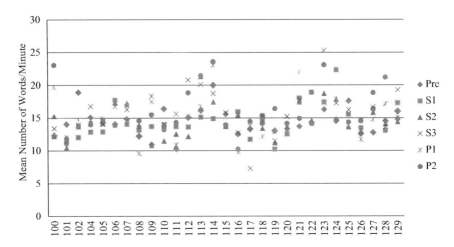

Figure 4.6 Writing fluency scores for individual L2 French participants

with French L1 speakers (Mann-Whitney U tests) showed small effects at Presojourn (p = .024, d = .82) and Insojourn 2 (p = .088, d = .67) because French L1 speakers were quicker writers than the learners, but only marginal effects were found at Insojourn 1 (p = .385, d = .07) and from Insojourn 3 onwards (Insojourn 3, p = .732, d = .17; Postsojourn 1, p = .692, d = .05; Postsojourn 2, p = .516, d = .10).

Figure 4.6 shows individual results for written fluency, showing limited change for most individuals, reflecting the group results.

4.3.3 Accuracy development in speech: French group

Accuracy in the L2 French oral narratives was analysed with two global measures of overall morphosyntactic accuracy: percentage of error-free Analysis of Speech Units (ASUs) and percentage of error-free clauses. We also analysed L2 French participants' use of three advanced learner features, *Imparfait* (IMP) and *Passé Composé* (PC) (in oral narratives) and subjunctive (SUBJ) (in interviews), as more fine-grained measures of accuracy.

First, as Figure 4.7 shows, the percentage of error-free clauses shows an initial accuracy increase for the L2 French group between Presojourn (M = 44.6%) and Insojourn 1 (M = 60.9%) that then remains stable though to Postsojourn 2 (Insojourn 2, M = 60.3%, Insojourn 3, M = 64.2%, Postsojourn 1, M = 63.9%, Postsojourn 2, M = 63.3%). These descriptive scores suggest that accuracy is quick to develop and the gains made during the year abroad were maintained once participants returned home for their final year of their degree. Indeed, comparisons between these different test phases (Friedman test) show a significant effect for time on learners' error-free clause accuracy ($X^2(5)$ = 27.455, p = .000). Post hoc

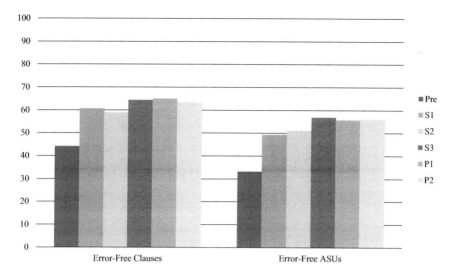

Figure 4.7 Mean percentage of error-free clauses and error-free ASUs for L2 French group, oral narrative

tests (Wilcoxon Signed Rank tests) showed small to medium-sized effect sizes for change between Presojourn and each subsequent testing phase (p ≤ .001, d ≥ .75), and, as expected, only marginal effects were found between all other testing phases (p ≥ .05, d ≤ .19). In terms of the individual results, Figure 4.8 shows a lot of variation across the groups, with some learners making a lot of development over time (e.g., 112 and 118) and others with a number of learners showing less accurate performance over time (e.g., 121 and 110). In general, however, the majority of individuals make clear development.

Our results for error-free ASUs indicate a very similar developmental trajectory (Figure 4.7). AS-unit accuracy appears to increase between Presojourn (M = 33.3%) and Insojourn 1 (M = 49.9%), and then is relatively stable through until Postsojourn 2 (Insojourn 2, M = 53%, Insojourn 3, M = 56.6%, Postsojourn 1, M = 54.4%, Postsojourn 2, M = 55.9%). Friedman tests showed a significant effect for time on learners' accuracy of error-free ASUs ($X^2(5) = 32.267$, p = .000). Post hoc tests (Wilcoxon Signed Rank tests) confirmed that the biggest increase in accuracy scores was between the Presojourn and all other testing phases (small to medium effect sizes, p ≤ .001, d ≥ .79), and as reported for clause accuracy, marginal effects were found between all other testing phases (Insojourn 1–Postsojourn 2, p ≥ .05, d ≤ .32). In terms of the individual results, Figure 4.9 confirms that the majority make clear gains (see e.g. 112, 118). However, the maintenance of these gains is quite variable over time. It also seems that Presojourn performance is not a strong predictor of development.

For our more fine-grained measures, we begin with percentage accuracy of *Imparfait* (IMP) use in appropriate contexts (in the oral narratives), shown in

86 *Linguistic development in French*

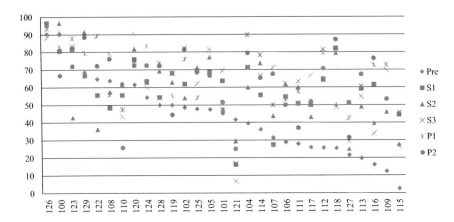

Figure 4.8 Percentage of error-free clauses for individual L2 French participants, oral narrative

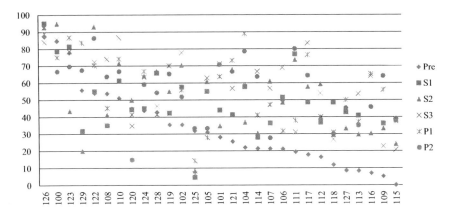

Figure 4.9 Percentage of error-free ASUs for individual L2 French participants, oral narrative

Figure 4.10. Again we see the greatest increase between Presojourn (M = 41.2%) and Insojourn 1 (M = 55.6%), with a more gradual rise thereafter. Friedman tests showed a significant effect for time on learners' appropriate use of IMPF ($X^2(5)$ = 25.910, p = .000). Post hoc tests (Wilcoxon Signed Rank tests) showed a marginal effect between the Presojourn and Insojourn 1 (p = .021, d = .49) and small-sized effects between Presojourn and other testing phases (p ≤ .003, d ≥ .64), but only marginal-sized effects between the other testing phases (Insojourn 1– Postsojourn 2, p ≥ .05, d ≤ .35). These findings are in line with our findings for the global accuracy measures. In terms of individual performance, Figure 4.11 presents a very mixed picture, with the most development made by those scoring at the lower end of the scale at Presojourn.

Linguistic development in French 87

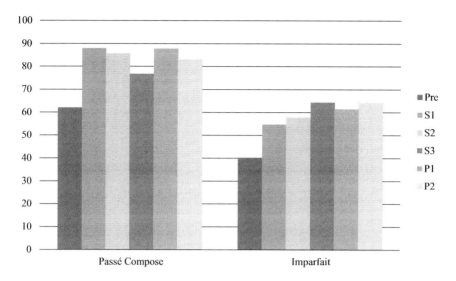

Figure 4.10 Mean percentage of accurate *Passé Composé* and *Imparfait* use for L2 French group, oral narrative

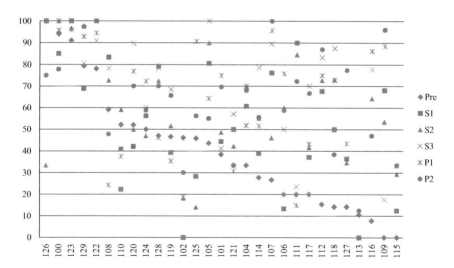

Figure 4.11 Percentage of appropriate *Imparfait* use for individual L2 French participants

For PC use in the oral narratives, there was greater accuracy at Presojourn (M = 63.1%) than for IMP use (M = 41.2%). However, despite this difference, our results presented in Figure 4.10 showed very similar patterns of development, namely a large increase in PC accuracy between Presojourn (63.1%) and Insojourn 1 (M = 88.9%), and a high-level, stable performance thereafter. Our analysis (Friedman test) showed a significant effect for time for appropriate PC use ($X^2(5) = 43.042$, p = .000). Post hoc tests (Wilcoxon Signed Rank tests) showed small effect sizes between Presojourn and all other testing phases (p ≤ .04, d ≥ .44). We also found marginal effect sizes between test phases including Insojourn 3 because of slightly lower accuracy scores at that point (Insojourn 1–Insojourn 3, p = .005, d = .54; Insojourn 2–Insojourn 3, p = .001, d = .43; Insojourn 3–Postsojourn 1, p = .009, d = .44). Differences between all other test phases were negligible (p ≥ .05, d ≤ .24). As for individual performances, Figure 4.12 shows much clearer development across the group than for the IMP results, with many learners scoring at ceiling after Presojourn.

To examine productive oral use of subjunctive (SUBJ) by the L2 French group, the full series of L2 interviews was analysed. All triggers/appropriate contexts for SUBJ use were identified, and the extent to which SUBJ was used in these contexts was calculated. SUBJ forms are infrequent in L1 speaker usage; O'Connor DiVito (1997) found that they appeared in just 2% of clauses in a corpus of spoken French. As reported in McManus and Mitchell (2015), the LANGSNAP participants produced around 1 subjunctive token per 1,000 words. Subjunctive use was most productive on either side of the sojourn, with less frequent use insojourn. Participants of higher proficiency (as measured by the French EIT) used SUBJ somewhat more frequently than those of lower proficiency, but individual participants' oral use of SUBJ did not appear to change significantly over time. Our analysis of SUBJ syntactic triggers revealed that although learners used 32 different triggers, they were not used in equal proportion. In fact, just five of them account for 64% of all SUBJ contexts in L2 speech (*falloir que, vouloir que, ne pas penser que, avant que,* and *pour que*).

Taken together, therefore, our findings for global measures of accuracy in spoken L2 French indicate that accuracy among these relatively advanced learners increased early in the sojourn, though not to 100% accuracy, and the level

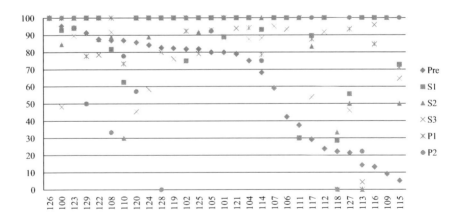

Figure 4.12 Percentage of appropriate *Passé Composé* use for individual L2 French participants

achieved was then maintained or increased more gradually throughout the sojourn and after returning home. This was also true for sojourners' control of the IMP/PC distinction, but not for their control of SUBJ, where there was little evidence for development, at least in oral production.

4.3.4 Accuracy development in writing: French group

Our analysis of written accuracy in the argumentative essays focused on a) mean percentage of error-free clauses and b) mean percentage of error-free T-units, similar to our analysis of oral accuracy (but using T-units instead of ASUs). We also examined use of SUBJ as a more fine-grained measure.

First, for production of error-free clauses, compared with our other results, there was much less variation over time in L2 writing (Figure 4.13). In particular, there was little change between the first two survey points, Presojourn (M = 63.8%) and Insojourn 1 (M = 66.3%), unlike those found for several other measures, including EIT, Speech Rate and error-free clauses in speech. Instead, our analysis shows marginal change over time on this measure: Insojourn 2, M = 67.2%; Insojourn 3, M = 68.6%; Postsojourn 1, M = 71.8%; Postsojourn 2, M = 67.7%. Friedman tests for the percentage of error-free clauses in L2 writing showed no significant change over time ($X^2(5) = 10.420$, p = .064). Figure 4.14 shows relatively little substantial development at the individual level.

Accuracy levels were generally lower for T-units than for clauses. The T-unit analysis presented in Figure 4.13 shows variation throughout the whole testing period, starting with an improvement between Presojourn (M = 34.2%) and

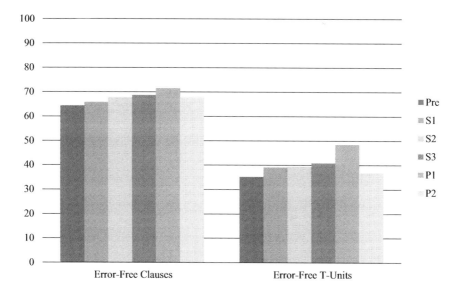

Figure 4.13 Mean percentage of error-free clauses and error-free T-units for L2 French group, argumentative essay

90 Linguistic development in French

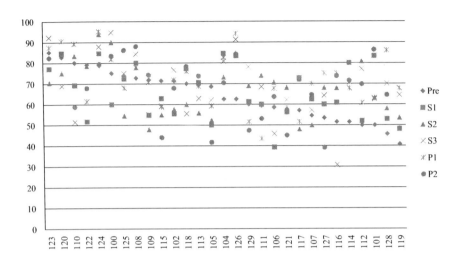

Figure 4.14 Percentage of error-free clauses for individual L2 French participants, argumentative essay

Insojourn 1 (M = 40.9%), similar to findings for oral accuracy (as measured in ASUs). Accuracy then remained stable through Insojourn 2 (M = 39%) and Insojourn 3 (M = 40.8%), and improved on returning home to the instructional context (Postsojourn 1 M = 49.9%).

Our statistical comparison of the different survey points (Friedman tests) showed a significant effect for time for percentage accuracy of error-free T-units ($X^2(5)$ = 14.005, p = .016). Post hoc tests (Wilcoxon Signed Rank tests) showed marginal-sized effects between Presojourn and all Insojourn survey points (p ≥ .05, d ≤ .27) and Postsojourn 2 (p = .787, d = .08). There was a small effect between Presojourn and Postsojourn 1 (p = .007, d = .67). Effects between the Insojourn survey points were all marginal (p ≥ .05, d ≤ .03). In terms of the individual results, Figure 4.15 indicates a lot of variation in the group, with a large proportion of learners exhibiting both development and regression for this measure, although it does appear that those scoring low at Presojourn are typically the ones making the most development over time.

Concerning use of the subjunctive, this form was more frequent in writing than in speech, with SUBJ tokens occurring at a rate of 3 per 1,000 words (again in line with L1 usage: O'Connor DiVito, 1997). Although we saw little change over time in speaking, a somewhat different picture emerged in writing, suggesting participants' increasing ability to vary their linguistic choices in different genres. Firstly, written accuracy for SUBJ increased during the sojourn. Secondly, the range of subjunctive triggers increased. For example, it was noted earlier that just five triggers accounted for most SUBJ contexts in speech, whereas in writing these same triggers are infrequent (e.g., *falloir que* is used only 8% of the time and *vouloir que* is never used). In fact, while verb triggers dominated our speech

Linguistic development in French 91

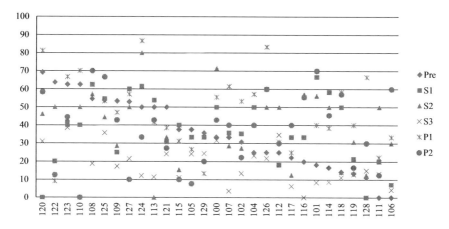

Figure 4.15 Percentage of error-free T-units for individual L2 French participants, argumentative essay

sample (e.g., *falloir que*), conjunction triggers were most frequent in writing (e.g., *bien que*). (See McManus & Mitchell, 2015 for fuller details.)

Overall, the L2 French written accuracy findings present an unclear picture which may have been influenced somewhat by task effects, such as one essay topic being easier to write about than another. That said, the picture we can take away from this analysis is that, in contrast to oral accuracy, written accuracy seems fairly stable throughout the study. We found no evidence of large increases in accuracy between Presojourn and Insojourn 1, as we have for other measures (e.g., EIT).

4.3.5 Development of syntactic complexity: French group

Syntactic complexity has been analysed in the written data only (argumentative essays). Results for three measures of syntactic complexity are presented here: 1) the ratio of clauses to T-units, 2) mean length of T-unit and 3) ratio of finite clauses to all clauses. A higher ratio of clauses to T-units, production of longer T-units, and a lower ratio of finite clauses to all clauses are accepted in the literature as indicators of greater written complexity, though it has to be accepted that these measures are all to some degree interrelated (Wolfe-Quintero et al., 1998).

The ratio of clauses to T-units is presented in Figure 4.16. The highest mean scores were found for Insojourn 2 (M = 2.88) and Postsojourn 2 (M = 2.83) (Junk Food prompt), the lowest scores for Insojourn 1 (M = 2.53) and Postsojourn 1 (M = 2.45) (Marijuana prompt), and middling scores for Presojourn (M = 2.71) and Insojourn 3 (M = 2.56) (Gay Marriage prompt). While Friedman tests showed a significant effect for time for this ratio ($X^2(5) = 24.469$, p = .031), post hoc tests (Wilcoxon Signed Rank tests) generally showed marginal effect sizes, with the exception of a small effect obtaining between Postsojourn 1 and Postsojourn 2 (p = .004, d = .72). Comparisons between groups (Mann-Whitney U tests) showed only marginal-sized effects between L1 and L2 French performances at each testing phase (p > .05, d ≤ .38).

92 Linguistic development in French

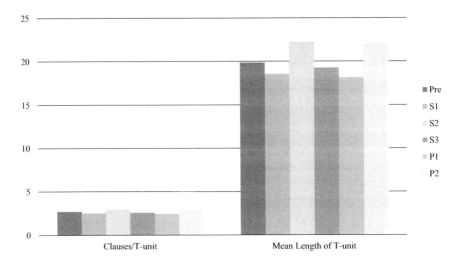

Figure 4.16 Mean ratio of clauses to T-units and mean length of T-unit for L2 French group (over time) argumentative essay

Figure 4.17 shows that scores are almost identical for each pair of survey points sharing the same task (for both French L1 speakers and L2 learners). It therefore seems likely that a task effect is the main factor leading to variation in participants' performance that is, there is little or no underlying change.

In terms of individual performance, Figure 4.18 indicates a lot of variation, with many learners exhibiting both development and regression over time. Furthermore, it appears not to be the case for this measure that lower scores at Presojourn led to greater development over time than for those scoring higher at Presojourn.

Our second measure of written syntactic complexity was mean length of T-unit (MLTu). Although Figure 4.16 suggests some (limited) variation over time, no clear improvement was detectable, and successive performances of individual tasks resembled each other closely: Presojourn (M = 19.89) and Insojourn 3 (M = 19.25); Insojourn 1 (M = 18.69) and Postsojourn 1 (M = 18.12); Insojourn 2 (M = 22.00) and Postsojourn 2 (M = 21.82). Our analysis (Friedman tests) revealed a significant effect for time ($X^2(5) = 24.469$, p = .000). Post hoc tests showed only marginal effects for time between the Presojourn and all other testing phases (p ≥ .02, d ≤ .34). Marginal effects were found between the insojourn phases because the MLTu score at Insojourn 2 was the highest (Insojourn 1–Insojourn 2, p = .002, d = .54; Insojourn 2–Insojourn 3, p = .029, d = .43). A small-sized effect was found between Postsojourn 1 and Postsojourn 2 (p = .001, d = .79) because MLTu scores at Postsojourn 2 were significantly higher than for Postsojourn 1. Similar to our clauses/T-unit ratio for syntactic complexity, French L2 learner comparisons with the French L1 speakers for MLTu (M = 19.86) showed that between-group performance was not significantly different (Figure 4.19); there were marginal-sized

Linguistic development in French 93

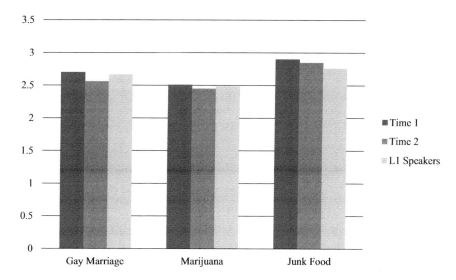

Figure 4.17 Complexity in French writing: Ratio of clauses to T-units by prompt, L2 French group and L1 French group

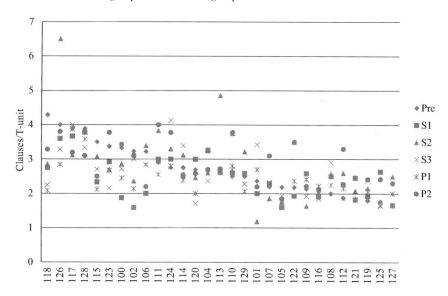

Figure 4.18 Ratio of clauses to T-units for individual L2 French participants, argumentative essay

effects at every survey phase (Presojourn, p = .629, d = .01; Insojourn 1, p = .885, d = .05; Insojourn 2, p = .499, d = .28; Insojourn 3, p = .380, d = .12; Postsojourn 1, p = .837, d = .07; Postsojourn 2, p = .421, d = .32).

In terms of the individual results, Figure 4.20 shows very large degrees of development for participant 126, an L1 Spanish speaker on a university placement,

94 Linguistic development in French

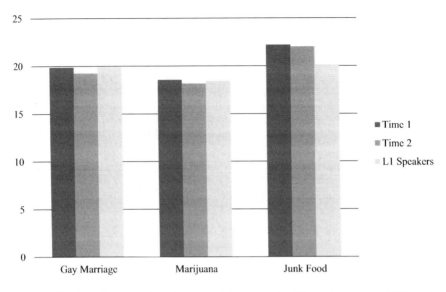

Figure 4.19 Complexity in French writing: Mean length of T-unit by prompt, L2 French group and L1 French group

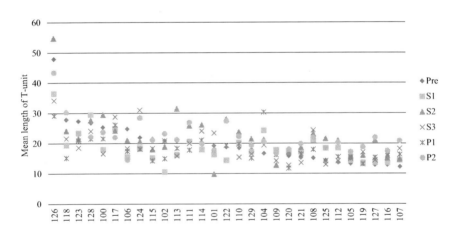

Figure 4.20 Mean length of T-unit for individual L2 French participants

but there is very little comparable development across the group. On the whole, development seems comparatively modest and influenced to a large extent by performance at Presojourn.

Finally, for syntactic complexity, increased complexity will be reflected in a reduced ratio of finite clauses to all clauses. In the L2 French writing samples, this ratio varied across time (see Figure 4.21). It should be recalled, however, that the same task was administered at Presojourn and Insojourn 3, at Insojourn 1 and Postsojourn 1, and at Insojourn 2 and Postsojourn 2. As the scores are almost

Linguistic development in French 95

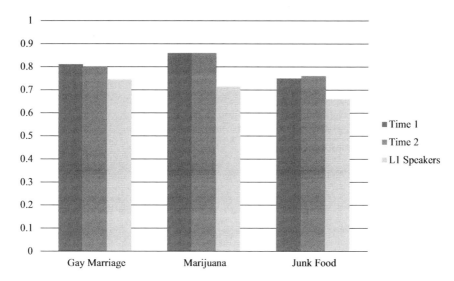

Figure 4.21 Mean ratio of finite clauses to all clauses for L2 French group and L1 French group, argumentative essay

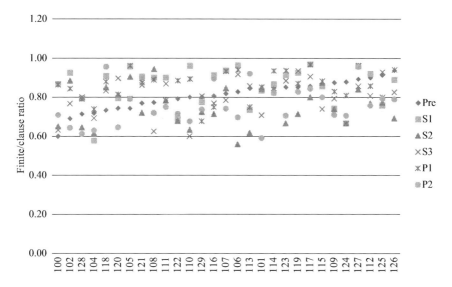

Figure 4.22 Ratio of finite clauses to all clauses for individual L2 French participants, argumentative essay

identical for each pair of survey points sharing the same task, it seems likely that task is the main factor leading to variation in participants' performance (i.e., there is little or no underlying change), and this was confirmed in statistical analyses, not shown. It is notable, however, that there is a continuing difference between

96 *Linguistic development in French*

L1 and L2 groups, with L1 performances reflecting somewhat greater complexity on this measure on all three tasks. In terms of the individual results, Figure 4.22 also shows that scores over time fall below and above Presojourn scores, indicating that development is less clear-cut for this measure, at the individual level.

Taken together, these results pattern similarly with our findings for written accuracy, suggesting little sustained development over time in writing. However, it is important to note that our writing samples may be influenced by task effects, and also to note the limitations of drawing all writing samples from a single genre. This issue is considered further in Chapter 5, with reference to L2 Spanish, where similar task effects were found.

4.3.6 Development of lexical complexity: French group

As explained in Chapter 3, we analysed lexical complexity using D, a measure of lexical diversity, computed using the CLAN program VocD. In the case of the French group, we report this analysis for the L2 oral interviews only. In these interviews, D scores increased steadily over time, peaking at Insojourn 2 (see Figure 4.23 for detail). Friedman tests showed a significant effect for time on D scores in the oral interview ($X^2(5) = 53.604$, p = .000). Post hoc tests (Wilcoxon Signed Rank tests) showed a small effect size between Presojourn and Insojourn 1 (p < .001, d = .78) and medium effects for Presojourn–Insojourn 2 (p < .001, d = 1.25) and Presojourn–Insojourn 3 (p < .001, d = 1.14). We found medium effects between Insojourn 2 (when D scores peaked) and the

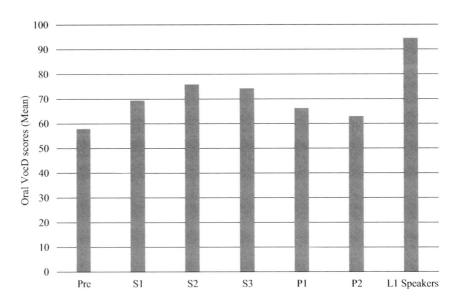

Figure 4.23 Mean lexical diversity scores (D) for L2 French group (over time) and L1 French group, oral interview

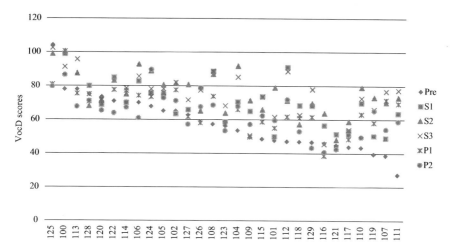

Figure 4.24 Lexical diversity scores (*D*) for individual L2 French participants, oral interview

Postsojourn phases, because *D* scores were significantly lower at both Postsojourn points (Insojourn 2–Postsojourn 1, p = .000, *d* = .76; Insojourn 2–Postsojourn 2, p = .000, *d* = 1.06). Differences between Presojourn and the Postsojourns were marginal for Postsojourn 1 (p = .002, *d* = .57) and for Postsojourn 2 (p = .030, *d* = .35). Comparisons with L1 French speakers (Mann-Whitney U tests) showed very large differences due to higher L1 scores (Mean = 94.37), with large effect sizes for *D* at every test phase (Presojourn, p < .001, *d* = 4.13; Insojourn 1, p < .001, *d* = 2.65; Insojourn 2, p < .001, *d* = 2.28; Insojourn 3, p < .001, *d* = 2.32; Postsojourn 1, p < .001, *d* = 3.13; Postsojourn 2, p < .001, *d* = 3.64).

In terms of the individual results, Figure 4.24 contrasts sharply with the syntactic complexity results, in that almost everyone made very clear progress over time. It also seems that it was the learners with lower *D* scores at Presojourn who made the largest developmental strides (e.g., 111 and 107).

4.3.7 Receptive lexical development: French group

We tested learners' receptive lexical knowledge at Presojourn and Insojourn 3 using X-Lex v2.05 (Meara & Milton, 2005), described in Chapter 3. Table 4.2 shows learners' mean X-Lex performance. Our analysis (Wilcoxon Signed Rank tests) showed no difference between Presojourn and Insojourn for X-Lex corrected scores (Z = −.894, p = .371, *d* = −.03). Although participants recognized more infrequent vocabulary at Insojourn 3, they also chose more of the fake words, which lowered their scores, and this explains the pattern for individual results presented in Figure 4.25, where roughly half the participants who took the test showed improvement but half achieved lower scores.

98 Linguistic development in French

Table 4.2 Summary results of the French X-Lex test

	Mean score	SD	Range
Presojourn	3225.86	534.79	2200–4250
Insojourn 3	3208.33	626.52	2050–4150

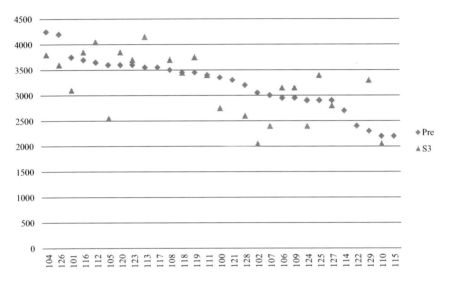

Figure 4.25 X-Lex test scores for individual L2 French participants at Presojourn (n=29) and at Insojourn 3 (n=24)

4.4 Conclusion

In this chapter we presented L2 French learners' linguistic development in terms of general proficiency, fluency, accuracy and complexity. Our findings have shown clear development in a variety of measures, but with important differences between them. In line with previous research, we found that lexical complexity and oral fluency were quick to develop, with the largest changes most often reported between Presojourn and Insojourn 1, with less dramatic change over time between the Insojourn survey points. In terms of accuracy development, however, our findings contrast with some previous studies which have found little benefit for accuracy during study abroad. For example, our findings showed significant improvement for error-free ASUs, particularly between Presojourn and Insojourn 1, in striking contrast to some other studies showing gradual accuracy gains. We also found evidence of more accurate past tense use. In terms of written syntactic complexity, however, our findings are less clear, showing little overall change, but we believe these findings to be complicated by task effects.

In the next chapter we examine L2 Spanish linguistic development, where comparisons between our L2s will also be presented.

Note

1 We are very grateful to Amanda Huensch for her help with the fluency analysis presented in this chapter.

References

Ågren, M., Granfeldt, J., & Schlyter, S. (2012). The growth of complexity and accuracy in L2 French: Past observations and recent applications of developmental stages. In A. Housen, F. Kuiken, & I. Vedder (Eds.), *Dimensions of L2 performance and proficiency: Complexity, accuracy and fluency in SLA* (pp. 95–120). Amsterdam: John Benjamins.

Allen, H. W. (2010). Language-learning motivation during short-term study abroad: An activity theory perspective. *Foreign Language Annals, 43*(1), 27–49.

American Council on the Teaching of Foreign Languages (ACTFL) (2012). *Oral proficiency interview familiarization manual*. White Plains, NY: ACTFL.

Bartning, I. (1997). L'apprenant dit avancé et son acquisition d'une langue étrangère. *Acquisition et Interaction en Langue Etrangère, 9*, 9–50.

Bartning, I. (2009). The advanced learner variety: 10 years later. In E. Labeau & F. Myles (Eds.), *Advanced learner variety: The case of French* (pp. 11–40). Oxford: Peter Lang.

Bartning, I. (2012). Synthèse rétrospective et nouvelles perspectives développementales: Les recherches acquisitionnelles en français L2 à l'Université de Stockholm. *Language, Interaction and Acquisition, 3*(1), 7–28.

Bartning, I., Forsberg Lundell, F., & Hancock, V. (2012). On the role of linguistic contextual factors for morpho-syntactic stabilization in high-level L2 French. *Studies in Second Language Acquisition, 34*(2), 242–267.

Bartning, I., & Schlyter, S. (2004). Itinéraires acquisitionnels et stades de développement en français L2. *Journal of French Language Studies, 14*(3), 1–19.

Carroll, J. B. (1967). Foreign language proficiency levels attained by language majors near graduation from college. *Foreign Language Annals, 1*(2), 131–151.

Cohen, A. D., & Shively, R. L. (2007). Acquisition of requests and apologies in Spanish and French: Impact of study abroad and strategy-building intervention. *The Modern Language Journal, 91*(2), 189–212.

Coleman, J. A. (1996). Residence abroad and its impact. In J. A. Coleman (Ed.), *Studying languages: A survey of British and European students* (pp. 59–90). London: Centre for Information on Language Teaching and Research.

Collentine, J. (2004). The effects of learning contexts on morphosyntactic and lexical development. *Studies in Second Language Acquisition, 26*(2), 227–248.

Collentine, J. (2009). Study abroad research: Findings, implications and future directions. In M. H. Long & C. J. Doughty (Eds.), *The handbook of language teaching* (pp. 218–233). Chichester: Wiley-Blackwell.

De Clercq, B. (2015). The development of lexical complexity in second language acquisition: A cross-linguistic study of L2 French and English. In L. Roberts, K. McManus, N. Vanek, & D. Trenkic (Eds.), *EUROSLA Yearbook Volume 15* (pp. 69–94). Amsterdam: John Benjamins.

DeKeyser, R. (2007). Study abroad as foreign language practice. In R. DeKeyser (Ed.), *Practice in a second language: Perspectives from applied linguistics and cognitive psychology* (pp. 208–226). Cambridge: Cambridge University Press.

DeKeyser, R. (2010). Monitoring processes in Spanish as a second language during a study abroad program. *Foreign Language Annals, 43*(1), 80–92.

DeKeyser, R. (2014). Research on language development during study abroad: Methodological considerations and future perspectives. In C. Pérez-Vidal (Ed.), *Language acquisition in study abroad and formal acquisition contexts* (pp. 313–326). Amsterdam: John Benjamins.

Dewaele, J.-M. (Ed.). (2005). *Focus on French as a foreign language*. Clevedon: Multilingual Matters.

Dewaele, J.-M., & Regan, V. (2002). Maîtriser la norme sociolinguistique en interlangue française: Le cas de l'omission variable de ne. *Journal of French Language Studies, 12*(2), 123–148.

Dewey, D. P., Belnap, R. K., & Hilstrom, R. (2013). Social network development, language use, and language acquisition during study abroad: Arabic language learners' perspectives. *Frontiers: The Interdisciplinary Journal of Study Abroad, 22*, 84–110.

Duperron, L. (2007). Study abroad and the second language acquisition of tense and aspect in French: Is longer better? In S. Wilkinson (Ed.), *Insights from study abroad for language programs* (pp. 45–71). Boston: Thomson and Heinle.

Dyson, P. (1988). *The year abroad: The effect on linguistic competence of the year spent abroad by students studying French, German and Spanish at degree level*. London: Central Bureau for Educational Visits and Exchanges.

Forsberg Lundell, F., & Bartning, I. (2015). Successful profiles in high-level L2 French: C'est un choix de vie. In F. Forsberg Lundell & I. Bartning (Eds.), *Cultural migrants: Multiple perspectives on optimal second language acquisition* (pp. 59–82). Clevedon: Multilingual Matters.

Forsberg Lundell, F., Bartning, I., Engel, H., Gudmundson, A., Hancock, V., & Lindqvist, C. (2014). Beyond advanced stages in high-level spoken L2 French. *Journal of French Language Studies, 24*(2), 255–280.

Foster, P. (2009). Lexical diversity and native-like selection: The bonus of studying abroad. In B. Richards, D. Malvern, P. M. Meara, J. Milton, & J. Treffers-Daller (Eds.), *Vocabulary studies in first and second language acquisition* (pp. 91–106). Basingstoke: Palgrave Macmillan.

Freed, B. F. (1990). Language learning in a study abroad context: The effects of interactive and non-interactive out-of-class contact on grammatical achievement and oral proficiency. In J. Alatis (Ed.), *Linguistics, language teaching and language acquisition: The interdependence of theory, practice and research* (pp. 459–477). Washington, DC: Georgetown University Press.

Freed, B. F. (1995). What makes us think that students who study abroad become fluent? In B. F. Freed (Ed.), *Second language acquisition in a study abroad context* (pp. 123–148). Amsterdam: John Benjamins.

Freed, B. F., Dewey, D. P., Segalowitz, N., & Halter, R. (2004). The language contact profile. *Studies in Second Language Acquisition, 26*(2), 349–356.

Freed, B. F., Segalowitz, N., & Dewey, D. P. (2004). Context of learning and second language fluency in French: Comparing regular classroom, study abroad, and intensive domestic immersion programs. *Studies in Second Language Acquisition, 26*(2), 275–301.

Freed, B. F., So, S., & Lazar, N. (2003). Language learning abroad: How do gains in written fluency compare with oral fluency in French as a second language? *Association of Departments of Foreign Languages Bulletin, 34*, 34–40.

Godfrey, L., Treacy, C., & Tarone, E. (2014). Change in French second language writing in study abroad and domestic contexts. *Foreign Language Annals*, 47(1), 48–65.

Granfeldt, J. (2007). Speaking and writing in French L2: Exploring effects on fluency, complexity and accuracy. In A. Housen, M. Pierrard, & S. Van Daele (Eds.), *Proceedings of the conference on complexity, accuracy and fluency in second language use, learning and teaching* (pp. 87–98). Brussels: Contactforum.

Grey, S., Cox, J. G., Serafini, E. J., & Sanz, C. (2015). The role of individual differences in the study abroad context: Cognitive capacity and language development during short-term intensive language exposure. *The Modern Language Journal*, 99(1), 137–157.

Guijarro-Fuentes, P., Schmitz, K., & Muller, N. (Eds.). (2016). *The acquisition of French in multilingual contexts*. Bristol: Multilingual Matters.

Gunnarsson, C. (2012). The development of complexity, accuracy and fluency in the written production of L2 French. In A. Housen, F. Kuiken, & I. Vedder (Eds.), *Dimensions of L2 performance and proficiency: Complexity, accuracy and fluency in SLA* (pp. 143–170). Amsterdam: John Benjamins.

Guntermann, G. (1995). The Peace Corps experience: Language learning in training and in the field. In B.F. Freed (Ed.), *Second language acquisition in a study abroad context* (pp. 149–170). Amsterdam: John Benjamins.

Housen, A., Kuiken, F., & Vedder, I. (Eds.). (2012). *Dimensions of L2 performance and proficiency: Complexity, accuracy and fluency in SLA*. Amsterdam: John Benjamins.

Howard, M. (2002). L'acquisition des temps du passé en français par l'apprenant dit avancé: une approche lexicale. In E. Labeau & P. Larrivée (Eds.), *Les temps du passé français et leur enseignement* (pp. 181–204). Amsterdam: Rodopi.

Howard, M. (2005a). On the role of context in the development of learner language: Insights from study abroad research. *ITL International Journal of Applied Linguistics*, 148, 1–20.

Howard, M. (2005b). Second language acquisition in a study abroad context: A comparative investigation of the effects of study abroad and foreign language instruction on the L2 learner's grammatical development. In A. Housen & M. Pierrard (Eds.), *Investigations in instructed second language acquisition* (pp. 495–530). Berlin: DeGruyter Mouton.

Howard, M. (2005c). The emergence and use of the plus-que-parfait in advanced French interlanguage. In J.-M. Dewaele (Ed.), *Focus on French as a foreign language: Multidisciplinary approaches* (pp. 63–87). Clevedon: Multilingual Matters.

Howard, M. (2006a). The expression of number and person through verb morphology in French interlanguage. *International Review of Applied Linguistics*, 44(1), 1–22.

Howard, M. (2006b). Variation in advanced French interlanguage: A comparison of three sociolinguistic variables. *Canadian Modern Language Review*, 62(3), 379–400.

Howard, M. (2008). Morphosyntactic development in the expression of modality: The subjunctive in French L2 acquisition. *Canadian Journal of Applied Linguistics*, 11(3), 171–192.

Howard, M. (2009). Compétence sémantique et compétence socio-pragmatique en français L2: Le cas de l'apprenant avancé et son acquisition du futur, du subjonctif et du conditionnel. In O. Galatanu, M. Pierrard, & D. Van Raemdonck (Eds.), *Construction du sens et acquisition de la signification linguistique dans l'interaction* (pp. 87–104). Brussels: Peter Lang.

Howard, M. (2012). The advanced learner's sociolinguistic profile: On issues of individual differences, second language exposure conditions, and type of sociolinguistic variable. *The Modern Language Journal*, 96(1), 20–33.

Ife, A., Vives Boix, G., & Meara, P. M. (2000). The impact of study abroad on the vocabulary development of different proficiency groups. *Spanish Applied Linguistics*, 4(1), 55–84.

Isabelli, C. A., & Nishida, C. (2005). Development of the Spanish subjunctive in a nine-month study-abroad setting. In D. Eddington (Ed.), *Selected proceedings of the 6th* conference on the acquisition of Spanish and Portuguese as first and second languages. Somerville, MA: Cascadilla Proceedings Project.

Isabelli-García, C. (2010). Acquisition of Spanish gender agreement in two learning contexts: Study abroad and at home. *Foreign Language Annals, 43*(2), 289–303.

Kinginger, C. (2008). Language learning in study abroad: Case studies of Americans in France. *The Modern Language Journal, 92*(Special Issue), 1–124.

Kinginger, C. (2009). *Language learning and study abroad: A critical reading of research.* Basingstoke: Palgrave Macmillan.

Kinginger, C. (2011). Enhancing language learning in study abroad. *Annual Review of Applied Linguistics, 31,* 58–73.

Kinginger, C., & Blattner, G. (2008). Histories of engagement and sociolinguistic awareness in study abroad. In L. Ortega & H. Burns (Eds.), *The longitudinal study of advanced L2 capacities* (pp. 223–246). Abingdon: Routledge.

Kuiken, F., & Vedder, I. (2012). Syntactic complexity, lexical variation and accuracy as a function of task complexity and proficiency level in L2 writing and speaking. In A. Housen, F. Kuiken, & I. Vedder (Eds.), *Dimensions of L2 performance and proficiency: Complexity, accuracy and fluency in SLA* (pp. 143–170). Amsterdam: John Benjamins.

Lemée, I. (2003). Acquisition de la variation sociostylistique par des apprenants hibernophones de français L2: les effets d'une année à l'étranger. (PhD), University College Dublin.

Lindqvist, C., & Bardel, C. (2014). *The acquisition of French as a second language: New developmental perspectives.* Amsterdam: John Benjamins.

Lindqvist, C., Bardel, C., & Gudmundson, A. (2011). Lexical richness in the advanced learner's oral production of French and Italian L2. *International Review of Applied Linguistics in Language Teaching, 49*(3), 221–240.

Llanes, À. (2011). The many faces of study abroad: An update on the research on L2 gains emerged during a study abroad experience. *International Journal of Multilingualism, 8*(3), 189–215.

Magnan, S. S., & Back, M. (2007). Social interaction and linguistic gain during study abroad. *Foreign Language Annals, 40*(1), 43–61.

Magnan, S. S., & Lafford, B. A. (2012). Learning through immersion during study abroad. In S. M. Gass & A. Mackey (Eds.), *The Routledge handbook of second language acquisition* (pp. 525–540). Abingdon/New York: Routledge.

Marsden, E., & David, A. (2008). Vocabulary use during conversation: A cross-sectional study of development from year 9 to year 13 among learners of Spanish and French. *Language Learning Journal, 36*(2), 181–198.

McManus, K., & Mitchell, R. (2015). Subjunctive use and development in L2 French: A longitudinal study. *Language Interaction and Acquisition, 6*(1), 42–73.

McManus, K., Tracy-Ventura, N., & Mitchell, R. (2016). *L2 linguistic development before, during and after a nine-month sojourn: Evidence from L2 French and Spanish.* Paper presented at Second Language Research Forum, Columbia University, New York, September 2016.

Meara, P. M. (1994). The year abroad and its effects. *Language Learning Journal, 10*(1), 32–38.

Meara, P. M., & Milton, J. (2005). *X-Lex: The Swansea levels test.* Newbury: Express.

Meara, P., & Jones, G. (1990). Vocabulary size as a placement indicator. In P. Grunwell (Ed.), *Applied linguistics in society: British Studies in Applied Linguistics 3* (pp. 80–87). London: Centre for Information on Language Teaching and Research.

Milton, J., & Meara, P. M. (1995). How periods abroad affect vocabulary growth in a foreign language. *ITL Review of Applied Linguistics, 107/108,* 17–34.

Möhle, D., & Raupach, M. (1983). *Planen in der Fremdsprach.* Frankfurt am Main: Peter Lang.

Mora, J. C., & Valls-Ferrer, M. (2012). Oral fluency, accuracy, and complexity in formal instruction and study abroad learning contexts. *TESOL Quarterly, 46*(4), 610–641.

Mougeon, R., Nadasdi, T., & Rehner, K. (2010). *The sociolinguistic competence of immersion students*. Bristol: Multilingual Matters.

Nadasdi, T., Mougeon, R., & Rehner, K. (2008). Factors driving lexical variation in L2 French: A variationist study of automobile, auto, voiture, char and machine. *Journal of French Language Studies, 18*(3), 365–381.

O'Connor DiVito, N. (1997). *Patterns across spoken and written French: Empirical research on the interaction among forms, functions and genres*. Boston: Houghton Mifflin.

Paige, R. M., Cohen, A. D., & Shively, R. L. (2004). Assessing the impact of a strategies-based curriculum on language and culture learning abroad. *Frontiers: The Interdisciplinary Journal of Study Abroad, 10*, 253–276.

Perdue, C., Deulofeu, J., & Trévise, A. (1992). The acquisition of French. In W. Klein & C. Perdue (Eds.), *Utterance structure: Developing grammars again* (pp. 225–300). Amsterdam: John Benjamins.

Plonsky, L. (2015). Statistical power, p values, descriptive statistics, and effect sizes: A "back-to-basics" approach to advancing quantitative methods in L2 research. In L. Plonsky (Ed.), *Advancing quantitative methods in second language research* (pp. 23–45). Abingdon/New York: Routledge.

Plonsky, L., & Oswald, F. L. (2014). How big is "Big"? Interpreting effect sizes in L2 research. *Language Learning, 64*(4), 878–912.

Prévost, P. (2009). *The acquisition of French*. Amsterdam: John Benjamins.

Rees, J., & Klapper, J. (2007). Analysing and evaluating the linguistic benefit of residence abroad for UK foreign language students. *Assessment & Evaluation in Higher Education, 32*(3), 331–353.

Regan, V., Howard, M., & Lemée, I. (2009). *The acquisition of sociolinguistic competence in a study abroad context*. Bristol: Multilingual Matters.

Segalowitz, N., & Freed, B. F. (2004). Context, contact, and cognition in oral fluency acquisition. *Studies in Second Language Acquisition, 26*(2), 173–199.

Serrano, R., Llanes, À., & Tragant, E. (2011). Analyzing the effect of context of second language learning: Domestic intensive and semi-intensive courses vs. study abroad in Europe. *System, 39*(2), 133–143.

Serrano, R., Tragant, E., & Llanes, À. (2012). A longitudinal analysis of the effects of one year abroad. *Canadian Modern Language Review, 68*(2), 138–163.

Tavakoli, P., & Foster, P. (2008). Task design and second language performance: The effect of narrative type on learner output. *Language Learning, 58*(2), 439–473.

Tidball, F., & Treffers-Daller, J. (2007). Exploring measures of vocabulary richness in semi-spontaneous French speech: A quest for the Holy Grail? In H. Daller, J. Milton, & J. Treffers-Daller (Eds.), *Modelling and assessing vocabulary knowledge* (pp. 133–149). Cambridge: Cambridge University Press.

Towell, R., Hawkins, R., & Bazergui, N. (1996). The development of fluency in advanced learners of French. *Applied Linguistics, 17*(1), 84–119.

Valls-Ferrer, M., & Mora, J. C. (2014). L2 fluency development in formal instruction and study abroad. In C. Pérez-Vidal (Ed.), *Language acquisition in study abroad and formal instruction contexts* (pp. 111–136). Amsterdam: John Benjamins.

Van Compernolle, R. A., & Williams, L. (2012). Teaching, learning, and developing L2 French sociolinguistic competence: A sociocultural perspective. *Applied Linguistics, 33*(2), 184–205.

Véronique, D., Carlo, C., Granger, C., Kim, J. O., & Prodeau, P. (2009). *Acquisition de la grammaire du français langue étrangère*. Paris: Didier.

Wilkinson, S. (1998). Study abroad from the participants' perspective: A challenge to common beliefs. *Foreign Language Annals, 31*(1), 23–39.

Wilkinson, S. (2002). The omnipresent classroom during summer study abroad: American students in conversation with their French hosts. *The Modern Language Journal*, 86(2), 157–173.

Willis, F., Doble, G., Sankarayya, U., & Smithers, A. (1977). *Residence abroad and the student of modern languages: A preliminary survey*. Bradford: Modern Languages Centre, University of Bradford.

Wolfe-Quintero, K., Inagaki, S., & Kim, H.-Y. (1998). *Second language development in writing: Measures of fluency, accuracy and complexity: Technical Report 17*. Honolulu: Second Language Teaching and Curriculum Center, University of Hawai'i at Manoa.

Yager, K. (1998). Learning Spanish in Mexico: The effect of informal contact and student attitudes on language gain. *Hispania*, 81(4), 898–913.

Yang, J.-S. (2016). The effectiveness of study abroad on second language learning: A metaanalysis. *Canadian Modern Language Review*, 72(1), 66–94.

5 Linguistic development in Spanish

5.1 Introduction

This chapter is a companion to Chapter 4 on the development of L2 French. The chapter therefore is focused on the 27 LANGSNAP participants majoring in L2 Spanish, who spent their period of residence abroad in Spain or Mexico. Linguistic development is conceptualized in the same way, in terms of general proficiency, fluency, accuracy, syntactic complexity and lexical diversity. The chapter begins by briefly summarizing what is known from Spanish L2 study abroad (SA) research, and then describes in detail the participants' longitudinal linguistic development in Spanish. Evidence is provided regarding group profiles and rate of development over time, and also the extent of individual variation. The chapter concludes with a comparison between profiles of development in the two languages, highlighting their general similarity and considering reasons for this, but also discussing specific linguistic differences.

5.2 Background

Much of the research on Anglophone language learning during SA has focused on L2 Spanish with results pointing to clear advantages in the areas of fluency, lexis, and sociolinguistic awareness, but less so in grammar (Lafford & Uscinski, 2014). Most researchers have investigated the experience of university sojourners, typically measuring gains made after a semester abroad, although research focusing on gains made during short-term study abroad has become more popular in recent times. Studies investigating an academic year abroad (or longer) are much less common.

In this section we review research on Spanish SLA, focusing on Spanish learning when SA is involved. We mainly concern ourselves with studies of one semester or longer, and those which investigated the constructs under investigation in LANGSNAP (i.e., general proficiency, fluency, accuracy, syntactic complexity, and lexis). Studies of sociolinguistic/pragmatic development, of phonological development and of learning/communication strategy development in L2 Spanish are excluded. Most L2 Spanish SA studies we have found investigate North American university students who are primarily English L1 speakers.

5.2.1 General proficiency in L2 Spanish

The development of general L2 proficiency has been a major strand in the study abroad research literature since the 1970s. In many studies in this tradition, proficiency is assessed via an oral interview; North American researchers investigating L2 Spanish have commonly used tools such as the Foreign Service Institute (FSI) Oral Interview (e.g., Guntermann, 1995) and the ACTFL Oral Proficiency Interview (OPI) or Simulated Oral Proficiency Interview (OPI/SOPI: e.g., Hernández, 2010; Segalowitz & Freed, 2004). For example, Guntermann (1995) conducted one of the first longitudinal studies investigating informal learning by American sojourners abroad. Her nine participants had Peace Corps work placements in fisheries, laboratories, university classrooms, and so on in Central America. Like the LANGSNAP group, they were responsible for handling their own daily needs using local resources. Their language abilities were assessed after 8–10 weeks of intensive in-country Spanish language training via the Foreign Service Institute Oral Interview. At the end of this training, 8/9 participants received what Guntermann claims to be a score equivalent to Intermediate High on the OPI. Approximately one year later, all scored Advanced (4), Advanced Plus (3) and Superior (2). Hernández (2010) administered the SOPI, which uses audio and a test booklet to elicit speech samples, to his 20 participants who were spending a semester in Spain. The majority of the participants improved either one (n=11) or two or more levels (n=5) on the SOPI by the end of their stay.

Yager (1998) chose to assess proficiency development via native speaker judgements of one-minute excerpts from an oral picture narrative on three separate 7-point scales: general, grammar, and pronunciation. Participants were spending the summer in Mexico and were assessed at two time points, seven weeks apart. In contrast to most SA studies, participants had a variety of L1s, including English, Swedish, Japanese, Dutch, French, German and Norwegian. Results demonstrated significant group improvement on all three assessment scales. Out of the 30 participants, 19 showed significant improvement across all three scales.

Comparing contexts of learning (SA in Spain and at home (AH) in the United States), Segalowitz and Freed (2004) examined the oral proficiency development of two groups of university students, using the face-to-face OPI in weeks 1 and 14 of their programme. Results demonstrated statistically significant improvement for the SA group (n=22) but not for the AH group (n=18); however, gains involved an increase of only one level and not all students improved (12/22 in the SA group, 5/18 in the AH group). It is clear from the results of these longitudinal studies that residence abroad is beneficial for (oral) proficiency. It may also be more beneficial than instruction at home, although the research comparing the two contexts is limited.

5.2.2 Fluency in L2 Spanish (oral and written)

The development of oral fluency is one of the most consistent findings favouring SA when compared with AH instruction contexts. For example, the study by Segalowitz and Freed (2004) mentioned above also investigated SA vs. AH learners' development of L2 Spanish fluency and found that only the SA group made statistically significant gains on four out of seven oral fluency measures (speech rate, filler-free run, fluent run, and number of words in the longest turn); these gains were not influenced by the amount of reported language contact. García-Amaya (2009) found in a small-scale comparison study that SA learners were significantly different from AH learners on rate of speech, though not on filled pauses, repetitions and repairs. D'Amico (2010) found that her L2 Spanish learners on a short-term study abroad programme made significant improvements on speech rate and average length of fluent run in an informal oral interview, unlike an AH group who showed no evidence of development.

Other studies have focused on SA groups only, tracking the development of L2 Spanish fluency over the course of a semester. For example, Leonard (2015) investigated 39 participants who spent three months abroad. Her participants made significant improvements on most measures of fluency. Based on her findings related to pausing, she concluded that pausing behaviour may be related to personal speaking style rather than L2 skills.

There is a relative lack of research on writing development in SA research in general (exceptions include Freed, So, & Lazar, 2003; Pérez-Vidal, 2014; Sasaki, 2007, 2011, nearly all dealing with L2 English). Lord's case study of one participant investigated the development of written fluency and accuracy in L2 Spanish over the course of an academic year abroad (Lord, 2009). The participant wrote 27 weekly journals, about 200 words in Spanish each, on self-chosen topics. Written fluency was operationalized following Wolfe-Quintero, Inagaki, and Kim (1998) as the number of words per T-unit and the number of words per error-free T-unit. Results demonstrated no significant improvement over time in written fluency, in contrast to other studies of classroom learners, notably the work of De Haan and Van Esch (2005, 2008), who found continuous improvement over three years in the writing development of instructed Dutch learners of Spanish.

Based on the work reviewed here, there is a large amount of evidence that oral fluency in L2 Spanish improves as a result of SA, even after short-stay programmes. Very little research has focused on written fluency so far.

5.2.3 Accuracy in L2 Spanish (oral and written)

Accurate use of individual grammatical features has been the subject of a number of Spanish SLA studies. For example, several studies have investigated the development of the copulas *ser* and *estar* (Collentine & Asención-Delaney, 2010; Geeslin & Guijarro-Fuentes, 2005, 2006; Martínez-Gibson, Rodríguez-Sabater, Toris, & Weyers, 2010), grammatical gender (Alarcón, 2011; Montrul, Foote, & Perpiñán, 2008), the subjunctive (Gudmestad, 2012; Montrul, 2011), and tense and aspect (Domínguez, Tracy-Ventura, Arche, Mitchell, & Myles, 2013; Salaberry, 2008), among others. In L2 Spanish SA research, many studies have also focused on the development of grammatical accuracy, investigating mostly specific grammatical features and comparing contexts of learning (SA vs. AH). That research suggests that AH learners may have a slight advantage for grammatical development over those who undertake SA (for verb tense and for subordination: Collentine, 2004), or achieve very similar development (for grammatical gender and for number: Isabelli-García, 2010). Contrasting findings are, however, reported by Isabelli and Nishida (2005), who found that learners who spent nine months in the SA context learned significantly more than AH learners (Spanish subjunctive).

Some longitudinal studies with pre-post designs have also found evidence for accuracy gain during SA. In her study of Peace Corps volunteers, Guntermann (1995) investigated the development of grammatical contrasts known to be challenging for L1 English learners, including *ser* vs. *estar*, *por* vs. *para*, and preterit vs. imperfect. At the end of their initial language training, participants already scored high on *ser* (87%) and on preterit (86–91%). Accuracy rates on the other features all improved to similarly high levels over the sojourn. Grey, Cox, Serafini, and Sanz (2015) have also recently reported significant gains on a grammaticality judgement test for Spanish word order and for number agreement (but not for grammatical gender), in the course of a short (five-week) SA sojourn.

Lord (2009) also investigated the development of written accuracy in her single-subject SA case study. Accuracy was operationalized as the number of errors/T-unit and the percentage of error-free T-units, and improved significantly over time (in contrast to written fluency). The latter finding changed the most during the first semester and stabilized during the second semester. Lord is one of the few studies of Spanish SA research that has investigated accuracy focusing on the level of the T-unit or ASU, commonly studied in the general CAF literature. Analyses based on variationist sociolinguistic frameworks have also demonstrated change over time, when learners' production and performance on controlled preference tasks is compared to that of L1 speakers (Geeslin, Fafulas, & Kanwit, 2013; Geeslin, García-Amaya, Hasler-Barker, Henriksen, & Killam, 2012). Overall, recent research in varied frameworks is beginning to find that some areas of L2 Spanish grammar do in fact improve as a result of SA.

5.2.4 Syntactic complexity in L2 Spanish

The development of syntactic complexity has received little attention in L2 Spanish SA research. Except for a brief mention by Lord (2009) that her participants wrote less complex sentences over time, it is difficult to find research focusing on this construct. Although primarily a study of subjunctive accuracy, Isabelli and Nishida (2005) investigate a structure that is part of complex syntax. Compared to the AH group, the SA group produced more subordination after four months abroad, demonstrating improvement in syntactic complexity.

5.2.5 Lexical complexity in L2 Spanish

Despite very general understanding of its importance in language learning, only a limited number of SA studies have investigated vocabulary development. Ife,

Vives Boix, and Meara (2000) reported one of the first studies of vocabulary development in L2 Spanish, with British university students as participants, who were spending either a semester or a whole academic year abroad. They were categorized into intermediate and advanced learners based on previous length of studying Spanish, and all were exchange students at a partner institution. Two vocabulary assessments were adopted in this study. One was the Three Word Association Test (A3VT: Vives Boix, 1995), which consists of three sub-tests of 40 items each. Each item consists of three words, two associated with each other and one non-associate. Test takers must choose the misfit in each set. The second test required participants to translate the words in one of the A3VT sub-tests into their L1. The tests were administered before and after the sojourn abroad, showing significant improvement on both post-tests, for both intermediate and advanced participants. Analysis of the A3VT by length of stay demonstrated that those who stayed for two semesters greatly outperformed those who stayed for one, regardless of proficiency level. The authors conclude that

> for less proficient learners, two semesters rather than one could be the more desirable pattern of exposure, yet even one semester makes an appreciable difference
>
> (Ife, Vives Boix, & Meara, 2000, p. 16).

Productive use of vocabulary has received very little attention in the general Spanish SLA research and L2 Spanish SA research. Although lexical diversity has been investigated in the cross-sectional study of Marsden and David (2008) and in a study comparing different writing genres (Castañeda-Jiménez & Jarvis, 2014), to our knowledge there has been no study investigating the development of lexical diversity over time in L2 Spanish during residence abroad.

5.2.6 Summary

In sum, the literature investigating the development of L2 Spanish during SA tends to mirror the general study abroad literature. There is clear evidence that learners improve in their oral skills, that is, oral proficiency and fluency, while the evidence on grammatical development has been mixed. For some features SA appears to be beneficial (e.g., the subjunctive) but findings are inconsistent. Clearly more research is needed investigating specific grammatical features, as well as more global assessments of accuracy at the clause and T-unit/ASU level. Very little research has been conducted on the development of sojourners' writing skills during SA. Additionally, although some research has focused on vocabulary learning, it has primarily investigated knowledge via controlled vocabulary tests, rather than free production.

L2 Spanish seems to be one of the most studied languages during SA (see Yang, 2016), yet there is still a lot to learn about many aspects of sojourners' development insojourn and long-term retention postsojourn.

110 *Linguistic development in Spanish*

5.3 Spanish language development in the LANGSNAP project

This section is designed to provide an accessible general overview of L2 Spanish development and is organized by construct. First we provide overall group results for oral proficiency, followed by fluency, accuracy, syntactic complexity and lexical knowledge. Additionally, we have included graphs showing individual learner results, making it possible to track individual participants' performance at each data collection point. Where appropriate, results are compared with the L1 Spanish speaker group (n=10) on the same set of tasks. As for the L2 French findings, more detailed analyses of aspects of these results have been presented in other places; we refer to those publications where appropriate. Readers are referred to McManus, Tracy-Ventura, and Mitchell (2016) for fuller statistical analysis of CAF development.

5.3.1 Measurement of overall proficiency: The Spanish Elicited Imitation Test

As explained in Chapter 3, our main measure of L2 proficiency was the Spanish Elicited Imitation Test (EIT) created by Lourdes Ortega (Ortega, 2000; Ortega, Iwashita, Norris, & Rabie, 2002). We administered the French and Spanish EITs three times to the relevant groups, each approximately nine months apart, to limit any practice effects: at Presojourn, at Insojourn 2, and later at Postsojourn 1. Descriptive statistics for Spanish are presented in Table 5.1. As evidenced by the increase in the mean scores and decrease in the standard deviation, there was continued improvement over time on oral proficiency. Results of a repeated measures ANOVA (time as independent variable) demonstrated a significant effect for time: $F(2,25) = 82.76$, $p < .001$. Post hoc comparisons demonstrated significant differences between all three survey points with very large effect sizes based on Plonsky and Oswald (2014)'s discipline-specific benchmarks for Cohen's d: Presojourn–Insojourn 2: $p < .001$, Cohen's $d = 1.76$; Presojourn–Postsojourn 1: $p < .001$, Cohen's $d = 2.54$; Insojourn 2–Postsojourn 1: $p < .001$, Cohen's $d = 1.37$.

Figure 5.1 presents the individual learner scores on the Spanish EIT. As shown, there was considerable variation among the learners in the amount of gain made between survey points. Most participants made the largest gains between Presojourn and Insojourn 2, although there were a few, like participant 157, who made

Table 5.1 Summary results of the Spanish Elicited Imitation Test

	Mean score	SD	Range
Presojourn	85.15	11.73	59–108
Insojourn 2	99.78	8.17	76–113
Postsojourn 1	104.89	7.69	90–117

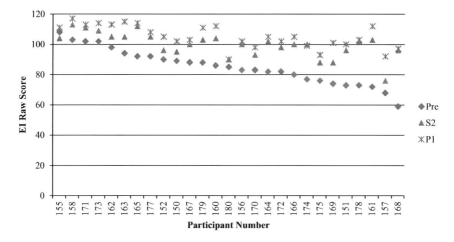

Figure 5.1 EIT scores for individual L2 Spanish participants at Presojourn, Insojourn 2 and Postsojourn 1

a bigger improvement between Insojourn 2 and Postsojourn 1, and 169 who improved about the same amount between each test. Interestingly, the participant who scored the lowest at Presojourn, 168, made tremendous gains by Insojourn 2 and maintained those gains at Postsojourn 1.

The lowest score at Presojourn in percentage terms was 49% (59/120), whereas the lowest score at Postsojourn 1 was 75% (90/120), demonstrating substantial improvement. In sum, the group and individual results on the Spanish EIT suggest that the Spanish participants continued to improve in their general proficiency throughout the year.

5.3.2 Fluency development in speech: Spanish group

Huensch and Tracy-Ventura (in press) investigated oral fluency development in the Spanish picture-based narrative data, using measures of speed, breakdown, and repair fluency (Bosker, Pinget, Quené, Sanders, & De Jong, 2013; Skehan, 2003; Tavakoli & Skehan, 2005). The main findings were that statistically significant gains were made in speed fluency and a few measures of breakdown fluency (i.e., mean duration of silent pauses within ASUs, number of silent pauses per second, and number of filled pauses per second), but not in repair fluency. In what follows we will provide more detail about two of the speed fluency results, comparing group means to the native speaker results (see Figure 5.2) and examining individual learner results over time (Figures 5.3–5.4).

The global measures of oral fluency reported here are Speech Rate (SR: total number of syllables/total speaking time in seconds) and Mean Length of Run (MLR: average number of syllables produced between silent pauses). Results for both measures are presented in Figure 5.2. These show that the highest gains

112 *Linguistic development in Spanish*

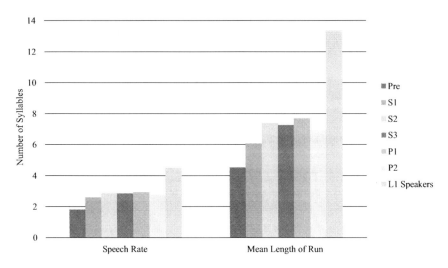

Figure 5.2 Mean Speech Rate (syllables per second) and Mean Length of Run (syllables between silent pauses) for L2 Spanish group (over time) and L1 Spanish group

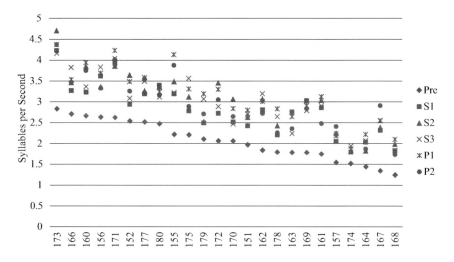

Figure 5.3 Speech Rate scores for individual L2 Spanish participants, oral narrative (n=24, three participants excluded for technical reasons)

were achieved at Insojourn 2, and also that the gains made abroad were maintained throughout the Postsojourn period. However, comparing these results to the productions of the L1 Spanish participants, it is clear from Figure 5.2 that the sojourners remained significantly different from the L1 group at all points.

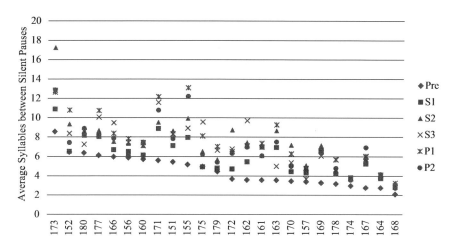

Figure 5.4 Mean Length of Run for individual L2 Spanish participants, oral narrative (n=24)

Individual results for SR (Figure 5.3) and MLR (Figure 5.4) demonstrate that, overall, most participants improved over time in both. Gains happened quickly for both measures, as evidenced by the large gap between Presojourn scores and all the other data points. Pairwise comparisons demonstrated significant differences between Presojourn and all other rounds for both measures, as well as between Insojourn 1 and all other rounds except Postsojourn 2. These results suggest that both SR and MLR peaked at Insojourn 2 for the L2 Spanish group. By Postsojourn 2 they were possibly starting to show signs of attrition, yet they were still speaking much more fluently than at Presojourn. In sum, these results suggest that participants made important gains in different measures of speed fluency as a result of residence abroad.

5.3.3 Fluency development in writing: Spanish group

We operationalized written fluency as the number of words produced per minute, dividing the total number of words by the time it took individual participants to write their argumentative essay. (In this computer-based task, writing time was automatically logged in seconds.)

Figure 5.5 shows group mean performances on this measure for L2 Spanish over all six data collection points. For comparison, results from the L1 speakers are also included. The change over time in group performance for written fluency was significant based on results of a repeated measures ANOVA, $F(5,22) = 6.03$, p = .001. Post hoc comparisons demonstrated that the Presojourn was significantly different (p < .05) from all rounds except for Insojourn 1. The effect sizes (Cohen's d) for the pairwise comparisons ranged from .69 to 1.10, suggesting medium to

114 *Linguistic development in Spanish*

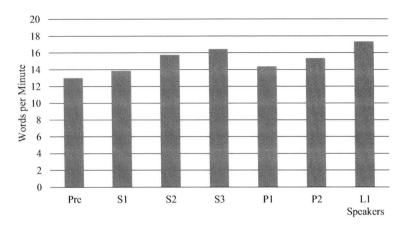

Figure 5.5 Mean writing fluency scores for L2 Spanish group (over time) and L1 Spanish group

large effects, with the largest occurring between Presojourn and Insojourn 3. These results demonstrate that the gains participants made in written fluency were maintained over time. Comparing the participants' written fluency to the Spanish L1 speakers' written fluency on the same tasks, significant differences were found at Presojourn ($p < .001$, Cohen's $d = 1.35$), Insojourn 1 ($p = .001$, Cohen's $d = 0.94$), and Postsojourn 1 only ($p = .03$, Cohen's $d = 0.64$). At Insojourn 2 and 3 and Postsojourn 2, the difference between the number of words produced per minute between sojourners and L1 Spanish speakers was not statistically significant. This suggests that the Spanish LANGSNAP participants had made considerable improvement in their written fluency as a result of residence abroad and that instruction during their final year of university helped to maintain these gains.

Individual results for written fluency are provided in Figure 5.6. Once again, there is considerable individual variation among the L2 Spanish participants on this measure. Most participants show improvement over time, yet there are examples of participants who produced fewer words per minute throughout the year abroad than they did Presojourn. For example, participant 155 wrote with the greatest fluency of all the participants at Presojourn, but never wrote so fast again until Postsojourn 2. In contrast, Participants 150, 161, 171 and 173 show large increases over time while others change little, such as 158, 162 and 175.

In sum, the results for written fluency suggest that the group as a whole improved significantly during the sojourn and maintained their gains once they returned home, and wrote at similar rates to L1 speakers after five months abroad. However, there was considerable individual variation, with evidence also that some learners did not improve from Presojourn levels until they returned to language classes at the home university, as well as participants who showed almost no change throughout the whole project.

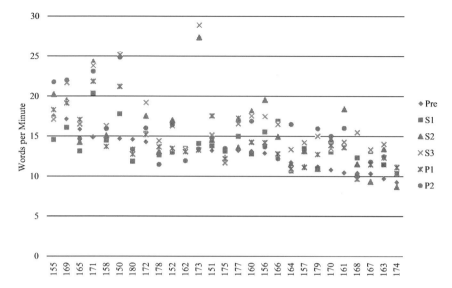

Figure 5.6 Writing fluency scores for individual L2 Spanish participants

5.3.4 Accuracy development in speech: Spanish group

In this section we examine the development of grammatical accuracy in spoken Spanish, again using the sequence of oral narratives. In this analysis, accuracy was operationalized in three ways: 1) the percentage of error-free clauses within the overall narrative, 2) the percentage of error-free Analysis of Speech Units (ASUs), and 3) accurate use of past tense morphology (preterit and imperfect).

Group results for the percentages of error-free ASUs and error-free clauses are summarized in Figure 5.7. As the figure shows, LANGSNAP participants made a large improvement in grammatical accuracy on both these (related) measures from Presojourn to Insojourn 1, but changed little during the rest of their time abroad. Interestingly, they improved once more after returning home and taking language classes again.

These changes over time for percentages of both error-free clauses and error-free ASUs were significant based on the non-parametric Friedman test (error-free clauses: χ^2 (5) = 67.593, p < .001; error-free ASUs: χ^2 (5) = 47.818, p < .001). Post hoc tests for error-free clauses demonstrated significant differences between the Presojourn and all other rounds (p < .001 for all), all with very large effect sizes (Cohen's *d* ranged from 1.15 to 1.90), in addition to Insojourn 1–Postsojourn 1 (p < .001, *d* = 1.05), Insojourn 1–Postsojourn 2 (p < .001, *d* = .99), Insojourn 3–Postsojourn 1 (p < .001, *d* = .91), and Insojourn 3–Postsojourn 2 (p < .001, *d* = 99). The only post hoc tests that were significant for error-free ASUs were between the Presojourn results and all other rounds (p < .001 for all; Cohen's *d* ranged from 1.21 to 1.88). In sum, the results for accurate clauses and ASUs

116 *Linguistic development in Spanish*

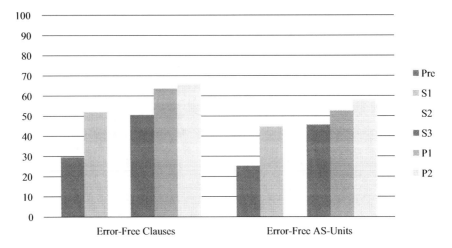

Figure 5.7 Mean percentage of error-free clauses and error-free ASUs for L2 Spanish group, oral narrative

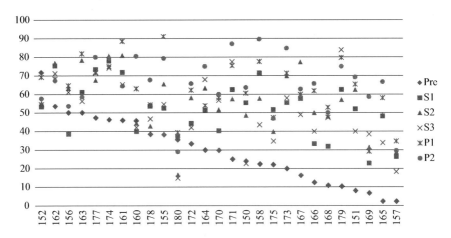

Figure 5.8 Percentage of error-free clauses for individual L2 Spanish participants, oral narrative

suggest that residence abroad was beneficial for improving general accuracy, and that instruction contributed to maintaining the gains made following return to the home university.

Individual participant scores are also provided for these measures in Figures 5.8 and 5.9, which show a great deal of individual variation and a large spread of scores. Nearly all of the participants show improvement over time from Presojourn accuracy levels in percentage of error-free clauses (Figure 5.8) and ASUs (Figure 5.9). Those who scored highest at Presojourn tended not to improve as

Linguistic development in Spanish   117

much as those who started much lower, although not all of those participants who started very low made large gains.

The narratives were also analysed for accurate use in context of two forms of the past tense in Spanish, the preterit (PRET) and the imperfect (IMPF). As explained in Chapter 3, past tense usage was selected for special investigation, as the aspectual contrast found in both French and Spanish presents well-known challenges for Anglophones (Comajoan Colomé, 2014). As shown in Figure 5.10, results for the group means for both forms show mostly gradual improvement over time in percentage terms. The Presojourn levels are 65% for PRET and 55% for IMPF, but by Postsojourn 2 they are both over 80%. The large gains made with

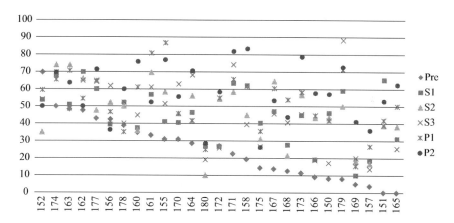

Figure 5.9 Percentage of error-free ASUs for individual L2 Spanish participants, oral narrative

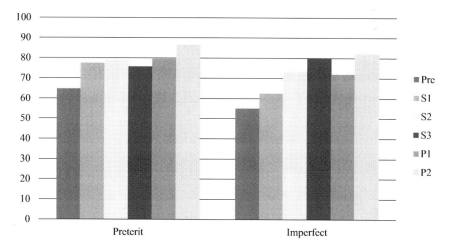

Figure 5.10 Mean percentage of accurate preterit and imperfect use for L2 Spanish group, oral narrative

118 Linguistic development in Spanish

IMPF decrease somewhat at Postsojourn 1 but rebound at Postsojourn 2. A nonparametric Friedman test demonstrated that the change over time was significant for both forms: PRET χ^2 (5) = 19.153, p = .002; IMPF χ^2 (5) = 37.609, p < .001. Post hoc comparisons for PRET were significant between Presojourn–Postsojourn 2 (p < .001, Cohen's d = .90) and Insojourn 3–Postsojourn 2 (p = .004, d = .78), and for IMPF between Presojourn–Insojourn 3 (p < .001, d = .80), Presojourn–Postsojourn 2 (p < .001, d = .89), Insojourn 1–Insojourn 3 (p < .001, d = .92), and Insojourn 1–Postsojourn 2 (p < .001, d = .99). Results for IMPF demonstrate that improvement was more gradual than for PRET but that the gains made with both forms during the sojourn were sustained after the sojourn.

Individual results for PRET and IMPF are provided in Figures 5.11 and 5.12. Results for PRET demonstrate that a majority of the participants were rather

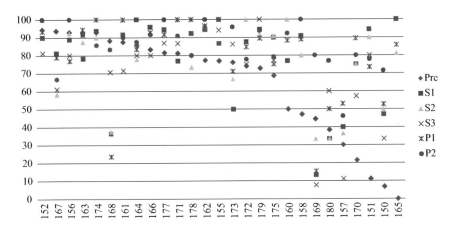

Figure 5.11 Percentage of appropriate preterit use for individual L2 Spanish participants

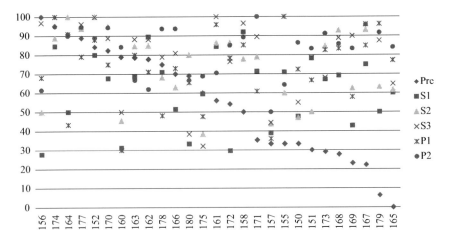

Figure 5.12 Percentage of appropriate imperfect use for individual L2 Spanish participants

Linguistic development in Spanish   119

accurate at Presojourn (over 70%) and continued to improve over time. In contrast, there was more variation with IMPF, particularly for those students who started off with higher accuracy levels initially. Those who started off lower continued to improve over time.

In sum, the results for accuracy on the oral picture-based narratives demonstrate that the L2 Spanish group made significant gains during residence abroad on global measures, as well as on two specific grammatical features, PRET and IMPF. Similar to the other results presented thus far, there was considerable variation among participants in the extent of gains made, but in general these gains were maintained during their final year of university.

5.3.5 Accuracy development in writing: Spanish group

Accuracy in written Spanish was also examined, in the argumentative essays, and operationalized as the percentage of error-free T-units per individual text and the percentage of error-free clauses (again, two somewhat related measures).

Figure 5.13 displays the group results for percentage of error-free clauses per individual text and percentage of error-free T-units. In contrast to the results presented thus far, participants did not appear to make gains in written accuracy over time on these measures. Instead, their percentage accuracy levels initially decreased from Presojourn levels, rose somewhat at Insojourn 3, and decreased again during their final year of university. For error-free T-units, the decrease over time in accuracy was significant based on results of a non-parametric Friedman test, χ^2 (5) = 15.743, p = .008; the post hoc tests demonstrated a significant difference between the Presojourn and Insojourn 1 results only (p = .001, Cohen's d = .73). The result of the Friedman test for error-free clauses was also significant,

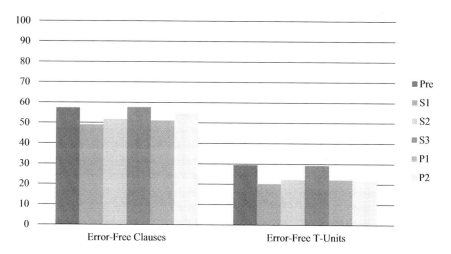

Figure 5.13 Mean percentage of error-free clauses and error-free T-units for L2 Spanish group, argumentative essay

120 *Linguistic development in Spanish*

χ^2 (5) = 17.328, p = .004; the post hoc tests demonstrated significant differences between Presojourn–Insojourn 1 (p = .005, d = .60) and Insojourn 1–Insojourn 3 (p = .006, d = .58). In sum, these findings suggest that the LANGSNAP Spanish participants' accuracy levels in the written argumentative essay did not improve during residence abroad, nor after they returned to their home university.

Individual results are displayed in Figures 5.14 and 5.15 and show much more variation across time than might be expected from the group means. Only a few participants, such as 170 and 175, show little change over time. Not surprisingly, participants were somewhat more able to produce error-free clauses than complete error-free T-units; the lowest score for error-free clauses is just over 20%, whereas for error-free T-units it is 0%. Very few participants scored more than 50% on error-free T-units. Lastly, accurate production in the writing task often decreased from Presojourn levels, a finding that contrasts with outcomes for

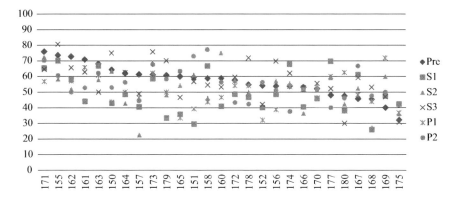

Figure 5.14 Percentage of error-free clauses for individual L2 Spanish participants, argumentative essay

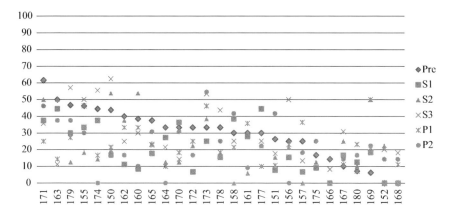

Figure 5.15 Percentage of error-free T-units for individual L2 Spanish participants, argumentative essay

the oral narrative, where participants almost always showed improvement from Presojourn levels. In sum, the results for writing accuracy show little change over time and suggest that for these L2 Spanish participants, residence abroad was not beneficial for the overall accuracy of their written production.

5.3.6 Development of syntactic complexity: Spanish group

Syntactic complexity has been analysed in the written data only. Results for two measures of syntactic complexity are presented here: the ratio of clauses to T-units and mean length of T-unit. A higher clause to T-unit ratio, and production of longer T-units, are viewed as indicators of greater written complexity (Wolfe-Quintero et al., 1998).

As shown in Figure 5.16, there appears to be little change over time in the ratio of clauses to T-units produced by the L2 Spanish group. Although the results of a repeated measures ANOVA comparing change over time were statistically significant ($F(5,22) = 4.93$, $p = .004$), only one post hoc test was significant: the difference between Presojourn and Postsojourn 2 ($p = .007$, Cohen's $d = .80$). Results for mean length of T-unit show more obvious change over time, particularly a large increase at Insojourn 2 and Postsojourn 2, and a significant effect for time was found ($F(5,22) = 29.2$, $p < .001$). As might be expected based on Figure 5.16, several significant post hoc results were found: Presojourn–Insojourn 2 ($p < .001$, Cohen's $d = 1.23$), Presojourn–Postsojourn 2 ($p < .001$, Cohen's $d = 1.26$), Insojourn 1–Insojourn2 ($p = .006$, Cohen's $d = .77$), Insojourn 1–Postsojourn 2 ($p = .001$, Cohen's $d = .87$), Insojourn 2–Insojourn 3 ($p = .002$, Cohen's $d = .74$), Insojourn 3–Postsojourn 2 ($p < .001$, Cohen's $d = .74$), Insojourn 2–Postsojourn 1 ($p = .018$, Cohen's $d = .68$), and Postsojourn 1–Postsojourn 2 ($p = .003$, Cohen's $d = .80$).

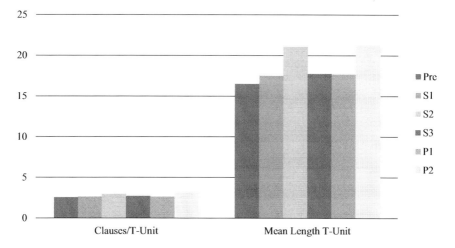

Figure 5.16 Mean ratio of clauses to T-unit and mean length of T-unit over time, L2 Spanish group, argumentative essay

122 Linguistic development in Spanish

Interestingly, the higher scores at Insojourn 2 and Postsojourn 2 came from the same prompt (Junk Food). These scores were significantly different from all the other scores but not from each other, suggesting that the prompts may have had an influence on syntactic complexity. When all performances were compared pairwise for the same prompts, no significant change was found, though each prompt was repeated one year later. Therefore, the results appear to suggest overall that there was no development over time in participants' syntactic complexity.

It is interesting to compare these L2 findings with those for the L1 Spanish group. Figure 5.17 displays the results for ratio of clauses/T-unit for all performances with each individual prompt (i.e., two performances by sojourners and one performance by the L1 Spanish group). Similar results for mean length of T-unit are displayed in Figure 5.18. Statistical tests made it clear that both groups produced more complex syntax in the Junk Food essay.

A comparison with the L1 Spanish group demonstrated significant differences in the ratio of clauses/T-unit on all rounds except for Insojourn 1, Insojourn 3 and Postsojourn 2. For mean length of T-unit, the differences between the two groups were significant for all survey points.

Individual data for clause/T-unit ratios and mean length of T-unit are given in Figures 5.19 and 5.20 respectively. The figures show considerable fluctuation over time in the scores of those participants who produced more syntactically complex language at Presojourn. In comparison, those who initially scored lower primarily improved over time. The individual results also confirm that a majority of participants produced the most complex language at Insojourn 2 or Postsojourn 2 in response to the Junk Food prompt.

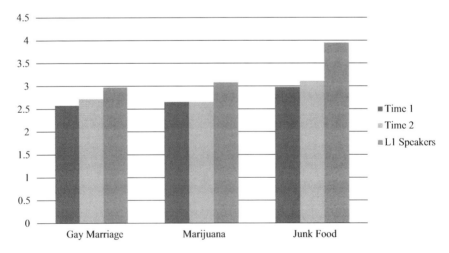

Figure 5.17 Complexity in Spanish writing: Ratio of clauses to T-units by prompt, L2 Spanish group and L1 Spanish group

Linguistic development in Spanish 123

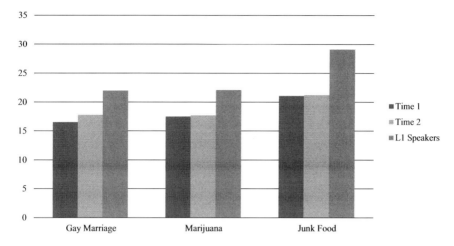

Figure 5.18 Complexity in Spanish writing: Mean length of T-unit by prompt, L2 Spanish group and L1 Spanish group

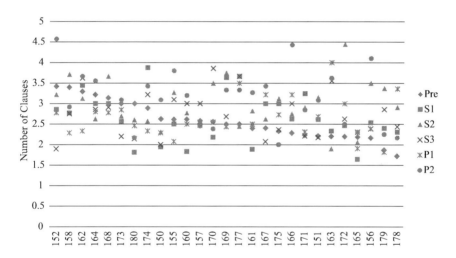

Figure 5.19 Ratio of clauses to T-units for individual L2 Spanish participants, argumentative essay

5.3.7 *Development of lexical complexity: Spanish group*

The development of lexical complexity in the Spanish LANGSNAP data is analysed using the measure of lexical diversity, D, computed using the VocD program in CLAN. The measure was applied to the oral narratives, the oral interviews and the argumentative essays, from all six survey points.

124 *Linguistic development in Spanish*

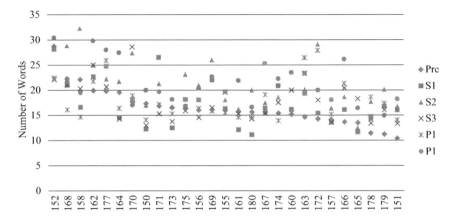

Figure 5.20 Mean length of T-unit for individual L2 Spanish participants, argumentative essay

As described more fully by Tracy-Ventura, Mitchell, and McManus (2016), an interaction was found between time and task which suggests that *D* scores changed differently over time in the different task types. For example, the *D* scores for the interview improved from Presojourn to Insojourn 1, and those gains were maintained over time (see Figure 5.21). Results for the narratives also suggest that learners improved from Presojourn to Insojourn 1 and then mostly maintained those gains over time. In contrast, no major differences occurred in writing, though a slight improvement was noticeable for the second iteration of each writing task. As in the results for syntactic complexity, the L1 data provided further support that the variety of prompts used for the oral narrative and argumentative essay might have affected use of vocabulary differently. Here, we select the *D* scores in the interviews for discussion in more detail.

The change over time in *D* scores for the interview was significant based on a non-parametric Friedman test (χ^2 (5) = 26.80, p < .001), and post hoc tests found a significant difference between Presojourn and all Insojourn data points: Presojourn–Insojourn1 (p = .003, Cohen's *d* = .70), Insojourn 2 (p = .001, Cohen's *d* = .65), Insojourn 3 (p = .001, Cohen's *d* = .63). Upon return to the home university, however, there were possible indications of attrition, as *D* scores at Postsojourn 1 and Postsojourn 2 were not significantly different from Presojourn. At all data points, the L2 Spanish sojourners were significantly different from the L1 group.

Individual results for each participant are shown in Figure 5.22. As evidenced in the graph, the range of *D* scores over time is rather narrow compared to some of the other analyses presented thus far. Most participants scored the lowest at Presojourn and highest whilst abroad. The largest gains were made by participant 165, who had the lowest *D* score at Presojourn, similar to 173 and 157. In sum, the results for development of lexical diversity on the oral interview suggest that

Linguistic development in Spanish 125

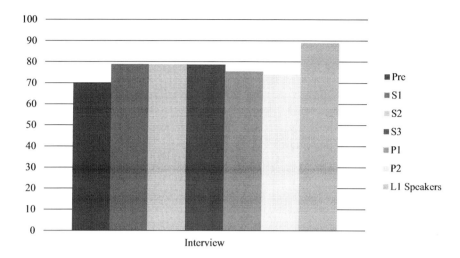

Figure 5.21 Mean lexical diversity (D) scores for L2 Spanish group (over time) and L1 Spanish group, oral interview

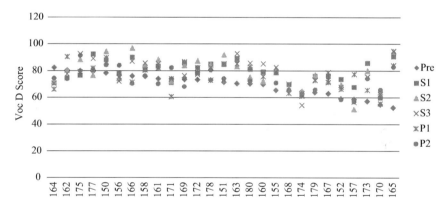

Figure 5.22 Lexical diversity scores (D) for individual L2 Spanish participants, oral interview

the L2 Spanish participants made improvements during their sojourn abroad but that they had difficulty maintaining these gains once they returned home.

5.3.8 Receptive lexical development: Spanish group

In addition to analysing productive vocabulary, we investigated vocabulary recognition using the Spanish version of the Swansea X-Lex levels test (Meara & Milton, 2005). Participants took the test at Presojourn and at Insojourn 3. As shown in Table 5.2, participants' scores on the Spanish version of the test

Table 5.2 Summary results of the Spanish X-Lex test

	Mean score	SD	Range
Presojourn	2700.00	746.53	900–4100
Insojourn 3	3453.70	560.89	2350–4350

improved between these two points (the highest possible score is 5000), and the standard deviation also decreased. The change over time was significant (based on a paired samples t-test, t(26) = –5.02, p < .001, Cohen's d = .99) and primarily due to participants recognizing more infrequent vocabulary over time, which coincided with them producing more infrequent vocabulary as well. (For more details see Tracy-Ventura, 2014.)

Individual participant data for the X-Lex results are shown in Figure 5.23. As shown in the figure, the majority of the participants improved at Insojourn 3, although there were a few whose score decreased, most notably participant 152. Interestingly, her raw score at Insojourn 3 was higher than at Presojourn, 4850 vs. 4100 respectively, but her adjusted score was much lower, 2600 vs. 4100, because she chose a much higher number of the fake words at Insojourn 3, nine vs. one. In sum, the results for vocabulary recognition show significant overall improvement as a result of residence abroad.

To summarize the findings for the L2 Spanish LANGSNAP group, as in previous research, there is strong evidence that their oral abilities improved, particularly in proficiency and fluency, as well as in vocabulary knowledge and use. In contrast to much of the previous Spanish SA research, our participants also improved in accuracy on the oral narrative task for the general measures of error-free clauses and error-free ASUs, in addition to use of the imperfect. Several of the improvements which took place insojourn were also maintained during their final year of university instruction; for example, results for error-free clauses improved significantly from Insojourn 3 to Postsojourn 2. Taken together, these results demonstrate that residence abroad had a positive impact on the oral abilities of the Spanish LANGSNAP group, and that continuing language instruction postsojourn was beneficial for maintaining the gains made. In writing, however, a different picture emerged. The only gain made in written abilities was in the area of writing fluency, but accuracy and complexity did not change during their stay abroad. This is likely due to limited writing practice among most participants, as documented through the Language Engagement Questionnaire (see Chapter 7). Interestingly, when comparing learners' syntactic complexity with the L1 Spanish group, at least for the ratio of clauses/T-unit, there were some survey points where no differences were found. This suggests that the L2 Spanish participants were already rather good at producing complex syntax in writing. They still appeared to differ from the L1 group on the mean length of T-unit, however.

Linguistic development in Spanish 127

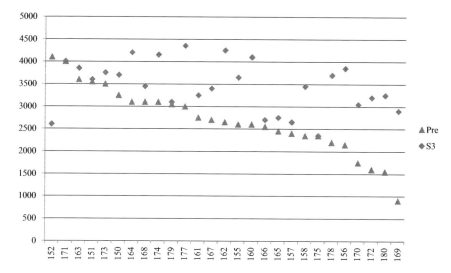

Figure 5.23 X-Lex test scores for individual L2 Spanish participants at Presojourn and at Insojourn 3

5.4 Comparing linguistic development in the French and Spanish groups

In this final section, we compare the learning outcomes achieved by our two learner groups and previous SLA research on residence/study abroad, finding both similarities and differences. Results for our measure of oral proficiency, the EIT, were similar across the two groups. This measure was administered three times (Presojourn, Insojourn 2 and Postsojourn) and significant differences were found between each round for both groups. This is a robust finding (e.g., all effect sizes for the L2 Spanish group were more than 1.0) providing strong evidence for continuing improvement in oral proficiency throughout the sojourn. This finding provides further evidence in support of residence abroad as beneficial for proficiency development (e.g., Guntermann, 1995; Hernández, 2010; Kinginger, 2008; Segalowitz & Freed, 2004; Yager, 1998). In contrast to some previous research, nearly all of the LANGSNAP participants showed clear improvement over time. That is, while there is individual variation in the amount of gains made, all but a very few improved throughout the year.

Results for oral fluency, as measured by Speech Rate and Mean Length of Run, were also quite similar between the two LANGSNAP groups, and support previous research demonstrating fluency development as a major outcome of residence/study abroad (D'Amico, 2010; García-Amaya, 2009; Segalowitz & Freed, 2004; Towell, Hawkins, & Bazergui, 1996). Both of the LANGSNAP groups demonstrated significant improvement by Insojourn 1; the Spanish group continued to show evidence of improvement, peaking at Insojourn 2, which was significantly different from Insojourn 1. Both groups maintained these early gains throughout their stay abroad and into the postsojourn year. The Spanish group may have started to show early signs of attrition at Postsojourn 2, as there was no longer a significant difference from Insojourn 1. The French group may also have started to show signs of attrition, as a significant difference was found between Postsojourn 1 and Postsojourn 2. Although both groups appeared to make their main gains in oral fluency within the first few months, it seems they consolidated these gains over time due to their continued use of their L2s during the rest of their stay abroad. This finding echoes the results of Serrano, Tragant, and Llanes (2012), whose longitudinal study of L2 English sojourners also showed early improvement in oral fluency that was maintained throughout the rest of their year abroad.

In contrast to oral fluency, little previous research has investigated the development of writing fluency during residence/study abroad. Both L2 groups in LANGSNAP made gains in writing fluency, albeit not in exactly the same way. The Spanish group demonstrated gradual improvement over time abroad, whereas the French group made large improvements between Insojourn 2 and Insojourn 3. These findings are in line with Freed, So, and Lazar (2003), who found that an SA group improved on other measures of French writing fluency (number of words per essay and number of T-units) significantly more than an AH group. Sasaki (2007) also found that her SA group improved more in English L2 writing fluency (words per minute and number of words in the text) than an AH group. Our results also support those of Serrano et al. (2012), who found more gradual and significant improvement in writing fluency (operationalized as words/T-unit). However, the results of both their study and ours suggest that gains in writing fluency take longer to appear than those in oral fluency.

Switching now to accuracy on the oral narrative, our results demonstrate that both groups made similar improvements. For error-free ASUs, the difference between Presojourn and all subsequent rounds was statistically significant, thus demonstrating once again early gains that were maintained throughout the year and into the postsojourn instructed year. As mentioned above, the L2 Spanish group continued to improve on error-free clauses after the sojourn, but these results were not found for the L2 French group. These results contrast with those from previous research demonstrating few or no gains in accuracy (DeKeyser, 2010; Isabelli-García, 2010; Mora & Valls-Ferrer, 2012), and also from those of Serrano et al. (2012), who found that their participants improved in accuracy in the second half of their year abroad.

We also analysed the LANGSNAP participants' use of two past tense forms (*Passé Composé* vs. *Imparfait* in French; preterit vs. imperfect in Spanish). Both groups started more accurate with the perfective forms (*Passé Composé*, preterit), achieving around 60% accuracy, compared to imperfective forms (*Imparfait*, imperfect). By the end of their sojourn, the Spanish group was using both forms with about the same accuracy (87% preterit, 82% imperfect), whereas the French group was still more accurate at producing the *Passé Composé* than *Imparfait* (83% vs. 64% respectively). Both groups made significant improvements in use of both forms over time. The French group made gains quickly that were maintained over time. The Spanish group showed more gradual development, particularly for the imperfect. Howard (2005) also found that his SA group improved significantly in use of the French *Passé Composé* and *Imparfait*, and Guntermann (1995) found improvement in the use of the preterit and imperfect. So far the use of the subjunctive has been analysed for the French LANGSNAP group only; results showing little change over time appear to contrast with those of Isabelli and Nishida (2005) for L2 Spanish, who found evidence of development over their nine-month study.

In contrast to improvements found in oral accuracy, results for the argumentative writing task showed little change over time. The Spanish LANGSNAP group actually appeared to get worse between Presojourn and Insojourn 1 on both accuracy measures, but they recovered after that, showing little change between rounds and between repetitions of the same exact prompt. The French group's written accuracy did not change over time. Similar results were also found for written complexity when task effects were taken into consideration. The Junk Food prompt inspired more complex syntax in Spanish, both for the Spanish L1 and L2 participants, and this was also the case, though to a lesser degree, for the French L1 and L2 participants. These results differ from Serrano et al. (2012), whose participants improved in both written accuracy and complexity during the second half of their year abroad. Our social data provide a possible explanation, showing that many participants practised very little L2 writing during the sojourn.

Finally, results for vocabulary use were mostly similar between the two LANGSNAP groups. Both showed significant improvement on our measure of lexical diversity, D, between Presojourn and Insojourn 1, and this was maintained over time. However, results for our measure of lexical knowledge, X-Lex, differed between the two groups. This measure was only administered at Presojourn and Insojourn 3. The Spanish group improved significantly between the two time periods but the French participants did not. This difference may be due to the French group's higher Presojourn mean score of 3225, compared to 2700 for the Spanish group. These results mostly point to improvements as a result of residence/study abroad, in line with much of the previous research on L2 vocabulary development in SA (Ife et al., 2000; Milton & Meara, 1995; Serrano et al., 2012).

In conclusion, these LANGSNAP project results offer further evidence that residence/study abroad is beneficial for improving oral skills in several specific ways, particularly in regard to fluency, accuracy and lexis. It also appears that many of these gains were made within the first few months abroad, perhaps due to the fact that our participants were already at least of intermediate proficiency – that is, they already possessed the prerequisite declarative knowledge which could be proceduralized through L2 practice when abroad (DeKeyser, 2010). Our pioneering results for writing demonstrate little change over time except in writing fluency, perhaps due to improved efficiency in retrieval of lexical items. The findings also demonstrate the benefits of longitudinal studies lasting more than one semester, in that (like Ife et al., 2000, and Serrano et al., 2012) we have been able to investigate the important question of how much time is needed to evidence improvement in the different skill areas.

References

Alarcón, I. V. (2011). Spanish gender agreement under complete and incomplete acquisition: Early and late bilinguals' linguistic behavior within the noun phrase. *Bilingualism: Language and Cognition, 14*(3), 332–350.

Bosker, H. R., Pinget, A.-F., Quené, H., Sanders, T., & De Jong, N. (2013). What makes speech sound fluent? The contributions of pauses, speed and repairs. *Language Testing, 30*(2), 159–175.

Castañeda-Jiménez, G., & Jarvis, S. (2014). Exploring lexical diversity in second language Spanish. In K. L. Geeslin (Ed.), *The handbook of Spanish second language acquisition* (pp. 498–513). Chichester: Wiley Blackwell.

Collentine, J. (2004). The effects of learning contexts on morphosyntactic and lexical development. *Studies in Second Language Acquisition, 26*(2), 227–248.

Collentine, J., & Asención-Delaney, Y. (2010). A corpus-based analysis of the discourse functions of ser/estar+ adjective in three levels of Spanish as FL learners. *Language Learning, 60*(2), 409–445.

Comajoan Colomé, L. (2014). Tense and aspect in second language Spanish. In K. L. Geeslin (Ed.), *The handbook of second language Spanish* (pp. 235–252). Chichester: Wiley Blackwell.

D'Amico, M. L. (2010). *The effects of intensive study abroad and at home language programs on second language acquisition of Spanish*. (PhD), University of Florida.

De Haan, P., & Van Esch, K. (2005). The development of writing in English and Spanish as foreign languages. *Assessing Writing, 10*(2), 100–116.

De Haan, P., & Van Esch, K. (2008). Measuring and assessing the development of foreign language writing competence. *Porta Linguarum: revista internacional de didáctica de las lenguas extranjeras, 9*, 7–22.

DeKeyser, R. (2010). Monitoring processes in Spanish as a second language during a study abroad program. *Foreign Language Annals, 43*(1), 80–92.

Domínguez, L., Tracy-Ventura, N., Arche, M., Mitchell, R., & Myles, F. (2013). The role of dynamic contrasts in the L2 acquisition of Spanish past tense morphology. *Bilingualism: Language and Cognition, 16*(3), 558–577.

Freed, B. F., So, S., & Lazar, N. (2003). Language learning abroad: How do gains in written fluency compare with oral fluency in French as a second language? *Association of Departments of Foreign Languages Bulletin, 34*, 34–40.

García-Amaya, L. (2009). New findings on fluency measures across three different learning contexts. In J. Collentine (Ed.), *Proceedings of the 11th Hispanic Linguistics Symposium* (pp. 68–80). Somerville, MA: Cascadilla Proceedings Project.

Geeslin, K. L., Fafulas, S., & Kanwit, M. (2013). Acquiring geographically-variable norms of use: The case of the present perfect in Mexico and Spain. In C. Howe (Ed.), *Selected Proceedings of the 15th Hispanic Linguistics Symposium* (pp. 205–220). Somerville, MA: Cascadilla Proceedings Project.

Geeslin, K. L., García-Amaya, L., Hasler-Barker, M., Henriksen, N., & Killam, J. (2012). Variability and the L2 acquisition of perfective past time reference in Spanish in an abroad immersion setting. In K. L. Geeslin & M. Díaz-Campos (Eds.), *Selected Proceedings of the 14th Hispanic Linguistics Symposium* (pp. 197–213). Somerville, MA: Cascadilla Proceedings Project.

Geeslin, K. L., & Guijarro-Fuentes, P. (2005). The acquisition of copula choice in instructed Spanish: The role of individual characteristics. In D. Eddington (Ed.), *Studies in the acquisition of the Hispanic languages: Papers from the 6th conference on the acquisition of Spanish and Portuguese as first and second languages* (pp. 66–77). Somerville, MA: Cascadilla Press.

Geeslin, K. L., & Guijarro-Fuentes, P. (2006). Second language acquisition of variable structures in Spanish by Portuguese speakers. *Language Learning, 56*(1), 53–107.

Grey, S., Cox, J. G., Serafini, E. J., & Sanz, C. (2015). The role of individual differences in the study abroad context: Cognitive capacity and language development during short-term intensive language exposure. *The Modern Language Journal, 99*(1), 137–157.

Gudmestad, A. (2012). Acquiring a variable structure: An interlanguage analysis of second language mood use in Spanish. *Language Learning, 62*(2), 373–402.

Guntermann, G. (1995). The Peace Corps experience: Language learning in training and in the field. In B.F. Freed (Ed.), *Second language acquisition in a study abroad context* (pp. 149–170). Amsterdam: John Benjamins.

Hernández, T. A. (2010). The relationship among motivation, interaction, and the development of second language oral proficiency in a study-abroad context. *The Modern Language Journal, 94*(4), 600–617.

Howard, M. (2005). Second language acquisition in a study abroad context: A comparative investigation of the effects of study abroad and foreign language instruction on the L2 learner's grammatical development In A. Housen & M. Pierrard (Eds.), *Investigations in instructed second language acquisition* (pp. 495–530). Berlin: DeGruyter Mouton.

Huensch, A. & Tracy-Ventura, N. (in press). L2 utterance fluency development before, during, and after residence abroad: A multidimensional investigation. To appear in *The Modern Language Journal, 101*(2).

Ife, A., Vives Boix, G., & Meara, P. M. (2000). The impact of study abroad on the vocabulary development of different proficiency groups. *Spanish Applied Linguistics, 4*(1), 55–84.

Isabelli, C. A., & Nishida, C. (2005). Development of the Spanish subjunctive in a nine-month study-abroad setting. In D. Eddington (Ed.), *Selected proceedings of the 6th conference on the acquisition of Spanish and Portuguese as first and second languages* (pp. 78–91). Somerville, MA: Cascadilla Proceedings Project.

Isabelli-García, C. (2010). Acquisition of Spanish gender agreement in two learning contexts: Study abroad and at home. *Foreign Language Annals, 43*(2), 289–303.

Kinginger, C. (2008). Language learning in study abroad: Case studies of Americans in France. *The Modern Language Journal, 92*(Special issue), 1–124.

Kinginger, C. (2009). *Language learning and study abroad: A critical reading of research.* Basingstoke: Palgrave Macmillan.

Lafford, B. A., & Uscinski, I. (2014). Study abroad and second language Spanish. In K. L. Geeslin (Ed.), *The handbook of Spanish second language acquisition* (pp. 386–403). Chichester: Wiley Blackwell.

Leonard, K. R. (2015). *Speaking fluency and study abroad: What factors are related to fluency development?* (PhD), University of Iowa.

Lord, G. (2009). Second-language awareness and development during study abroad: A case study. *Hispania, 92*(1), 127–141.

Marsden, E., & David, A. (2008). Vocabulary use during conversation: A cross-sectional study of development from year 9 to year 13 among learners of Spanish and French. *Language Learning Journal, 36*(2), 181–198.

Martínez-Gibson, E. A., Rodríguez-Sabater, S., Toris, C.M., & Weyers, J.R. (2010). To be: A study of ser and estar in second language learners of Spanish. *Southern Journal of Linguistics, 30*(1), 52–77.

McManus, K., Tracy-Ventura, N., & Mitchell, R. (2016). *L2 linguistic development before, during and after a nine-month sojourn: Evidence from L2 French and Spanish*. Paper presented at Second Language Research Forum, Columbia University, New York.

Meara, P. M., & Milton, J. (2005). *X-Lex: The Swansea levels test*. Newbury: Express.

Milton, J., & Meara, P. (1995). How periods abroad affect vocabulary growth in a foreign language. *ITL Review of Applied Linguistics, 107/108*, 17–34.

Montrul, S. (2011). Multiple interfaces and incomplete acquisition. *Lingua, 121*(4), 591–604.

Montrul, S., Foote, R., & Perpiñán, S. (2008). Gender agreement in adult second language learners and Spanish heritage speakers: The effects of age and context of acquisition. *Language Learning, 58*(3), 503–553.

Mora, J. C., & Valls-Ferrer, M. (2012). Oral fluency, accuracy, and complexity in formal instruction and study abroad learning contexts. *TESOL Quarterly, 46*(4), 610–641.

Ortega, L. (2000). *Understanding syntactic complexity: The measurement of change in the syntax of instructed L2 Spanish learners.* (PhD), University of Hawaii at Manoa.

Ortega, L., Iwashita, N., Norris, J., & Rabie, S. (2002). *An investigation of elicited imitation tasks in crosslinguistic SLA research.* Paper presented at the Second Language Research Forum, Toronto, Canada.

Pérez-Vidal, C. (Ed.). (2014). *Language acquisition in study abroad and formal instruction contexts.* Amsterdam: John Benjamins.

Plonsky, L., & Oswald, F. L. (2014). How big is "Big"? Interpreting effect sizes in L2 research. *Language Learning, 64*(4), 878–912.

Salaberry, M. R. (2008). *Marking past tense in second language acquisition: A theoretical model.* London: Continuum.

Sasaki, M. (2007). Effects of study-abroad experiences on EFL writers: A multiple-data analysis. *The Modern Language Journal, 91*(4), 602–620.

Sasaki, M. (2011). Effects of varying lengths of study-abroad experiences on Japanese EFL students' L2 writing ability and motivation: A longitudinal study. *TESOL Quarterly, 45*(1), 81–105.

Segalowitz, N., & Freed, B. F. (2004). Context, contact, and cognition in oral fluency acquisition. *Studies in Second Language Acquisition, 26*(2), 173–199.

Serrano, R., Tragant, E., & Llanes, À. (2012). A longitudinal analysis of the effects of one year abroad. *Canadian Modern Language Review, 68*(2), 138–163.

Skehan, P. (2003). Task based instruction. *Language Teaching, 36*(1), 1–14.

Tavakoli, P., & Skehan, P. (2005). Strategic planning, task structure, and performance testing. In R. Ellis (Ed.), *Planning and task performance* (pp. 239–273). Amsterdam: John Benjamins.

Towell, R., Hawkins, R., & Bazergui, N. (1996). The development of fluency in advanced learners of French. *Applied Linguistics, 17*(1), 84–119.

Tracy-Ventura, N. (2014). *A longitudinal study of lexical sophistication in a residence/study abroad context.* Paper presented at the Second Language Research Forum, University of South Carolina, SC.

Tracy-Ventura, N., Mitchell, R., & McManus, K. (2016). The LANGSNAP longitudinal learner corpus: Design and use. In M. Alonso Ramos (Ed.), *Spanish learner corpus research: Current trends and future perspectives* (pp. 117–141). Amsterdam: John Benjamins.

Vives Boix, G. (1995). *The development of a measure of lexical organisation: The association vocabulary test.* (PhD), University College of Swansea.

Wolfe-Quintero, K., Inagaki, S., & Kim, H.-Y. (1998). *Second language development in writing: Measures of fluency, accuracy and complexity: Technical Report 17*. Honolulu: Second Language Teaching and Curriculum Center, University of Hawai'i at Manoa.

Yager, K. (1998). Learning Spanish in Mexico: The effect of informal contact and student attitudes on language gain. *Hispania, 81*(4), 898–913.

Yang, J.-S. (2016). The effectiveness of study abroad on second language learning: A metaanalysis. *Canadian Modern Language Review, 72*(1), 66–94.

6 Social networks and social relationships during the sojourn

6.1 Introduction

This chapter draws on both quantitative and qualitative evidence to develop an account of the evolving social networks in which LANGSNAP participants were engaged during their time abroad.

Section 6.2 presents quantitative findings from the Social Networks Questionnaire (SNQ) which participants completed at Insojourns 1, 2 and 3 (see Chapter 3 for details). We start with an analysis of sojourners' overall network size (Section 6.2.1), with a particular focus on the contexts where contacts were made and on the languages(s) used. Then we examine network durability, that is, how frequently sojourners interacted with network contacts in their different languages (Section 6.2.2), as well as network intensity, that is, the people they reported to be their most frequent/closest contacts (Section 6.2.3). In Section 6.2.4 we introduce a Social Network Index for each language (L1 and L2) which summarizes different aspects of SNQ data, provides an overview of social network change over time, and can be used to explore relationships between social networking and L2 development (see Chapter 9).

In Section 6.3, we complement the quantitative SNQ results with qualitative analysis of sojourners' comments on social networking, drawn from the interview data from Presojourn to Insojourn 3. In Section 6.3.1, we review their Presojourn hopes for social networking. In 6.3.2, we examine how the insojourn domestic setting and early leisure contacts facilitated network formation. In 6.3.3–6.3.6, we examine different types of insojourn social contact (with international and local peers, with other locals and with romantic partners). In 6.3.7, we examine the maintenance of relations with family and friends from home.

6.2 Social networking: The quantitative findings

6.2.1 Size of sojourners' social networks

The first analysis presented here concerns sojourners' evolving network size (Dewey, Belnap, & Hilstrom, 2013). Through SNQ, at each survey point, sojourners reported on the numbers of contacts they were interacting with at the time in five different contexts: daytime work or study, organized free time, general free time, home life, and virtual. They also reported the language(s) used with individual contacts in each context (L1, L2 and L1-L2 mixed). We present findings concerning network size for each country separately in Tables 6.1–6.3.

Tables 6.1–6.3 show the number and percentage of contacts made across the five contexts through each language (L1, L2 and L1-L2 mixed). Firstly, in the France group (Table 6.1), the Total column shows that L1-using contacts were reported most frequently overall throughout the sojourn, with L2 users in second place. For this group, the highest numbers of L2-using contacts were found in the workplace or university (Range: 36.2%–44.4%). The majority of contacts with mixed L1-L2 language use were also found in those contexts (Range: 51.8%–54.0%), and contacts using only L1 were infrequent (Range: 7.7%–11.9%). Organized free time (covering activities such as sports) was also a highly favourable context for L2-using contacts, though absolute numbers were small. Considerable numbers of L2 users and mixed-language users were also encountered during general free time (e.g., travelling, "going out"), with some increase at midsojourn, though there was also extensive contact with L1 users in this setting. Contacts made in the home setting were fewer, but fairly evenly divided by language. Finally, the virtual context contained the vast majority of L1-using contacts, and very few L2- or mixed-language contacts. To sum up, the majority of the French group's L2 contacts were found in the daytime location of the university, school or other workplace, with some spillover to general free time.

For the Spain group (Table 6.2), total numbers of L1- and L2-using contacts were almost equal throughout the sojourn. In Spain, a high proportion of home life contacts were L2 users, and they were also the most frequent contacts during general free time categories. At work or university and in organized free time, all types of contact were encountered, but mixed-language contacts predominated; language contacts in virtual contexts, as in France, predominantly used L1.

For the small Mexico group (Table 6.3), L2 contacts predominated overall (see "Total" column). The fact that they were all English-language teaching assistants is reflected in the work/university context, where L1 and mixed-language

Table 6.1 Network size by language and context (% and number of reported contacts): France group (n=29)

		Work/ university	Organized free time	General free time	Home life	Virtual	TOTAL
Insojourn 1							
L2	% (n)	44.4 (76)	14.0 (24)	19.9 (34)	14.0 (24)	7.6 (13)	100.0 (171)
L1	% (n)	7.7 (17)	0.5 (1)	30.3 (67)	9.5 (21)	52.0 (115)	100.0 (221)
Mixed	% (n)	51.8 (56)	7.4 (8)	18.5 (20)	16.7 (18)	5.6 (6)	100.0 (108)
Insojourn 2							
L2	% (n)	36.2 (63)	14.9 (26)	28.2 (49)	14.9 (26)	5.8 (10)	100.0 (174)
L1	% (n)	11.9 (25)	2.9 (6)	29.5 (62)	10.5 (22)	45.2 (95)	100.0 (210)
Mixed	% (n)	53.2 (41)	11.7 (9)	23.4 (18)	9.1 (7)	2.6 (2)	100.0 (77)
Insojourn 3							
L2	% (n)	44.0 (55)	12.8 (16)	22.4 (28)	12.8 (16)	8.0 (10)	100.0 (125)
L1	% (n)	10.7 (19)	2.2 (4)	27.5 (49)	12.4 (22)	47.2 (84)	100.0 (178)
Mixed	% (n)	54.0 (34)	6.3 (4)	27.0 (17)	9.5 (6)	3.2 (2)	100.0 (63)

136 *Social networks and social relationships*

Table 6.2 Network size by language and context (% and number of reported contacts): Spain group (n=18)

		Work/ university	Organized free time	General free time	Home life	Virtual	TOTAL
Insojourn 1							
L2	% (n)	21.7 (33)	16.3 (25)	32.0 (49)	22.2 (34)	7.8 (12)	100.0 (153)
L1	% (n)	9.6 (15)	8.9 (14)	22.9 (36)	3.2 (5)	55.4 (87)	100.0 (157)
Mixed	% (n)	38.2 (50)	18.3 (24)	29.8 (39)	6.1 (8)	7.6 (10)	100.0 (131)
Insojourn 2							
L2	% (n)	22.8 (28)	6.5 (8)	37.4 (46)	29.3 (36)	4.0 (5)	100.0 (123)
L1	% (n)	13.5 (17)	5.6 (7)	26.2 (33)	3.1 (4)	51.6 (65)	100.0 (126)
Mixed	% (n)	46.9 (46)	18.5 (18)	20.4 (20)	7.1 (7)	7.1 (7)	100.0 (98)
Insojourn 3							
L2	% (n)	25.6 (30)	6.8 (8)	34.3 (40)	28.2 (33)	5.1 (6)	100.0 (117)
L1	% (n)	13.5 (16)	7.6 (9)	24.6 (29)	5.1 (6)	49.2 (58)	100.0 (118)
Mixed	% (n)	43.5 (37)	14.1 (12)	25.9 (22)	4.7 (4)	11.8 (10)	100.0 (85)

Table 6.3 Network size by language and context (% and number of reported contacts): Mexico group (n=9)

		Work/ university	Organized free time	General free time	Home life	Virtual	TOTAL
Insojourn 1							
L2	% (n)	31.8 (28)	1.2 (1)	30.7 (27)	26.1 (23)	10.2 (9)	100.0 (88)
L1	% (n)	27.7 (13)	2.1 (1)	10.6 (5)	14.9 (7)	44.7 (21)	100.0 (47)
Mixed	% (n)	46.8 (22)	4.3 (2)	25.5 (12)	6.4 (3)	17.0 (8)	100.0 (47)
Insojourn 2							
L2	% (n)	19.1 (18)	10.6 (10)	29.8 (28)	22.3 (21)	18.1 (17)	100.0 (94)
L1	% (n)	27.3 (15)	7.3 (4)	14.5 (8)	7.3 (4)	43.6 (24)	100.0 (55)
Mixed	% (n)	34.9 (23)	7.6 (5)	36.3 (24)	10.6 (7)	10.6 (7)	100.0 (66)
Insojourn 3							
L2	% (n)	14.8 (12)	14.8 (12)	29.6 (24)	21.0 (17)	19.8 (16)	100.0 (81)
L1	% (n)	25.6 (11)	0.0 (0)	18.6 (8)	7.0 (3)	48.8 (21)	100.0 (43)
Mixed	% (n)	35.6 (16)	4.4 (2)	37.8 (17)	11.1 (5)	11.1 (5)	100.0 (45)

contacts predominated. L1-using contacts also predominated in the virtual context, though numbers of L2-using virtual contacts increased during the sojourn (unlike for the France and Spain groups). At home and in general free time, L2 contacts predominated throughout for the Mexico group. Few contacts were reported for organized free time at Insojourn 1, but when more contacts were reported (at Insojourns 2 and 3), they were mostly L2 users.

Overall, there were both differences and similarities amongst the groups. The group in France had the smallest L2-using networks, and the group in Mexico the largest; this can be connected to differences in the nature of contacts found in the home setting, as well as during general free time. Second, the workplace or university generally promoted contact with L2 and mixed-language users, but the role of English language assistant also promoted the use of L1 in this setting. Finally, L1-using contacts dominated the virtual context, regardless of other country differences.

6.2.2 Strength of network ties

Next, we examined the strength of sojourners' ties with their network contacts, the equivalent of "durability" in the studies of Dewey and colleagues (Dewey et al., 2013; Dewey, Bown, & Eggett, 2012). We determined network tie strength using sojourners' SNQ responses concerning the frequency and duration of their interactions with network contacts. *Strong ties* were those where interaction was reported to occur "every day" or "several times a week". *Medium ties* were those where interaction occurred "a couple of times a week", and also "a few times a month" when the duration was longer than three hours (in total, not per interaction). Lastly, contacts where interactions occurred "a few times a month", and for less than three hours in total, were classified as *Weak ties*. So, for example, we classified as *Weak* sojourner 167's relationship with Person A because the reported interaction was "a few times a month" for a total of two hours (over that period), whereas 167's relationship with Person B was reported as "a few times a month" for seven hours and was classified as *Medium*. An overall analysis of tie strength is presented in Table 6.4.

At Insojourn 1, the table shows solid numbers of strong ties for each language option (including mixed) for each country, but with some differences. For instance, at Insojourn 1, the most frequent strong ties were L1-based for the French group (21.6%), but L2-based for the groups in Spain (19.1%) and Mexico (33.3%). This pattern continued up to Insojourn 3 for the France and Mexico groups, but for the Spain group, while the percentage of L2-based strong ties remained fairly constant over time (19.1% → 20.1% → 19.4%), that of L1-based strong ties increased substantially at Insojourn 3 (16.3% → 16.2% → 22.8%). Strong L1-based ties were low throughout for the Mexico group (15.5% → 9.6% → 13.2%). In terms of mixed language use, the highest percentages for strong ties were consistently found in the Mexico group (19.4% → 18.7 → 16.3%), with lower percentages in France (13.4% → 10.1% → 10.6%) and Spain (13.5% → 14.8% → 14.6%).

These findings complement many of the findings reported in Section 6.2.2. It appears that although the France group reported high numbers of L2-using contacts at work/university, their strongest ties were with English-using contacts, found overwhelmingly in general free time and virtual contexts. The Mexico and Spain groups reported that their strongest ties were L2-based, and the highest proportions of their L2-using contacts were found in general free time and at home.

6.2.3 Intensity of social networks: The "Top 5"

The last part of the SNQ asked participants to list "the top five people with whom you interact the most", and to state in what language(s) they did so. The

Table 6.4 Strength of network ties, by language: Strong, medium and weak (% of total Top 5 contacts per group, mean numbers of Top 5 contacts per individual)

		L2			L1			Mixed			Total
		Strong	Medium	Weak	Strong	Medium	Weak	Strong	Medium	Weak	
Insojourn 1											
France	%	15.6	14.9	1.5	21.6	16.5	7.1	13.4	7.8	1.5	100.0
	M(SD)	3 (1.6)	3 (2.3)	1.2 (.4)	4.2 (2.5)	3 (1.8)	3.7 (1.9)	2.7 (1.3)	2.3 (1.2)	1.2 (.4)	
Spain	%	19.1	10.8	3.0	16.3	15.2	6.4	13.5	12.7	3.0	100.0
	M(SD)	4.1 (2.2)	3 (2.3)	1.4 (.7)	3.5 (.25)	3.4 (2.1)	2.1 (1.4)	3.3 (1.9)	3.3 (2.9)	3.7 (2.1)	
Mexico	%	33.3	10.1	3.1	15.5	8.5	3.1	19.4	7.0	0.0	100.0
	M(SD)	4.8 (2)	1.9 (.7)	1.0 (0)	2.2 (2.4)	1.8 (.8)	1.3 (.6)	2.8 (1.8)	1.3 (.8)	0.0 (0)	
Insojourn 2											
France	%	15.3	14.9	5.3	19.7	17.5	8.6	10.1	6.5	2.2	100.0
	M(SD)	3.0 (2.3)	3.4 (1.8)	2.4 (1.7)	3.3 (1.8)	2.9 (1.8)	3.0 (1.8)	2.5 (1.3)	1.6 (.8)	1.8 (1.1)	
Spain	%	20.1	10.6	3.9	16.2	16.5	5.6	14.8	9.9	2.5	100.0
	M(SD)	3.6 (1.8)	2.5 (1.5)	1.6 (.8)	2.9 (1.5)	3.4 (1.7)	1.8 (1.4)	3.2 (2.4)	2.8 (2.0)	1.4 (.9)	
Mexico	%	26.5	10.8	9.6	9.6	11.4	4.2	18.7	7.2	1.8	100.0
	M(SD)	4.9 (4.6)	2.0 (1.3)	4.0 (3.2)	2.0 (1.3)	2.1 (.3)	1.8 (.9)	3.4 (3)	3.0 (2.2)	1.0 (0)	
Insojourn 3											
France	%	18.5	16.2	3.1	23.8	15.1	5.6	10.6	6.2	0.8	100.0
	M(SD)	3.3 (2.2)	3.6 (2.8)	1.4 (.7)	3.4 (1.9)	2.5 (1.5)	1.8 (1.5)	2.2 (1.3)	2 (1)	1 (0)	
Spain	%	19.4	10.4	6.3	22.8	10.4	5.6	14.6	7.8	2.6	100.0
	M(SD)	3.5 (2.1)	2.2 (1.3)	1.9 (1.4)	3.4 (2.2)	2.5 (1.4)	1.7 (1.1)	3.3 (2.5)	2.1 (1.6)	1.8 (.9)	
Mexico	%	30.2	12.4	8.5	13.2	9.3	3.9	16.3	5.4	0.8	100.0
	M(SD)	4.3 (2.9)	2.3 (1.5)	2.2 (1.3)	2.4 (1.1)	1.5 (.8)	1.3 (.5)	2.6 (1.5)	1.4 (.5)	1.0 (0)	

Table 6.5 Mean Top 5 contacts, by language (standard deviations)

	L1	L2	L1-L2 mixture
Insojourn 1			
France	2.3 (1.5)	1.2 (0.9)	1.4 (1.4)
Spain	1.8 (1.2)	1.9 (1.3)	1.1 (1.1)
Mexico	2.0 (1.0)	1.9 (1.5)	1.1 (0.8)
Insojourn 2			
France	2.1 (1.6)	1.5 (1.5)	1.3 (1.4)
Spain	1.8 (1.4)	2.0 (1.1)	1.1 (0.9)
Mexico	2.0 (1.4)	1.0 (1.0)	2.0 (1.4)
Insojourn 3			
France	2.6 (1.7)	1.2 (1.3)	1.0 (1.4)
Spain	2.1 (1.3)	1.8 (1.2)	0.9 (0.9)
Mexico	2.0 (1.7)	1.6 (1.1)	1.4 (1.0)

list provided evidence for network intensity (Dewey et al., 2013) by identifying active relationships with close friends, romantic partners, and family members. Table 6.5 shows group means for these intensive relationships conducted in L1, L2 or mixed mode, from Insojourn 1 to Insojourn 3.

Table 6.5 suggests that at each survey point, there was considerable stability in the make-up of the most intensive relationships across all country groups, in terms of the languages used. Throughout the sojourn, around two in five of the Top 5 across the whole cohort were L1 users, and around three in five were L2 or mixed-language users. The only exception was the French group, where the proportion of L1 users was slightly higher at Insojourn 1 and Insojourn 3. This general finding reflects the reality of bilingual/multilingual practices, throughout the sojourn.

6.2.4 Two Social Networking Indices

Our final quantitative analyses summarize main dimensions of the social networking data in two Social Network Indices (SNIs), one for L2-using network contacts and the other for L1-using contacts. In constructing these SNIs, we followed the broad approach of Milroy (1980, 1987), who used social networks as an analytic tool to explain patterns of linguistic behaviour, in the context of Belfast, Northern Ireland. Milroy constructed a 6-point Network Strength Scale to measure participants' degree of integration into the community. This scale was based on how far an individual fulfilled the following conditions:

1. Membership of a high-density, territorially based cluster;
2. Having substantial ties of kinship in the neighbourhood;
3. Working at the same place as at least *two* others from the same area;
4. Having the same place of work as at least two others of the same sex from the area;
5. Voluntary association with workmates in leisure hours.

140 Social networks and social relationships

Here, Condition 1 is an indicator of density, and Conditions 2–5 are indicators of multiplexity. As Milroy notes, "the scale is capable of differentiating individuals quite sharply. Scores range from zero for someone who fulfils none of the conditions (although zero is rare), to five for several informants who fulfil them all" (Milroy, 1980, pp. 142–143).

To summarize our own participants' degree of integration, we designed scales appropriate to the temporary sojourner context, taking account of 1) network size, 2) strength of network ties, 3) multiplexity and 4) intensity (Top 5). The criteria for our L2 Social Network Index (SNIL2) were:

1. Having at least two people from place of work/study with L2/mixed interaction;
2. Having at least two strong L2 ties;
3. Having at least three ties with L2/mixed interaction in any free time context (organized and/or general);
4. Having at least one L2/mixed tie in two different contexts (excluding home life);
5. Having at least three people from Top 5 with L2 interaction.

The criteria for the L1 Social Network Index (SNIL1) were:

1. Having at least two people from place of work/study with L1 interaction;
2. Having at least two strong L1 ties;
3. Having at least three ties with L1 interaction in free time contexts;
4. Having at least one L1 tie in two different contexts (excluding home life);
5. Having at least three people from Top 5 with L1 interaction.

In sum, our SNIs integrate the extent to which L1- and L2-using contacts are established in different contexts, and the extent to which the same contacts appear across different contexts, as well as information about frequency of interaction with those contacts. Here, we present overviews of the SNI information for L2 and for L1, organized by country group and by survey point. Tables 6.6 (SNIL2) and 6.7 (SNIL1) show group mean scores for each criterion (maximum score = 1) as well as a group mean SNI score (maximum score = 5).

For SNIL2, all groups easily satisfied Criterion 1 (at least two contacts at work/university with L2 or mixed interaction) throughout the sojourn. For Criterion 2 (two strong L2 contacts) and Criterion 3 (three contacts in free time with L2 or mixed interaction), scores for the France group were moderate throughout, while the Spain and Mexico groups scored highly. On Criterion 4 (multiplexity, i.e., the same L2 contacts are encountered in different contexts), only the Mexico group scored highly throughout. Finally, on Criterion 5 (intensity, i.e., 3 or more L2-using contacts named among the Top 5), no group scored strongly (though the France group mean score did rise from a very low starting point). The overall SNIL2 mean scores shown in the Total column reinforce earlier evidence

Social networks and social relationships 141

for a gradient in the strength of L2-using social networks, with the France group consistently the lowest, and the Mexico group the highest at Insojourn 2 and Insojourn 3.

Table 6.7 provides an overview of the strength of L1-using networks across the three groups. This table shows that all groups regardless of location sustained a regular commitment to L1 networking. However, comparison of Tables 6.6 and 6.7 also shows that that SNIL1 mean scores were somewhat below SNIL2 scores throughout; that is, L1 networking was sustained alongside active L2 networking. The most notable between-group differences apparent in Table 6.7 are the relatively high Mexico score for Criterion 1 (reflecting their workplace role as

Table 6.6 Group scores for L2 Social Network Index (SNIL2)

		Criterion 1	Criterion 2	Criterion 3	Criterion 4	Criterion 5	Group mean SNIL2
Insojourn 1							
France	M (SD)	1.00 (.00)	.62 (.49)	.48 (.51)	.48 (.51)	.03 (.19)	2.6 (1.1)
Spain	M (SD)	1.00 (.00)	.89 (.32)	1.00 (.00)	.61 (.50)	.44 (.51)	3.9 (1.1)
Mexico	M (SD)	1.00 (.00)	.89 (.33)	1.00 (.00)	.78 (.44)	.22 (.44)	3.9 (0.8)
Insojourn 2							
France	M (SD)	.89 (.31)	.45 (.51)	.55 (.51)	.48 (.51)	.28 (.45)	2.7 (1.4)
Spain	M (SD)	.78 (.43)	.83 (.38)	.72 (.46)	.33 (.49)	.33 (.49)	3.0 (1.2)
Mexico	M (SD)	1.00 (.00)	.89 (.33)	1.00 (.00)	.89 (.33)	.22 (.44)	4.0 (0.7)
Insojourn 3							
France	M (SD)	.86 (.36)	.54 (.51)	.54 (.51)	.54 (.51)	.18 (.39)	2.6 (1.4)
Spain	M (SD)	.83 (.38)	.72 (.46)	.72 (.46)	.56 (.51)	.28 (.46)	3.1 (1.4)
Mexico	M (SD)	.78 (.44)	1.00 (.00)	.89 (.33)	.78 (.44)	.22 (.44)	3.7 (1.0)

Table 6.7 Group scores for L1 Social Network Index (SNIL1)

		Criterion 1	Criterion 2	Criterion 3	Criterion 4	Criterion 5	Group mean SNIL1
Insojourn 1							
France	M (SD)	.14 (.35)	.79 (.41)	.55 (.51)	.21 (.41)	.55 (.51)	2.2 (1.2)
Spain	M (SD)	.28 (.46)	.67 (.49)	.28 (.46)	.39 (.50)	.33 (.49)	1.9 (1.6)
Mexico	M (SD)	.56 (.53)	.78 (.44)	.33 (.50)	.33 (.50)	.22 (.44)	2.2 (1.2)
Insojourn 2							
France	M (SD)	.24 (.44)	.72 (.46)	.48 (.51)	.45 (.51)	.45 (.51)	2.4 (1.7)
Spain	M (SD)	.39 (.50)	.72 (.46)	.22 (.43)	.50 (.51)	.28 (.46)	2.1 (1.6)
Mexico	M (SD)	.44 (.53)	.56 (.53)	.33 (.50)	.33 (.50)	.22 (.44)	2.2 (2.2)
Insojourn 3							
France	M (SD)	.21 (.41)	.76 (.44)	.52 (.51)	.34 (.48)	.49 (.51)	2.3 (1.6)
Spain	M (SD)	.28 (.46)	.72 (.46)	.28 (.46)	.39 (.50)	.44 (.51)	2.1 (1.8)
Mexico	M (SD)	.56 (.53)	.78 (.44)	.44 (.53)	.56 (.53)	.33 (.50)	2.7 (1.7)

teachers of English), and the relatively high France scores for Criterion 3 and Criterion 5, reflecting higher dependence on L1 contacts during free time and also a relative lack of emotionally significant L2 network contacts.

Overall, our Social Network Index analyses confirm the existence of differences between the groups with regard to L1 and L2 networking. The Spain and Mexico groups appeared to be more successful than the France group in developing L2- and mixed-using contacts outside of the work/university context. In Section 6.3 we examine the insojourn interview data to derive explanations for the development and maintenance of different types of social relations during the sojourn.

6.3 Making and sustaining social relationships during the sojourn

6.3.1 *Presojourn hopes*

In the Presojourn interview, LANGSNAP participants were asked about their hopes and plans for social networking when abroad. Supported by the preparatory course offered by the home university, participants had reflected on the social possibilities of the different placement types, and on strategies for making new friends. While several declared themselves open to varied types of social contacts, most sojourners prioritized making friends with locals of a similar age and life stage to themselves. This was seen as central to accessing the target language skills they valued, and to developing their desired L2 "young sojourner" identity (see Chapter 8). Participants going on student exchanges in France and Spain, and also those going to teach in Mexico, saw access to a student population as a big advantage:

> Pero um pensaba que sería más útil um hablar con los estudiantes de mi edad, de salir con ellos, de merodear con ellos, todo eso um en vez de hablar todos los días con los menores en inglés porque ya puedo hablar inglés
>
> (156/PREQ3).

> [I thought it would be easier to talk to students my age, go out with them, hang around with them, all of that instead of talking everyday with young kids in English because I can already speak English.]

This group hoped to meet local students in class and in student accommodation, as well as through tandem exchanges, student organizations and leisure activities such as sport or music. Some did acknowledge that getting to know locals might not be straightforward. Participant 169 had consulted Erasmus contacts in Home City:

> No me gustaría tener solamente amigos Erasmus. Um pero yo sé que será difícil. Y he hablado con algunos amigos um Erasmus de España que estudian

aquí. Y me han dicho que ehm es un poco difícil. Pero como ellos son amigos con yo puedo hacer amigos españoles también

(169/PREQ7).

[I wouldn't like only having Erasmus friends. But I know that it will be difficult. I've talked to some Erasmus friends from Spain that are studying here. And they've told me that it's a bit difficult. But since they're friends with me, I can make Spanish friends too.]

The language teaching assistants' group going to France or Spain hoped that the teachers they encountered would be friendly, and might also be a source of introductions to younger people. They expected to befriend other language assistants, and again, hoped to meet locals through activities such as music or sports:

Des profs et les familles des profs peut-être, parce que j'espère que tous les profs sont très sympas. Et euh je pense parce que je serai dans une (.) école secondaire, peut-être il serait aussi des autres assistants là aussi peut-être. Mais ça serait très bon

(106/PREQ7).

[Teachers and teachers' families maybe, because I hope the teachers are nice. And I think that because I will be in a secondary school, maybe there will be other assistants there too maybe. But that would be very good.]

Those going to Spain were hopeful of finding Spanish flatmates, and a few of those going to France hoped to do the same. The nine participants going to Mexico knew they would be placed with host families, but were hopeful that these could offer access to young adult networks too:

Porque trabajaría en la universidad y enseñaré a los alumnos y yo estaré cerca de la misma edad de los alumnos espero que me hagan amigos durante las clases, y [. . .] que no hará tan formal como las clases de aquí [. . .]. sí y la familia tiene tres hijos eh uno de diecinueve años, que es mi edad. Y así espero que mi xxx que mi – he olvidado la palabra – pero espero que es un amigo mía

(160/PREQ7).

[Because I will be working in the university and I will teach students, I will be close to the same age as the students, so I hope they'll befriend me during the classes [. . .] that it won't be as formal as the classes here [. . .] Yes and the family has three children, one is 19 years old, which is my age. And I hope that – I forgot the word – but I hope that he becomes my friend.]

144 *Social networks and social relationships*

A few of the eight workplace interns already had local contacts. More generally, they also hoped for flatshares with local people, and for friendly colleagues at work:

> La fille stagiaire qui est dans mon place en ce moment elle a dit que euh je mangerai à la cantine avec des autres stagiaires des autres départements dans l'entreprise. Donc j'espère qu'il y aura des gens sympas là comme ça. Mais à part de ça je ne sais pas trop. Mais j'espère que je vais trouver un logement avec des étudiants français sympas
>
> (128/PREQ7).

[The girl who is an intern there at the moment has said that euh I will eat in the canteen with other interns from other departments in the company. So I hope there will be some nice people around like that. But apart from that I don't really know. But I hope I will find somewhere to live with some friendly French students.]

6.3.2 *Potential for early social contacts: The domestic and leisure domains*

As we have just seen, sojourners' generally preferred option for living was to find a flatshare with local young people, replicating to some extent their experience as British university students. However, this proved to be a straightforward option only for sojourners destined for Spain.

With only one exception, all sojourners in Spain did live in shared apartments, and in 10/17 cases, their flatmates were local students or young professionals. (The others mostly shared apartments with student flatmates of mixed nationalities; only one Spain-based sojourner lived in an all-Anglophone flat.) In France, cheap institutional accommodation was offered to many of the participants, and 11/29 took up the offer. However, almost all of these sojourners found themselves sharing this accommodation with other language assistants or international exchange students. Only three sojourners in France managed to find flatshares with locals, in all cases with young professionals rather than students; only one of these flatshares survived without conflict to the end of the year. A further seven sojourners in France undertook flatshares either with mixed nationality groups or with other Anglophones, and four found studios and lived alone there.

The "homestay", much studied in SA research, was a generally dispreferred option. However, host families were prearranged for the Mexico group, in consultation with their host academic institution. Five others also ended up with host families (one in Spain, four in France), either on the recommendation of their host institution, or because of difficulties in finding flatshares. These host families were typically middle-class professionals; five in Mexico, and two in Europe, were teachers' families, while two others in Europe involved leading local figures in art and culture.

Once a place to live had been found, sojourners had to accomplish a number of practical activities, such as opening a bank account, getting a local mobile phone or internet account, getting a social security number (NIE: Spain) or applying for student housing benefit (CAF: France). These activities provided immediate interests in common with other sojourners and reasons to try to contact them:

> La plupart de ma groupe d'amis ici sont anglais ou irlandais ou britanniques euh ou des Etats Unis euh. Parce que il y a un groupe sur Facebook pour tout les assistants ici qui a été très utile. Parce que la première semaine euh que moi je n'ai pas eu des amis du tout. Et donc c'était très dur de rencontrer les autres gens qui ont dû ouvrir les comptes bancaires et des choses comme ça. Et c'était mieux de faire ça ensemble
>
> (114/V1Q7).

> [Most of my group of friends here are English or Irish or British or from the US euh. Because there is a Facebook group for all the assistants here which has been very useful. Because the first week I did not have any friends at all. And so it was very hard to meet other people who had to open bank accounts and things like that. It was better to do all that together.]

Once the first flurry of settling in was over, however, both exchange students and language assistants realized they had a good deal of leisure time to fill. (This was less true for the workplace interns, who almost all had a full working week.) In many respects they set out to reproduce the leisure activities they were used to in Home City. That is, in the domestic setting, they would cook and eat shared meals; chat and watch TV, films and drama series with housemates; message, Skype or telephone with family and friends in England, or (in a few cases) read novels.

Outside the home setting, sojourners described going for a coffee with friends, going into town perhaps to shop, or doing some form of physical activity (gym, dance classes, running, playing sport or athletics). When spring advanced, sojourners talked about going to the beach, walking in town or the country, and sunbathing in the park. A few joined choirs or undertook other creative activities (pottery, drama, instrumental music); others joined student associations; two spoke about organized religious activities (Bible study). In the evenings, and particularly at weekends, "going out" in groups was considered normal, to restaurants, bars, nightclubs or the cinema:

> Aparte de eso sigo estudiando mucho. xxx cosas normales, hablando con amigos y saliendo un poco. Saliendo por las tardes un poco pa(ra) tomar algo, para ser sociable
>
> (156/V3Q1).

> [Besides that, I keep studying a lot. xxx normal things, talking with friends and going out a bit. Going out in the afternoons a little to drink something, to be social.]

146 *Social networks and social relationships*

All of these activities might be considered extensions, with variations, to the kinds of activities sojourners would engage in as students in Home City. The final, highly popular leisure theme was, however, much more distinctive to a sojourn abroad: the theme of touristic travel, discussed more fully below.

6.3.3 Friendships with international peers

Facebook groups, and introductory events organized by school districts or universities, provided early meeting places where assistants and exchange students could meet up with their peers (if not living with them already). These meetings led to the formation of enduring relationships, which provided friendship and social support for many participants throughout the year. In France and Spain, only two assistants described their social life without any reference to other assistants:

> La verdad es que solo conozco a los profesores probablemente. Sí [. . .] y también mis amigas ingleses y americanas que conozco que también son auxiliares de conversación. [. . .] Um Claire y Donna les conocí cuando fuimos a City SJ para el curso introductorio
>
> (151/V1Q7).

[The truth is that I only know the teachers probably. Yes [. . .] and also my English and American friends that I know that are also teaching assistants. Claire and Donna I met when we went to City SJ for an introductory course.]

Similarly for exchange students in France and Spain, the overwhelming majority talked about other Erasmus students as part of their domestic and leisure network:

> Normalement on regarde ensemble toutes ensemble avec les autres Erasmus euh une film français les soirées um après une dîner ensemble quelquefois. Normalement moi et 107 on mange toujours ensemble. Mais normalement, plusieurs fois trois ou quatre fois à chaque semaine, on mange avec les autres Erasmus. Normalement c'est ici en fait. Et euh on essaie inviter des autres étudiants français
>
> (112/V1Q3).

[Usually we watch together, all together with the other Erasmus, a French film in the evening, after having dinner together sometimes. Usually myself and 107, we always eat together. But usually, several times three or four times each week, we eat with the other Erasmus. It is usually here in fact [in own apartment]. And euh we try to invite other French students.]

Student and assistant sojourners explained the prominence of other sojourners in their personal networks on several grounds. Firstly, they were passing through shared circumstances of upheaval and arrival, and the emotional support offered by other sojourners was helpful. Many also found the international mix among

Erasmus students in France and Spain positive in itself, and appreciated the opportunities offered for intercultural exchange:

> Je pense que ça c'était une des plus euh les choses les plus enrichissants de cette année. C'est que on a dans le groupe des amis les gens de tout le monde (111/V3Q4).

> [I think that was one of the most enriching things about this year. It's that we have in our group, some friends who are from all over the world.]

Thirdly, sojourners acknowledged that their way of life was anyhow somewhat different from that of local peers, who often went home at weekends. These issues, which predisposed student and assistant sojourners toward international friendships and made breaking into local friendship groups more challenging, were summed up by participant 156:

*156: Bueno la mayoría son de Erasmus. son alemanes o como franceses o (.) pues son todos muy (.) todos quieren aprender español. Pues no hablan nada salvo español, y sí todos muy agradables [. . .] La gente que están de aquí también pues te ayuda mucho porque saben que no sabes nada como (.) y también la mayoría hablan o aprenden inglés pues quieren ser amigos contigo para que aprovechen de tu inglés también.
[Well the majority are Erasmus. They're Germans or French they're all very (.) all want to learn Spanish. So they don't speak anything but Spanish and all are really nice. [. . .] The people that are here too they help a lot because they know that you don't know anything like (.) and also the majority speak or are learning English so they want to be friends with you so that they can take advantage of your English too.]
*NTV: Y a veces sales con ellos los fines de semana?
[And do you sometimes go out with them on the weekends?]
*156: Sí bueno intentaba unas veces. Pero también salen mis amigos de Erasmus. pues hablo con ellos la mayoría porque ya les conozco. Y con los españoles normalmente en la universidad porque allí tenemos que hablar.
[Yes well I tried a few times. But my Erasmus friends go out too. I mostly talk with them because I already know them. And with the Spaniards normally at the university because there we have to speak.]
*NTV: No se mezclan mucho los grupos?
[The groups don't mix much?]
*156: Mmm no de verdad no. No mucho porque – no sé. Los grupos aquí de españoles ya son hechos. xx ya tiene amigos. Ya tienen su grupo. Y es bastante fijado. Y por los fines de semana la mayoría de la gente que va a la Uni son de pueblos fuera de City SC. O sea cerca pero no viven en City SC. Van a sus casa con sus padres los fines de semana. O si tienen un día libre o (.) pues por eso la mayoría de los fines de semana no puedo salir con ellos porque no están. Sí. Pero sí hablamos mucho. Y tengo intercamb – eh tandems y todo.

Pues hablo bastante español con españoles en vez de con español alemán o español

(156/V1Q7).

[No, honestly no. Not much because – I don't know. The Spanish groups here are already established. They already have friends. They have their group and it's rather set. And on the weekends the majority of the people that go to the university are from towns outside of City SC, close, but they don't live in City SC. They go to their family home on the weekends. Or if they have a day free or (.) for that reason the majority of the weekends I can't go out with them because they're not here. Yeah, but we do talk a lot. And I have exchanges – eh tandems and things. So I talk quite a lot of Spanish with Spaniards instead of German Spanish or Spanish.]

Finally, sojourners' enthusiasm for travel at weekends and in other breaks also shaped their social networks, and affected the extent of local integration. Touristic trips to other cities and regions were seen as a positive cultural feature of the sojourn; only four sojourners from among all assistants and exchange students in France and Spain made no mention of such trips. Touristic travel was normally undertaken with other sojourners, or sometimes with visiting family members, and might take place locally, or involve a visit to other Home City sojourners in more distant locations:

*110: Ou si c'est un mercredi parce que l'après-midi c'est libre, donc euh on va dans une autre euh ville qui est proche de City FC et qui est bon, parce qu'il y a plein de petits villes à côté. Donc de temps en temps on visite euh une petite ville qui est proche en bus ou en train euh ça c'est bon oui.
[Or if it is Wednesday because the afternoon is free, then euh we go to another euh town which is close to City FC and which is good, because there are a lot of little towns nearby. So from time to time we visit a little town nearby by bus or by train, euh that is good yeah.]
*JS: Il s'agit de quelles sortes de villes, qu'est-ce-que vous faites dans ces villes?
[What kind of towns, what do you do in these towns?]
*110: Hum seulement visiter hum voir les structures les monuments ce qui est typique de ces villes. Euh nous allons euh hum à une petit bar ou café euh (110/V2Q4).
[Hum just visit, see the buildings and the monuments, whatever is typical. And we go to a little bar or a café euh.]

A después la navidad, en enero, um yo fui a París con 161, quien está en City SM. Y um nos encontramos nuestras otras amigas quienes um están en Francia este año. Encontramos y hicimos todas las cosas turísticas en París

(151/V2Q1).

[And after Christmas, in January, um I went to Paris with 161, who's in City SM, and um we met up with our other friends who are in France this year. We met up and we did lots of touristy things in Paris.]

Such travel obviously reinforced contacts among sojourners, and reduced somewhat the opportunities for networking beyond this social group.

The sojourners in Mexico were undertaking their language assistantships under very different conditions, mostly in contexts with far fewer other foreigners, and where security was sometimes an issue, though in practice their leisure activities broadly resembled those of sojourners in Europe (including sport and visits to the beach, and evenings out in restaurants and bars). Several were working in pairs in particular institutions, and some lived together with the same host family (155 and 175, 157 and 177). Sojourners 162 and 178 lived with different host families in the same city, and were often together. Most of this subgroup reported close friendships throughout the sojourn, including mutual long-distance visiting and other leisure/cultural travel:

*AMM: Con quién pasas la mayor parte de tu tiempo?
[With whom do you spend the majority of your time?]
*155: Uh pues con 175 creo porque vivíamos juntos y fuimos a la escuela juntos (V3Q4).
[Uh well with 175 I think because we were living together and we were at the school together.]

This closeness was acknowledged by 157 to be problematic, in terms of integration with Mexican contacts:

*AMM: Um con quién pasas la mayor parte de tu tiempo?
[With whom do you spend the majority of your time?]
*157: Con las chicas [177 and another Home City sojourner]. Sí. Sí. Es difícil porque quiero practicar un poco platicar con la gente y hablar un poco más. Pero es difícil porque siempre tengo dos inglesas (V3Q4).
[With the girls [177 and another Home City sojourner]. Yeah, yeah, it's difficult because I want to practice a little, chat with people and speak a bit more. But it's difficult because I always have two English girls there.]

On the other hand, very unlike participants in Europe, only three people in Mexico mentioned finding new Anglophone friends other than those from Home City.

The experiences of the workplace interns were the most diverse. Three of these in France lived alone in studio flats (116, 125 and 128); both working sojourners in Spain, plus one in France, shared accommodation with locals (100 and 150) or a mixed group including locals (158); and the remaining two both lived with international students, one in a residence (102) and one in a flatshare (124). When at work, only 124 (in a provincial French town) worked with local colleagues only. Both 116 and 158 were teaching English, and were thus in contact with other English teachers or language assistants at work; 150 worked for different small mixed-nationality firms in Madrid; the rest were based in two large international organizations, with numbers of Anglophone interns, and other international staff. In these settings, the interns stuck together:

> Cette stagiaire et tous les autres c'est des CDI [contrat à durée indéterminée]. [. . .]. Elle mangerait toujours toute seule. Donc elle vient toujours manger

avec nous. Donc elle est carrément à deux mètres de nous hein. C'est le même bureau, on est le même étage. Donc on commence à connaître assez bien toutes ces personnes là

(100/V1Q7).

[This intern and all the others are on short-term contracts [. . .]. She would always eat by herself. So she always comes to eat with us. So she is really just two metres away from us. It is the same office, on the same floor. So we are getting to know all these people pretty well.]

Thus all of the working sojourners had access to potential English/international networks, either through their home setup or else through the workplace. Most of them were also based in big cities, with many leisure options, including potential contact with other Home City sojourners. However, as a group they undertook little touristic travel; only 116 found the time for a ski trip (with family), and a visit to Paris from her provincial French city. These conditions led to the development of quite diverse social networks.

Four of the workplace interns in France started the year by developing a supportive network of Anglophone intern friends. Sojourners 116 and 125 continued to spend much of their leisure time in these groups throughout the year, but 102 and 128 started romantic relationships with French male partners, which reduced the time spent with a wider group. Sojourner 124 also associated with international sojourners throughout the year, though in her case these were exchange students and assistants. Sojourner 100 associated with other interns during work hours, but spent most of his leisure time with his French relatives (with whom he lived). In Spain, 150 was active in several separate social networks, including an English-medium network centring on a sporting club, and a Spanish-medium network centring on her former au pair family. The life of 158 centred largely round two poles: her apartment and the language school where she worked, where her closest friend was another English teacher.

6.3.4 Friendships with local peers

The sojourners were in no doubt that networking with local peers was central to the success of their stay abroad. When asked at Insojourn 3 about the most important influences on their L2 development, almost all of them put local relationships at the top of the list. But how did sojourners achieve this strongly desired goal?

The first option was to try to build networks in a domestic setting. As we saw in the last section, at the start of the year, 13 sojourners were living in flats with local people only (10 of these in Spain, and three in France); a further six were living in mixed flats, including at least one local person. Altogether, 14 sojourners were living with host families, and four of these included at least one similar-aged young person.

Of those sojourners living in a flatshare with at least some locals, a majority reported at Insojourn 1 that flatmates were friendly, chatted with them in the flat, and might eat with them there. In later interviews, a number reported increasing intimacy with local flatmates; thus, for example, seven sojourners in Spain reported that they spent most leisure time with one or more flatmates, and four reported that they had been invited to a flatmate's home town and met family members there. Our data did not allow detailed capture of how these friendships got started, except in rather general retrospective accounts, where "luck" was prominent:

> I think my year has been so good because I was really lucky. I found that flat with Lucía [Spanish young professional] after two days. Then I met Claire and Donna the two English girls after a couple of days because we had an [assistants'] induction day in City SJ, and then our group just kind of fell into place. Everyone met each other and then everybody liked each other and everybody liked hanging out together and everybody made friends and it was just luck. It was really strange just how well everything has been going
> (151/RI).

*152: Obviously I was really lucky to get on with certainly one of my Spanish flatmates as well, and she is really friendly and stuff, so she introduced me to all of her groups and stuff, and yeah because they are mainly Spanish and seeing the Spanish side of things as well, it's just definitely the best part and the luckiest part.
*NTV: So she is one particular person that you think has made a difference?
*152: Yeah (152/RI).

A sketch of increasing domestic intimacy with local flatmates was offered by 172:

> Entonces estoy en casa más que antes. Y (.) no sé qué hacemos. Pero tienen más deberes que yo. Y hacen muchas cosas así uh en casa. Y después comemos juntas. Veamos la tele o una película. Pero una, mi compañera que se llama Malena no puede ver una película entera sin dormir. [laugh] Normalmente es solo Mariangela y yo que estamos en el salón
> (172/V2Q5).

[Now I'm at home more than before. And I don't know what we do. But they have more homework than I do. And they do many things at home. And after we eat together. We watch the telly or a film. But one, my flatmate called Malena, can't watch an entire film without falling asleep. [laugh] Normally it's only Mariangela and I that are in the living room.]

Not all flatshares led to positive networking, however. The male exchange student 156 began a flatshare with local female students, but he did not find them friendly, and had found other, more sociable flatmates by Insojourn 3. Some of the flatshares were with local young professionals rather than with students. These might lead to strong friendships (as for 151), but those few flatshares which broke down dramatically were all of this type (and incidentally involved mixed-gender groups).

For exchange student sojourners, the university campus was another key potential source of local networks. Shared courses offered one entry point:

*168: Y también en la univercidad@n cuando ehm hacemos trabajo en grupos está bien porque [. . .] trabajo con uh estudiantes españoles que está muy bien porque tienen que hablar conmigo. [. . .] Sí. Uh he encontrado mucha gente. [And also in the university when ehm we do group work it's good because [. . .] I work with Spanish students and that's really good because they have to talk with me [. . .] yeah, uh I've met many people.]
*NTV: Y has salido con ellos?
[And have you gone out with them?]
*168: [. . .] Sí. Solo para tapas pero sí (V1Q7).
[Yes. Only for tapas but yeah.]

When classes were small, it was also easier to get to know classmates:

Et après en italien on est quatre filles. Il y a une Ecuadorienne et les autres sont Françaises. Elles sont très gentilles. Et puisqu'on est quatre seulement on s'est oui euh connu assez bien euh oui

(126/V2Q5).

[And after that, in Italian there are four girls. There is one from Ecuador and the others are French. They are very nice. And because we are only four we have got to know each other quite well euh yeah.]

In Mexico, 177 found not only good friends on campus, but also a boyfriend in class:

*177: Tenemos dos amigos muy muy muy buenos de la uni MC que se llaman um Lisa y Manuel. Y sí. siempre que podamos hacemos cosas con ellos. Pero últimamente han estado muy ocupados con sus exámenes al final del año, con sus proyectos finales.
[We have two very very very good friends from uni MC that are called Lisa and Manuel. And yeah. Whenever we can we do things with them. But lately they've been very busy with their final exams, with their final projects.]
*AMM: Y su novio es mexicano?
[And your boyfriend is Mexican?]
*177: Sí sí sí. Es de mi clase de portugués (V3Q4).
[Yes, yes, yes. He's from my Portuguese class.]

However, as the above quote suggests, the rhythm of classroom friendships could be affected by differences in study patterns:

*KMcM: Et tu passes la plupart du temps avec qui?
[And you spend most time with whom?]
*121: Euh avec mes colocataires euh parce qu'elles sont euh aussi des Erasmus. Parce que les étudiants français euh n'ont pas le temps de – parce qu'ils ont beaucoup de cours plus que les Erasmus. Euh par exemple les étudiants français a sept heures ou huit heures de cours par jour mais moi j'ai (.) trois heures quatre heures (121/V2Q5).
[Euh with my flatmates because they are Erasmus as well. Because the French students don't have the time – because they have lots more courses than the Erasmus. Euh for example the French students have seven hours or eight hours of classes every day but I have (.) three hours four hours.]

The tandem language exchange was another important route to local peer networking adopted by many student and assistant sojourners. The structured tandem exchange has an instrumental aspect (an hour of my English for an hour of your French/Spanish), but obviously flourished best where partners found interests in common. Sojourner 156 explained how he used a tandem partnership as a way of entering a friendship group:

*NTV: And what experiences do you think have been the most beneficial in your Spanish learning here?
*156: Euh attaching myself to a group of Spanish people I think, just that just that in itself just gives you a lot more opportunity to speak Spanish, listen to Spanish, have people to talk in Spanish at you, ehm see films, watch telly together, just general discussions and stuff.
*NTV: How did you get that group of friends?
*156: They're in a class of mine actually, and one of them euh became a tandem friend, and then he was already in a group. So I kind of went out with, he invited me along to an event and then everybody else was there and from there it – But yeah just being in a group of Spanish people, you either speak Spanish or you don't speak, so.
*NTV: So you told me you were the one that initiated the tandem.
*156: Yeah.
*NTV: So you took a risk right?
*156: I took a – well I mean I was pretty sure that he'd say "yes" because he learns English so who turns down that opportunity to speak? I think if I was in England I wouldn't turn down an opportunity to speak Spanish. So I guess it was a risk in some ways, but it was calculated (RIQ2).

A small number of sojourners also participated in student associations and campus volunteering activities, which in some cases led to extensions of their social networks. A few sojourners with serious interests in music and sport found that these gave access to intensive local networks. Sojourner 129 described making her first musical contact, in the kitchen of her student residence:

> Un des premiers gens que j'ai rencontré euh un Français qui s'appelle André. Il habite sur mon étage. Euh à ce point là je connais personne. Euh j'étais dans ma chambre. C'était le deuxième jour. J'étais un peu isolée, j'étais un peu triste de n'être pas en Angleterre. Et donc j'ai pensé que xxx "je vais me s'asseoir dans la cuisine et je vais attendre quelqu'un". Donc j'ai attendu et André est entré et j'ai dit "Tu t'appelles comment? Qu'est-ce-que tu fais?" Ehm ehm j'ai découvert que on aime les deux la musique. Il joue de la guitare, je joue de la clarinette. Donc on a joué ensemble un peu. Maintenant on est amis. Euh le jour après on est allé en centre avec quelques de ses amis qui étaient Français aussi pour jouer la musique dans un pub irlandais
> (129/V1Q1).

> [One of the first people I have met euh a French guy called André. He lives on my floor. And at this point I don't know anyone. Euh I was in my room. It was the second day. I was a bit lonely, I was a bit sad not to be in England. And so I thought xxx "I am going to sit in the kitchen and wait for someone". So I waited and André came in and I said, "What is your name? What do you do?" Ehm I found out that we both like music. He plays guitar and I play clarinet. So we played together a bit. Now we are friends. And the next day we went into the centre with some of his French friends to play music in an Irish pub.]

Two female sojourners (108 and 167) sought out local sporting clubs and became heavily involved throughout the year, training several evenings a week as well as taking part in regular competitions. Unsurprisingly, these individuals became very strongly networked with fellow club members and spent much informal leisure time with them also. The engagement of 167 with her team was evident in her account of a recent basketball game:

> Y yo creo que las chicas son muy – me incluyen en todo. Y [. . .] no me olvidan. Y eso (.) a mí me gusta. Es como (.) fuimos a un partido hace dos semanas. Y uh nuestro entrenador no pudo venir. Entonces estábamos solas las chicas. Y yo como soy la viejita del equipo y yo tenía que hacer un poco como el entrenador, un poco decir quién tiene que hacer qué, dónde jugamos, si hacemos presión, o si hacemos defensa en zona. Y he intentando pues [?] animar un poco las chicas porque a veces estamos todo el tiempo perdiendo. Es que las chicas no quieren jugar. No tienen ganas. Pero este partido fue el mejor partido de todo el año, de todo el año porque hemos jugado muy muy bien muy bien. [. . .] Eh todas las chicas me han dicho que – sabes? "Mejor que hay alguien que anima"
> (167/V2Q11).

[And I think that the girls are very – they include me in everything. And [. . .] they don't forget me. And this, I like it. It's like (.) we went to a game two weeks ago. And our coach couldn't come. So us girls were alone. And since I'm the oldest on the team, I had to do a bit of the coaching, a little telling them who had to do what, where to play, if we create pressure, or if we play defensively. And I tried well to liven them up some because sometimes, we're always losing. So then the girls don't want to play. They don't feel like it. But this game was the best game of the entire year, of the entire year because we played very very well [. . .] all the girls told me – you know, "Better that there's someone who inspires us".]

Informal rugby or football, running, and gym visits were all cited by other individuals as sources of local acquaintances of varying closeness. Creative and artistic activities (pottery, drama, choir), as well as regular visits to local bars, led in some cases to local acquaintanceships as well.

Finally, a few participants were introduced to local peers by host families, by other mentors or by international friends. For example, participant 105 (assistant) sought her school mentor's help in meeting local students, and got some introductions, which eventually led to a flatshare and friendship with a local student. Another assistant, 120, managed to meet local students by attending some classes at a nearby university, and assistant 101 was introduced to local students by another sojourner. In Mexico, participant 162 described the son of his host family as his "Mexican brother":

Mmm creo que no hay nada más una persona con que [?] paso como la mayoría del tiempo. Pero en el trabajo la mayoría paso con A, mi supervisor. Y en la casa normalmente estoy con Damián porque es de mi edad. Tenemos como muchos intereses en común. Y por eso nos llevamos muy bien

(162/V2Q5).

[I don't think there's just one person with whom I spent the majority of my time. But at work, I spent most of the time with A, my supervisor. And at home normally I'm with Damián because he's my age. We have many common interests. And that's why we get along really well.]

Sojourners might eventually belong to several separate local peer networks:

La mayor parte del tiempo sería con mi compañera de piso que se llama Paula y con compañeras de clase también, por ejemplo Edaline o uh Caridad o María. Porque depende de si estoy en mi piso o en la universidad

(152/V3Q4).

[The majority of the time I'd be with my flatmate whose called Paula and with my classmates too, for example Edaline or Caridad or Maria. Because it depends on whether I'm at my flat or at the university.]

> Euh ça dépend ça vraiment dépend c'est difficile à dire parce que (.) c'est comme, au foyer je suis avec mes amies qui habitent au foyer. Donc je mange avec mes amies là. Mais par contre euh en centre ville hum j'aime bien sortir avec les étudiantes comme j'ai ces amies hum. Mais aussi j'ai les amis au collège, euh les amis avec qui je travaille au collège. Donc parfois je vois ces amis, c'est difficile à dire
>
> (101/V3Q4).

> [Euh well it depends it really depends it is hard to say because (.) it is like, at the residence I am with my friends who live at the residence. So I eat with my friends there. But on the other hand in town hum I like going out with the students, like I have these friends hum. But also I have friends at the school euh the friends I am working with at the school. So sometimes I see those friends, it is hard to say.]

When with these local networks, sojourners generally undertook similar activities to those undertaken with international peers. The exception was touristic travel, which almost always took place with international peers, or family/friends from England. Any travel carried out with local friends normally involved visits to family, or local events such as festivals.

6.3.5 Informal social relations with other age groups

In this section we explore sojourner relations with other age groups than their own. A key site for this was the host family, even though this was not the preferred lifestyle choice of most sojourners. We have already seen how 162 developed close relations with adult members of his host family. The remainder of the Mexican group mostly kept on good terms with their hosts, who most often were teachers (and sometimes connected with their institution). However, relations did not appear especially close. One problematic issue for sojourners was the preference of some teacher hosts for speaking English, while another was the suburban location of most homes. However, the main issue was a feeling of lacking personal independence, expressed even by 162:

> Me ha gustado mucho vivir con una familia. Pero si tuviera otra oportunidad, tal vez porque ya haya experimentado vivir con una familia, me gustaría ver algo diferente, no? Tener más indepencia. Tengo mucha independencia con esta familia. Pero (.) de todos modos es diferente vivir solo con amigos, no? Y si pudiera – o aún si fuera a quedar otro año creo que me mudaría
>
> (162/V2Q12).

> [I've really enjoyed living with a family. But if I had another opportunity, maybe because I've already experienced living with a family, I would like to so something different, no? Have more independence. I have a lot of

independence with this family. But (.) anyway it's different living with friends, no? And if I could – or if I were to stay another year, I think I would move.]

Three sojourners did move out: 171 to a house shared with same-aged peers, and 157 and 177 to their own apartment. By Insojourn 2, 160 was spending most of his time at his local girlfriend's family home. There was only one overt disagreement with a host family, however: 155 and 175 reported that visitors were barred from their shared house, following a party.

The few homestays in Europe (n=6), undertaken with greater freedom of choice than those in Mexico, showed stronger cross-generational links. Intern 100 lived by choice with relatives outside Paris. Intern 150 sought out her former au pair family, for regular contact and support during her time in Madrid, and finally moved in with them for a short time before returning home. Exchange student 104 had sought a flatshare, but ended up living with the cultural director of the local city, his wife and daughter, and another lodger. This family involved him in all family meals and social occasions, invited him to cultural events and supported his interest in studying music; he reported a positive relationship with his male host in particular. The three assistants undertaking homestays also liked the families and engaged in social activities with them. (One of these, 173, is the subject of a case study in Chapter 9.)

Eighteen sojourners (mostly language assistants) also reported at some point that they were undertaking private tutoring in English. For a few, this was also a route to friendship with further families:

> I taught a few tutorials euh tutees. Ehm one family was in English and I spoke with them in English all the time, so it wasn't fantastic for my French, although they are always willing to help with the problems I have, which is nice ehm. But the other one was a little girl I taught for two hours every week, but I had to be driven to her house. So [. . .] when I first met this family, "Oh do you – how much do you want to get paid?" "I don't know, I don't care, I just want to be part of a family!" And one of my friends told me I was being a bit silly [. . .] but they really took to heart what I said, and they let me be part of their family. I spoke to them for at least an hour every time in French, car journeys, and then we would have tea and cake afterwards, they would send me pictures of their family, talk about their English side of their family, all in French with the mum. I became friends with this little girl's big brother who took me on a few nights out with all of his French friends, bought us lots of drinks and spoke loads and loads in French. So I think making friends with that family was possibly the best thing I've ever done
>
> (106/V3RI).

Six assistant sojourners reported friendships with teacher colleagues which extended outside the working day, including invitations for home dinners, as well

158 *Social networks and social relationships*

as evenings out. A contact like this helped 119, who had struggled with establishing worthwhile peer relationships, to feel more settled:

> Je n'ai pas voyagé beaucoup pendant les dernières deux mois. En fait j'ai décidé que je voudrais rester et profiter de City FB, les choses que je peux faire là-bas. Euh je mange le dîner avec une professeur euh euh chaque semaine hum et sa fille, euh oui ça c'est bien. Donc j'ai oui je pense que alors je suis plus bien intégrée euh qu'avant, je suis plus contente pour ça oui
>
> (119/V3Q3).

> [I have not travelled much for the past two months. In fact I decided that I would like to stay put and enjoy City FB, the things I can do there. Euh I am eating dinner with a teacher every week hum and her daughter, yeah that is good. So I yeah I think that now I am much better integrated than before, I am happier because of that, yeah.]

Almost all sojourner interns developed good social relations with their workplace colleagues, joining them for regular lunch breaks and coffee breaks. In a minority of cases only, this extended to social activities outside work:

> Eh tengo esos nuevos amigos del trabajo eh con los que juego paddle. Son muy majos. Son cinco hombres españoles. Vienen de Zaragoza de Madrid de Barcelona. Y llevamos muy bien. Y me enseñan muchas frases eh colocualis@n
>
> (150/V1Q7).

> [I have these new friends from work with whom I play paddle. They're really cool. They're five Spanish guys. They're from Zaragoza, Madrid, Barcelona. And we get along really well. And they teach me many colloquial phrases.]

We have already noticed the older mentors met through flatshares by a few sojourners, and the serious sports practitioners developed strong relationships with older club staff as well as with fellow team members. Through her interest in folk music, 129 networked exceptionally widely. She gave an example of an all-night music session:

> J'ai un ami qui a une péniche ehm. [. . .] Et de temps en temps il fait les sessions musicales dans le péniche, euh c'était magnifique. On a joué toute la nuit euh um à côté du feu ehm. C'était euh un péniche qu'il euh vient de rénover, donc c'était comme quelque chose de l'histoire de euh *le Hobbit*. On a joué jusqu'à cinq heures le matin. C'était magnifique. [. . .] Et c'était génial parce-qu'il y avait les gens de toutes âges, de toutes modes de vie, euh des jeunes et des vieux, des jeunes, euh des gens entre les deux
>
> (129/V3Q4).

> [I have a friend who has a barge ehm [. . .] And from time to time he has musical sessions on the barge, it was wonderful. We played all night euh

beside the fire ehm. It was a barge that he has just done up, so it was like something out of the story of The Hobbit. We played until five in the morning. It was wonderful. [. . .] And it was great because there were people of all ages, of all walks of life, euh young and old people, young people, euh people in between.]

Two sojourners specifically mentioned relationships with the elderly, as when 113 described her busy upcoming weekend:

Euh demain oh je vais voir des amis euh à City FN2 pour parler oui. [. . .] Mais ils sont âgés, très âgés, j'ai rencontré quand j'ai fait des recherches pour mon projet. Et – mais ils sont très gentils. Alors je vais aller au piscine. Et dimanche je ferai un cours du cardio au centre boxe thaï. L'élève qui j'enseigne le mercredi j'enseigne aussi le dimanche. Et puis je mange le repas avec sa famille

(113/V2Q2).

[Euh tomorrow I am going to see friends at City FN2 for a chat yes. [. . .] But they are old, very old, I met [them] when I did research for my project. And – but they are very nice. Then I will go to the swimming pool. And on Sunday I will do a class at the Thai boxing centre. The pupil I teach on Wednesdays I teach as well on Sundays. And then I eat a meal with their family.]

6.3.6 Gender and romantic partnerships

In the home culture, British students expect to have active and equal friendships with both sexes, and to undertake many activities in mixed-sex groups (Finn, 2013). In addition, many are sexually active, usually within the context of a committed relationship, though short-term sexual encounters are also not uncommon (Arnett, 2014). It seemed that sojourners generally expected that relations with the opposite sex would work similarly, at least as far as same-aged student peers were concerned. While some women did find themselves exposed to rather more street harassment abroad than they were used to at home, sojourners generally seemed able to manage gendered relationships with confidence.

Concerning the development of romantic partnerships, however, we have only limited evidence from the LANGSNAP interviews. It is likely that not all emotional relationships were disclosed, especially short-term ones. Nonetheless, a number of participants did speak about committed relationships with opposite-sex partners, and here we explore the implications for their social and linguistic integration insojourn. (No sojourner spoke about a same-sex partnership.)

Three of the 10 male sojourners in the cohort spoke about long-term English girlfriends and described how they kept in touch during the sojourn. It seemed sojourners 161 and 170 were already partners before they both went to Spain, and they sustained the relationship throughout the sojourn. When in his Spanish city, 170 spent his leisure time with a circle of male friends; at weekends he regularly visited 161 in her (different) city, or else travelled with her to visit other Spanish cities and regions. Sojourners 156 and 175, on the other hand, sustained relationships with girlfriends based in England throughout the sojourn. The girlfriend of 175 visited him in Mexico twice, once for Christmas and once for a lengthy Easter vacation trip. This English girlfriend did not know Spanish, so the first visit to his Mexican base was socially somewhat awkward, illustrating some of the difficulties of trying to merge home and insojourn networks:

> Nos encontremos en De Efe [. . .] y uh pasemos como dos días aquí para conocer el ciudad y ver las monumentos y cosas así. Y después regresamos a City MS para que pudiéramos pasar tiempo con mi familia y para que mi novia pudiera conocer a mucha gente allá, mis amigos y – antes estaba un poco incómodo porque obviamente yo estaba hablando y comunicando con mucha gente aquí en México y ella eh mi novia no la conocía. Entonces se estaba un poco difícil
>
> (175/V3Q4).

> [We met up in DF and uh we spent like two days there to get to know the city and see monuments and things like that. And after we returned to City MS so that we could spent time with my family and so that my girlfriend would meet a lot of people there, my friends and – before it was a little uncomfortable because obviously I was speaking and interacting with a lot of people in Mexico and she, my girlfriend, didn't know them. So it was a little difficult.]

In contrast, Mexican sojourner 160 quickly found himself a local girlfriend and spent most of his time with this partner, her family and her friends. Describing himself as "el novio perfecto" (V2Q1), his integration seemed very complete. Once classes were finished toward the end of the sojourn, he sketched a typical lazy day spent together:

> Me levanto como las nueve diez. Me desayuno. Este y viene mi novia. Salimos a la calle. Este tal vez hagamos un poquito de yoga, que es un parte principal de free time. Tienes que ser muy flexible. Y [?] después vamos a la playa, nadamos, como bajamos, nada más. Como unas horas en la playa, después vamos a su casa a comer. Como dormir una siesta nada más. Todo tranquilito
>
> (160/V3Q2).

> [I wake up around nine ten. I have breakfast. And my girlfriend comes. We go out. Perhaps we do a bit of yoga, which is a major part of free time. We have to be very flexible. And later we go to the beach, swim, we walk down, nothing more. Like a few hours at the beach, after we go to her house to eat, like have a nap, nothing else. Very relaxing.]

His plans for the future involved (at least) saving up toward a return visit.

Out of the 48 women sojourners, seven talked about previously established relationships with English boyfriends, which persisted throughout the sojourn. (Two others mentioned breakdown in such relationships, however.) Some of these women sojourners' English partners came to visit them briefly at their sojourn location. More often, however, these visits involved travel to touristic destinations, such as Paris or Bruges.

Another nine described new relationships with French or Mexican boyfriends; two others hinted at similar relationships. Three of the women sojourners in France provided fairly full accounts of these romantic relationships. Sojourner 102 was the only one to describe how she met her partner – in the bank, when she went to open an account! Over the period of the sojourn, she spent increasing amounts of time with him in his apartment, and saw somewhat less of her (international) friends. When she went to England for her birthday, her family took steps to include him:

> Euh bon le weekend de mon anniversaire était très bien pour moi. Je suis rentrée en Angleterre hum oui. Je suis partie le matin de mon anniversaire, et j'ai rencontré ma famille à l'aéroport. Et euh le soir on est allé manger dans une très bon restaurant. Et en fait mon copain il était là. Et je savais pas qu'il venait, donc c'était une belle surprise [. . .] Et le samedi j'ai eu une surprise de – bon, je vais dire une "porte ouverte" pour ma maison en fait. C'était une journée avec la champagne, les cupcakes hum. Et tout ma famille tous mes amis étaient invités de venir quand ils veut euh. Donc c'était bien, j'ai raconté tous mes nouvelles à mes amis, à ma famille. Donc c'était trop bien
> (102/V3Q5).

> [Euh well my birthday weekend was really good for me. I went back to England, yeah. I left on the morning of my birthday and i met my family at the airport. And in the evening we went to eat in a really good restaurant. And in fact my boyfriend was there. And I did not know that he was coming, so it was a lovely surprise [. . .] And on the Saturday I had a surprise – well, I will say an "open house" in fact. It was a whole day with champagne, cupcakes hum. And all my family all my friends were invited to come when they want. So it was good, I told all my news to my friends, to my family. So it was really good.]

The French boyfriend of 107 became part of her international social group at her French university (which also included her flatmate, sojourner 112). In the later part of the sojourn, he joined her on a touristic trip with her parents, and she later spent a week at his family home, meeting his mother and home friends; by this time she was also partly living in his apartment. Similarly, 128 reported spending less time with international friends as her romantic relationship developed toward the end of the sojourn. (See fuller case study account for 128 in Chapter 9.)

162   Social networks and social relationships

These brief examples confirm the power of committed romantic partnerships to influence cultural integration, noted by other researchers (e.g. Trentman, 2015); sojourners such as 102, 107, 128 and 160 (and their partners) had exceptionally rich opportunities for cross-cultural experiences. On the other hand, sojourners who stayed loyal to partners from the home culture might be distanced from local networks and be somewhat more predisposed to touristic activities as an exclusive couple when their partners were around.

6.3.7 Sustaining relationships with home friends and family

Even though most sojourners had already been living away from home for two years as university students and had previously spent time abroad, it was clear that home friends and family remained of considerable emotional importance throughout the sojourn. As described more fully in Chapter 7, however, contemporary sojourners could Skype, phone or message family and friends as often as they wanted to. The isolation reported by past sojourner cohorts (Coleman & Chafer, 2010) did not affect this generation:

> I thought I would be a lot more homesick which I haven't really at all, but because, that might be because of Skype as well, which means you – basically means you can see them as much as you need
>
> (162/RI).

In addition to the internet, the ease of contemporary travel and its relative affordability in Europe also meant that many sojourners had regular face-to-face contact with family and home friends. Without any exception, all of the sojourners in Europe who mentioned the Christmas holiday reported visits to family. The Mexico-based group were the only ones who found this impractical. Several of them got together for Christmas instead; a group of six sojourners toured Chiapas, and 162 and 178 also made a New Year trip. The parents and grandparents of 157 came to visit at Christmas, and so did the English girlfriend of 175.

Many family members and other friends made trips at other times to visit sojourners in Europe; a few sojourners introduced these home contacts to their new insojourn networks, but often these visits were – once again – occasions for touristic travel. For example, 151 summed up a busy schedule of visits at Insojourn 2, culminating in a trip to Morocco with her parents:

> Regresé a Inglaterra para la navidad. Y vi a toda mi familia. Y después la navidad, en enero, um yo fui a París con 161, quien está en City SM. Y um nos encontramos nuestras otras amigas quienes um están en Francia este año. Y hicimos todas las cosas turísticas en París. Y la semana pasado vino aquí mi novio. Y el fin de semana pasada uh vinieron aquí mis padres. [. . .] Nos divertimos muy bien. Y fui a Tánger con mis padres
>
> (151/V2Q1).

[I went back to England for Christmas, and I saw all my family. And since Christmas, in January, I was in Paris with 161, who is in City SM. And we met our other friends who are in France this year. And we did all the touristic things in Paris. And last week my boyfriend came here. And last weekend my parents came [. . .] We had a good time. And I went to Tangier with my parents.]

Overall, these accounts of home network maintenance confirm the trends seen in the questionnaire responses. It is clear that young adult sojourners worked to maintain home networks, both virtually and through mutual travel, and found emotional support in this. The visits of friends and family may also have biased sojourners a bit further in favour of touristic travel, and thus potentially limited the deepening of networks in the locality of the sojourn. However, both of these factors (home contact, plus touristic travel) seem central to the contemporary sojourner experience, whatever their unintended consequences for network building in the new location.

6.4 Conclusion

The quantitative analysis presented in this chapter shows that all placement settings offered potential for development of new L2 or mixed-language-using social networks (though the role of language assistant facilitated new L1 networking alongside). It was possible to develop both the network diversity and the L2 network intensity, which have been suggested as facilitating L2 gain (Baker-Smemoe et al., 2014; Gautier & Chevrot, 2015). However, geographical location influenced networking patterns to some extent. In Mexico, sojourners maintained an intensive Home City Anglophone network, but otherwise were also quite quickly engaged in L2 or mixed networks with locals; they developed the largest/most diverse L2 networks over time. In France and Spain, most sojourners actively networked with international peers, both Anglophone and others. In Spain, however, the domestic setting frequently provided entry to local L2-using networks, unlike in France, where L2 networking was more likely to begin in the daytime setting or evening leisure settings. Some new relationships in all geographical locations progressed to high intensity (notably romantic partnerships, but also some peer friendships with individual locals or internationals). All sojourners meanwhile actively maintained L1 home networks, through virtual means and face-to-face visiting.

The qualitative analysis provides further detail about the motivations which drove sojourners to seek particular types of network (e.g., with international peers), but also about how sojourners could use agency to enter and develop local networks. Overall, it can be seen that they universally sustained a complex mix of local, international and home networks. It is the relative strength, durability and intensity of these different networks, that is, their quality, not their mere presence or absence, which is likely to determine access to L2 practice and – ultimately – L2 gain. The quality of sojourners' networks will be revisited in Chapter 9, where case studies of individual "high gainer" participants are presented.

References

Arnett, J. J. (2014). *Emerging adulthood: The winding road from the late teens through the twenties* (2nd ed.). Oxford: Oxford University Press.

Baker-Smemoe, W., Dewey, D. P., Bown, J., & Martinsen, R. A. (2014). Variables affecting L2 gains during study abroad. *Foreign Language Annals, 47*(3), 464–486.

Coleman, J. A., & Chafer, T. (2010). Study abroad and the internet: Physical and virtual context in an era of expanding telecommunications. *Frontiers: The Interdisciplinary Journal of Study Abroad, 19*, 151–167.

Dewey, D. P., Belnap, R. K., & Hilstrom, R. (2013). Social network development, language use, and language acquisition during study abroad: Arabic language learners' perspectives. *Frontiers: The Interdisciplinary Journal of Study Abroad, 22*, 84–110.

Dewey, D. P., Bown, J., & Eggett, D. (2012). Japanese language proficiency, social networking, and language use during study abroad: Learners' perspectives. *Canadian Modern Language Review, 68*(2), 111–137.

Finn, K. (2013). Young, free and single? Theorising partner relationships during the first year of university. *British Journal of Sociology of Education, 34*(1), 94–111.

Gautier, R., & Chevrot, J.-P. (2015). Social networks and acquisition of sociolinguistic variation in a study abroad context: A preliminary study. In R. Mitchell, N. Tracy-Ventura, & K. McManus (Eds.), *Social interaction, identity and language learning during residence abroad*. EUROSLA Monographs 4 (pp. 169–184). Amsterdam: European Second Language Association.

Milroy, L. (1980). *Language and social networks*. Oxford: Blackwell.

Milroy, L. (1987). *Language and social networks*. (2nd ed.). Oxford: Blackwell.

Trentman, E. (2015). Negotiating gendered identities and access to social networks during study abroad in Egypt. In R. Mitchell, N. Tracy-Ventura, & K. McManus (Eds.), *Social interaction, identity and language learning during residence abroad*. EUROSLA Monographs 4 (pp. 263–280). Amsterdam: European Second Language Association.

7 Language practices insojourn

7.1 Introduction

In this chapter, we examine the language practices in which sojourners engaged, in the target L2, in English, and in other languages. Again, we begin by presenting quantitative findings from the Language Engagement Questionnaire, followed by analysis of interviews. Complementing the social networking focus of Chapter 6, our main focus here is on sojourners' L2 practices, and how these were negotiated in a broadly multilingual environment; we also document the social purposes for which sojourners continued to use English, both as L1 and also as lingua franca.

7.2 Language engagement: The quantitative survey

In this section, we summarize the quantitative results from the Language Engagement Questionnaire (LEQ), administered during each of the three Insojourn surveys. The design of the LEQ was described in Chapter 3. Internal consistency was checked using Cronbach's alpha and results at each administration were above .70 (.81, .76, and .84 respectively). The results of the LEQ are presented by language and by country. In Sections 7.2.1, 7.2.2 and 7.2.3 we describe the use of French, Spanish and English in France, Spain and Mexico respectively. In Section 7.2.4 we summarize sojourners' use of other languages.

7.2.1 French and English use in France

Results for the group in France (n=29) are presented first in Table 7.1. Some of these findings have been presented previously in McManus, Mitchell, and Tracy-Ventura (2014). Here we provide the mean scores for all 26 activities listed in the LEQ at each administration, for both French and English. The first point to notice is the consistently bilingual behaviour of the group, with both French and English typically in daily use throughout the sojourn, and English being reported at higher frequency for many activities. The most frequently reported activities are similar across the two languages and primarily involve interaction with another interlocutor, whether virtual or face-to-face.

166 *Language practices in sojourn*

Table 7.1 France group language use: Mean frequencies for L2 and L1 activities, Insojourn 1–3

Activity	Insojourn 1 French	Insojourn 1 English	Insojourn 2 French	Insojourn 2 English	Insojourn 3 French	Insojourn 3 English
Engage in small talk	4.83	4.14	4.66	4.25	4.61	3.82
Engage in service encounters	4.46	0.66	4.03	0.82	4.54	0.68
Engage in long casual conversations	4.07	4.38	3.79	4.11	3.79	3.93
Browse the internet	3.83	4.90	3.79	4.79	3.93	4.75
Read text messages	3.79	4.52	3.86	4.25	3.79	4.32
Read emails	3.76	4.52	3.79	4.57	3.79	4.57
Write text messages	3.76	4.55	3.83	4.22	3.79	4.32
Write emails	3.69	4.24	3.69	4.24	3.46	4.29
Use social networking sites	2.86	4.69	3.59	4.69	3.14	4.61
Listen to talk radio	2.83	1.28	2.39	1.00	2.36	1.11
Listen to music	2.79	4.38	3.03	4.43	3.04	4.46
Have short phone conversations (<5 mins)	2.79	2.62	3.03	2.79	3.25	2.96
Read newspapers	2.76	1.38	2.86	1.43	2.96	2.07
Read magazines	2.55	1.17	2.55	0.89	2.50	1.21
Participate in organized social activities	2.48	0.86	2.14	0.61	1.64	0.46
Write reports (e.g., work, academic)	2.41	1.97	3.07	1.46	2.36	0.86
Read literature (e.g., fiction, poetry)	2.34	2.55	2.21	2.36	2.29	2.29
Watch television	2.24	2.93	2.31	3.07	2.25	2.93
Read academic texts	2.17	1.76	2.83	2.75	2.18	1.86
Use instant messaging	2.17	3.48	2.55	3.57	2.32	3.32
Watch films	2.07	2.00	2.00	2.00	1.93	2.04
Teach a class	2.03	2.14	1.66	2.46	1.57	2.25
Listen to lectures	1.38	0.41	1.34	0.29	0.71	0.14
Have long phone conversations (>5 mins)	1.31	2.66	1.55	2.61	1.61	2.93
Participate in seminars/language classes	1.10	0.38	1.10	0.25	0.75	0.04
Write for leisure (e.g., journal)	0.45	2.07	0.66	2.00	0.46	1.54

Note: 5 = every day, 4 = several times a week, 3 = a couple of times per week, 2 = a few times per month, 1 = rarely, 0 = never

The two most frequently reported activities for French, each with a group mean score of 4.00 or above throughout the sojourn, were *Engage in small talk* and *Engage in service encounters*. *Engage in long casual conversations* was third at Insojourn 1 but later dropped to seventh, although still on average occurring several times a week. A large majority (25) reported engaging in L2 small talk every day, compared to 15 for service encounters and 10 for long casual conversations. Sojourners did report doing some more solitary activities in French quite frequently, including *Browsing the internet* (several times per week) and *Listening to music/talk radio* (a couple of times per week), although they generally reported these two activities more often in English. *Engaging in service encounters* was predictably rare in English. The sojourners reported *Reading* (newspapers, magazines, academic texts) somewhat more often in French than English. However, they preferred to *Use social networking sites* and *Use instant messaging* in English, reported almost daily and a few times a week respectively.

The least frequent activities in French varied somewhat by placement type. These were *Writing for leisure* (19/29 reported never doing it), *Participating in seminars/language classes* (only 6/29 reported this several times per week, all from the student subset), and *Having long phone conversations* (one intern sojourner reported doing this daily, in all three surveys). Unsurprisingly, the least frequent activities in English were attending formal classes and participating in organized social activities.

Among the group in France, there was little change in these broad language use patterns over time. The only major exception was the observable increase in academic reading and writing at Insojourn 2, coinciding with the research project required by the home university. At Insojourn 3 many student sojourners had already finished studying, and this is reflected in a decline in reporting of French-medium classes.

7.2.2 Spanish and English use in Spain

Results for the group in Spain (n=18) are displayed in Table 7.2, and again show consistent bilingual language practice throughout the sojourn. The most frequent

Table 7.2 Spain group language use: Mean frequencies for L2 and L1 activities, Insojourn 1–3

Activity	Insojourn 1		Insojourn 2		Insojourn 3	
	Spanish	English	Spanish	English	Spanish	English
Engage in small talk	4.67	2.94	4.67	3.22	4.78	3.00
Engage in long casual conversations	4.33	3.47	4.00	3.56	4.33	3.44
Read text messages	4.17	4.22	3.94	4.22	3.78	4.22
Write text messages	4.17	4.22	3.94	4.17	3.71	4.22
Listen to music	3.89	4.33	3.61	4.50	3.33	4.50
Watch TV	3.83	2.72	4.06	2.89	3.83	2.67
Engage in service encounters	3.83	0.22	4.06	0.33	4.11	0.22
Read emails	3.67	4.17	3.94	4.39	3.67	4.17
Use social networking sites	3.67	4.89	4.00	4.67	3.83	4.83
Browse the internet	3.56	4.44	4.00	4.44	3.89	4.44
Have short phone conversations (<5 mins)	3.06	2.89	3.00	3.00	3.11	3.33
Participate in seminars/language classes	2.94	1.17	2.17	0.44	2.00	0.50
Write emails	2.89	3.56	3.17	3.56	2.61	3.67
Use instant messaging	2.89	4.00	3.00	4.06	3.22	4.00

(*Continued*)

168 *Language practices insojourn*

Table 7.2 (Continued)

Activity	Insojourn 1 Spanish	Insojourn 1 English	Insojourn 2 Spanish	Insojourn 2 English	Insojourn 3 Spanish	Insojourn 3 English
Write reports	2.78	1.17	2.88	1.00	2.39	0.56
Read newspapers	2.61	0.89	2.22	1.56	2.24	1.28
Participate in organized social activities	2.5	0.65	2.00	0.44	2.00	0.67
Listen to lectures	2.33	0.72	2.39	0.44	2.06	0.17
Listen to talk radio	2.28	0.78	2.06	1.00	1.72	0.94
Read academic texts	2.06	1.67	2.44	2.33	1.94	1.94
Watch films	2.00	1.39	1.83	1.39	2.33	1.53
Read magazines	1.89	0.78	1.72	1.00	1.56	0.94
Read literature	1.56	1.89	1.56	2.00	1.61	1.89
Have long phone conversations	1.39	3.67	1.56	3.39	1.44	3.33
Teach a class	0.72	2.39	0.94	2.94	0.89	2.72
Write for leisure	0.61	1.33	0.44	1.11	0.44	0.72

Note: 5 = every day, 4 = several times a week, 3 = a couple of times per week, 2 = a few times per month, 1 = rarely, 0 = never

uses of Spanish (with mean scores over 4.00 throughout the sojourn) were *Small talk* and *Long casual conversations*, plus reading and writing text messages. At Insojourn 2, the number of highly frequent Spanish-medium activities rose to six, with *Watch TV, Engage in service encounters, Use social networking sites* and *Browse the internet* replacing texting, though the number declined again at Insojourn 3. This group reported listening to music in L2 much more often than the France group (several times per week), as well as watching more television in Spanish (several times per week, compared to only a few times per month for the French group).

Comparing the use of Spanish and English, sojourners in Spain reported more use of Spanish in small talk, long casual conversations and service encounters at all three surveys. Additionally, they reported listening to lectures and talk radio more often in Spanish, as well as reading newspapers and magazines. There were, however, some reading activities (i.e., reading academic texts or literature) where they did not show a language preference. Long phone conversations were frequent in English (at least a few times per week) but not in Spanish. Most very frequent activities in English involved technology, including using social networking sites, browsing the internet and listening to music. As we have seen, participants often reported doing these activities in Spanish too, although slightly less often, which suggests that when they were alone they did not always prefer to use English.

Like the France group, the results for the Spain group show little change over time, apart from changes relating to the home university project and the routine of the academic year.

7.2.3 Spanish and English use in Mexico

Results for the group in Mexico are displayed in Table 7.3. This group shows the highest intensity in terms of use of Spanish (with 6, 10 and 8 activities having a mean score of 4.00 minimum, at the three survey points). Comparing the most frequent L2-medium activities with the other two groups, however, we find few differences. The most notable difference is that all sojourners in Mexico reported having short L2 phone conversations at least several times per week.

Comparing use of L2 and L1, small talk, texting, short phone conversations, long phone conversations and attending social events were all consistently of higher frequency in Spanish than in English for the Mexico group. Casual conversation and listening to music were common in both languages. Reading and writing emails and browsing the internet occurred more often in English, though, than in the other groups. Because all Mexico participants were teaching assistants, *Teach a class* occurred as a high-frequency English activity.

Table 7.3 Mexico group language use: Mean frequencies for L2 and L1 activities, Insojourn 1–3

Activity	Insojourn 1 Spanish	Insojourn 1 English	Insojourn 2 Spanish	Insojourn 2 English	Insojourn 3 Spanish	Insojourn 3 English
Engage in small talk	5.00	3.78	5.00	2.89	4.78	3.11
Read text messages	4.44	3.33	4.44	3.67	4.67	3.67
Write text messages	4.44	3.22	4.44	3.67	4.78	3.67
Engage in service encounters	4.33	0.67	4.67	0.22	4.67	0.44
Have short phone conversations	4.22	2.22	4.22	2.44	3.78	2.89
Engage in long casual conversations	4.00	4.00	4.56	3.89	4.67	3.44
Browse the internet	3.78	4.44	4.00	4.67	4.00	4.33
Listen to music	3.78	4.56	4.22	3.89	3.67	4.44
Use instant messaging	3.78	3.44	4.22	4.11	4.67	4.11
Use social networking sites	3.67	3.89	4.33	4.33	4.33	3.78
Watch TV	3.33	3.11	2.78	2.33	2.56	2.89
Read emails	3.33	4.44	3.22	4.56	3.33	4.44
Write emails	3.00	4.33	3.11	4.00	2.89	3.67
Watch films	2.67	2.00	2.67	2.89	2.44	2.56
Read newspapers	2.33	1.22	2.56	1.56	2.22	1.67
Read academic texts	2.00	2.33	2.44	2.11	1.33	0.89
Read magazines	2.00	1.22	2.00	0.78	2.00	0.78
Participate in organized social activities	2.00	0.56	2.22	0.33	2.22	0.56
Listen to talk radio	1.89	0.33	2.89	0.67	2.11	1.00
Participate in seminars/language classes	1.89	2.22	1.00	0.89	1.11	1.11
Read literature	1.78	1.56	2.33	1.33	2.00	1.44
Write reports	1.78	1.33	3.56	0.78	0.89	0.56
Teach a class	1.67	4.44	1.78	4.00	1.11	2.56
Have long phone conversations	1.44	1.22	2.33	1.56	2.89	2.22
Write for leisure	0.67	1.11	0.89	0.89	0.56	0.78
Listen to lectures	0.56	0.33	0.33	0.11	0.22	0.00

Note: 5 = every day, 4 = several times a week, 3 = a couple of times per week, 2 = a few times per month, 1 = rarely, 0 = never

170 *Language practices insojourn*

As with the other groups, there were few changes over time for the Mexico group, apart from those stimulated by the home university project. However, engaging in long casual conversations in Spanish slowly increased over time, as did use of instant messaging in Spanish, perhaps reflecting intensifying social networking with locals.

7.2.4 Other languages used in France, Spain and Mexico

Table 7.4 provides an overview of sojourners reporting use of additional languages at one or more survey points. Four sojourners in France reported using Spanish regularly at Insojourn 1 and Insojourn 2. One of these (126) was an L1 Spanish speaker; the others were also studying Spanish in Home City. Of the four participants who reported regular use of German, three were also studying German in Home City and one was sojourning near the German border (126). Two sojourners were studying Italian in France, one as a beginner (107), the other (129) continuing her studies from home. The one person who reported regular use of a Scandinavian language (108) was an L1 speaker. At Insojourn 3, sojourner 104 reported some use of Japanese (listening to music and watching Japanese films and anime).

In Spain, seven participants reported regular use of French at Insojourn 1. All of these participants were studying French in Home City, and five continued to take French language classes during the sojourn; sojourner 163 was taking classes in Russian. Two other sojourners in Spain were L1 Polish speakers (158 and 165) and used this language for family contact, and they also reported some use of other languages (German and Italian). Sojourner 180, who was working in a bilingual English/Basque school, reported hearing Basque regularly and seeing it written

Table 7.4 LEQ responses for use of various languages in France, Spain and Mexico

Languages	France (n=29)			Spain (n=18)			Mexico (n=9)		
	S1	S2	S3	S1	S2	S3	S1	S2	S3
English	29	29	29	18	18	18	9	9	9
French	29	29	29	7	8	6	3	3	3
Spanish	4	4	2	18	18	18	9	9	9
Italian	2	2	2	1	1				
German	4	3	2	2	2	1			
Finnish	1	1	1						
Japanese			1						
Polish				2	2	2			
Basque				1	1	1			
Russian				1	1	1			
Valenciano					1	2			
Portuguese							1	1	1
Welsh							1	1	1

Note: S1 = Insojourn 2, S2 = Insojourn 2, S3 = Insojourn 3

in notices, textbooks and computers. At Insojourn 2, one student (166) living in the province of Valencia reported regular use of Valenciano. By Insojourn 3, both she and participant 173 reported regular use, mostly related to listening and reading emails. A few others commented on encounters with Valenciano in interview but did not record this in LEQ.

Several sojourners in Mexico were studying French back home, and three reported regular use of the language at each survey point. Participant 177 was studying Portuguese and continued her studies in Mexico. Participant 157 reported communicating in Welsh with her family back home. Two participants said in interview (but not in LEQ) that they were attending a Mayan language class.

7.3 Qualitative accounts of language practices

7.3.1 Introduction: Structure and agency in language choice

Despite very similar expectations presojourn, the quantitative data deriving from the LEQ show clear between-group differences in levels of L2 engagement from the three different locations: Mexico (highest engagement), Spain (intermediate) and France (lowest). We attribute these group differences to underlying sociocultural/structural differences between the sojourner experience in these three locations, partly to do with immediate living conditions and partly to do with broader sociolinguistic factors, combining to produce the somewhat different patterns of social networking detailed in Chapter 6.

However, these broad differences are not deterministic of individual participants' language choices, in settings which are all multilingual to some degree. In the rest of this chapter, we focus on the agency of individual sojourners (Block, 2013), exploring how in apparently similar social settings, different language practices could be negotiated. In Section 7.3.2 we explore participants' accounts of how they negotiated access to French and Spanish and used them in a range of settings. In following sections we explore their practices in English (7.3.3), and in other languages/regional varieties (7.3.4).

7.3.2 Negotiating the use of French and Spanish

In this section we examine learner agency in gaining access to informal L2 practice, in a number of key settings: the home (7.3.2.1), the placement (7.3.2.2), language skills exchanges (7.3.2.3), service encounters (7.3.2.4) and the specialist domains of sport and music (7.3.2.5). We conclude by considering sojourners' efforts to use French or Spanish as a lingua franca with their international peers (7.3.2.6).

7.3.2.1 L2 practices in domestic settings

Participants were very enthusiastic predeparture about the idea of sharing accommodation with local peers, on grounds of the opportunity for target language

172 *Language practices insojourn*

use, hopefully with congenial interlocutors. Several (female) sojourners in Spain reported finding rich conversation opportunities very quickly with their new local flatmates:

> Pero son chicas muy majas muy simpáticas. Y a veces hablamos cuando estamos juntos en el piso. Hablamos de los novios, los chicos, los trabajos, los problemas y todo. Es muy bien. Son chicas muy bien
>
> (167/V1Q1).

> [But they're very cool and very nice girls. And sometimes we chat when we're together in the flat. We chat about boyfriends, guys, work, problems and everything. It's really good. They're really great girls.]

The first encounters could be a linguistic shock, but this wore off soon, and time with supportive flatmates helped develop L2 confidence:

> Um (.) paso la mayoría de mi tiempo con mis compañeras de piso y sus amigos. Um la mayoría de sus amigos um son del mismo curso que estudio de comunicación audiovisual, y pues tengo clases con ellas o ellos. Um (.) la mayoría son chicas, [. . .] y son muy majas. Y um me incluyen en <toda la vida> [?]. Um he ido al cine con ellas, a una fiesta en un albergue con un chico para su cumpleaños. Sí. Mmm siempre tratan de um hablar conmigo y um uh asegurar que entiendo todo lo que hablan [?]
>
> (172/V1Q7).

> [Um I spend the majority of my time with my flatmates and their friends. The majority of their friends are in the same course as me, audiovisual communication, and so I have classes with them. The majority are girls [. . .] and are really cool. And they include me in <everything> [?]. I've been to the cinema with them, to this guy's birthday party. Yeah, mmm they always try to talk to me and um make sure that I understand everything that they say.]

It was rare to live with classmates, as 172 did, but this had the advantage of providing further Spanish-medium activities in common, such as preparing group work together.

Not all local flatmates were so friendly and supportive, however. In some such situations, sojourners (n=7) demonstrated agency by making a mid-year move (or even two); in most cases their declared motivation was to find a more favourable home environment for Spanish/French use. We saw in Chapter 6 how male sojourner 156 moved from one flat to another in quest of more sociable Spanish flatmates. Female sojourner 119 also moved out of an all-assistant flat in order to sublet from a male French young professional. She was still planning the move at Insojourn 1, and described her hopes:

> Ok euh j'ai fait la connaissance de Gabriel il y a une mois euh à une soirée de Halloween euh. Oui euh il est très gentil et sympa. Euh nous avons beaucoup

en commune, et euh nous parlons en français et en anglais. Euh c'est bien pour moi puisque il est français, donc je peux faire la connaissance de plus de gens français. Euh puisque il y a une danger que je peux seulement parler anglais, puisque la plupart de mes amis euh sont les assistants euh anglophones. Et pour moi je voudrais pratiquer mon français, euh puisque euh j'ai le but euh d'être courant euh par fin de l'année [. . .] Uh je pense que ce serait très bien quand j'habite avec lui oui

(119/V1Q7).

[I got to know Gabriel a month ago at a Halloween party. Yeah, he is very nice, and kind. We have a lot in common, and we speak in French and in English. That's good for me because he's French, that way I can get to know more French people, because there's a danger that I'll only speak English, since the majority of my friends are English-speaking assistants. And I would like to practise my French because my aim for the end of this year is to be fluent [. . .] Uh I think that would be very good when I live with him.]

In the event, language practices within this flatshare led to conflict, as 119 described a bit later:

J'essaie de parler en français tout le temps, mais euh par exemple euh euh il passait (.) six mois au Canada avant. Donc euh il aime beaucoup de parler en anglais et c'est très agaçant pour moi, parce que um je [lui] ai dit que je veux parler en français tout le temps, ça c'est la raison que euh je voulais habiter au centre ville avec lui. Et euh si je comprends pas quelque chose parce que il parle très vite tout le temps, euh il décide de parler en anglais comme je suis stupide et je peux pas comprendre. Donc j'ai dit les choses comme "Gabriel, je peux comprendre, c'est juste que tu parles très vite, tu es dans une autre pièce dans euh l'appartement donc c'est difficile pour moi. Mais euh ce n'est pas très bien, ce n'est pas très gentil de toi de parler en anglais parce que euh je me sens que mon français c'est très nul, je peux pas communiquer", les choses comme ça. Mais je suis très persistant

(119/V2Q1).

[I try to speak in French all the time, but, for example, he spent six months in Canada before. So, he enjoys speaking English and that is very annoying for me, because I have said to him that I want to speak in French all of the time, that's the reason why I wanted to live with him in the city centre. And if I don't understand something because he's speaking too fast all of the time, then he decides to speak in English as if I'm stupid and I don't understand. So I have said things like "Gabriel, I can understand! It's just that you're speaking very fast, and you're in a different room in the flat, and so that's difficult for me. But it's not very nice if you speak English because I feel like my French is rubbish, as if I can't communicate", things like that. But I'm very persistent.]

Clearly even in the home, locals' interest in practising English could clash with sojourners' motivation to practise French.

Another complication regarding home L2 practice was regional linguistic variation. Flatmates in Spain might not always speak standard Castilian:

> Pues cuando estoy hablando con una persona de City SG o de Madrid me viene más fácil para entenderlos. Pero por ejemplo porque vivo con un andaluz, y es de City SS, a veces es bastante difícil para entenderle ehm por el acento. Y cuando estoy [?] con sus amigos y todos son andaluces y están hablando de prisa pues puede ser un poco difícil
>
> (170/V1Q5).

> [Well when I'm talking with a person from City SG or from Madrid, it's easier to understand them. But for example because I live with an Andaluz, and he's from City SS, sometimes it's rather difficult to understand him due to his accent. And when I'm with his friends and all are Andaluces, and they're talking quickly, well then it can be a bit difficult.]

Even within host families, language choice might also require some negotiation; thus the "Mexican brother" of 162 was keen to practise English. However, rich opportunities for L2 practice were on offer. For example, exchange student 104 formed a close social relationship with his hosts, leading to extensive L2 practice opportunities with them, both at home and on a variety of cultural and leisure excursions. His male host in particular liked serious discussions about philosophy, music and politics; consequently, 104 was stimulated to read more widely and to inform himself about current affairs through French radio and television. In this house, unusually, English was explicitly discouraged:

> Well in the beginning English was sort of forbidden in a sort of jokey way. But it had a serious purpose, in that I relied on it much less and I am much more likely to switch automatically to thinking in French
>
> (104/RIQ2).

In Mexico, most sojourners remained on polite terms with their host families, but increasingly found leisure activities and associated L2 practice outside the home. The main exception was 162, who as we have seen, became good friends with the bilingual son of the family, and who also ate lunch daily with the (monolingual) mother. While his "Spanish brother" was keen to practise English some of the time, he introduced both 162 and fellow sojourner 178 to monolingual friends and supported their learning of Spanish, correcting 162 in ways he found helpful: "With Damián and *ser* and *estar* he's always on top of me, and he will shout at me if I say *estar* when it should be *ser*" (162/RIQ4).

Finally, there were two cases in France where language assistants lived in institutional accommodation with French fellow residents only, and found practice opportunities there. Sojourner 101 was living cheaply in a residence for young working women. At first she was very negative about this experience, saying in her first interview that she had nothing in common with the 16- and 17-year-olds around her. However, by Insojourn 2, chatting with some of these girls had become valued L2 practice. Somewhat similarly, male sojourner 127 lived in the boarding house of a rural *lycée;* on weekday evenings he interacted in French with a group of resident *surveillants*, eating with them and watching sport together on TV.

7.3.2.2 Engaging with L2 through placement roles

In this section we examine the L2 practices which could be negotiated around the different placement types. Some linguistic tension was inevitably associated with these roles, given that the language assistants and workplace interns in particular had been recruited for their L1 skills and were expected to operate bilingually during the working day.

In schools, language assistants had a teaching commitment of only 12 hours per week, so that they typically visited the school only two to three days per week. In some cases, this time commitment was split between different schools. Teachers varied in how welcoming they were, and in their own language practices. Thus some teachers wanted to practise their own English with the assistant, whereas elsewhere, teachers either spoke little English or were more accommodating of sojourners' preference for L2. In some but not all schools, teachers tried to involve sojourners in staffroom conversation and invited them on outings. Thus the opportunities available for informal L2 use depended partly on the particular school context, and partly on assistant sojourners' own responses to these.

At the start of the sojourn, the staffroom itself generally presented a major linguistic challenge:

> Pour moi le plus difficile est dans le cantine avec tous les professeurs, parce que tout le monde parle très vite et en même temps. Ça c'est les choses les plus difficiles pour moi. Parce que je dois écoute et répondre, c'est – mais je pense que c'est normal de trouver des difficultés avec ça
>
> (109/V1Q5).

> [For me, the most difficult is in the canteen with all of the teachers, because everyone is speaking really fast, and all at the same time. Those are the most difficult things for me. Because I need to listen and respond. But I also think it's normal to find difficulties with that.]

> El problema más grande es um hablar con los otros profesores en la sala de profesores en el instituto. Porque um cuando hay mucha gente, muchos españoles hablando muy rápido, um y hablan de cosas que no entiendo muy bien como – no sé – como la enseñanza. Y porque son mayores es difícil. Es que no tengo nada que ver con ellos. Y me cuesta mucho intervenir en una conversación con la gente que están hablando muy rápido y – para mí es la cosa más difícil
>
> (161/V1Q5).

[The biggest problem is speaking with the other teachers in the teachers' room at the school. Because when there's a lot of people, many Spaniards speaking very quickly, um and they're talking about things I don't understand very well – I don't know – like about teaching. And because they're older, it's difficult. It's that I don't have anything in common with them. And it's hard for me to jump into a conversation with people who are speaking very quickly and – for me that's the thing that's most difficult.]

Assistant 161 was aware that her teacher colleagues went to a local café at midday, but they had not invited her to accompany them, and at first she did not feel brave enough to suggest it herself. The mentor of assistant 106 was often absent, and she was unclear to begin with about her detailed timetable. Like 161, she was too timid at first to solve the problem verbally. Instead, her solution was to sit with a novel in the staffroom, waiting to be told what to do next.

However, assistants realized that the staffroom and in particular the lunch hour with teachers offered access to informal L2 conversation, and tried to capitalize on this:

Je mange le déjeuner à l'école avec les autres enseignants. Le déjeuner est deux heures à l'école. C'est très bizarre pour les Anglais d'avoir deux heures pour déjeuner, mais pour moi c'est très agréable parce que je prends ce temps de parler avec les autres enseignants. Alors parce que je suis là-bas trois fois par semaine ça veut dire j'ai six heures de conversation en français. Et euh euh tout le monde se détend tout le monde parler de le weekend de les autres enseignants de les enfants. Ça j'aime bien, le déjeuner à l'école

(111/V2Q2).

[I have lunch at school with the other teachers. The lunch break is for two hours at the school. It's very strange for English people to have two hours for lunch, but for me it's very pleasant because I take this time to speak to the other teachers. So, as I'm there three times per week, that means I have six hours of conversation in French. And everyone relaxes, everyone talks about the weekend and the other teachers and the children. I like that, lunch at the school.]

Where teachers preferred to speak some English, however, sojourners might feel constrained to follow these preferences. For example, early on, 119 described accepting the use of English by teachers, in spite of expressing her own preference for French. Over time, however, she reported greater L2 engagement:

En ce moment j'essaie de rester au lycée pour toute la journée. Euh j'ai commencé de manger dans le salle de profs, située dans la cantine avec les autres professeurs. Donc je peux parler le français, je peux écouter des discussions français, et il y a beaucoup qui sont très typiques, euh surtout xx du sujet de euh l'enseignement. Euh il y avait un grève il y a deux trois semaines, euh j'ai écouté la raison pourquoi, les choses comme ça

(119/V2Q2).

[At the moment I try to stay at the school for the whole day. I have started to eat in the staffroom, which is in the canteen with the other teachers. So I can speak French and I can listen to French discussion, and a lot of the discussion is pretty typical, especially that about teaching. Two weeks ago, there was a strike, I listened to the reasons for the strike, and things like that.]

By Insojourn 2, 105 was spending time between classes chatting to friends in the school counsellors' office. Similarly, in Spain, 161 started accompanying the teachers to their midday off-campus break. Others became increasingly involved in activities such as school trips and lunchtime clubs, accessing further opportunities for L2 use. A few took lifts with teachers to school (an hour of Spanish conversation each way, noted 167). Others accepted social invitations from teachers, which led to additional L2 practice. For example, 109 felt she had made a linguistic breakthrough at dinner with a teacher's family:

Oui et un femme m'a invité pour le diner vendredi dernier [. . .] avant quand j'étais chez elle j'étais un peu timide, et je ne voulais pas parler beaucoup parce que j'avais peur de faire des erreurs tout ça. Euh oui mais le semaine dernière j'avais une débat avec son mari euh en ce qui concerne euh l'importance pour les personnes anglais d'étudier les langues étrangères. Oui, parce que il a dit que c'est pas nécessaire parce que tout le monde parle anglais. "Alors pourquoi tu étudies le français?", tout ça et oui. Alors j'avais une débat avec lui. Alors ça c'était assez significatif je pense oui

(109/V2Q6).

[Yes, a lady invited me for dinner last Friday. [. . .] Before, when I was at her house I was a little timid and I didn't want to speak much because I was scared to make mistakes. Yeah but last week I debated with her husband about the importance for English people to study foreign languages. Yes, because he said that it's not necessary because everyone speaks English. He asked, "Why are you studying French?", and all that. So I debated with him and that was quite significant I think.]

Two assistants (119 and 167) were engaging in language exchanges with younger teachers, who were also described as friends. Finally, as discussed in Chapter 6, teachers might provide introductions to local peers, as possible friends and L2 interlocutors. However, some assistants seemed to spend little time in their schools other than class hours, throughout the sojourn, and never reported any extended L2 practice there. (An example was assistant 113, whose experiences are described as a case study in Chapter 9.)

As in domestic settings, socializing with teachers in certain parts of Spain brought sojourners into contact with regional languages. In the school where 173 was working, Valenciano was commonly spoken:

> Eh y los profesores cuando están juntos hablan valenciano. Y luego se dan cuenta que yo estoy aquí, y cambian a castellano. Y luego dos minutos después vuelven a hablar en valenciano. Y luego están diciendo "ah! Terence está aquí", y vuelven al castellano. Pero a los dos minutos xxx vuelven al valenciano. xxx entiendo un poco, pero no sé decir nada.[. . .] Estoy aprendiendo un poco
>
> (173/V2Q7).

> [And the teachers when they're together they speak Valenciano. And later they realize that I'm here and then change to Castilian. And then two minutes later they go back to speaking Valenciano. And then they're saying "Ah, Terence is here" and go back to Castilian. But two minutes later they're back to Valenciano. xxx I understand a bit but I don't know how to say anything. [. . .] I'm learning a bit.]

Sojourner 173 still had partial access to Castilian in school. However, 180 faced a greater challenge, working in two different Basque-medium schools:

> Pero no escucho español todo el día, porque los niños y los profesores hablan en euskera. También en el recreo, cuando los niños estaban jugando, los otros profesores juntas estaban hablando en euskera. Y yo siento un poquito que no puedo uh hablar con ellas. Y es difícil. Por eso sería mejor para mí [. . .] si la escuela fue en español
>
> (180/V1Q10).

> [But I don't hear Spanish the whole day because the children and the teachers speak in Euskera. Also during recess, when the children are playing, the other teachers speak to each other in Euskera. And I feel a bit like I can't talk to them and it's really difficult. That's why it would be better for me [. . .] if Spanish was spoken at school.]

As we saw in Section 7.2, the Mexico group reported the richest patterns of L2 use. Almost all (7/9) were assistants in universities, which provided them with access to similar-aged students as well as to staff colleagues, as potential L2 interlocutors. They generally reported using a mix of English and Spanish in campus-based friendship groups, but clearly the mix included extensive L2 practice in most cases. Sojourner 162 was working in a major city, in a private language school for adults:

> Aquí se puede hablar con casi cualquier persona en la calle – o no tanto en la calle pero en la escuela, todos los profes me platican. Y en los trabajos que he tenido en Inglaterra no siempre ha sido así
>
> (162/V1Q4).

[Here it's possible to speak with just about anyone in the street – or not as much in the street but at the school, all the teachers chat with me. And in the jobs I've had in England, it hasn't always been like that.]

By Insojourn 3, 162 was saying that he had found the best workplace friends of his life in Mexico; along with his "Mexican brother" Damián and his friends, these work associates were clearly central to his L2 practice.

In the case of the Mexico sojourners generally, therefore, the workplace offered an immediate point of access to local social networks and related opportunities to use Spanish. However, as time progressed, references to teachers and other professional contacts as L2 interlocutors were gradually supplanted by references to local students and young adults.

For the student sojourners in Europe, the situation was very different. Many international students frequented all of the campuses they attended:

> Je m'attendais pas à ça, le nombre d'étrangères à la fac et partout. Et c'était genial, mais oui oui à la fin on se sent identifiée avec les autres étrangères qui sont dans la même situation. Mais oui ça je m'attendais pas à ça
> (126/V3Q10).

[I was not expecting that, the number of foreigners at university and everywhere. And it has been nice, but, yes, you feel grouped together with the other foreigners who are in the same situation. I was not expecting that.]

As we saw in Chapter 6, host institutions positively promoted cohesion among the international student group, and friendships quickly developed among them:

> Conozco muchos Erasmus, y por eso es una buena cosa, porque vivimos la misma estilo de vida. Pero por otro lado sería mejor que hable con españoles para aprender mas de su cultura y como hablar como español
> (166/V1Q4).

[I know a lot of Erasmus and that's a good thing because we live the same kind of life. But on the other hand, it would be better for me to speak with Spaniards to learn more about their culture and how to speak like them.]

Some sojourners did try to make French or Spanish the lingua franca of their Erasmus networks, as we discuss below in 7.3.2.5. In Spain, it was also possible to meet international students who themselves had Spanish as their first language; thus, 163 was using the language to interact with Colombian and Mexican girls, describing how they went shopping together and even watched the Home City football team together on TV. Sojourner 166 met a group of Mexican students at an Erasmus introductory event and discovered they shared her Christian faith; she regularly joined in Spanish-medium religious and social activities with this group throughout the semester they remained in Spain.

180 *Language practices in sojourn*

A small number of student sojourners took positive steps to avoid other Erasmus students, primarily to avoid use of English as a lingua franca. However, most were hoping to develop local contacts and L2 opportunities in addition to Erasmus friendships. Here, sojourners realized that they needed to be proactive:

> Alors l'effort doit venir de l'étudiant Erasmus pas des autres, parce que ils ont déjà des amis, et ils ont déjà des soirées. Alors il faut faire vraiment un effort pour euh les inviter, euh de faire le premier pas je dirais, parce que ils se rendent pas compte parfois qu'on est seul là. Ils sont jamais peut-être sortis de la France. Ils savent pas. Alors [il faut] pas attendre euh que les gens oui se rapprochent de toi parce que ça marche pas normalement
>
> (126/V3Q10).

> [So the effort should come from the Erasmus student and not from the others, because they already have friends and they already have parties. You really need to make the effort to invite them and to take the first step, I would say. They don't notice that you are alone. Perhaps they have never left France, so they don't know. You must not wait for French people to come and approach you because it doesn't usually work like that.]

But how could sojourners make themselves attractive/interesting as interlocutors, in a challenging environment? Some had reflected on linguistic self-presentation within the classes they were attending, and the academic impression they were making on both lecturers and fellow students:

> Porque tenemos que hablar enfrente de los otros españoles. Y a veces es más difícil porque yo sé cómo hablar sobre temas más comúnes. Pero cuando es algo específico o para analizarlo no tengo el vocabulario para analizar. Y por eso enfrente de como treinta otras jóvenes que saben su lengua y tal me cuesta mucho. Eh por eso es un poco difícil
>
> (152/V1Q11).

> [Because we have to talk in front of other Spaniards. And sometimes it's more difficult because I only know how to talk about very common topics. But when it's something specific or to be analysed, I don't have the vocabulary to analyse. Therefore, in front of like 30 other young people who know their own language, I find it hard. For that reason it's a bit difficult.]

Sojourner 152 went on to explain her strategies, which included taking an active part in group work, showing herself to be competent, and making a positive contribution:

> Eh también porque estamos trabajando un uh trabajo en grupo para una asignaturas hicimos un poco de trabajo. Y luego fuimos uh de tapas también todas juntas. Así es mejor. [. . .] Y lo que he encontrado es que um si trabajas

bien aquí la gente española están más dispuesta a trabajar contigo en el trabajo en grupo y tal

(152/V1).

[Also because we are working on a group project for one of our modules, we did a bit of work. And then we went to have some tapas all together. It's better that way. [. . .] What I have found out is that, if you work well, the Spanish people are more willing to do group work with you and so forth.]

Several sojourners commented that a translation class was a favourable place to get talking with local students because of the distinctive linguistic contribution they could make.

Acquaintances made in the classroom mostly led only to daytime L2 interaction on campus, but there were exceptions. By Insojourn 2, 156 was regularly engaging with local classmates in varied types of L2 interaction:

NTV: Y con quién pasas la mayor parte de tu tiempo?
[And who do you spend most of your time with?]
*156: Con mis compañeros de clase supongo, que hay algunos que – bueno, son amigos también. Pues después de clase vamos a tomar algo, a seguir charlando, y si tenemos proyectos pues los hacemos juntos. Si tenemos trabajos, el mismo trabajo, nos ayudamos, a lo major (156/V2Q5).
[With my classmates I suppose, since there are those who are my friends too. So after class we go to have a drink, to carry on talking, and if we have projects, we do them together. If we have assignments, the same assignment, we help each other, perhaps.]

Sojourner 156 believed that being an English speaker had made him attractive to these classmates to begin with. However, once integrated within the group, this was a rich opportunity to hear and use challenging Spanish:

En grupo hay un tendencia que yo no hablo mucho, porque (.) yo tengo que pensar un poco más que ellos. Pues una vez que haya pensado en lo que quiero decir, ya ha pasado esa parte de la conversación, xxx o sea alguien más lo ha dicho lo que iba a decir. Pues es la tendencia en grupo

(156/V2Q10).

[In a group, I tend not to say a lot because I have to think a bit more than them. And by the time I have thought about what I want to say, that part of the conversation is already over, I mean someone else has said what I was planning to say. So that's the tendency when we are in a group.]

Like the language assistants, the workplace interns had been recruited by their host organizations because of their English language skills, and they were often working alongside other nationalities. (Sojourner 150 in Spain first had an

182 *Language practices in sojourn*

American boss, then a French one, and 125 worked in university administration with several different nationalities.) Thus, the workplace not only required some use of English for professional activity, but also typically offered a multilingual social environment. In these settings, the interns like the language assistants made somewhat varied language choices. Some used predominantly L2, while others became members of mixed social groups, where leisure talk was multilingual. Two (116 and 128) socialized with workmates predominantly in English.

7.3.2.3 Accessing informal L2 practice through skills exchange: Tandems and individual tutoring

A key practice where sojourners could access L2 use was that of tandem exchanges, and 18 sojourners reported these. A few sojourners reported taking part in group events, where on a given evening, people met to practise a variety of languages:

> Um pero fuimos a ese grupo que se llama México Babel. Es como un grupo de estudiantes que uh se reunen <todos los dos> [?] semanas y es para practicar inglés, español, francés, cualquier la lengua. Y conozco muchas personas de aquí, como muchos mexicanos que quieren hablar inglés. Y yo quiero hablar con ellos en español. Y es bueno porque los mexicanos tienen como claros y contactos
>
> (171/V1Q7).

> [Mmm, but we went to that group that is called Mexico Babel. It's like a group of students that get together, every week, and it's to practice English, Spanish, French, any language. And I know many people from there, like lots of Mexicans who want to speak English. And I want to speak Spanish with them, and it's good because Mexicans have like contacts.]

More often, sojourners found individual tandem partners through classes, from websites and noticeboards, or through personal recommendations, for example, by mentor teachers. These arrangements could be quite informal:

> J'ai rencontré deux jeunes tunisiennes qui sont oui très sympas très accueillantes. Et on essaie de se voir une ou deux fois par semaine juste pour parler le français un peu d'anglais un peu de français. [. . .] Euh oui tous les gens sont très sympas. Et ils savent que j'ai vraiment envie de parler français. Donc euh (.) oui ils sont très acceuillants pour ça
>
> (102/V1Q7).

> [I have met two young Tunisian girls who are very nice and very welcoming. We try to see each other once or twice a week, just to speak French, a little English and a little French. [. . .] Everyone is very nice and they know that I really want to speak French. So euh (.) yes they are very welcoming for that.]

Depending on the extent of shared interests, some tandems faded away, but others might be very productive and long-lasting. For example, 152 found a tandem through a webpage set up by the host university, early in her stay; this pair were still meeting weekly at Insojourn 2. Sojourner 167 sustained her tandem with an English teacher until Insojourn 3, by which time he was bringing a friend along as well. Sojourner 126 found that her tandem partnerships did not necessarily last long, but she continued to find new ones throughout her stay and regularly reported that this was her best opportunity to speak French. Despite socializing regularly with classmates, 156 rated individual tandems as his best language-learning opportunity (because he had more opportunity to speak, in a one-to-one setting).

Another common sojourner practice was (paid) private language tutoring; both assistants and exchange students reported teaching English to individual schoolchildren, host family members or other locals. Many found the money useful, and for language assistants in particular, some tutoring could fill up an otherwise rather empty weekly schedule; by the end of her stay, 180 was giving private classes for 10 hours each week. Most sojourners did not explicitly mention any linguistic benefit to themselves. However, occasional comments made it clear that private lessons involved bilingual practices:

> Y también hablo – pues supongo que hablo más español en mis clases de inglés (.) particulares. Porque son chicos pequeños, y obviamente a veces necesito hablar en español para que entiendan
>
> (170/V3Q7).
>
> [And I also speak, I suppose I speak more Spanish in my private English classes, because they are small children, and obviously, I sometimes need to speak Spanish for them to understand me.]

We have already described in Chapter 6 how some sojourners in France became socially involved with the families of children they were tutoring and got the chance to speak "loads of French in a very natural environment" (106/R1Q2).

7.3.2.4 *Service encounters*

Leading a "young adult" life in France and Spain meant taking part in a range of service encounters (confirmed in the LEQ as well). Immediately on arrival, those renting apartments had to negotiate with landlords and prospective flatmates and also sort out utilities and the internet. Sojourners in France were often eligible to apply for a state rental subsidy (from the *Caisse d'Allocation Familiale*, or CAF); those in Spain needed to get an identity number (the Número de Identificación de Extranjero (NIE) number). Sojourners wanted to set up bank accounts and mobile phone contracts; exchange student sojourners had to negotiate university administration processes in order to identify and sign up for suitable courses.

Assistants had to master school timetables, pedagogic practices and disciplinary procedures. Sojourners in Mexico had to settle into a new work environment and learn about administrative procedures.

Sojourners gave vivid accounts of these processes, which they had sometimes never experienced at home, and which in any case worked differently in the new settings. They had to be conducted in L2, with officials who did not always seem particularly welcoming or cooperative. At this time, many sojourners were having difficulty both with understanding everyday interlocutors and with making themselves understood. Several described linguistic preparation and rehearsal before attempting service encounters:

> Oui je sais pas si ma langue a amélioré, mais je pense que je suis plus confidante, parce que avant j'avais la peur de parler en français. En fait quand j'ai arrivé euh je n'ai pas voulu entrer dans la banque, et j'ai resté à l'extérieur de la banque pour je pense une demi-heure, euh de décider qu'est-ce que je vais dire quand j'ai entré. Mais maintenant j'ai pas le peur de le faire. Je pense que ça c'est la différence la plus grande
>
> (111/V1Q12).

> [I don't know if my language has improved, but I think that I am more confident, because before I was scared to speak French. In fact when I arrived I didn't want to go into the bank, and I waited outside the bank for I think half an hour, deciding what I am going to say when I went in. But now, I'm not scared to do that. I think that's the biggest difference.]

However, many sojourners also reported a strong access of confidence once they had succeeded in negotiating these early challenges. Sojourner 177 said she did not like the telephone, even in English, but had overcome these feelings to talk to possible landlords:

> Para mí el reto más grande que hasta ahora he tenido que (.) sobresaltar um es alguna de que soy muy orgullosa. La semana pas[ada], porque estamos buscando un departamento para compartir 157 y yo, tuve que um llamar por teléfono en castellana. Y a mí no me gusta mucho uh llamar alguien por teléfono en inglés. Um entonces sí, para mí fue un reto muy grande
>
> (177/V1Q5).

> [For me the biggest challenge I have gone through until now is one I am very proud of. Last week, because we are looking for a flat to share, 157 and me, I had to make a phone call in Spanish. And I don't like to speak to people on the phone in English, so, yeah, for me, it was a big challenge.]

Once settled in the new location, sojourners naturally continued to engage in more routine service encounters, which continued to challenge their L2 capacities and provide practice opportunities. Several told anecdotes about failures to make themselves understood in service settings, or when purchasing small items. Thus, 104 could not pronounce the word "muffin" in a sufficiently French way for a baker to serve him, and 126 created confusion at the hairdresser's through an error of grammatical gender:

*KMcM: Oui et euh as-tu rencontré quelques difficultés langagières?
[Yes and have you met any language difficulties?]

*126: Euh oui parfois (.) à cause de ma prononciation euh. Euh oui ils comprennent pas ce que je veux dire, mais oui je trouve toujours une façon de le dire, ou je le dis en anglais parfois. Je suis allée la deuxième semaine dans un coiffeur. Et j'ai demandé "Combien combien coûte un [MASC] coupe?" Et je voulais dire "une [FEM] coupe". Et il me disait "le cou?", beaucoup de choses. Et je disais "non un [MASC] coupe". Alors les choses comme ça, et ouais. Mais c'était drôle (126/V1Q5).
[Yes, sometimes, due to my pronunciation. They don't understand what I want to say, but I find a way to say it or I sometimes say it in English. The second week here, I went to the hairdresser's. And I asked, "How much does a haircut cost?" And I intended to say "une [FEM] coupe". And he said to me, "the neck?", and lots of other things. And I said, "No, un [MASC] coupe". So things like that, yeah. It was funny!]

A few participants had to handle more complex service encounters in the course of the year, such as disputes with landlords, incidents of theft or fraud, and medical incidents. Shortly after arriving in Mexico, for example, 178 needed treatment for appendicitis and found herself using Spanish in a completely new register. A few also had dealings with the police; 117 had to report a burning car, and in Mexico, 171 had several times been stopped by police when driving at night, and had to acquire routines for extracting herself.

In general, handling these incidents through L2 contributed to sojourners' growing sense of self-efficacy, both as L2 users and independent adults. Sojourner 122 vividly described a dispute with her local CAF office:

Je veux pas parler de CAF parce que ça m'a vraiment énervé. Euh j'y suis allée à peu près six fois. Et maintenant ils vont couper euh mes allocations dans deux parce que je suis en colocation et tout ça. Et je vais recevoir un lettre qui dit "Oh mais parce que tu n'as pas été honnête on va prendre une moitié de ton argent", ce qui n'est pas vrai parce que je suis honnête dès le début, et c'est CAF qui est nul. Mais euh avant, je n'aurais pas eu le confiance de faire un truc comme ça, même en anglais, de dire "Non c'est vous qui êtes trompés, c'est pas moi, et je vais pas dire que je suis coupable ici. Oui je vais vous payer l'argent, mais il faut accepter que c'est vous qui êtes nuls quoi". Et avant je n'aurais pas eu la confiance de faire cela. Il est simple maintenant de dire quand je suis pas d'accord avec les gens. Ça m'a vraiment aidé je crois

(122/V2Q7).

186   *Language practices in sojourn*

[I don't want to talk about the CAF because that really annoyed me. Euh I went there almost six times. And now they are going to cut my support in half because I'm sharing a flat, and I'm going to receive a letter saying "Oh, because you haven't been honest we are going to take half of your money", which isn't true because from the very beginning I have been honest, and it's CAF that is rubbish. But before I would not have had the confidence to do something like that, even in English, to say, "No, it is you that have made the mistake here, it is not me, and I'm not going to say that I'm the guilty one. I'm going to pay, but you need to admit that it's you who are rubbish". And before I would not have had the confidence to do that. It is easy now to say when I disagree with people. This experience has really helped me I think.]

This aggressive stance may have lacked intercultural sensitivity, but it certainly reflected growing confidence in her ability as an L2 user.

7.3.2.5 Accessing informal L2 practice through sport and music

Sport (whether playing or watching) has been mentioned already as a means of accessing local social networks. All of the sojourners concerned saw their sports-derived networks as one of their major openings for L2 practice. Entering these networks demanded a certain amount of pre-existing social and linguistic self-confidence, however. Sojourner 169 provided an unusually immediate description of how she had broken into a predominantly Spanish-speaking network when attending a kayaking event:

> Eehm fui a un kayak un evento de kayak nocturno, y ehm he hecho una broma con un hombre que estaba trabajando como instructor, ehm porque hemos chocado las barcas y del kayak, y um he hecho una broma que él no sabe cómo hacerlo, y tiene que aprender antes de ir al kayak, porque yo estoy haciendo perfectamente. Y sí, y um después de este hemos hablado un poco más y él me ha introducido a muchos de sus amigos y yo a él. Y ahora tenemos un grupo muy largo de – una mezcla de italianos españoles ingleses franceses
> (169/V1).

[Mmm. I went to a kayak, to a kayak night event, and I made a joke to a man who was working as an instructor, because our boats crashed into each other, our kayaks and I joked and said to him he didn't know how to do it properly, because I was doing it perfectly. And yes, after this we talked a bit more and he introduced me to lots of his friends and I to mine. And now we have a large group of – a mixture of Italians, Spanish, English and French.]

We saw in Chapter 6 how 129 showed similar self-confidence when she used her musical abilities to find local student friends. In turn, this led her into membership of city-wide folk music networks with exceptionally rich opportunities for L2 practice with varied interlocutors. It seems that conscious possession of a non-linguistic talent contributes to the positive agency needed to access local networks and related L2 practice opportunities, at least at the very start of the sojourn.

7.3.2.6 Lingua franca usage of French and Spanish

A concern that English would predominate as lingua franca in international networks was expressed by numbers of participants at Presojourn. However, on campus, at Insojourn 1, several sojourners referred to using French or Spanish routinely with international friends:

> Euh jusqu'à maintenant euh beaucoup d'Allemands et Allemandes, ce qui est bien parce que j'aime parler un peu d'allemand. Je suis débutant quand même. Et ils sont drôles, euh ils sont très sarcastiques, ça marche pour moi. Mais (.) euh principalement Espagnols et Italiens, et tout le monde parle français. On a dit "on va pas parler anglais", tout le monde veut pratiquer
> (126/V1Q7).

> [Up to now, lots of Germans, which is good because I enjoy speaking a little German. I'm a beginner, though. And they're funny, they are very sarcastic and that works for me. But, mainly Spanish and Italian people, and everyone speaks French. We say that "we are not going to speak English". Everyone wants to practise.]

> Mmm realmente solo tengo una amiga aquí que se llama Lena. Pero es de Alemania así. Mmm sí. Aunque hablamos en español, es como un español roto porque no somos nativos así, pero creo que ayuda
> (179/V1Q7).

> Mmm [I really only have one (girl) friend here, who is called Lena. But she's from Germany, so, yeah, although we speak Spanish to each other, it's like broken Spanish because we are not native speakers, but I think it helps.]

A timid sojourner, such as 106, might in the beginning actually prefer other learners as her interlocutors:

> Et aussi je suis plus timide avec les Français parce que je sais que je fais des erreurs. Et avec les autres gens qui ont français comme deuxième langue je suis plus à l'aise parce que je sais que ils font les mêmes erreurs
> (106/V1Q5).

> [And also I'm more timid with the French speakers because I know that I make mistakes. And with others who speak French as a second language like me I'm more relaxed because I know that they make the same mistakes.]

This did not routinely apply, however, and there were many settings where English was accepted as the normal lingua franca:

> En fait j'ai imaginé que je parlerais plus euh de français, et pour le premier moitié de septembre j'ai parlé que l'anglais. Avec tous les étudiants Erasmus, on parle toujours en anglais
>
> (112/V1Q7).

> [In fact, I thought that I would be speaking more French, and for the first half of September I only spoke English. We always speak English with all of the Erasmus students.]

Among language assistants in Europe, there was considerable bias toward the use of English when at leisure; assistant sojourners quickly found new English, North American or Irish assistant friends, and (mostly) spoke English with them. However, where they worked alongside assistants from other language backgrounds, some did refer to the use of French or Spanish as lingua franca:

> Euh je préfère passer les soirées avec Natalie, elle est canadienne, Anne elle est anglaise aussi. Les deux travaillent dans les écoles primaires. Mais ce qui est bon c'est que euh il y a aussi une fille espagnole qui ne parle pas l'anglais. Alors quand nous sommes ensemble vraiment nous sommes obligées vraiment de parler euh le français, parce que c'est pas poli pour la fille espagnole
>
> (122/V1Q7).

> Euh [I prefer to spend the evenings with Natalie, she's Canadian, Anne, she's also English. Both of them work in primary schools. But what's good is that there is also a Spanish girl who doesn't speak English. So when we're together we are obliged to speak French, because it's not polite for the Spanish girl.]

Flatshares with mixed nationalities could also offer the option of lingua franca usage. 163 referred to the use of Spanish with one particular French flatmate, and 169 became very good friends with an Italian flatmate (her "Italian sister") with whom she spoke Spanish:

> Si somos solo, ella y yo, hablamos en español. A veces ella me dice algo muy simple como "Qué tal?", pero en inglés, y yo respondo en inglés. Pero si es una conversación larga, hablamos en español
>
> (169/V2Q5).

> [If it's only her and me, we speak Spanish. Sometimes she says something very simple, like "How are you?" but in English, and I reply in English. But if it's a long conversation, we speak Spanish.]

Overall, then, it seems that sojourners with active agency could find similarly motivated learner-interlocutors and engage in L2 lingua franca use with them. However, use of L2 in these relationships could be unstable, and liable to give way to English, even where intentions were positive. In France, 107 and 112 were sharing a flat with two Turkish girls; at first they all spoke French together, but later on, English came to predominate.

7.3.3 Using English

In many cases, as we have seen, English was central to sojourners' placement roles. Here we explore how sojourners also used English for private and leisure purposes with other Anglophones (7.3.3.1) and as a lingua franca with international friends (7.3.3.2). We finally examine conflict and negotiation around the use of English in service encounters and with local interlocutors more generally (7.3.3.3).

7.3.3.1 English in old and new Anglophone relationships

The quantitative survey shows that sojourners made very extensive use of the internet in English; here, a key function was the maintenance of long term home networks. 177 drew a picture of herself together with two other sojourners, finishing each day by making home contact, and others described similar L1 contact routines:

> Hacemos algo por la tarde, por ejemplo cenamos en un restaurante o vamos a la (.) no sé, ir al cine. Eh por la noche a menudo estamos por ejemplo todas juntas en una sala con nuestros computadores, escribiendo emails uh sean a los padres, o nuestros padres, o amigos
>
> (177/V1Q3).

> [We do something in the evening, for example, we have dinner at a restaurant or we go to the (.) I don't know, to the movies. At night we are usually all together in a room with our computers, writing emails to our parents, to our parents or to friends.]

> I get to Skype my boyfriend most days and I get to speak to my mum every week, like it is so much easier. Thank God for the internet, thank God
>
> (151/R1).

When family, partners and friends visited, English was normally spoken: "Y pasé dos semanas con mis papás. Entonces hablaba inglés" (155/V3). Additionally, sojourners normally spoke English together. This led to some questioning, in particular in Mexico, about whether it was wise to live together, but no one felt this strongly enough to separate. In Europe, most sojourners had regular contact with other Anglophone peers, apart from the Home City group, and in almost all cases it is clear that they spoke English together, whether in domestic settings, "going out", or undertaking touristic travel. Occasional attempts to use the target language between Anglophones were mentioned, but it was clear that these were fragile and unlikely to be sustained.

7.3.3.2 English as a lingua franca

The use of English as a lingua franca among student sojourners in various European countries is well documented (Dervin, 2013; Kalocsai, 2011). For our sojourners, we have seen that in some settings, other lingua franca choices were available. However, the interview data suggest that English as lingua franca was indeed the unmarked form of communication in mixed groups, at least in student settings. For example, housemates 107 and 112 mentioned switching into French when the local boyfriend of 107 was around; this not only implied that they spoke English together, but also implied the predominant use of English within their wider international group. More direct comments on the use of ELF were made by a few sojourners. Assistant 120 was using English with new international friends from the local university: "Euh j'ai des amis du Sciences Po à City FM, mais eux bien sûr ils parlent l'anglais" (120/V1Q3). Sojourner 165 was an exchange student in a setting where Erasmus students followed a distinct programme:

> Conozco muchísima gente aquí, solo pensaba que voy a usar español más. Pero como te dijo, no tengo tantos amigos españoles porque todos mis clases son específicamente para la gente Erasmus, es como español, traducciones, geografía de España. Y por eso todos mis compañeros son de Erasmus. Entonces normalmente hablamos en inglés, a veces en español, pero es más fácil en inglés
>
> (165/V1Q7).

> [I know a lot of people here, but I just thought I was going to use Spanish a lot more. But as I said to you, I don't have that many Spanish friends, because most of my classes are specifically for Erasmus students, it's like Spanish, translation, Spanish geography, and that's why all my classmates are Erasmus. So we normally speak in English, sometimes in Spanish, but it's easier to do it in English.]

Overall, the choice of lingua franca seemed an area where individual agency could influence practice to some degree, but where some use of ELF was structured into the wider environment wherever international sojourners were numerous.

7.3.3.4 Conflict and negotiation around the use of English

While sojourners accepted or preferred the use of English with Anglophones, in most cases, and with international peers in many others, most of them had very different feelings about the use of English with locals. We have seen that in professional settings, local colleagues quite often wanted to practise English, in competition with sojourners' wish to practise French or Spanish. Sojourners might feel uncomfortable about this, but often did not feel able to negotiate a different practice:

> Normalement je parle avec les profs qui sont français, mais ils veulent pratiquer l'anglais avec moi. Donc je parle avec eux en français, et ils parlent avec moi en anglais
>
> (110/V2Q7).
>
> [Usually I talk to the teachers who are French, but they want to practise English with me. So I speak to them in French, and they speak to me in English.]

At leisure, sojourners also found it frustrating that service personnel would often ignore their own efforts to speak French or Spanish, and use English regardless:

> Euh la seule chose que euh j'ai rendu compte, que euh j'ai surprise, que beaucoup de gens qui rend compte que je parle anglais veut euh parler avec moi en anglais. Par exemple euh dans beaucoup de restaurants, si euh (.) ceux qui travaillent là euh peut écouter que je parle en anglais, si je demande quelque chose en français, euh ils me répondent en anglais. Et ça c'est un peu euh (.) pour moi je n'aime pas ça. J'ai parlé en français, et j'ai essayé de parler en français, mais ils me parlent en anglais. C'est un peu impoli en mon avis. Mais pour eux c'est pour pratiquer l'anglais je pense
>
> (110/V1Q4).
>
> [So the only thing that I have noticed, and that I have surprise, is that lots of people who notices that I speak English wants to speak English to me. For example, in a lot of restaurants, if the people working there can hear that I'm speaking English, and if I ask for something in French, they reply in English. And that euh (.) well I don't like that. I spoke in French, and I tried to speak in French, but they speak back to me in English. That's not polite in my view, but for them it's to practise their English I think.]

It seemed in several accounts that service personnel had observed intragroup use of English by the sojourners themselves, and were attempting to accommodate to this. However, some sojourners (like 110) attributed this use of English to selfish motives on the part of their interlocutor, who they saw as wishing to practise, at the expense of their own opportunity. By the end of the year, however, some sojourners reported greater persistence in L2 use, which indicated their language preferences much more clearly to service personnel:

> At the beginning even when I wanted an ice cream, they would just reply to me in English, even though I'd asked them in perfect French, or even if

192 *Language practices insojourn*

it wasn't perfect it was definitely understandable. And I knew that and they knew that, but they'd still say "Right, that will be one euro twenty", and you'd be like "Well". And it's just I think it's rude personally, and then then you get to the stage where you don't, like I'm quite a shy individual so then I'll reply in English, I'll do what they want me to do. But then I got to the stage where I thought, "Well I'll still reply to them in French", even though they just ignored the fact and they've spoken to you in English. And now people don't talk to me in English, which is the progression, which is nice

(128/RIQ5).

Non-confrontational negotiation around language choice seemed more feasible with peers, whether local or international:

Euh je trouve que tout le monde veut euh parler en anglais au début, mais si je dis "Non je veux parler en français", on est sympathique et on le fait. Et je pense que euh ça c'est pas la stéréotype de les Français, que on est ouvert et on veut parler avec xxx. Mais c'est mon expérience

(111/V1Q4).

[Euh I find that everyone wants to speak English at first, but if I say "No I want to speak French", they are sympathetic and they do it. And I think that isn't the stereotype of French people, to be open and to be willing to talk xxx. But that is my experience.]

It seems that distinctive strategies and levels of confidence were needed when exercising language preferences with strangers such as service personnel, which were only gradually acquired.

7.3.4 Using additional languages

A number of sojourners enrolled in formal language classes while insojourn, usually in university settings. The languages mentioned were French (in Spain: n=3); German (n=3); Italian (n=4); "Mayan" (n=2: which language was not specified); Portuguese (n=1); Russian (n=1); and Spanish (in France: n=2). Post-sojourn, 113 and 119 were off to China and 127 to Germany, for a further brief sojourn. Small numbers also reported undertaking tandems in some of these additional languages, and occasionally using them informally. The sojourners with first languages other than English (108, 158 and 165) spoke their home language when opportunity arose.

It is noticeable that with the exception of "Mayan", all of the languages sojourners studied formally were international standard languages which could be found on the home curriculum as well. In several cases, therefore, sojourners were keeping in touch with a language that they would be studying in their final university year.

As far as regional languages were concerned, 157 and 177 did not clearly explain their reasons for taking a Mayan course. Sojourner 157 showed rather equivocal motivation: "Es que no quiero hablar maya, pero quiero decir que puedo hablar maya" [It is not that I want to speak Mayan, but I would like to say that I can speak Mayan]. She found the language difficult, and remarked that the greatest benefit for her was that the teacher taught through Spanish. Sojourner 177 was filling her time with a variety of classes: "Estoy disfrutando de las oportunidades que tengo en la escuela, como las clases de portugués y de maya y las clases de baile" [I am taking advantage of the opportunities in the school, like the classes in Portuguese and in Mayan, and the dance classes] (177/V2Q1). In contrast, 129 in France was focusing her university research project on the Breton language. She travelled to Breton-speaking districts and joined in a demonstration in favour of minority language rights; it is not clear that she attended any classes in the language, but her pro-minority-language stance was exceptional.

In parts of Spain, sojourners were confronted with minority languages directly in their daily lives; those in Catalonia, in Valencia and near the Basque country encountered the respective regional languages in daily communication. Attending university in Catalonia, and socializing primarily in an international circle (where she spoke English, Polish and German, as well as Castilian), 165 found she could largely ignore the existence of Catalan:

> La gente habla catalán en las calles, pero normalmente en español también. Cuando voy a una tienda, cuando ven que no soy española no catalana no hablan catalán, normalmente hablan español o inglés, pero sí, no es ningún problema catalán
>
> (165/V1Q2).
>
> [People speak Catalan in the streets, but normally in Spanish too. When I go to a shop, when they see I am not Spanish or Catalan, they don't speak Catalan, they normally speak Spanish or English, but yeah, Catalan is not a problem.]

Things were very different for 180, however, who was placed as assistant in two Basque-medium schools. As we have seen, she felt herself linguistically isolated in this setting, and frustrated by the limited opportunity to use Castilian. By the end of her stay she had mastered some phrases in Basque, but she believed the language was too difficult to learn informally and was not motivated to seek a formal class.

Two male sojourners (156 and 173) were well integrated in local communities in Valencia, but with the complication that Valenciano was their associates' usual language. By the end of the sojourn, 173 was claiming to understand Valenciano well, and he quoted some expressions in interview, reflecting his strong commitment to his immediate local setting. Sojourner 156 was much less accommodating. His clear objective was to learn Castilian, he objected to the use of Valenciano in university communications, and he found that it was inhibiting and frustrating to be among Valenciano speakers (even though by Insojourn 3, at least, he could understand them):

> Es que escuchando como pasivamente a conversaciones en Málaga a lo mejor o en Madrid sería posible aprender un poco así, pero aquí no es posible porque todo el mundo habla entre sí en valenciano, y no me ayuda para nada. Y sí, es un poco difícil a veces unirme a un conversación que ya existe, o que ya ha comenzado, porque si han comenzado en valenciano me siento un poco maleducado como interrumpir, como quiero que cambien
>
> (156/V2Q11).

> [It is just that that listening passively to conversations in Málaga maybe or in Madrid, it would be possible to learn a bit, but here it is not possible because everyone speaks Valenciano to each other and that doesn't help me at all. So yeah, it's a bit difficult, sometimes, to join an ongoing conversation or one that had started [before I joined], because if they had started speaking Valenciano, I feel it's rude to interrupt, as if I want them to switch.]

Sojourner 156 liked many aspects of his city, but he said more than once that if he had known the strength of Valenciano there, he would have studied somewhere else.

7.4 Conclusion

The quantitative evidence presented early in this chapter confirms that sojourners' language practices were consistently bi- or plurilingual throughout their stay. The qualitative evidence goes some way to explaining these complex practices. English was spoken actively throughout, by virtually all sojourners, to sustain emotional and social ties with home and to develop relationships with other Anglophone sojourners, and in many cases, with a wider network of international peers. The value of English as tradable cultural capital was understood and exploited not only within sojourners' placement roles, but also in forging relationships and earning L2-using opportunities with locals, including students, professional mentors, and host and other families.

Alongside this ongoing use of English, most sojourners made considerable efforts to find interlocutors and occasions for L2 use. The structural-social factors facilitating L2 use varied geographically, however, and to some extent also by placement role, and were closely related to variation in social networking opportunity.

Within a given sociolinguistic framework, sojourners had to demonstrate agency in order to negotiate L2 use. We have seen examples of "high agency" sojourners who proactively engaged with local flatmates, families, classmates, colleagues and teacher mentors; who sought leisure environments which were monolingual or L2-dominant; and who made their language preferences known to local acquaintants, to international peers and to strangers (e.g., in service encounters). There were also examples of "low agency" sojourners, who failed at times to accept invitations or to express language preferences, avoided venues such as school staffrooms or tools such as the telephone, and in general rarely ventured beyond Anglophone networks. In between, many sojourners resorted to tandems and organized activities such as choirs or dance classes, as a relatively controlled means of accessing at least some L2 practice. Even active agency could not always create easy access to L2; however, as shown in the individual case studies presented below in Chapter 9, persistence and flexibility could, over time, develop L2 practice even in structurally difficult settings.

References

Block, D. (2013). The structure and agency dilemma in identity and intercultural communication research. *Language and Intercultural Communication, 13*(2), 126–147.

Dervin, F. (2013). Politics of identification in the use of lingua francas in student mobility to Finland and France. In C. Kinginger (Ed.), *Social and cultural aspects of language learning in study abroad* (pp. 101–126). Amsterdam: John Benjamins.

Kalocsai, K. (2011). The show of interpersonal involvement and the building of rapport in an ELF community of practice. In A. Archibald, A. Cogo, & J. Jenkins (Eds.), *Latest trends in English as a Lingua Franca research* (pp. 113–138). Newcastle Upon Tyne: Cambridge Scholars Publishing.

McManus, K., Mitchell, R., & Tracy-Ventura, N. (2014). Understanding insertion and integration in a study abroad context: The case of English-speaking sojourners in France. *Revue Française de Linguistique Appliquée, 19*(2), 97–116.

8 L2 identity and the ideal L2 self

8.1 Introduction: The foundations of L2 identity

Like the British undergraduates studied by Stolte (2015), Busse (2013) and Busse and Williams (2010), the LANGSNAP participants had enjoyed their school experiences of languages, and more than half had ended up as languages specialists at A level, the academic school-leaving examination. (20/27 members of the LANGSNAP Spanish group and 13/29 members of the French group had studied at least two languages successfully up to A2 level or International Baccalaureate level, usually a combination of French and Spanish.) When asked at Presojourn about target language use outside the classroom, all participants mentioned prior experience of one or more French- or Spanish-speaking countries. Many had visited for family holidays, or with their school, while some had travelled independently (e.g., as au pairs, to do voluntary work or to take a summer language course). Several members of the Spanish group had previously attended a short SA programme in Mexico arranged by the university. Thus, their favourable personal biographies clearly predisposed them to language learning including an extended sojourn abroad (Lörz, Netz, & Quast, 2016; Stolte, 2015).

The LANGSNAP project distinguished between personality, seen as a largely stable construct, and identity, described in Chapter 2 as more fluid, socially constructed and contextually determined. As described in Chapter 3, the LANGSNAP sojourners completed the 91-item Multicultural Personality Questionnaire (MPQ) of Van der Zee and van Oudenhoven (2000) at Presojourn and at Postsojourn 1. The MPQ tests five dimensions of personality: Cultural Empathy (CE), Openmindedness (O), Social Initiative (SI), Emotional Stability (ES) and Flexibility (F). Detailed findings from this questionnaire survey are reported elsewhere (Tracy-Ventura, Dewaele, Koylu, & McManus, 2016). Briefly, it turned out that the only personality dimension which showed significant (positive) change between the two administrations was Emotional Stability – a measure of participants' sense of self-confidence and self-efficacy. However, the LANGSNAP participants had already scored highly presojourn, on Cultural Empathy in particular. Perhaps unsurprisingly, these well-motivated and specialist languages students seemed already very open to new cultural experiences before actually experiencing their year abroad.

In this chapter we focus on the social construction of sojourners' identity throughout and following the sojourn, drawing on the interview data collected throughout, and in particular on the reflective interviews conducted in English at Insojourn 3.

8.2 Traditional demographic factors: Gender, nationality, culture and social class

In Chapter 2 we reviewed discussions of gender, nationality and social class in previous SLA-focused study abroad literature. None of these were prominent topics in any of the Insojourn interviews. This does not mean that these factors were neutralized; it is clear, for example, that both social class and gender have played an important prior role in language majors' long-term educational choices. During the sojourn it is clear that participants continued to enact gendered as well as national identities – for example, in their friendship networks and choice of romantic partners. But how far, if at all, were sojourners' norms and expectations for each of these factors significantly challenged during the sojourn abroad?

8.2.1 Gender

In the Presojourn interview, participants were asked if they expected their gender to affect their experience abroad. Most did not expect this; while several said, for example, that women would need to take more precautions than men when going out at night, this opinion was often qualified by the view that this was the case at home as well. A few women reported that they had been advised to change their style of dress (jeans in place of short skirts); small (and roughly equal) numbers felt it would be easier for males and for females to make friends. But it was clear that overall, these participants expected a gendered experience similar to young adult life in Britain. All participants discussed gender in binary terms (male/female); there was no disclosure throughout the project of any issues relating to LGBT identities.

When interviewed Insojourn, sojourners in France and Spain, male and female, clearly felt they could live daily life in their residential localities, undertake their programme of work or study, form friendships, and travel freely in groups without major gender-based restrictions. A few women complained about lack of late-night public transport, which restricted their leisure activities. A few confirmed the usefulness of the advice on dress offered by the home university, and a few mentioned offensive comments and/or behaviour from strange men in the street. Two women in France described men as "very pushy" in their sexual expectations:

> Bon je suis sûre que tout le monde peut-être a dit la même chose, je sais pas. Mais je dirais que les hommes sont beaucoup plus directs, je suis obligée d'être un peu moins moi, quoi. Moi en fait je peux pas être un ami aux hommes, parce que c'est comme quand je suis amie avec les hommes, les hommes me voient comme je veux coucher avec haha et pfff bon
>
> (122, V1).

[Well I am sure that everyone has maybe said the same thing, I don't know. But I would say that men are much more direct, I have to be a bit less myself. In fact I can't be a friend to men, because it seems like when I am friendly with men, the men see me as if I want to sleep with them ha ha well.]

Several female assistants in France also reported difficulties in establishing professional authority with some older male students:

*114: Et ils sont pas très sympas, dans les couloirs dans les cantines ils ont toujours une phrase anglais, des gros mots, des choses comme ça qu'ils veut dire à moi. Oui c'est pas très sympa.
[And they are not very nice, in the corridors and in the canteen they always have an English expression, something very rude, those kinds of things that they want to say to me. Yeah, it is not very nice.]
*KMcM: Est-ce-que tu penses que c'est parce que tu es une femme ou parce que tu es jeune?
[Do you think it is because you are a woman or because you are young?]
*114: Euh je pense que peut-être c'est les deux euh un peu hum (114/V2Q7).
[Euh I think maybe it is both a bit hum.]

However, participants who described relations with males as somewhat problematic frequently commented that similar issues might be encountered at home, and they described a range of coping strategies. The particular concerns of the assistants diminished as the year progressed.

Gender seems to have affected female sojourners' experience somewhat differently in Mexico. In the workplace and on campus, as in Europe, the five female sojourners felt free to make male friends, and some started romantic partnerships with Mexican men. However, four out of five also talked about street harassment as an ongoing problem; two of this group, who had acquired Mexican partners, were startled to find themselves ignored – as they saw it – when accompanying them in service encounters:

Fui a una tienda con mi novio, y yo pregunté al vendedor algo, no? Pero él respondió a mi novio, y me ignoró, y como, "Pues estoy aquí, te estoy hablando, no?" O no sé. Como por la calle te gritan cosas, no? A veces es gracioso pero a veces no. Entonces para mí diría que este reto es como acostumbrarse a sentir o acostumbrarse a estar tratada diferente que antes, no?
(171/V2Q7)

[I went to a shop with my boyfriend and I asked the shop assistant something, right? But he replied to my boyfriend, and completely ignored me, and I was like "Well, I am here, I am talking to you, aren't I?" Or I don't know. Like how on the street they shout things at you, don't they? Sometimes it's funny, but sometimes it isn't. So for me, I would say that this challenge is all about getting used to feeling, or getting used to being treated differently than before.]

Otherwise, all those participants who found local romantic partners generally described these relationships in very positive terms – for example, as opening doors to welcoming families and "authentic" life more generally. Little in the way of culture shock appeared to attach to these relationships, which typically involved fellow students.

8.2.2 Nationality and culture

Here we deal together with sojourners' perceptions of nationality and culture. In interview, they were willing to make judgements on perceived national and cultural characteristics, though these were generally limited to comments on practices in everyday interaction. The language they used was often drawn from long-standing national stereotypes.

In France, several sojourners commented positively on what they saw as a generally more relaxed way of life. The pre-eminent example given concerned practices during mealtimes, which were commonly described as more sociable than the rapid lunch breaks, for example, experienced in England, and linked to different attitudes to work:

> Quand je travaillais en Angleterre c'est plus like hum on doit travaille travaille travaille tout le temps, on doit manger le déjeuner seule au bureau euh comme ça. Mais ici en France c'est plus hum sociable avec les autres gens. Et c'est plus – oui je pense que c'est bien oui
>
> (116/V2).

> [When I worked in England it was more like you must work work work all the time, you must eat your lunch alone at your desk like that. But here in France it is more sociable with other people. It is more – yeah, I think it is good, yeah.]

Sojourners who had got to know families made similar comments:

> Euh je crois qu'ils ont une façon de vivre qui est vraiment – euh euh c'est focalisé sur la nourriture et la convivialité. Euh les deux choses euh vont [ensemble], euh ils font le bon ménage en fait, parce que on se rassemble le matin pour prendre un bon petit déjeuner en famille, avant de partir séparément tous les travaux diverses. Hum le déjeuner c'est vraiment un lieu de rencontre pour manger ensemble
>
> (104/V2).

> [Euh I think they have a way of living which is really – euh it is centred on food and conviviality. The two things go together, they have a good home regime in fact, because everyone gets together in the morning to have a nice family breakfast, before going off separately to work. Hum lunch is really a meeting point to eat together.]

Others linked this sociability to a greater French interest in politics and willingness to engage in extended discussions. A few compared this favourably with student nights out in England:

> Avant quand j'étais à Home City j'avais pas vraiment envie de sortir beaucoup parce qu'il y a pas beaucoup des endroits très sympa, et en plus les étudiants étaient pas trop – ils voulaient um boire beaucoup. [. . .] Mais pour moi j'arrive pas à boire beaucoup déjà. Et je trouve que c'est beaucoup plus sympa de parler avec les gens. Et là à Paris especialement avec les Français c'est plutôt on boit pour le plaisir. Et après on parle beaucoup [. . .] là j'ai envie de sortir
>
> (128/V2).

> [Before when I was in Home City I did not really want to go out a lot because there are not very many nice places. And the students were not very – they wanted to drink a lot [. . .]. And I find it is much nicer to talk to people. And in Paris especially with French people it is more that you drink for pleasure. And afterward you talk a lot [. . .] here, I want to go out.]

Sojourners' opinions were more divided on French people's general friendliness and politeness. Here, opinions might be qualified by region:

> Mais enfin je trouve que ici au Nord tout le monde est vraiment acceuillant, un petit peu comme dans le film *Bienvenue chez les Ch'tis* euh, que que euh oui les gens sont supers
>
> (108/V2).

> [But I really find that here in the north everyone is really welcoming, a bit like in the film *Bienvenue chez les Ch'tis*, euh, that yes, people are great.]

> I've become more assertive and to an English person maybe a bit rude, I don't know, but Parisians are just very rude, they can be very rude
>
> (128/RI).

Several thought that the French people they encountered in service settings were often not very interested in understanding or assisting foreigners:

> On Saturday I had to go to the police station, I was trying to explain to the policeman something that I wanted to say, it wasn't something particularly important but it just really annoyed me that I couldn't get it out, and I felt like he was a bit like "Oh she's just a little English girl, she doesn't really know what she is trying to say", and that really annoyed me
>
> (107/RI).

A good number of participants saw French administrative processes and attitudes as unnecessarily bureaucratic and slow. Opening a bank account was a common example:

> You know I managed to do it by myself but it was – euh there was a lot of toing and froing there, you know, I needed an *attestation d'hébergement* and things like that, and it was then going to the secretary of the school and getting things off of her and – Bureaucracy is a nightmare in France, I think a lot of people have said that, and I totally agree with them
>
> (127/RI).

The commonest opinion expressed by sojourners in Spain was that life was more "relaxed" than in England; Spanish people were perceived as generally friendly. Aspects of lifestyle were seen as very different, notably the style and timing of meals, and related opening hours of shops and offices, and a few sojourners in Spain never became reconciled to these. Several referred to traditional stereotypes of Spanish behaviour, mostly in positive terms:

> If I had gone to France or maybe gone to Germany it would have been kind of similar [to the UK] you know, it's a kind of similar way of life but here in Spain it's very different, you've got like your siestas, you've got your staying out all night, you've got the weather, you've got the tapas, and it's – and the way that people do things is different, there is no rush to do anything, it is very very relaxed and I think that has been the best thing like just doing it differently for a whole year
>
> (164/RI).

It was an intern who took the most negative view:

> The worst basically [are the] disappointments which come from from what you thought before about Spain and Spanish people, which are the stereotypes basically, that they are so relaxed, that they just go out, they are so funny, they are lovely to be around. But when you have to live here you don't want it to be always like that, you actually want them to do something that they are supposed to do as well [. . .] the work ethics as well, how they work, how they deal with things, they just sort of – they don't plan, they don't analyse, they just do things however just to get them done, and they don't do them on time, they just do them later and later and it doesn't matter, and they are not bothered, [. . .] they just carry on
>
> (158/RI).

Participants in Mexico also described people generally as friendly, open and relaxed; again, a few criticized bureaucracy and inefficiency (e.g., when seeking a motorcycle license). As we have seen, some women sojourners perceived sexist attitudes in Mexican male behaviour and found this uncomfortable throughout their stay. Nonetheless, several members of this group clearly developed strong local attachments and expressed complex feelings about returning home:

> El pensamiento de regresar a Inglaterra es muy difícil también, porque no sé si me voy a sentir como feliz de estar con mi familia o si voy a querer re–, creo que sí, voy a querer regresar. Pero (.) como luchando con este pensamiento, es como – es algo raro, no? Y no es algo que he experimentado (.) jamás en mi vida
>
> (162/V3Q6).

> [The thought of going back to England is very difficult too, because I don't know if I am going to feel, like, happy to be with my family or if I am going to wish I were ba–, I think I will want to be back. But, (.) like battling with this thought, it's like something odd, isn't it? And not something I have experienced before (.) ever in my life.]

The LANGSNAP sojourners had little to say about locals' perceptions of their own British identity. The only issue raised which was regularly connected to being "English" was that of language choice. Many sojourners reported frustration with assumptions that as Anglophones, English people would prefer to speak English, and/or would not be capable of making themselves understood in the target language:

> Well sometimes when you start speaking, or often I find just like they can tell just by the way you are, by the way you dress, ehm – and often when they realize that you are English, even teachers at school that weren't English teachers, they would sometimes speak to me in English, and I'd be like, I would try you know, I'd make sure I spoke back in French, but because they wanted to practise their own English – which makes it a bit difficult
>
> (120/RI).

> Porque parezco extranjera [laugh], y no hay forma de esconderlo. [laugh] A veces es difícil porque todos – es como estamos en una situación con mucha gente, estamos platicando, y (.) um – no sé – alguien me presenta a su familia o algo, y siempre dicen a mi amigo "Habla español?" y yo como [laugh] "Háblame". Y sí, a veces la gente piensa que no puedo hablar español y todo eso
>
> (179/V3Q6).

> [Because I look like a foreigner [laugh], and there's no way to hide it [laugh]. Sometimes it's difficult because everyone – it's like when we are in a situation with lots of people, we are talking and, I don't know, someone introduces me to their family or something and they always say to my friend: "Does she speak Spanish?" and I'm like [laugh] "Speak to me!" And yes, sometimes people think I can't speak Spanish and all that.]

Some of the non-British LANGSNAP participants reported the same issue, however, suggesting that this was a reaction to perceived language proficiency and preferences rather than to nationality per se.

It can be seen in the foregoing quotations that sojourners generally talked about national characteristics in quite stereotyped and particularistic ways. However, a small number talked at greater length, and with a relativistic perspective, about broader cultural values. For example, 166 talked at length about Spanish and British attitudes toward animals and treatment of animals. She had gone to witness a village bull-running event (with fire tied to the bull's horns), and had discussed this both with a teacher in class and also with a Venezuelan friend; knowing the historical background, and how the bulls are trained for the event, helped her distance herself from the immediate British reaction of "Oh no that's animal cruelty that's bad" (166/RI). She referred in particular to the helpfulness of a presojourn ethnography course in Home City, as she explained why she could now live uncomplainingly with people who smoked:

166: I'm – definitely I am more tolerant. I notice this for example with my flatmates. Now all my flatmates [in Spain] have smoked, and before in England I would be like "eughh" and make a big fuss you know. I didn't, I wouldn't be with smokers at all because I didn't like it. But here I am like, I don't know, little things I am more tolerant of, and I try to understand. I try not to get angry about things before I try to understand it, and then make my judgement of it, rather than get angry or whatever.

*NTV: What do you think has helped you get to that point?

*166: I think the course I did last year for ethnography in university really helped me this year [. . .] because it taught you to analyse it from a lot of different points of view, because if you only judge it from your point of view, well, my experience of life is not what the people who are doing this kind of thing know. They are doing it from their reasoning not mine. So if I don't find out why people do things, then of course it will be weird and strange to me (166/RI).

8.2.3 Social class and ethnicity

As we have seen, British languages majors come from relatively advantaged social class backgrounds, with previous experience of foreign travel and so on. Some differences did emerge within the LANGSNAP group, in terms of the economic resources available to individuals. Some participants could travel freely, take ski trips, rent cars or purchase furniture for individually rented apartments, while others lived in the cheapest available accommodation and found the small financial subsidies available to them very important for both short- and long-term needs. However, it seemed that solidarity around their shared sojourner identity generally prevailed, with few intragroup disputes being reported in interview.

It was the assistants' group in France who were most likely to mention social class difference as affecting their daily professional routine. Those working in a *lycée professionel* or a *lycée technique* were likely to refer to lack of motivation for learning English and poor school discipline, which they often attributed to social disadvantage among their students. One participant compared class sizes with her own private-school experience in England:

> L'équivalent du lycée pour moi en Angleterre, *high school* pour moi c'était assez strict. C'était privé, donc c'était différent à ici. Je pense que c'est le nombre d'étudiants dans une classe parce que pour moi euh à l'équivalent du Bac il y avait huit ou neuf étudiants par classe. Ehm et j'ai eu de la chance maintenant je sais, parce que maintenant il y a quelques classes ici de trente-cinq et c'est impossible
>
> (114/V2).

> [The equivalent school for me in England was high school, and it was quite strict. It was a private school, so different to here. I think it is the number of students in a class, because for me when I was doing school-leaving exams there were eight or nine students in a class. Ehm I was lucky I realize now, because now there are some classes of thirty-five here, and that is impossible.]

Another (106) was placed in a high-achieving *lycée* in a wealthy neighbourhood. She characterized her students as "très riches" and the owners of horses and designer clothes; nonetheless, some students misbehaved, though in this situation the school authorities took immediate strong action to support her. On the other hand, sojourner 123 clearly enjoyed planning motivating tasks for a variety of classes in a disadvantaged *collège* and did not report experiencing discipline problems there.

Despite the multiracial nature of contemporary France and Spain, sojourners rarely referred to ethnicity in interview. Participant 108 enjoyed living in a district with many immigrants in her northern French city. Participant 123 particularly enjoyed working with newly arrived migrant schoolchildren at her *collège*; she was given complete responsibility for teaching English to a small group who had studied the language before coming to France, while the regular teacher taught the other new arrivals. Exceptionally, participant 105 talked at length about entrenched racist attitudes in her southern city between ethnic French and ethnic Maghreb-origin citizens. At Insojourn 2, she talked about her initial shocked reactions to ethnic tensions in the very large *lycée professionel* where she was working:

> Au début j'étais "Oh c'est affreux vous êtes tous racistes et je peux pas euh le supporter", mais maintenant je comprends les deux côtés, et je suis plus euh ouvert je pense. Mais de toute façon je reste choquée par l'ambiance ici. Mais oui je pense que c'est parce que, à l'université par exemple dans les cours de l'immigration, des choses comme ça, on a appris des choses au sujet de ça. Mais je pensais que c'était un peu exagéré [. . .] mais non, c'est la vérité. Mais je pense que c'est le même en Angleterre, dans certains quartiers en Angleterre. Il y a le même problème donc mais oui
>
> (105/V2).

[In the beginning I was "Oh it's awful, you are all racist and I can't stand it", but now I understand both sides, and I am more open I think. But anyhow I am still shocked by the atmosphere here. But yes I think that it's because, at university for example in the classes about immigration, we did learn stuff about it. But I thought it was a bit exaggerated [. . .] but no, it's the truth. But I think it is the same in England in some districts. There is the same problem, yeah.]

She eventually used her research project for the home university as a way of developing a more nuanced and historically grounded understanding of the situation, adding to the small numbers who mentioned their academic studies as helpful in preparing them for intercultural encounters and intercultural reflection.

8.2.4 Traditional demographic factors: Conclusion

Overall, the data show that the LANGSNAP sojourners were challenged in relatively limited ways, as far as traditional demographic and cultural identity factors were concerned, unlike, for example, the female North American sojourners studied by Kinginger (2009), Trentman (2015) or Plews (2015). They noticed and commented on some differences in everyday cultural practices, but on the whole they adapted themselves successfully to these. The main exceptions involved the language assistant group, who were forced to acknowledge challenges deriving from gender, social class and ethnicity in developing their professional identity as educators; and the more general experience of being pigeonholed as an Anglophone, in spite of personal aspirations to multilingualism. In the next section we examine the "sojourner" identity itself.

8.3 The sojourner identity

8.3.1 The temporary sojourner

The general pattern of living of the participants described in Chapters 6 and 7 reflects a core "Anglophone international sojourner" identity, similar to that of the "new strangers" of Murphy-Lejeune (2002). The social networks we have described in Chapter 6 were largely aligned with this core identity. There we saw how most sojourners in France and Spain quickly joined an international network offering shared backgrounds and interests, emotional support and companionship, on all types of placement. In Mexico, the Home City sojourners collaborated to sustain a smaller network of this type among themselves. The "temporary sojourner" identity was also reflected in participants' enthusiasm for travel and tourism, described in Chapter 6 and also noted in previous studies (Adams, 2006; Papatsiba, 2006).

Some participants felt that local people reinforced this identity, with stereotypes of the "Erasmus student". Sometimes this stereotyping was positive, as

206 *L2 identity and the ideal L2 self*

described by a few participants in small towns. However, it was more often felt to be negative – for example, in administrative service encounters (in police stations, hospitals, banks, social security offices, etc.), where several participants in France reported an unhelpful reception. A few exchange students felt that their Erasmus status meant they were not taken seriously by their teachers, though others gave positive accounts of integration into worthwhile courses. Workplace intern 125 felt it was inevitable for her to be perceived as an outsider, given her temporary status (in an international business school):

> Well, I don't belong to Paris because I don't live there, and I don't belong to the campus because I am a foreign student and an intern, and therefore there is – I don't go to classes with all the students here. And I don't particularly belong in the workplace because I'm an intern, and I am leaving in two months, and everyone knows that. And they know that I am going to have a replacement, so for them it is just like a rolling carpet of interns. So no, a year – a year is not enough to belong in a place
>
> (125/RI).

8.3.2 *The student identity downshifted*

The LANGSNAP sojourners already had a strongly developed student identity before departure. However, there is considerable evidence that during the sojourn, this wider student identity receded. When asked at Presojourn about their objectives and expectations, virtually all participants mentioned improvement in their language skills as their main (or in some cases, sole) objective; many explicitly prioritized the development of oral fluency. To this, a general reference to cultural experience was commonly added, and many also spoke about the objective of making local friends of similar age to themselves. Becoming more independent and travelling were commonly mentioned too. (Almost everyone going to Mexico in particular spoke about some aspect of self-development and becoming more independent.)

When asked more specifically about the reasons for their choice of placement type, all of the prospective interns mentioned their wish to gain practical experience of the world of work:

> Oui je voudrais ehm bénéficier d'une haute niveau linguistique pour ma français ehm apprendre le français familier et aussi le français professionnel aussi. Ehm je voudrais ehm être plus courageuse en parlant le français aussi. Ehm et je voudrais développer mes compétences ehm en ce qui concerne la vie professionnelle, une vie travail, une vie dans (.) l'entreprise. Ehm (.) et je voudrais m'amuser beaucoup
>
> (102/Pre).

> [Yes I would like to benefit from a high linguistic level for my French, learn informal French and also professional French. Ehm I would like to be braver

when speaking French as well. And I would like to develop my abilities as far as professional life is concerned, working life, company life. Ehm (.) and I would like to have a great time.]

Almost everyone going to Mexico made it clear that the destination itself was the attraction, and the type of work (as language assistants) was a secondary concern. However, many of the language assistants going to Europe said they hoped to discover whether they were suited to teaching as a profession, and/or that the prospect of earning some money was important. Several interns and assistants also found the idea of a break from academic study appealing:

*AGM: Euh pourquoi as tu choisi de faire assistante de langue l'année prochaine? [Why did you choose to be a language assistant next year?]
*122: Pour commencer je ne voulais plus faire euh des études. Euh j'en ai marre des études ici. Il y a trop de travail toujours. Et aussi je voulais apprendre aux élèves à parler l'anglais, parce que je veux qu'ils aient le même passion pour la langue comme moi. Euh je veux le partager. Alors si je peux aider les élèves à vouloir apprendre l'anglais je serai très contente (122/Pre).
[To start with I did not want to study any more. I am fed up with studying here. There is always too much work. And also I wanted to teach children to speak English, because I want them to have the same passion for language as I do. I want to share it. So if I can help pupils to want to learn English I will be really pleased.]

In the case of these two groups, any wider "student" identity was clearly downplayed temporarily. But even among the participants who were continuing the student role, as exchange students in a French or Spanish university, only a small minority had related their choice of institution abroad to a study plan beyond language improvement. Our example comes from 108, already a sojourner in England:

Ici en Angleterre je fais des études européens aussi euh aussi bien que les langues, et à City FL2 je pourrais ehm faire des études européens. Euh je aussi voudrais faire ehm un master après ma licence, et je le voudrais faire dans le domaine de ehm um de politique de l'environnement et de développement durable. Mais je n'ai rien fait dans ce domaine euh. Et alors à City FL2 je pourrais prendre les cours euh qui est ehm ehm oui dans ce domaine, par exemple les cours dans le développement durable et le politique européen de l'environnement oui

(108/Pre).

[Here in England I am doing European studies as well as languages, and at City FL2 I could do European studies. Euh also I would like to do a masters degree after my bachelors, and I would like to do it in environmental politics and sustainable development. But I have not done anything in this field.

And so at City FL2 I could take courses in this domain, for example courses in sustainable development and European environmental politics, yeah.]

Several did explain that their choice of university allowed them to continue to improve their skills in other languages; others described studying when abroad as a fallback solution (work placements were hard to get, they did not relate well to children, etc.). Overall, many prospective exchange students also seemed to see the student role as a minor dimension of the sojourner experience. For example, the language-learning strategies they expected to use when abroad, described in the Presojourn interview, were largely informal and related to the spoken language, just like the other groups. Little curiosity was shown regarding alternative academic cultures and study traditions.

Once abroad, it is clear that for the interns and the language assistants, their home "student" identities remained largely in the background. Three of the Mexico-based assistants did sign up for language classes at their host university, and one assistant in Spain (174) found a French class; otherwise the sole academic activity referred to by assistants based in Europe was the compulsory research project for the home university. However, the exchange student group did sustain a somewhat clearer student identity insojourn. Studying might not be very intensive, but importance was attached to balancing activities, and at least passing courses:

*164: Los exámenes en enero um (.). sí, y (.).
 [The exams in January, yes, and (.).]
NTV: Fueron difíciles?
 [Were they difficult?]
*164: Algunas sí, ehm (.) es que (.) – porque viajé durante estes@n meses, bueno en enero y febrero, los fin de semanas. Entonces no tenía mucho tiempo a estudiar por los exámenes. Bero sí, eh aprobé los todos, entonces (.) da igual (164/V2Q7).
 [Some were, ehm (.) what happened was (.) because I travelled during those months, well in January and February and on weekends. So I didn't have much time to study for the exams. But, I did pass them all, so it doesn't really matter.]

A majority of student sojourners were attending language, linguistics and/or translation classes, and they frequently talked about investing effort and benefiting from these. A minority sustained a broader student identity, reporting successful studies in international development, music, history or mathematics. Others, however, tried to do this but were not successful, either because they were not allowed to enrol in classes which interested them, or because they did so but received failing grades. Finding relevant content courses at a manageable level of difficulty was referred to by many as a major challenge. For example, 121 took a history course in France, but dropped this in favour of extra language classes, on receiving a failing grade in the first few weeks.

Overall, therefore, it seems that for most sojourners, their general "student" identity was reduced largely to a "L2 learner" identity when abroad, with just a few exceptions among the university-based group. However, this was to change following the return to the home university (see Section 8.5).

8.3.3 Coming of age

We have already noted that a significant change in participants' personality was documented through the MPQ survey, in the area of Emotional Stability – a measure of participants' sense of self-confidence and self-efficacy (Tracy-Ventura et al., 2016). This finding was abundantly confirmed by the interview data. Virtually all sojourners stated very emphatically that they felt they had matured and become more independent, and some compared themselves favourably with their stay-at-home friends. They described many practical aspects of domestic life that they had learned to manage, as well as increased confidence when travelling or getting to know new people, and adapting to new work situations; they felt less dependent on parents and friends, and several told anecdotes about handling emergencies successfully (an attempted mugging, a theft, a bank fraud, a fire in the street, health problems, difficulties with landlords, etc.). Several country-dwellers in England felt they had adjusted to the practicalities of big-city life; almost everyone felt capable of living and working abroad again, in a new environment. As 129 put it, "I feel like the world's my oyster now, while before perhaps I was a bit scared to live abroad, and now it doesn't faze me" (RI). Many expressed pride in what they saw as distinctive accomplishments:

> Euh I think I've learnt a lot of life skills from this year abroad, ehm which at the time may have seemed like the worst thing in the world, but at the same time I now think have provided me with an amazing experience, euh and have made me see what I myself can achieve and has made me really excited for going to China and doing it all again but with friends this time so that's good ehm [. . .] like you're completely independent in this context, and you think that you're independent when you come to uni, but I don't think you realize [. . .] that you're really really not that independent when you are coming to university. [. . .] I mean I have a lot of friends (at Home City) who are amazing, and ehm you know they love what they study, but if you would say to them "Go and live in France for seven months" they wouldn't do it, and like it's not even like France is very far away. But euh I think it takes a particular type of person to be able to go and persevere and to do the experience as a whole, and at the same time do it all in a foreign language. And yeah I mean it's definitely made me consider living in a foreign country when I've graduated
>
> (119/RI).

There is thus abundant evidence for an increased sense of personal autonomy, independence and self-efficacy, which develop through the sojourner experience and can be summarized as "coming of age".

8.4 The L2 self

In this section we examine more closely the place of language in participants' current and desired identity, that is, their identity-related L2 proficiency (Benson, Barkhuizen, Bodycott, & Brown, 2013) and their descriptions of future, ideal L2 selves. (Participants' practices as language learners and language users, included by Benson et al. as a strand of L2 identity, have been described already in Chapter 7.)

8.4.1 Identity-related L2 proficiency

Benson et al. (2013) introduce the concept of identity-related L2 proficiency, to capture the dimensions of target language proficiency which are most valued by L2 learners and users. For Benson et al., sociolinguistic and pragmatic dimensions of language are central to this concept. Here, we summarize the dimensions mentioned as important for self-realization by the LANGSNAP sojourners, which range somewhat more widely. The picture presented derives primarily from the Insojourn 3 reflective interviews.

Overall, there were four dimensions of L2 proficiency which emerged as strikingly important for the LANGSNAP participants. Unsurprisingly, the participants referred most frequently to listening comprehension, and to oral fluency and intelligibility, not as neutral skills, but as key to successful life as a sojourner.

*KMcM: So how do you think this year has influenced your learning of French?
*125: I think for speaking and listening skills euh huge huge influence, because euh I've had to speak and listen to survive every day. And I think they've really improved, euh (.) my listening, euh for example on the telephone so without seeing someone euh someone's face I can still understand them. I can understand like guys' voices, like male and female voices, whereas before I found male voices kind of harder to understand. And yeah even if someone is kind of walking away from me or something, I can generally pick up what they are trying to tell me which is good (125/RI).

> I feel like when I first arrived in France, I would often say things and people would not understand me, euh not necessarily because I was making really big errors or anything, but you know, due to pronunciation, or just the fact that I wasn't very confident in what I was saying. [. . .] and then people they kind of immediately assume that they're not going understand you, when you first start speaking. And I think that I'm a lot more perseverant now. [. . .] Ehm it's not very often that someone says "I really don't understand what you're saying"
>
> (119/RI).

Secondly, sojourners talked about the social importance of being able to sustain conversational interaction, in a way interesting to themselves and their interlocutor(s):

> I think fluency more than more than anything, euh just being able to hold a conversation that doesn't get slowed down to the point of being ridiculous, ehm which I think I was doing at the start. You know, when someone asks you a question and you think about what they just said to you, you formulate your answer and you try and say it, whereas now they sort of say it to me and I have got the answer. I think that's the main key thing, xxx being able to have a conversation at a normal pace
>
> (156/RI).

> Euh I have been able to use it to talk about stuff that I like with people, I can explain now in detail about like folk music, like an interest in history. I mean, in a lesson [. . .] we started discussing Nostradamus, just like I had a question, and I was able to understand all about how it was written in old French and just simple stuff like that, which wouldn't be simple at all at the beginning of the year
>
> (104/RI).

> Now I have a lot of conversations about lots of different themes, like for example like football, I can have a proper conversation about football in Spanish, whereas before I didn't really know what the word for "offside" was or "half time" or "foul", or you know, silly things. I mean it's a silly example, but it shows how from speaking to people [. . .] it's how you learn
>
> (167/RI).

The third dimension of proficiency strongly valued by these sojourners was mastery of idiomaticity, colloquial language and slang, seen as key to establishing a "young adult" identity:

NTV: Any other [. . .] sort of activities that you think were useful?
*172: Euh yeah I think like yeah watching TV. And like just spending time with them and their friends I think helps more, because it's more like a social situation with people my age, so it's more the Spanish that I would need, rather than in school where you would learn the practical stuff. Well I guess you still need it obviously, but to fit in a bit more you need more of the younger colloquially language thing, I think (172/RI).

Here, we find clear motivation for the well-documented acquisition of sociolinguistic variation in French during the sojourn abroad (Regan, Howard, & Lemée, 2009). Numerous sojourners also told anecdotes of acquiring and using idiomatic phrases, swear words, and so on, for example on the sports field:

> I used to play rugby, that was good, because I met people there who spoke obviously like quite colloquial Mexican Spanish, so I learnt a few ehm expressions from there, not all of them particularly polite. We went to the football as well, in the stadium in City MS, and I learnt a lot of swear words

there. But it's quite, it's quite, I don't know, I mean it's good to be able to express yourself in the same way that you would in English

(155/RI).

However, sojourners had also developed some awareness that use of informal registers might be problematic for themselves as outsiders. Some self-censored their use of informal language, and others reported conflicting advice or negative reactions from locals:

> I have learnt like a lot of slang and stuff but only so that I can understand it. I don't use it, because I think if I use it I sound silly, I do, because like even the few words that I use, like people laugh when I say them, because it is like "it doesn't sound right coming out of her mouth"
>
> (178/RI).

> We had a language assistant who said "Oh people in France never say *je ne sais pas*. Some people say *je ne sais pas*, but most of them just go *sais pas*". And I tried to be a good student and take that on board, and this lady just laughed and laughed at me saying, "You sound like a proper commoner, don't never ever do that again"
>
> (106/RI).

Similar issues arose around the acquisition of regional language features, also noticed/discussed by a substantial subgroup. Some sojourners saw this as problematic for L2 sojourner identity, once again, but others were pleased to identify with a particular region or language variety:

> Ehm I've learned that there were certain things that I was saying that I was taught by my friends but they are very northern. Like they all spoke *Chti*, and things that – ehm certain things that I would say. And I went to Nice last week and Cannes, and there was an accent difference, like a serious accent difference. So I think I've learned very northern things, and sort of they put "*quoi?*" on the end of every phrase in the north, and in the south everyone was like "What are you talking about?" So I think I've without realizing it, I've learned a bit of a dialect in France. But I quite like that, it's quite fun
>
> (114/RI).

The fourth area widely mentioned as important was vocabulary. Most talked in general terms about vocabulary growth, but those who were more specific almost always connected this with the need for colloquial language, and gave as examples the learning of vocabulary relevant to daily life (getting a car fixed, getting medical care, cooking, etc.):

> I think it's a little bit lame, but there is ehm there is a show on, *Cauchemar en Cuisine,* that I just love so that really helps. We learned lots of cooking vocabulary from that
>
> (114/RI).

One area of L2 proficiency which was downgraded in importance among sojourners' priorities was grammar. A few participants said that their grammar had improved:

> I'm getting more of a feel about sort of which past tenses to use, and sometimes I use subjunctive without having to go, "Hang on subjunctive, right hang on, how do I do subjunctive again?" and that has always been a really good signal for me. I mean the first time that I realized that I'd used subjunctive without thinking about it, I was quite proud of myself
>
> (167/RI).

However, a larger group commented that they had not invested much effort in this domain: "In Spanish the grammar has gone a bit to the side" (152/RI). The skills of reading and writing were also relatively marginal to sojourner L2 identity. Writing was mentioned most often in the context of the research project for the home university, and occasionally when describing the exchange student and workplace intern experience. Reading was the least mentioned skill, though private leisure reading in French or Spanish was mentioned by a minority (thrillers, or women's magazines), and some academic reading was undertaken for the home research project:

> I think my writing is still not very good, but I didn't need to write, so it was kind of – yeah that was one of the things that was always going to be left behind I think. But yeah, until – until it was the year abroad project and then I was like "Ooh I should really have been doing this before"
>
> (117/RI).

Participants' preoccupation with developing informal L2 proficiency, and relative indifference toward L2 literacy, connect with the relative lack of attention paid to more formal registers of language. A few teaching assistants referred to their need for a professional style of speech for use in the classroom, and some workplace interns also spoke about the need to master particular genres:

> So I had to ehm learn quite a lot of new vocab especially in the first three months like office vocab especially just day-to-day stuff that I didn't know before. [. . .] And kind of like the etiquette for writing emails and reading emails, but especially for writing emails, how to write them properly depending on who is receiving it, and I think it has really improved in general
>
> (125/RI).

214   L2 identity and the ideal L2 self

However, among the exchange students, though most were taking language classes, only a very small number explicitly talked about mastery of academic language as part of the L2 identity they were aiming to achieve.

8.4.2 An interim ideal L2 self

In the Presojourn interviews, as we have just seen, sojourners focused largely on improvement of oral proficiency and fluency, and during their stay, they prioritized the development of conversational ability, idiomaticity and the mastery of informal registers of language. By the end of the stay (Insojourn 3), they were generally feeling very positive about their language improvement and current capabilities. Some of them did reflect on earlier over-expectations:

> All through second year like we were doing like tests and things and I was getting my marks and thought "It's fine, I've got a year abroad, I'll be fluent by the fourth year". And there is no way in hell that I'm any way near fluent, and I think I put far too much pressure on the year abroad, and I thought I would come back speaking like a French person, which now on reflection was obviously really naive and stupid
>
> (113/RI).

There was, however, a general feeling of confirmed motivation for languages, arising from a generally successful experience:

> I think it has made me sort of appreciate my degree a bit more than I did before. Because well before I was kind of like "Oh I like French and I like German so I'll do French and German". And then you know I was going along quite happily, not doing particularly brilliantly, not doing really badly, just kind of there. And then being in France kind of made me think "Actually I do like the fact that I have an ability that other people don't have, and I can be useful"
>
> (117/RI).

Most participants had come to terms with a non-native speaker identity, prioritizing that of an informal young adult L2 communicator. At this point (end of sojourn), they still had only limited thoughts about longer-term aspirations for L2 identity:

> Euh I mean obviously there is still a lot of stuff that I lack, but I understand everything a lot better. And ehm as I said, my goal is to be able to do it in a business situation so that I can go to Spain, South America, wherever, and speak confidently over a business table and negotiate things, because that's what I want to do in the future sort of thing. So I think it is coming towards that ehm yeah
>
> (175/RI).

I'd quite like to sound a bit more native and grown-up

(152/RI).

8.5 The return to study

When interviewed at the start of their final university year (Postsojourn 1), many participants expressed some feelings of social dislocation. Over half the participants returning from France used the word "bizarre" when talking about their perceptions; a few commented that the sojourn was like a dream or something that had never happened. A very large majority reported missing some aspect of life abroad, or missing international friends. A few said they missed the independence they had enjoyed abroad; however, many reported at the same time that they enjoyed reintegrating with home social networks, and the return to a familiar way of life. Half a dozen sojourners expressed no regrets at all about their return.

Some of these feelings of dislocation expressed during the Postsojourn 1 interview concerned the return to study. Some were expecting to enjoy the new academic year socially and/or in terms of challenging study. However a few participants also referred to anxiety, alienation from academic work, or a sense of being left behind by past classmates who had now graduated.

8.5.1 Foregrounding of student identity

The final interview (Postsojourn 2) took place in the spring of the participants' final year of study. By this point, most participants had settled down into a "student" identity once again and were keen to achieve well. This was evident firstly in how they talked about their academic work; substantial numbers spoke positively about the final year language programme. Their successful Insojourn experiences had contributed to this:

> Mais aussi um j'adore mes cours orales ici. Euh je crois que je parle bien français. Et euh ma lectrice m'a dit que dans ma classe on parle le plus que tous les classes. Donc j'aime bien ça. Et normalement je blague beaucoup, mais je blague en français. Donc je crois que euh mon attitude a changé, car avant mon séjour en France j'étais très paresseux pendant les classes. Je voulais pas parler français avec les Anglais euh. Et maintenant c'est le contraire en fait euh. Euh je suis plus passionné pour le français je crois
>
> (127/PS2).

> [But as well I love my oral classes here. Euh I think I speak French well. And my tutor has told me that my class is the most talkative of all, and I like that. Normally I tell a lot of jokes, but I do it in French. So I think my attitude has changed, because before my sojourn in France I was very lazy in class. I did not want to speak French with English people. But now it is the contrary in fact. Euh I am more passionate about French I think.]

216   L2 identity and the ideal L2 self

Most participants were supplementing their classes with informal self-initiated activities, including use of target language media, extensive reading, and interactions with French or Spanish speakers. These took the form either of tandem language exchanges or other forms of social interaction with current Erasmus students at Home City, or of regular communication with L2-speaking friends, partners, and so on, either based in England or abroad. Twelve participants had revisited France or Spain already; a much larger number were maintaining contacts with friends abroad via Facebook and other social media. A small minority reported dissatisfaction or lack of engagement with their current L2 classes, feeling – it seemed – that they had little to learn there. This group generally reported investing most academic effort in other subjects, including their non-sojourn L2.

Secondly, the re-emergence of a strong student identity was evident in the social cohesiveness of the Postsojourn group. Friendship networks had necessarily changed, since most friends from other programmes had now graduated. (In the UK most degrees are finished in three years.) The great majority described strong networking among their Postsojourn cohort, who in many cases were living together. The shared experience of the sojourn was a contributing factor:

> Entonces ahora tengo más amigos que están en mi curso porque solamente están ellos aquí eh en Home City, y sí, pienso que (.) tenemos más en común las personas que han pasado el año en extranjero, y tenemos muchas conversaciones sobre lo que hicimos, y sí, paso más tiempo con ellos ahora que pienso que en el segundo año cuando estaba con mis compañeras de casa (.) que hacen cursos diferentes
>
> (180/PS2).

> [So now I have more friends who are in my course because they are the only ones who are here in Home City, and yes, I think that we, the people who have spent a year abroad, have more in common and we have lots of conversations about what we did, and yes, I spend more time with them now, I think, than in second year, when I was with my housemates who were doing different courses.]

8.5.2 Transnational futures

In both the Postsojourn interviews, participants were asked to comment on their future life plans. At Postsojourn 1, many spoke in general terms about the possibilities of further travel, living abroad in the future, and/or undertaking further study. A few talked about possible career choices, with teaching most frequently mentioned, followed by international business. With the exception of 150, who was actively seeking business internships, none had so far taken any practical steps toward future study or employment:

*129: Je sais pas si je voudrais travailler en France ou en Angleterre. Mais um (.) je sais que (.) si je travaillais en Bretagne je serais très heureuse. Euh donc peut-être c'est quelque chose que je considère maintenant que je n'ai pas considéré avant.
[I don't know if I want to work in France or in England. But um (.) I know I would be very happy to work in Brittany. Euh so maybe that is something I am considering now which I did not consider before.]

*KMcM: Et tu sais ce que tu veux faire?
[And do you know what you want to do?]

*129: Um pas exactement um (.) euh non je sais pas encore (129/PS1).
[Not exactly, no I don't know yet.]

> Pero no hay [?] planes como fijos. Tengo que concentrarme en la universidad porque sin la licencia no puedo hacer nada
>
> (155/PS2/Q8).
>
> [But there's no, like fixed plans. I have to concentrate on university because without a degree I can't do anything.]

By Postsojourn 2, a minority were making applications for further study or employment as translators, teachers, lawyers, management trainees in business, and so on:

> Je compte retourner à Paris. Donc euh je suis déjà en train de postuler pour certains (.) jobs un peu marketing voilà. Sinon il y avait un autre poste là chez Institute il y très peu de temps aussi. J'aurais un an à Home City, et tu fais un an à Paris. Donc ça pourrait être assez intéressant, si c'est un peu rel[atif à la] gestion
>
> (100/PS2).
>
> [I plan to go back to Paris. So euh I am already applying for some jobs in marketing. If not, there was another job there at Institute a little while back. I would have one year in Home City and then you do one year in Paris. So that could be quite interesting, if it has to do with management.]

However, even at Postsojourn 2 there were many who were not yet ready to make long-term career decisions. These participants were often promising themselves an interim period of working in subprofessional jobs or doing short-term English language teaching, to relax, earn money, travel, and so on before applying for professional training or work: "Je voudrais une carrière mais pas encore" [I'd like a career but not yet] (129/PS2). Whether or not participants had started to make career decisions, however, a vision of the self as an active and confident L2 user generally continued to apply. At the end of the sojourn, only a very small minority had said that they definitely preferred living in England and were unlikely to live abroad again. During the Postsojourn interviews, a majority described aspirations to spend time in an L2-speaking destination soon after graduating:

*NTV: Y cuáles son tus planes para después de que te gradúes?
[And what plans do you have after graduation?]
*156: Uh voy a volver a España para enseñar con el British Council. [. . .]
[I am going to go back to Spain to teach for the British Council. [. . .]
*NTV:Y por qué decidiste volver a España?
[And why have you decided to go back to Spain?]
*156: Eh (.) no quería un empleo real, así que – [laugh] sí, la mejor opción me pareció volver a España, seguir viviendo allí, mejorar el español, perfeccionarlo (156/PS2Q8).
[I didn't want a real job, so [laugh] yeah, the best option, seemed to me, was to go back to Spain, continue living there, improve my Spanish, perfect it.]

A further group were contemplating living/studying abroad, but in completely new locations. For example, 105 was hoping to work in international development and had already arranged a short-term VSO placement in Asia; 113 was off to China for a further year as a language assistant and hoped eventually to become a diplomat. These ambitions were closely related to the development of a broadly multilingual L2 self:

> I love being able to communicate, I love being able to be in another country and to be able to communicate, so I want to be able to go to other countries and be able to communicate. I think it is so important ehm yeah
>
> (105/RI).

Only a small number were considering specialist language professions (language teaching or translation), but many more expressed aspirations to use their L2 in some way at work:

> Prefería utilizarlo en un ambiente laboral. Eso es mi sueño, pero no sé si va a pasar o no
>
> (163/PS2).
>
> [I would prefer to use it in the workplace, that's my dream, but I don't know if that will happen or not.]

The potential of multilingualism to sustain and develop international friendships was also commonly mentioned:

> Pues si voy a estar en Londres voy a tener un montón de amigos españoles porque hay un montón de españoles en Londres ahora mismo. Hablaré con los amigos que tengo
>
> (150/PS2).
>
> [Well if I'm going to be in London, I'm going to have many Spanish friends because there's lots of Spanish people in London right now. I will talk to those friends I already have.]

L2 identity and the ideal L2 self 219

However, while most participants were enthusiastic about a multilingual future, very few of them envisaged a long-term return to settle and integrate in one particular L2-using destination (exceptions here were 160, with his commitment to a Mexican romantic partner, and 173, who was maintaining intensive contact with his host family in Spain). That is, when thinking long-term, participants primarily envisaged using their languages in a British-based or global work context:

> Espero um que lo usará mucho en mi trabajo, como en un trabajo para una empresa um que tiene clientes en España o algo, pero una empresa inglesa que tiene um clientes en España, y puedo hablar con ellos y escribir con ellos y todo eso. Entonces no es a un nivel muy alto como traducción uh en que tengo que pensar mucho. [laugh] Pero es el uso diario <de el español> [?]. Pero no sé si voy a um encontrar algo como así
>
> (168/PS2).

> [I hope I will use it a lot in my job, like in some job in a company that has Spanish clients or something, but an English company that has clients in Spain, and I can talk to them and write to them and all that. So not to a very high level like translation for which I will have to think a lot [laughs] but everyday Spanish. But I don't know if I'm going to find something like that.]

Several participants made it clear that they saw their future L2 self as plurilingual, and that they might use three or more languages at work in their future life. Participants 164, 166 and 167 referred to future use of both French and Spanish; 158 was planning to train as a Polish/English interpreter, but hoped to maintain her Spanish too; and 177 expected to use a range of languages in her chosen career in international development.

8.6 Conclusion

This qualitative investigation of interview data has confirmed that the LANGSNAP sojourners had much in common with the "new strangers" of Murphy-Lejeune, and that "coming of age" was an important dimension of their identity development. Their placement roles and peer social networks offered sufficient support for them as temporary members, to move comfortably between cultures, with few direct challenges to their sense of self as far as gender and nationality were concerned (unlike, e.g., some American sojourners in studies reviewed in Chapter 2). Culturally, most continued to seek out encyclopedic knowledge (through travel), and to comment in fairly stereotypical ways on contrasting aspects of daily life; only a minority developed more reflective and interpretive intercultural perspectives, as in the cohorts studied, for example, by Jackson (2012) or Papatsiba (2006). The tensions between "coming of age" and becoming an intercultural speaker, noted by Kinginger (2010), were also present in this cohort.

As for the L2 self more specifically, the sojourners' most typical aspiration was to become a competent multilingual, with oral fluency adequate for independent adult life in the standard variety of at least one language additional to English. Most sojourners did not aspire to integrate fully in the society of residence, though there were exceptions; they had set aside their home "student" identity in order to undertake the sojourn, but they returned to this very readily postsojourn. Neither did they wish to pass as native speakers of the L2; however, they wanted to be able to function as independent users, both in-country and elsewhere. They wanted to master informal registers in the target language, appropriate to their age group, like the sojourners studied by Regan et al. (2009). However, they were often ambivalent about regional varieties and accents, pleased to develop some awareness of these, but not generally motivated to acquire them (as in studies by Iino, 2006, or Garrett & Gallego Balsà, 2014). Thus, overall, the plurilingual practices of the sojourners confirm that for most, their ideal L2 self encompassed fluency in standard varieties of one or more "supercentral" languages in the global language system described by de Swaan (2001), alongside their existing mastery of English, the hypercentral language in the system. However, they were not hurrying to enter specialist multilingual careers, nor to capitalize instrumentally on their new skills. They had grown greatly in terms of self-efficacy and saw their personal plurilingualism as a reassuring asset and a key to future mobility and choice, in terms of lifestyle, career and self-realization.

References

Adams, R. (2006). Language learning strategies in the study abroad context. In M. A. DuFon & E. Churchill (Eds.), *Language learners in study abroad contexts* (pp. 259–292). Clevedon: Multilingual Matters.

Benson, P., Barkhuizen, G., Bodycott, P., & Brown, J. (2013). *Second language identity in narratives of study abroad*. Basingstoke: Palgrave Macmillan.

Busse, V. (2013). An exploration of motivation and self-beliefs of first year students of German. *System*, 41(2), 379–398.

Busse, V., & Williams, M. (2010). Why German? Motivation of students studying German at English universities. *The Language Learning Journal*, 38(1), 67–85.

de Swaan, A. (2001). *Words of the world*. Cambridge: Polity Press.

Iino, M. (2006). Norms of interaction in a Japanese homestay setting: Toward a two-way flow of linguistic and cultural resources. In M. A. Dufon & E. Churchill (Eds.), *Language learners in study abroad contexts* (pp. 151–173). Clevedon: Multilingual Matters.

Jackson, J. (2012). Education abroad. In J. Jackson (Ed.), *The Routledge handbook of language and intercultural communication* (pp. 449–463). Abingdon/New York: Routledge.

Kinginger, C. (2010). American students abroad: Negotiation of difference? *Language Teaching*, 43(2), 216–227.

Lörz, M., Netz, N., & Quast, H. (2016). Why do students from underprivileged families less often intend to study abroad? *Higher Education*, 72(2), 153–174.

Murphy-Lejeune, E. (2002). *Student mobility and narrative in Europe: The new strangers*. New York: Routledge.

Papatsiba, V. (2006). Study abroad and experiences of cultural distance and proximity: French Erasmus students. In M. Byram & A. Feng (Eds.), *Living and studying abroad: Research and practice* (pp. 108–133). Cleveland: Multilingual Matters.

Plews, J. (2015). Intercultural identity-alignment in second language study abroad, or the more-or-less Canadians. In R. Mitchell, N. Tracy-Ventura, & K. McManus (Eds.), *Social *interaction, identity and language learning during residence abroad. EUROSLA Monographs 4* (pp. 281–304). Amsterdam: European Second Language Association.

Regan, V., Howard, M., & Lemée, I. (2009). *The acquisition of sociolinguistic competence in a study abroad context*. Bristol: Multilingual Matters.

Stolte, R. (2015). *German language learning in England: Understanding the enthusiasts*. (PhD), University of Southampton.

Tracy-Ventura, N., Dewaele, J.-M., Koylu, Z., & McManus, K. (2016). Personality changes after the 'year abroad'? A mixed methods study. *Study Abroad Research in Second Language Acquisition and International Education, 1*(1), 107–127.

Trentman, E. (2015). Negotiating gendered identities and access to social networks during study abroad in Egypt. In R. Mitchell, N. Tracy-Ventura, & K. McManus (Eds.), *Social interaction, identity and language learning during residence abroad. EUROSLA Monographs 4* (pp. 263–280). Amsterdam: European Second Language Association.

Van der Zee, K. I., & van Oudenhoven, J. P. (2000). The Multicultural Personality Questionnaire: A multicultural instrument for multicultural effectiveness. *European Journal of Personality, 14*(3), 291–309.

9 The L2 impact of the sojourn experience

9.1 Introduction

In this chapter we draw together the two main strands of the LANGSNAP project: the language learning gains made by the sojourners overall (Chapters 4 and 5), social aspects of the sojourner experience, and sojourner identity (Chapters 6, 7 and 8). In Section 9.2, we explore statistical relationships between findings of the Social Networking Questionnaire (SNQ), the Language Engagement Questionnaire (LEQ), and selected measures of L2 performance. In 9.3, we introduce the concept of L2 gain scores, and again explore relationships between these scores with SNQ and LEQ. Using gain score information, we identify a group of "high gainers" for each language. In 9.4, we adopt a case study approach to provide qualitative portraits of eight "high gain" sojourners, and explore in more depth the significance for individual L2 development of social relationships and of sojourner agency, L2 engagement and identity. In 9.5 we make brief proposals as to the qualities of L2 networking and engagement that appear to "push" advanced L2 development.

9.2 Relations among social networking, language engagement and L2 development: The quantitative evidence

As explained in earlier chapters, we gathered quantitative data concerning sojourners' social networking and language engagement through two questionnaires (SNQ and LEQ). In the case of social networking, we then calculated an integrated Social Networks Index (SNI) for L2 and another for L1.

9.2.1 Relations between SNI, LEQ and L2 performance measures

Here, we explore the relationships between the SNI (L2/L1), the Language Engagement Questionnaire (LEQL2/L1) results, and the linguistic performance of all participants over time. To undertake this analysis, we selected four linguistic measures to represent different domains of L2 development: Elicited Imitation (EI) for general proficiency, Speech Rate for fluency, % Error-Free Clauses for spoken accuracy, and % Error-Free Clauses Writing for written accuracy. We explored relations between each of these measures Presojourn and at end sojourn, with each other and with mean scores for SNIL2, SNIL1, LEQL2 and LEQL1. Correlations between all of these measures are presented in Table 9.1 (Spearman's rho).

Table 9.1 shows that significant relationships exist among the various linguistic measures, and also among the social behaviour measures. Plonsky and Oswald (2014) suggest that correlation coefficients close to .25 should be considered small, .40 medium, and .60 large (p. 889). Of the linguistic measures, the EI scores at Presojourn and Postsojourn 1 correlate significantly with each other (a "large" finding) and also with the Speech Rate scores (at Presojourn and Insojourn 3: "medium"). The accuracy measures in speech and writing are also all significantly related (though correlations are mostly "small"). The Presojourn Speech Rate scores are significantly related to the Presojourn accuracy scores for speech, but this relationship is "small" and disappears at Insojourn 3. Of the social behaviour measures, the SNIL2 measure correlates positively with LEQL2 ("medium"), and negatively with the two L1 measures (SNIL1 and LEQL1: "small").

A small number of significant relationships also emerged between selected linguistic measures and social behaviour measures. There were positive correlations at end sojourn between (1) EI scores and mean SNIL2 scores (r_s = .28, p = .037), (2) Speech Rate and SNIL2 (r_s = .32, p = .022), and (2) Speech Rate and LEQL2 (r_s = .40, p = .004). Following Plonsky and Oswald (2014), none of these findings are "large". Nonetheless, we view them as tending to confirm the general linguistic benefits of L2 networking and engagement when abroad, not always demonstrated in past studies.

9.3 Examining learning gains

As shown in Chapters 4 and 5, there was considerable individual variability in the final learning outcomes of the sojourn, confirming findings of many previous studies. Much of the variability in ultimate L2 achievement can be explained in terms of learners' level of proficiency presojourn. As seen above in Table 9.1, for most of the linguistic measures, there were significant positive correlations between Presojourn scores and later sets of scores on the same measures, suggesting that early high achievers kept their linguistic advantage throughout the study. This was confirmed when we identified a "top 10" of high achievers at Presojourn and end sojourn; eight out of 10 of the highest achievers at Presojourn retained this status at end sojourn.

However, in exploring relationships between sojourners' social experiences and their L2 development, absolute final L2 achievement is not the most helpful measure, and greater insights can be gained from studying sojourners' L2 progress. That is, whatever their starting point, the extent of learners' L2 gains should be affected by the extent of their investment in L2 learning during the sojourn. We now shift our attention therefore to the relative learning gains achieved by different participants from different starting points, and the relationship of these learning gains to the sojourn experience, as in the studies of Dewey, Bown, and Eggett (2012), Klapper and Rees (2012), and Dewey, Belnap, and Hilstrom (2013).

Table 9.1 Correlations between selected linguistic and social measures, Presojourn and end sojourn (Spearman's rho)

Measures	Presojourn EI score	Postsojourn EI score	Presojourn Oral % EF clauses	Insojourn 3 Oral % EF clauses	Presojourn Speech Rate	Insojourn 3 Speech Rate	Presojourn Writing % EF clauses	Insojourn 3 Writing % EF clauses	SNI L2	SNI L1	LEQL2	LEQL1
Presojourn EI score	1.00											
Postsojourn EI score	0.84**	1.00										
Presojourn % Oral EF clauses	0.10	0.04	1.00									
Insojourn 3 % Oral EF clauses	0.09	0.12	0.57**	1.00								
Presojourn Speech Rate	0.50**	0.27*	0.32*	0.15	1.00							
Insojourn 3 Speech Rate	0.51**	0.45**	0.17	0.15	0.76**	1.00						
Presojourn Writing % EF clauses	0.17	0.12	0.32*	0.31*	0.17	0.09	1.00					
Insojourn 3 Writing % EF clauses	0.11	0.11	0.37**	0.60**	0.17	0.17	0.36**	1.00				
SNI L2	0.24	0.28*	-0.21	-0.04	0.07	0.32*	-0.19	-0.03	1.00			
SNI L1	-0.22	-0.17	-0.22	-0.12	-0.15	-.015	-0.06	-0.05	-0.29*	1.00		
LEQL2	0.11	0.19	0.09	0.23	0.20	0.40**	-0.23	0.21	0.44**	-0.37**	1.00	
LEQ L1	-0.10	-0.18	-0.14	0.05	0.16	-0.02	-0.12	0.10	-0.30*	0.15	0.22	1.00

**p < .01, *p < .05

9.3.1 Defining learning gain scores

In order to investigate learning gains, we calculated gain scores for individual participants using the same subset of linguistic measures (Elicited Imitation, Speech Rate, % Error-Free Clauses (S) and % Error-Free Clauses (W)). These gain scores were defined as the differences between the scores obtained by individual participants on each measure, pre and end sojourn.

Table 9.2 presents an overview of gains for all 57 sojourners on the four linguistic measures. On the EI measure of proficiency, gain scores were always positive; however, on the two accuracy measures, some gain scores were negative, i.e. participants might be less accurate at Insojourn 3 than they had been at Presojourn. On the Speech Rate measure, gains were almost always positive.

9.3.2 Relations between SNI, LEQ and learning gain scores

Table 9.3 reports correlations between results for the SNI (both L1 and L2), for the LEQ (both L1 and L2), participants' Flexibility scores on the Multicultural Personality Questionnaire (MPQ), and gain scores on the four linguistic measures. Interestingly, the significant relationships among the different linguistic measures found when raw scores were correlated (see Table 9.1), do not obtain when gain scores are examined; it seems that gains on these measures are independent of each other. However, Table 9.3 shows significant positive correlations among SNIL2, LEQL2, and Speech Rate gain scores (all "small" to "medium"). This finding lends support to the view that both L2 social networking and L2 engagement promote L2 learning gain at least in the domain of fluency, in line with findings of, for example, Dewey et al. (2012); Hernández (2010); and Whitworth (2006). There is also a significant "small" correlation between LEQL2 and % Error-Free Clauses (W) ($r = .38$), probably because the highest scorers on LEQL2 were the most likely to record regular L2 writing in addition to other L2 practices.

The Flexibility subscores from the MPQ are also included in Table 9.3 because they also showed significant correlations with gain scores on three linguistic measures: EI, Speech Rate and % Error-Free Clauses (all "small": $r \geq .29$). (The other dimensions of MPQ did not show any similar relationships.) We do not have a full explanation for why this particular personality strand should connect with L2 development. However, the adaptability, enjoyment of the unfamiliar, and willingness to seek challenges which form part of the Flexibility construct are also noted by Klapper and Rees (2012) as characteristic of high gain sojourners, and presumably make them ready to actively exploit the learning opportunities on offer throughout the sojourn (Tracy-Ventura, Dewaele, Koylu, & McManus, 2016).

In order to make further progress in exploring relations between relative linguistic gain and the sojourn experience, we turn next to a qualitative case study approach. Participants who made strong relative gains, regardless of their linguistic proficiency at the start of the sojourn, are of special interest. In the next

Table 9.2 Overview of linguistic gain scores, Presojourn to end sojourn (all sojourners)

	Scores Pre-sojourn	Scores end sojourn	Mean gain scores	Gain score range
EI (Presojourn–Postsojourn 1)				
Mean	73.63	94.91	21.29	1–51
SD	18.85	15.48	10.00	
% Error-Free Clauses (S) (Presojourn–Insojourn 3)				
Mean	36.10	57.64	21.54	−35.00–73.44
SD	22.15	20.47	19.77	
% Error-Free Clauses (W) (Presojourn–Insojourn 3)				
Mean	60.93	62.04	1.11	−79.17–28.80
SD	11.63	16.78	17.25	
Speech Rate (Presojourn–Insojourn 3)				
Mean	2.03	2.80	0.77	−.04–1.89
SD	0.44	0.61	0.39	

section we explain how we selected a number of "high gainers" for each target language, who would become the subjects of individual case studies.

9.4 Explaining learning gains: A case study approach

9.4.1 Identifying the fastest-progressing sojourners

In order to identify a group of "top 10" gainers for each target language, we referred once again to the same four linguistic measures (Elicited Imitation, Speech Rate, % Error-Free Clauses (S), % Error-Free Clauses (W)). Scores on these four measures could not be directly combined, as they used different scales and units of measurement. We therefore ranked the participants within each language group for gains on each linguistic measure, and calculated participants' mean rank position across all four sets of gain scores. The "high gain" sojourners identified in this way are listed in Table 9.4 (French) and Table 9.5 (Spanish).

These high gainer groups include only a minority of participants who started their sojourn as high achievers, and the groups are correspondingly dominated by students and language assistants in France and Spain. (There had been a tendency for Presojourn high achievers in the French group to opt for workplace internships, and in the Spanish group, Presojourn high achievers were more likely to opt for a Mexico placement.)

In the next section, we review the qualitative data available for eight individual case studies, selected from among these "high gain" sojourners. In particular we will pursue the intensity of engagement in local networks and of L2 use, the role of sojourner agency and identity in promoting these, and the resulting drivers for L2 development. Material used for these case studies includes individual sets of presojourn and insojourn interviews, plus qualitative data from SNQ and LEQ.

Table 9.3 Relations among selected linguistic gain scores, SNI mean scores (L2 and L1), and LEQ mean scores (L2 and L1)

	EI Gain Presojourn to Postsojourn 1	EF Clauses Gain Presojourn to Insojourn 3	Speech Rate Gain Presojourn to Insojourn 3	Writing EF Clauses Gain Presojourn to Insojourn 3	SNI L2 mean score	SNI L1 mean score	LEQL2 mean score	LEQL1 mean score	Flexibility
EI Gain Presojourn to Postsojourn 1	1.00								
EF Clauses Gain Presojourn to Insojourn 3	0.23	1.00							
Speech Rate Gain Presojourn to Insojourn 3	−0.01	0.23	1.00						
Writing EF Clauses Gain Presojourn to Insojourn 3	−0.01	0.10	0.03	1.00					
SNI L2 mean score	−0.01	0.20	0.35**	.10	1.00				
SNI L1 mean score	0.09	0.10	0.09	−0.08	−0.29*	1.00			
LEQL2 mean score	0.03	0.15	0.31*	0.38**	0.44**	−0.37**	1.00		
LEQL1 mean score	−0.08	0.16	−0.16	0.13	−0.30*	0.15	0.22	1.00	
Flexibility	0.29*	0.35**	0.29*	0.04	0.08	0.08	0.05	0.17	1.00

** $p < .01$, * $p < .05$

228 *The L2 impact of the sojourn experience*

Table 9.4 Top 10 gainers at end sojourn (in rank order): French

Participant	Combined gain score rank	Sojourn type	High achiever (="top 10") Presojourn	High achiever (="top 10") end sojourn	SNIL2 **mean score**	SNIL1 mean score	LEQL2 mean score	LEQL1 mean score
112*	1	Student	No	Yes	3.33	4.00	82.67	73.67
107	2	Student	No	No	2.67	3.00	74.67	57.00
113*	3	Assistant	No	No	2.67	0.67	59.00	60.33
117	4	Assistant	No	No	3.33	1.67	76.00	74.00
105	5	Assistant	No	No	4.67	1.33	88.33	73.67
129	6=	Student	Yes	Yes	4.00	1.00	86.00	63.00
101	6=	Assistant	No	No	2.33	3.67	81.33	74.33
128*	8	Intern	No	Yes	1.67	1.67	81.00	100.00
102	9	Intern	Yes	Yes	3.00	2.67	75.00	62.67
108*	10	Student	Yes	Yes	4.67	0.00	86.33	57.00

* selected for case study
For comparison: overall mean for SNQL2 (French) = 2.61; overall mean for SNQL1 (French) = 2.29; overall mean for LEQL2 (French) = 69.89; overall mean for LEQL1 (French) = 69.12.

Table 9.5 Top 10 gainers at end sojourn: Spanish

Participant	Combined gain score rank	Sojourn type	High achiever (="top 10") Presojourn	High achiever (="top 10") end sojourn	SNQL2 mean score	SNQL1 mean score	LEQL2 mean score	LEQL1 mean score
179*	1	Assistant (M)	Yes	Yes	4.33	3.67	55.00	51.00
169	2	Student (S)	No	No	3.67	2.00	83.33	69.33
173*	3	Assistant (S)	Yes	Yes	5.00	3.67	70.67	75.67
168*	4	Student (S)	No	No	2.67	4.33	54.00	54.67
167	5=	Assistant (S)	No	No	4.67	1.67	65.67	58.67
151	5=	Assistant (S)	No	No	2.67	2.33	70.33	78.67
178*	7	Assistant (M)	No	No	3.67	1.00	74.67	68.67
166	8	Student (S)	No	No	5.00	1.00	91.67	45.33
156	9	Student (S)	Yes	Yes	4.33	2.67	92.67	55.33
161	10	Assistant (S)	No	Yes	2.33	3.33	79.00	61.00

* selected for case study; (M) = Mexico, (S) = Spain
For comparison: overall mean for SNQL2 (Spanish) = 3.52; overall mean for SNQL1 (Spanish) = 2.12; overall mean for LEQL2 (Spanish) = 73.91; overall mean for LEQL1 (Spanish) = 64.09.

9.4.2 Case studies of "high gain" sojourners

High presojourn achievers and high gainers

Terence (173) is our first example of a high-achieving participant at Presojourn, who also succeeded in making exceptional gains insojourn. He was a language assistant in an academy for young footballers, in the Valencia region of Spain. Terence had the maximum score for SNIL2, his score for SNIL1 was above average, and his scores for LEQL1 and LEQ2 were close to average. Before departure, Terence was anxious about making friends. However, he was offered accommodation in the family home of the female director of the academy, and he became exceptionally well integrated into host family life. He spent much of his leisure time with family members, socializing at home with his "Spanish mum", watching her teenage son play basketball, and at first going out in the evenings with the daughter of the family and her friends. (He found some independent local friends later on.) He also undertook some English tutoring for the son and daughter. Meanwhile, he maintained very active contact by internet with his own family and a small group of friends in England; throughout the sojourn he reported speaking every day to his mother, and his family visited him toward the end of the sojourn. However, he did not associate regularly with Anglophone or other international peers during the sojourn.

Terence was very well integrated in the football academy, spending breaks in the staffroom among the teachers, sharing an office with the English staff, and speaking a mix of Spanish and English with his colleagues. As time passed the balance shifted toward Spanish, and by Insojourn 3 he described it as "weird" if a teacher of English addressed him in English. He felt respected by the staff, who valued his opinion, invited him to their homes and generally looked after his welfare: "I have got like lots of Spanish mums" (173/RI). He also took part in a school trip to Italy, quite late in the sojourn, which led to new local friendships independent of those met through the host family. He made friends with the French language assistant, and they spent a good deal of time together in the earlier part of the sojourn, speaking a mix of Spanish and French together. Terence also took a very active interest in the professional football club to which the academy was attached, which was central to the life of the town; he reported attending many club games, including youth games involving his young students and colleagues' children. He responded to a request from the American supporters' association of the club to write an informal blog for them (in English) about his experiences of attending games and the emotional attachment of the town to the club; this became a regular commitment, which led in turn to further activity with the main club. At a major ceremony to honour the club manager, Terence found himself publicly representing this American group and presenting a message of congratulations in Spanish on their behalf.

Terence showed a general willingness to integrate into family life, without the reservations expressed by several of the LANGSNAP cohort, and in a way that is arguably more typical of younger sojourners (Kinginger, 2015). This provided him with a rich everyday engagement with Castilian (the host family were not from the region), as well as access to networks of young local people through the host family children. He showed the same willingness to engage with the life of the football academy, and the youth side of the football club itself; his willingness to blog for the American supporters' association, and to represent it in public, demonstrated growing personal confidence. This engagement with school and club led to considerable exposure to Valenciano, for example during staff meetings as well as on more informal occasions; however, Terence did not show any of the irritation felt by sojourner 156 at this complication of the linguistic environment. Instead he was pleased to have developed a good understanding of Valenciano, and was one of only two sojourners in the whole cohort who reported regularly watching TV and using social media in any regional language. Overall, Terence was one of the sojourners to show the greatest local attachment to a particular place or region (as opposed to aspirations toward a more internationalized multilingual self). This was evident in his immediate decision to return to watch his oldest school students' graduation ceremony, his wish to invite host family members to England, and his longer-term wish to return to the region:

> I have kind of like fallen in love a bit with Spain. I mean, [. . .] even the little town where I live, I love it so much, I feel really part of the community. I don't know, like I definitely would go back and visit there. And if a situation turned out where I could, I don't know, live there or live nearby, I would love to do that
>
> (173/RI).

This local attachment was clearly a powerful driver for L2 progress and was sustained through his final studies back in Home City; during his final year, Terence continued regularly to visit the city and the host family. It seems the clearest factor accounting for Terence's higher than average L2 gain, building on a relatively high L2 level predeparture.

Rosie (179) is our second example of a high achiever Presojourn who was also a high gainer. She worked as an assistant in a university language teaching centre in a state capital in Mexico. Her mean scores on SNIL2 and SNIL1 were above average, while her LEQL2 and LEQL1 scores were below average. Before going to Mexico, she spent five weeks in Spain working with a family as a holiday au pair, and she returned to the same family during the summer following her Mexico sojourn. She lived in Mexico with a host couple, who she referred to as her host "parents", and she socialized with them and with their wider family throughout the sojourn (though this diminished somewhat as other relationships developed). At the university, her role was primarily to run English conversation classes, which she found somewhat frustrating because student attendance was unreliable; toward the end of the sojourn especially, she felt she did not have enough work to do. However, she did contribute to other activities, such as a language course for local teachers. She also attended some university classes in Spanish language and linguistics, primarily as a way of meeting local students. In practice, she took some time to make local friends; at Insojourn 1 she reported that her only "real friend" was a German girl she had met in class (and with whom she used Spanish as lingua franca). Unfortunately, this girl left the country after the first semester:

> When she left it was a bit like "Oh now I've got no girl company". And like, I really like boys' company, but sometimes there are some things you can only talk about with girls. Or it is nicer, it is better to go shopping with girls and stuff
>
> (179/RI).

Otherwise, apart from her host family, she spent leisure time with the one other Home City language assistant in the city (Peter), together with a local male language teacher, David, presented as a significantly helpful figure when getting settled in the new city; she also filled time reading Spanish fiction. At Insojourn 1, it seemed overall that her local social network was quite small and undeveloped, though most contacts were primarily Spanish-using (apart from Peter). Her understanding of Spanish was better than Peter's, but she was not confident about speaking, and she said later that she had sheltered behind him and let him speak for both of them. She disliked the attention she attracted in the street, as a blue-eyed "*gringa*". At this point she also spent considerable time on the internet, keeping in touch with British friends, including daily contact with a boyfriend in England. At Christmas she joined the group trip to Chiapas by Home City sojourners, and in spring she holidayed in Cancún together with her mother.

By Insojourn 2, however, Rosie had broken off her relationship with her home boyfriend and started a new friendship with a local male student. She was in communication with this new friend Alejandro every day, both face-to-face and virtually. By Insojourn 3 she was describing him unambiguously as her boyfriend and spending even more time with him: visiting the city centre, walking in the park, going climbing, horse riding at his family farm, and watching films at Alejandro's house, as well as spending time with him on the internet. She was still reading fiction for pleasure, and still seeing David and Peter, but less frequently than before, as this single relationship intensified, and her confidence as a user of Spanish increased. She continued to express regret at her failure to make local female friends, however, a failure she attributed to cultural miscommunication:

> What's also really frustrating here is, I found it really hard to make girl friends, I have got a lot of boy friends, but I don't have any girl friends, just because the way I make friends is to joke, but girls here don't. Because of my sense of humour as well, they don't really understand it so much, so I more likely offend them or something
>
> (179/RI).

Rosie can be summed up as a high achiever and high gainer who was a below-average interactor during her Mexico sojourn, in terms of network diversity. She interacted at home with her host family, but made relatively few local friends outside. Initially she relied on a small number of other international peers for her social life outside the home, primarily her fellow Home City sojourner Peter, and her German but Spanish-speaking female friend; the (bilingual) male teacher colleague David who associated jointly with herself and Peter was her main local leisure contact. Over time, her immediate network did not become especially large, but it changed in character as she became more confident, and she finished the sojourn in an intensive relationship with a local boyfriend, though she failed to find the local female friends she wanted. She did not lack agency, as is evident from her voluntary attendance at university classes in Mexico, her complementary activity as an au pair in Spain, and her use of literature to gain additional Spanish input. However, her high gain seems to be attributable primarily to her engagement in a small number of rich Spanish-using relationships, which developed over time as she gradually gained in confidence.

Kirsten (108) was a national of a Nordic country who had migrated to England for her higher education. She was thus not an L1 speaker of English, exceptionally for the focus of this book. However, she is included partly to represent the increasing internationalization of UK higher education, and partly because of the clear example she presents of a high achiever and high gainer driven by an exceptionally strategic vision of a multilingual ideal self.

Kirsten had already studied through English for two years at Home City. Insojourn, she was an exchange student at a prestigious *Grande Ecole* in northern France. Her SNIL2 and LEQL2 scores were very high, and her SNIL1 and LEQL1 scores (for English) were below average. She set herself very clear strategic goals for her sojourn; having already studied at Home City, and having worked hard there to develop her English, she wanted the sojourn to be a French immersion experience, and she took steps to structure her life this way. Very unusually, she visited her destination city three months before the sojourn began, so as to find accommodation with locals; she found a room in the apartment of an older professional woman, who proved a helpful mentor throughout her sojourn.

Kirsten took her studies seriously, pursuing her academic interests in environmental studies and enrolling for an optional credit-bearing course at her destination institution. She largely avoided ELF-using Erasmus networks, and she mostly socialized on campus with a Japanese postgraduate student, with whom she used French as lingua franca; she also took part in some local student clubs. However, her main leisure activity was athletics, in which she was already proficient. She joined an athletics club in the destination city, trained and competed with them several times a week, and socialized regularly with her club coach, his partner and other club members. Kirsten was injured part way through the year and missed a major competition abroad as a result. However, this did not break her links with her fellow athletes, and she still travelled with the team to this event as a supporter. At the end of the academic year, Kirsten remained in the city as an intern, helping one of her lecturers to organize summer events.

Kirsten's French immersion was of course not complete. She maintained close relations by internet with her family (who visited too), and also with Home City

Anglophone friends, and so was regularly using her Nordic L1 as well as English. She experienced some personal/cultural challenges in addition to the huge disappointment of her sports injury; she found she was expected to be chatty and forthcoming in ways which felt alien to her upbringing, and she was sensitive to criticism and teasing, which she encountered from time to time (about her French, about her blonde hair, etc.). But overall, this is a case where resilience and strategic agency, plus an exceptionally well-developed long-term ambition for a multilingual L2 self, including multilingual academic proficiency, clearly drove investment, leading to accelerated L2 gain. It was very helpful that she had a special talent, athletics in this case; this led to an important role for Kirsten in a local network unconnected with the university, which greatly enriched her L2 experience. However, the steps she took to become locally integrated in domestic life, and to make a success of her academic studies, showed that Kirsten's success was primarily due to her strategic L2 vision, enriched by her athletics talent.

High gainers and moderate presojourn achievers

Nadia (112) is our first example of a moderate achiever Presojourn, who gained so much that she became a top 10 achiever by end sojourn. She was an exchange student in a small university town in south-west France. She was a high interactor, in both French and English, as was evident in her above-average scores for SNIL2, SNIL1, LEQL2 and LEQL1. Before starting her official exchange studentship she had spent three months working as a hotel receptionist in France, making her actual sojourn considerably longer than those of most other participants, and giving her a valuable reference point to compare with her exchange student experience. Nadia was living in university accommodation, sharing a flat with two international peers and another sojourner (107), who became and remained her closest female friend throughout the year. The accommodation was of reasonable quality, according to Nadia, but one snag was the lack of a TV set – as a substitute she was initially watching British television on her tablet, though later in the sojourn she shifted to watching French TV. She was keen to do well in her studies, and she enrolled for a mix of literature and history courses selected from the Year 1 and Year 2 curricula. At Insojourn 1 she expressed annoyance with one of her lecturers, a young man who joked publicly in class about Erasmus students' lack of background knowledge about French literature; however, her response was not to hide or to withdraw, but to prepare well and try to speak more in class. At this time, she also expressed some frustration at how long it was taking to make local friends. She had spent the first few weeks socializing only with Erasmus students, all through the medium of English, but together with 107 she was now trying to build a network including French speakers (including offering invitations to meals in the flat).

"Going out" in the evening with groups of friends was important for Nadia, despite some mildly unpleasant experiences (being followed in the street, etc.), and together with 107 she gradually succeeded in making a number of friends among local students (mostly male) through nightlife contacts and parties. The French friends' names mentioned by Nadia in her SNQ responses changed from visit to visit, however, and it seems she did not herself develop any single, long-term local friendship. Nonetheless, one of these male students, Julien, mentioned for the first time by Nadia at Insojourn 1, later became the regular boyfriend of 107, and was an important contact for both women – when he was around, French was normally spoken. Unfortunately the Insojourn 2 interview of Nadia is truncated, but it is clear that she felt a qualitative change had taken place by this time, so that she now had good access to a network of French friends; she told an anecdote about the first-ever party she and 107 had held specifically for "les Français". (Sadly, a neighbour complained about noise and nuisance!) By Insojourn 3, Nadia seemed to be associating mostly with Anglophones once again, travelling to Spain with other Erasmus students, visiting England, and focusing on writing up her university research project. However, the relationships with both 107 and Julien remained close and continued to offer access to a network of French acquaintances during the final days of the sojourn. Life had become more domestic and quiet, one consequence being that Nadia was now watching a good deal of French TV.

Nadia showed considerable agency in taking a summer job in France prior to the official sojourn. She described herself as using French intensively in this role, and she recounted how she had learned niceties of French politeness which she was now passing on to fellow sojourners. Some of her strong linguistic gain may be attributed to this period of work experience, therefore, and it certainly developed her sense of self-efficacy as an L2 communicator. Once she had moved to the position of exchange student, she led a much more bilingual existence, using English throughout the year with a valued network of Erasmus friends and in her close relationship with 107. However, she tried to study seriously and worked to become accepted as a regular student by lecturers and classmates, and move beyond the stereotype she perceived of being an Erasmus "*idiote*". Together with 107 she took initiatives to find French friends, succeeding mainly in getting to know local males through evening socializing. Julien became a long-term friend and focus for French-medium interaction, and their joint media-viewing habits shifted over time from English to French. Overall, Nadia shows that it is possible to live with international peers and to be an active member of the Erasmus social scene, with an identity including goals to do with "coming of age" and having a good time, while simultaneously developing a more serious L2 student persona, and gradually building local social links with "les Français". In this way she gained access to the informal young person's French that she most wanted to master in the short term:

> This is definitely much more euh much more practice for social level than for like say work level or something like that. [. . .] Euh for one thing it has improved my fluency massively, massively, and I imagine it does for everyone really. Euh although I have to say it has probably in some ways degraded my level of French, in that I drop all the *ne* and euh – and as for like conjugating

my verbs, I don't really think I take that much notice of it any more, but I think that is something that will come back once I get back to uni

(112/RI).

It seems likely, however, that the prior period of work experience was crucial in equipping Nadia with the initial language skills and sense of self-efficacy that made this dynamic combination possible.

Caroline (128) is our second example of a moderate achiever Presojourn who joined the high achievers group by end sojourn. She was a workplace intern in an international media company with its headquarters in a Paris business district, where she worked as personal assistant to a female manager. Before attending university she had spent six months as au pair in a provincial town in France, and this experience provided a point of comparison for her Paris sojourn. She had below-average scores on both SNIL2 and SNIL1, but these scores were affected by non-completion of parts of SNQ and so are not reliable. However, she had exceptionally high scores on both LEQL2 and LEQL1, seemingly reflecting intensive interaction in both languages. Caroline was keen to live in a flatshare with local professionals, and she tried two successive sublets in central Paris. She was asked to leave the first one when she requested a receipt for her deposit, and was housed temporarily by another (French) female intern, Clémence, who became a lasting friend (though this relationship was conducted mostly in English throughout). Caroline then sublet from a young male professional, but after a short time he became the flatmate from hell ("*le pire des pires des colocs*") in her view, and she extracted herself from the situation in January, with support from her father; after these experiences she rented a one-person studio for the rest of the sojourn.

At the first visit, Caroline described her busy week, involving long metro journeys every day, before work in a pressurized and bilingual environment, with French as the language of office communication, but where her own responsibilities included writing website material in English, checking English texts produced by others, and doing varied translations from French into English, including publicity material and a feature article about her boss. There were a number of Anglophone interns in the company, with similar roles (including sojourner 100), and she socialized mainly with these (in English) during the leisure moments of the working day. At weekends, she got together for long nights out with a wider group, partly international but still largely Anglophone, and including other Home City students sojourning in Paris. She was maintaining active contact by internet with her family in England, and also with a home boyfriend.

By Insojourn 2, Caroline felt she was earning her boss's confidence at work, and Caroline named her as one of her most important contacts (spending eight hours per day at the next desk, and routinely answering the phone on her boss's behalf). Her social life was changing also; long weekend nights out in an international, English-using group were fewer. She was now meeting Clémence weekly for an evening of mojitos and conversation; she had also broken with her English boyfriend and started a relationship with a local French man (Adam), so that increasingly she was spending her leisure time alone with him. Her confidence in using French was growing, or rather, she believed, recovering to what it had been during her six months as au pair. However, if she met French people who addressed her in fluent English, she still felt shy about replying in French. At Visit 3, Caroline was still socializing in English with her family very regularly by Skype, phone, and so on, and also with fellow Anglophone interns at her workplace. At home and at leisure, however, her life was very much centred on her deepening relationship with Adam, and she was seeing less of other friends, even Clémence.

Overall, the story of Caroline is largely a "coming of age" narrative. Following her earlier experience of life in France, she was willing to take risks in a number of ways, including undertaking an internship in a major company and chasing what seemed to be affordable lodgings in central Paris. She was proud of having established herself as a valued worker, and she talked in more general terms of the need to be forceful to survive daily life in Paris (her first sustained experience of big city life, including fighting daily for space on the metro and handling an attempted mugging, as well as dealing with informal rentals and their problems). However, she also relied throughout on her family for emotional and practical support. Socially, among her peer group, Caroline progressed from group partying to building closer relationships with a small number of people. Her workplace activity and in particular her relationship with her boss, and her personal relationship with Adam, provided intensive engagement with French; yet if a relationship could be conducted more smoothly in English (as apparently with Clémence), Caroline did not negotiate/insist on French, suggesting that for her, the motivation to build a multilingual identity could not be allowed to conflict with relationship building.

High gainers, moderate achievers

A majority of the participants with exceptionally high gain scores were moderate achievers both predeparture and at the end of the sojourn (n=11). In this section we examine how a selection of these sojourners achieved their gains.

Lucy (113) was the language assistant for two primary schools, in a small town in a rural area of northern France with a population of just a few thousand. Her scores for SNI and LEQ were below average both in L2 and in L1. She accepted an offer of low-cost accommodation from the school district; this turned out to be a room in the boarding accommodation *(internat)* of a local high school. In practice, her corridor was deserted apart from one other assistant, the school nurse, and occasional overnighting teachers. Unsurprisingly, Lucy found this accommodation somewhat lonely, though other assistants were living elsewhere in the *internat,* and she met up with them for meals in the canteen (she had no kitchen). It did not help that she broke her ankle early in the sojourn and was not very mobile for some weeks. At the primary schools, Lucy's timetable was arranged so that she completed all of her work on two days only, and did not spend a full day at either school. She enjoyed her work with the children and got an enthusiastic response from them, but it seemed she never became integrated into wider school life. For example, at Insojourn 1 she still did not know most teachers' names, and she admitted later that she had been too shy to accept their social invitations, especially following a direct rebuff by one teacher who did not want an assistant in his class. In her leisure time, together with other assistants, she explored the social resources of the small town. At the time of Visit 1, they had tried step classes and badminton at the local sports centre, and Lucy was hoping to join a theatre club. When they visited the town bars, her assistant group received a lot of attention from local males, some of it unwelcome. The best same-aged local contacts at this point were with students from a local college for the construction industry, who came from other parts of France, and who also had cars (public transport was very limited in the district). Lucy was hoping, for example, to visit local Christmas markets with these friends. But overall, at Insojourn 1 she was still reporting homesickness and culture shock, to a degree which surprised her, given her previous experience of living away from home. However, she supported her spirits by keeping in close touch with family and English friends by internet, travelling home twice during the sojourn, and going on a ski trip with her family during the school spring break.

By Insojourn 2, Lucy was delivering some lessons for a third school by video-conference but otherwise working in the same way. She was still living in the *internat*, though she now planned to move to a studio apartment later in the spring. Her closest associates were still her assistants' network, with whom she interacted in English; while her confidence in speaking French had grown, she still found casual conversation challenging, and felt this was a bar to developing local friendships. However, in other respects she had very much developed her routines, finding additional ways of integrating with the local community. She was now volunteering on Wednesday mornings in a club for primary school children, playing games and running craft activities, and on Friday afternoons she was helping in a homework club for secondary school students. She was tutoring a child privately twice a week and eating Sunday lunch with the child's family. For her university research project she had been meeting older community members, and this was leading to invitations to their homes. To her list of leisure activities, she had added swimming, Thai boxing, and pottery, plus helping to animate an English/Irish-themed evening at the local cultural centre.

Lucy finished her assistantship contract at the end of March, but after a trip home in April she returned to the same small town for five more weeks, after most other assistants had departed, to take up an internship at the same cultural centre. Here she staffed the reception desk and undertook a variety of admin tasks; she found her colleagues' ways of working bureaucratic, but they befriended her and took her on day trips at weekends. She could no longer continue her daytime voluntary work with children, but was still seeing socially some members of the local network she had developed doing this work. For the first time, at Insojourn 3, she included some local individuals in her "top 5" contacts, all from these groups. She ultimately left this small town with regret (for a summer language course in China), saying she had finally learned to appreciate the sincerity and warmth of the locals, and that she was just starting to become properly integrated.

Overall, Lucy presents the case of a sojourner who started her year abroad with limited communicative proficiency and low self-confidence, in a small-town context which lacked immediate appeal for young people. Opportunities to integrate were available early on (e.g., teachers' invitations), which she was not confident enough to exploit. However, she had sufficient resilience to persist in making herself busy and fill up her rather empty schedule, initially in company with other assistants. Starting with sports and trips to the local bars, she progressed to greater community involvement, getting engaged with children's activities, with her tutee's family, and with retired people. She did not explain how she got the job in the cultural centre, but it seems likely this arose through her other community contacts; while working there, for the first time, she was ready both linguistically and in terms of self-confidence to make local friends. At that point, her commitment to a multilingual/international L2 identity cut things short, as China called her away. But her case shows how personal resilience, and a willingness to engage flexibly in community activity with different age groups, could in combination lead to high L2 gain, in what seemed unpromising local circumstances.

Alice (168) was an exchange student in a historic city in Andalucia, Spain, which is also a major tourist destination. Her score for SNIL1 was well above average, while her scores for SNIL2, LEQL2 and LEQL1 were below average. She found a flatshare with three local students (two women, plus the boyfriend of one of these), and had the good fortune (she said) that this group became her close friends and remained so throughout the year. They studied in a different faculty, and she did not meet up with them during weekdays on campus; however, in the evenings they watched Spanish TV and films together, and at weekends she accompanied them for coffees, meals, tapas, or to the beach in summer. These flatmates were patient and helpful with her language problems (they also were language students, and one had been an Erasmus student herself). They included her when socializing with their friends; one flatmate took her home to another town in the region, showed her the sights, and introduced her to her family. Part way through the year, they changed flat as a group; when the male student quit the group, the three women still lived together. Throughout they maintained a monolingual Spanish-using home; it was only at the end of the year, when a Home City friend of Alice came to stay, that these flatmates revealed that they themselves could speak functional English.

On campus, Alice took her studies seriously. She took French language classes throughout the year, plus Spanish linguistics and history courses. She complained about the difficulty of finding courses at the right level; it was hard to get information about courses beforehand, and some turned out to be very challenging, others rather too easy. She failed some mid-year exams (a French to Spanish translation exam caused her big problems), but persisted in studying regularly, as did her flatmates.

The university was very popular with Erasmus students, and Alice spent her leisure time on campus largely among an Erasmus network including many Anglophones. In her first semester she made efforts to get to know Spanish classmates (group work activities in a course on teaching Spanish as a foreign language were helpful for this). She socialized with some of these classmates after class, but lasting friendships did not develop: "I think maybe because there are so many Erasmus, the Spanish don't really want to know, unless you're put in a group with them". By Insojourn 3 she reported having two separate sets of friends: her flatmates (and their wider network), and her Anglophone university network. This situation was reflected also in her qualitative SNQ returns. Alice did make some efforts to use Spanish as a lingua franca with other international Erasmus students, and reported attempted negotiations on this; however, "*es difícil*" [it's hard], as many were keen to practise their English. She was proud of her own Spanish language development, attributing much of this to her domestic and leisure life with her flatmates. At home she was completely at ease using Spanish with them, and when they were socializing in large groups outside, if her contributions to group conversations were slow or inappropriate, they all made a joke of it together.

Overall, Alice offers an example of a sojourner who made strong gains, despite being in a touristic city and on a campus popular with Erasmus students. She herself participated in this Erasmus scene, and she networked regularly in English with other international students (as well as sustaining home relationships very actively by internet). Despite some initial efforts, she failed to make lasting local student friends in class. However, the strong relations she developed with her local student flatmates and the entry point they offered to local life, as well as to Spanish media (TV, films, etc.), were central to her development of oral fluency. The contribution of this second, Spanish-medium network to her L2 gain was complemented by her studies (in French as well as in Spanish), reflecting her ambition for a multilingual ideal self. However, Alice was herself sceptical about the contribution of her university studies to her language development, attributing most if not all of her progress to her Spanish-using social network.

Heather (169) was an exchange student in a different, large city in Andalucía. Her personal scores for SNIL2, SNIL1, LEQL2 and LEQL1 were all above average, indicating a profile of intensive interaction and engagement in both English and Spanish. She was already familiar with other places in Spain; as a teenager, she had done work experience in a southern city, and immediately prior to the official sojourn, she had spent a month in Madrid, and was proud that she could pass herself off as a Madrid resident with new acquaintances, at least for the first few minutes. In her destination city, she lived in a very central apartment shared with four other women, two Italians and two English (one a fellow Home City student). She reported that a mixture of English, Spanish and Italian was spoken in the flat. However, she developed a lasting friendship with one of the Italian women, Gianna, and they sustained a mutual commitment to speaking Spanish as lingua franca together right through the year.

Heather found the university enrolment system confusing to start with, but she managed to locate Semester 1 courses in Spanish/English translation and interpreting, in Spanish literature, and in French language and culture. She found most of these courses interesting and had good relations with her teachers. The interpreting course was quite advanced, and she was the only English person in the class; she reckoned, however, that her Spanish was equal to her classmates' English, and this particular class made her feel welcome and a useful resource for the group. She had a substantial number of class hours on four days of the week, though she admitted that in Semester 1 she did not do much studying outside class. As far as her social life was concerned, in her SNQ questionnaire at Insojourn 1, Heather listed an exceptionally high number of student acquaintances of different nationalities, in addition to her flatmates: English, Italian, Belgian, Spanish and Latin American. In interview, she spoke about organizing dinner parties in her flat, turning her bedroom into a dining room for the occasion. She had joined an informal group of mixed nationalities which met for regular beach barbecues and other outings. Heather had met this group following a kayaking event, where she struck up a friendship with the instructor (see Chapter 7). At Insojourn 1, however, her "top 5" included one Spanish male friend, two English Erasmus friends, and two friends in England (one her boyfriend) with whom she Skyped frequently throughout the entire sojourn. She was also maintaining close contact with her family, who had already visited her and were planning further visits to the city. Her "top 5" pattern remained similar throughout the year, though individual names changed; she remained committed to her English boyfriend throughout.

By Insojourn 2, Heather could report success in her Semester 1 courses. Her social life continued with considerable intensity, though by now the crowd of acquaintances claimed at Insojourn 1 had reduced somewhat. It seemed she belonged primarily to two overlapping groups: an English Erasmus network including her Anglophone flatmates plus others met on campus, and an Italian Erasmus network met through her flatmate and friend Gianna (now her "Italian sister"). With the latter group, she consistently maintained the use of Spanish as lingua franca; with her Anglophone friends she said that a mix of Spanish and English was spoken on campus in the daytime, while English predominated during evening leisure. However, she also sustained Spanish contacts, including her landlord, who became a friend. Heather believed that she was using Spanish daily to a greater extent than most English sojourners she knew, and that her comprehension, for example of rapid group conversation, was consequently much better than theirs:

> Creo que en situaciones cuando estoy con un grupo quizá y alguien como un camarero o algo, alguien dice algo, yo comprendo lo que dice, y mis amigos están un poco confundidos, o no saben exactamente qué ha dicho. O entienden mal lo que él ha dicho y por eso creo que mi español personalmente ha mejorado. Porque antes pasa a mí también que yo estoy

un poco confundida, pero ahora más o menos comprendo la primera vez lo que dicen. Y algunos de mis amigos que no practican tanto puedes ver que sufren un poco cuando están en una situación completamente en español

(169/V2Q8).

[I think that in situations when I'm in a group maybe and someone like a waiter or something, someone says something, I understand what they say and my friends are still a little confused or they don't know exactly what he said. Or they misunderstood what he said and for that reason I think that my Spanish, personally, has improved. Because before it happened to me too, that I was a little confused, but now I more or less understand what they say the first time. And some of my friends who don't practice as much, you can tell that they suffer a bit when they're in a situation completely in Spanish.]

She identified positively with the city and its people, and accordingly was pleased to have acquired an accent reflecting regional identity, even though she thought that her previous Madrid-influenced accent was "more standard". When at leisure, she continued to entertain friends in her flat and was a regular in particular bars in the city, as she was proud to demonstrate to her visiting mother and aunt. Sociable and adventurous, she had also made a road trip to north-east Spain with a mixed group of male friends (Spanish, Belgian and Italian); attending the Cádiz carnival with a group of Erasmus friends, she had been involved in a violent incident, but was taken care of by these friends.

At Insojourn 3, Heather had already completed her studies and was enjoying staying on in the city for a spell of "*playa, comida, sol, amigos*" [beach, food, sun, friends], in company with her two remaining flatmates and other friends. Gianna was still her most constant friend and companion, though she generally spent her leisure time in a group. With Gianna, she still spoke Spanish almost entirely, though she was teaching her some English phrases (and in turn was learning a little Italian). She was speaking some French with a part-French flatmate, and she told an anecdote about helping two lost French boys, which had proved to her that she could still speak some (Spanish-influenced) French. She did not detail the courses she had taken in Semester 2, which she had found challenging in terms of workload, and not very enjoyable; she had worried about failure, but finally believed she had passed her exams successfully. She said that when on campus, she had been most regularly with a group of three English girls, but had succeeded in spending increased time with Spanish classmates too. She hoped that some of her Spanish friendships, as well as her Erasmus ones, might last beyond the sojourn.

Overall, Heather offers another example of exchange student life and L2 development in a university environment with a strong presence of international/Erasmus students. She built diverse and fluid networks and was willing to take social initiatives and risks. An active and varied multilingual social life was central to her immediate sense of identity:

> Quizá me gustaría pasar un poco menos de tiempo con ingleses. Pero la verdad es que no paso demasiado y que siempre estoy hablando en español también. Entonces tengo una mezcla bastante equilibrado
> (V2Q10).
>
> [Perhaps I would like to spend less time with English people. But the truth is that I don't spend too much and that I'm always speaking in Spanish too. So I have a rather balanced mix.]

She was somewhat ambivalent about the value of her formal studies, though she acknowledged the contribution of some classes both to language development and to social networking with locals. The intensive friendship with Gianna, including their pact to use SLF, must also have contributed positively to her language gain. She took special pride in the Spanish oral fluency she had developed through leisure time interaction; unlike many other sojourners, Heather had also developed some identification with the region, and she was pleased that this was now reflected in her locally influenced speech.

Megan (178) was a language assistant in the elementary section of a private bilingual school in a large city in Mexico. Her stay had an unlucky beginning as she had appendicitis in her second week. She was living with a teacher and her family in a pleasant district, though a long way from the city centre, which meant a complicated journey by public transport every day; she liked the family and maintained good relations with them, though as time passed she started to spend more time away from the home.

At school, Megan was expected to support the English teachers, helping children complete classwork (e.g., written exercises), hearing them read, or helping prepare them for international English examinations; she was also increasingly asked to act as a substitute to cover teacher absences. At first she was nervous in this role, but as she got to know the institution, and the children, she became very involved in their learning, found herself acting as an informal counsellor for them, and generally enjoyed her work more and more, so much so that she was starting to consider teaching as a career. She became well integrated with the staff as well, and she received many tokens of appreciation at the end of the year. Throughout, however, the teachers (some British, some Mexican) mostly spoke English with her, and she did not try to renegotiate this.

Outside the school, Megan was initially quite homesick, and she kept up frequent virtual contact with her family, boyfriend and other friends in England, as well as with other Home City sojourners in Mexico. (Another male sojourner, 162, was based in the same city.) However, by Insojourn 2 she had started to get to know a variety of locals. She had attended Day of the Dead ceremonies at a major university in the city and met some local students there; she had also joined a suburban gym near her home and went there most evenings after work, finding a number of friends among the staff and local gym members. She described staying at a Mexican friend's house at weekends, nearer the city centre, together with 162; they cooked together, and on one occasion when 162 and Megan prepared an English meal, this turned into an informal party. In the last weeks of her stay, Megan still counted 162 as her "best friend" of the sojourn, and they went out together with Mexican friends. However, she reported that her circle of acquaintances was still growing, in the immediate locality of her home; as well as her local gym friends, she now at last knew the neighbours, the local print shop people, and so on. She no longer worried, as she had in the beginning, about being so conspicuously fair and attracting attention in the street, but talked proudly instead about how people now sometimes assumed she was Mexican, just from a different part of the country. When her "Mexican mum" told her she was now sounding very Mexican, she took this as a compliment. Meanwhile, she was trying to read more in Spanish, and she had found her home university project a good stimulus to practise writing as well.

Alongside this increasing local integration, however, and personal investment in L2, Megan also pursued the partly conflicting aim of travel, always with other Anglophones. At Christmas, she joined the group of Home City sojourners touring Chiapas; at other times she visited other sojourners in Cancún and travelled with her parents elsewhere in the Yucatán. When she finished her contract in the school, her English boyfriend joined her, to undertake an extended trip around Central America before a final two weeks back in her sojourn city. Megan was pleased to introduce him to her local friends and found translating for him very easy, yet she seemed somewhat conflicted about this final trip: At what point was she really leaving, how would she handle her goodbyes, should the last two weeks be spent by herself and her boyfriend as tourists or with her local friends? She had been slow to settle in Mexico, but now:

> It would be hard to say I would change anything, because I loved it. Euh but I suppose I wish I'd loved it earlier, like it took a long time to get used to [. . .] but I don't know how I would change that. [. . .] [Now] I feel like this is where I live. I think the difference now is that at the beginning it was a trip, and now it is my life and I'm leaving it
>
> (178/RI).

Overall, Megan provides an example of a sojourner who progressed from feelings of cultural strangeness (expressed in worries about dress, as well as in self-consciousness about her fair skin and blue eyes) to social integration and identification with the particular location and country. As far as L2 learning was concerned, she showed somewhat limited agency at first – for example, accepting the decision of her teacher colleagues to speak mainly English with her, and relying on 162 for social support when entering into new contexts and social relationships. Over time, however, she gained professional confidence in her work at the school and felt increasingly comfortable in navigating a major city. She showed growing social adaptability and skill at developing new contacts through neighbourhood environments, beginning with the local gym. She also showed sensitivity about the challenges of developing intimate relationships through L2, reverting several times in interview to the challenges of resolving misunderstandings and disputes with friends. She was keen to develop a balanced proficiency in Spanish and practised reading and writing to assist this. At the same time she was pleased to speak in a Mexican style, and to be mistaken sometimes for a Mexican, reflecting her increasing social identification with the locality and people. She sustained active relations with Anglophone contacts back home, and also with her fellow Home City sojourners, with whom she travelled extensively. Yet the arrival of her English boyfriend seemed to confront her with some of the contradictions between two different identities, which were not fully resolved when the sojourn ended.

9.5 Discussion and conclusion

9.5.1 Overview of high gainer characteristics

These individual case studies confirm that the residence abroad experience is firmly a multilingual one, with at least two languages present in every sojourner's daily social and personal practices. They also confirm the challenges presented for Anglophone sojourners in particular, due to the international standing of English and the interest of many global citizens in practising it. However, they also shed light on how high L2 gains could be achieved by Anglophone sojourners, by a variety of different routes. Some common underlying themes emerge which help us understand their success.

To start with, it is clear that even within the high gainers group, sojourners differed considerably in their preparedness for the sojourn experience, in terms of self-confidence as well as L2 proficiency. Certain sojourners had previously worked or studied abroad and could draw on this previous experience as a point of comparison and source of self-efficacy (Kirsten, Nadia, Caroline and Heather). Others drew confidence from a special talent, whether music or sport, which they used to gain quick access to local networks (Kirsten). However, some other sojourners also managed to make good L2 gains, despite a less-than-confident beginning with reported loneliness and culture shock (Lucy, Rosie and Megan, none of them high achievers presojourn). The extended length of stay was very important in allowing such sojourners gradually to build self-confidence and increase their agency in seeking L2 opportunities.

We already know from earlier chapters that the environments in which sojourners found themselves on arrival might be more or less welcoming; the case studies provide fuller detail on this. Thus Terence, Megan and Rosie all found themselves placed in welcoming host families who proved compatible and offered social support, as well as plenty of L2 interaction (104 and 111 in France had similar experiences). Kirsten, Alice and Heather quickly found flatmates who were willing to become friends and spoke L2 consistently. However, Caroline experienced early failures when seeking compatible L2 speakers as flatmates, and others were housed in international-only accommodation (Nadia, Lucy). Caroline was made immediately welcome by her work colleagues, like most other workplace interns. However, the welcome offered by schools to newly arrived language assistants seemed quite variable; among the high gainers, Terence and Rosie were quickly integrated into the staff team, whereas Lucy had a very unfavourable timetable and (unusually) never became integrated into staff social life. Exchange student sojourners, such as Heather, often found local university administration baffling, and administrators unhelpful. As for getting to know local classmates, this was particularly difficult on campuses where international students were very numerous; some sojourners felt positively welcome only in small small classes/small groups (Alice), or where their English knowledge was an asset (Heather).

Another structural challenge, in terms of L2 gain, was sojourners' ongoing relations with family, friends and partners at home in English, with other Anglophone sojourners, and with wider networks of international peers. These relationships were valued yet needed management so that they did not crowd out L2 practices and relationships. And finally, the urge to travel also needed management.

The case studies detailed above make it clear that certain sojourner qualities were helpful in handling this range of contextual challenges. These included a strategic vision of the L2 self (Kirsten); active agency and initiative in accessing and sustaining L2 networks, whether diverse and/or intensive (all); social adaptability and flexibility (Caroline, Lucy, Megan, Rosie, Terence); and active management of lingua franca usage and of touristic travel (Heather).

9.5.2 Relationships as drivers of L2 development

Overall the case studies show that high gainers were motivated to manage their multilingual social environment, in favour of L2 engagement, and succeeded to a considerable degree in achieving this, if not always from the very beginning of the sojourn.

There is also considerable anecdotal evidence that intensive L2 networking was key to development, pushing sojourners to the limits of their L2 knowledge, and promoting investment in learning. Several high gainers told stories about incidents in valued relationships, connected with their own L2 limitations, which motivated them to improve. Examples concerned the performance of their professional/academic L2 identity; telling stories and being a good conversationalist; the expression of intimacy; and the management of misunderstandings. The following set of comments and anecdotes exemplify these challenges.

Performing professional identity

> I had to ehm learn quite a lot of new vocab, especially in the first three months. Like office vocab especially just day-to-day stuff that I didn't know before. And kind of like the etiquette for writing emails, and reading emails, but especially for writing emails, how to write them properly depending on who is receiving it, and I think it has really improved in general. [. . .] Before Christmas my colleagues

would check my emails before I sent them if it was an important email, now they don't, so that must indicate that fingers crossed, they trust my French. So that's different, that's an improvement in my writing I guess

(125/RI).

Being a good conversationalist

Le plus difficile pour moi c'est de raconter euh les histoires, les évènements passés. Je sais pas pourquoi, mais quand je parle avec mes collègues je veux leur dire euh les choses que j'ai fait la semaine dernière quelque chose, et je trouve difficile juste de décrire qu'est-ce-qui s'est passé. Je sais pas pourquoi, mais c'est toujours quand je raconte les histoires, c'est ça que je trouve difficile

(102/V2).

[The most difficult for me is to tell stories and past events. I don't know why, but when I talk to my colleagues I want to tell them what I did last week or something, and I find it difficult simply to describe what happened. I don't know why, but it is always when I tell stories, that is what I find difficult.]

Expressing/performing intimacy

Mais en fait le mercredi soir j'avais Adam qui m'a appelé en disant "Bon j'ai lu euh tout ce que tu as écrit [C's university assignment] et je pense qu'il y a des petits trucs, peut-être on doit parler un peu quoi, je suis un peu perdu". J'ai dit "D'accord", et jusqu'à cinq heures du matin il était là. On était là ensemble en faisant les petits modifications, et c'était trop mignon qu'il a fait ça, parce que franchement ça si j'étais lui je sais pas. [. . .] C'était vraiment quelque chose je pense de travailler comme ça la journée et la nuit

(Caroline/V3).

[But in fact on the Wednesday evening I had Adam who called me saying "Well I have read everything you have written [C's university assignment] and I think there are some little things, perhaps we should talk a bit, I am a bit lost". I said "Fine", and until five in the morning he was there. We were there together making the little changes, and it was so sweet that he did that, because honestly if I was him, I don't know [. . .]. It was really something I believe, to work like that all day and all night.]

Misunderstandings

Hace unos días de hecho he tenido como un problema con mi amigo porque había mal comunicación entre nosotros. Obviamente yo estaba pensando como si yo pudiera explicarlo en inglés podría como solucionar muy rápido porque podría explicarlo muy bien, muy como – no sé – cómo quería explicarlo. Obviamente este es un gran eh reto porque es muy difícil cuando hay [. . .] algo que tienes que explicarlo muy bien y no – no – no sabes cómo explicarlo como en una manera muy (.) um (.) – pero no sé – como muy (.) correcta. No sé. Como las palabras que necesito usar (.) son distintos

(178/V2).

[A few days ago in fact I had like a problem with my friend because there was bad communication between us. Obviously I was thinking if I were able to explain it in English, I could fix it quickly because I could explain it really well, really like – I don't know – like I wanted to explain it. Obviously this is a big challenge because it's very difficult when there's [. . .] something that you want to explain really well and you don't –don't – don't know how to explain it in a way very (.) um (.) – but I don't know – like (.) correctly. I don't know. Like the words I need to use are different.]

*128: J'étais fâchée contre Adam, pas comme d'hab(itude) [. . .] mais j'ai dit "Ça me gêne pas si tu me trompes!". J'avais pas l'intention de dire ça bien sûr, pas du tout, mais euh . . .
[I was annoyed with Adam, unusually [. . .] but I said, "I don't care if you cheat on me!". I did not mean to say that of course, not at all, but euh . . .]

*JS: Qu'est-ce-que tu voulais dire alors?
[So what did you mean to say?]

*128: En fait le soir (.) avant il a fait tomber une verre d'eau sur moi. Donc j'ai voulu dire "trempe", [pas] "trompe", voilà. Et j'arrivais pas à le dire. J'arrivais pas, c'est le différence entre le E et le je sais pas quoi. Et euh c'était pas du tout le bon phrase euh. Et en plus je savais que il y avait le possibilité qu'il va mal l'interpréter, parce que je sais très bien ce que ça veut dire. Et j'ai espéré que peut-être que dans le contexte de ce qu'on a parlé que euh (.) Mais non, il a dit euh "Bon c'est très xxx de toi de dire quelque chose comme ça, euh c'est sympa, mais en même temps on est pas dans un relation comme ça". J'ai dit "Oh il a pas compris" (Caroline/V3Q6).
[Well the night before he had spilled a glass of water on me. So I wanted to say "soak", [not] "cheat", that was it. But I couldn't say it. I couldn't, it is the difference between the E and the I don't know what [sound]. And it was not at all the right expression. And I knew that he might misunderstand, because I know very well what it means. And I hoped that maybe in the context euh (.). But no, he said, "Well, it is very xxx (?) of you to say something like that, it is nice, but at the same time we are not in that kind of relationship". I said "Oh, he didn't understand".]

In conclusion, this chapter has allowed us to make progress in linking together the social experience of the sojourn, and L2 development in a multilingual environment. By focusing on L2 gain, we have been able to show the overall importance of both diversity and intensity in L2 social networks for development of important aspects of L2, confirming and extending the suggestions of other researchers (Baker-Smemoe et al., 2014; Gautier & Chevrot, 2015; Klapper & Rees, 2012). Through a case study approach, we have been able to identify sojourner characteristics which promote L2 social networking, in a multilingual environment, separately or in combination: a clear vision of the ideal multilingual self, flexibility and resilience, emotional engagement (Kinginger, 2008; Pavlenko, 2005; Pellegrino Aveni, 2007). A strategic approach, and strong capacity for self-reflection, could help (Jackson, 2012), but these were not obvious characteristics of all high gainers; openness and responsiveness could also lead to intensive networking and in turn high gain. And finally, we have been able to sketch some aspects of intensive L2 relationships which challenge existing L2 proficiency and drive forward development. Deeper investigation of these relational dynamics is a major challenge for future research.

In the next chapter, we consider the implications of these findings for the professional design and management of the sojourn.

References

Baker-Smemoe, W., Dewey, D. P., Bown, J., & Martinsen, R. A. (2014). Variables affecting L2 gains during study abroad. *Foreign Language Annals*, 47(3), 464–486.

Dewey, D. P., Belnap, R. K., & Hilstrom, R. (2013). Social network development, language use, and language acquisition during study abroad: Arabic language learners' perspectives. *Frontiers: The Interdisciplinary Journal of Study Abroad*, 22, 84–110.

Dewey, D. P., Bown, J., & Eggett, D. (2012). Japanese language proficiency, social networking, and language use during study abroad: Learners' perspectives. *Canadian Modern Language Review*, 68(2), 111–137.

Gautier, R., & Chevrot, J.-P. (2015). Social networks and acquisition of sociolinguistic variation in a study abroad context: A preliminary study. In R. Mitchell, N. Tracy-Ventura, & K. McManus (Eds.), *Social interaction, identity and language learning during residence abroad*. EUROSLA Monographs 4 (pp. 169–184). Amsterdam: European Second Language Association.

Hernández, T. A. (2010). The relationship among motivation, interaction, and the development of second language oral proficiency in a study-abroad context. *The Modern Language Journal*, 94(4), 600–617.

Jackson, J. (2012). Education abroad. In J. Jackson (Ed.), *The Routledge handbook of language and intercultural communication* (pp. 449–463). Abingdon/New York: Routledge.

Kinginger, C. (2008). Language learning in study abroad: Case studies of Americans in France. *The Modern Language Journal*, 92(Special issue), 1–124.

Kinginger, C. (2015). Language socialization in the homestay: American high school students in China. In R. Mitchell, N. Tracy-Ventura, & K. McManus (Eds.), *Social interaction identity and language learning during residence abroad* (pp. 53–74). Amsterdam: European Second Language Association.

Klapper, J., & Rees, J. (2012). University residence abroad for foreign language students: Analysing the linguistic benefits. *Language Learning Journal*, 40(3), 335–358.

Pavlenko, A. (2005). *Emotions and multilingualism*. Cambridge: Cambridge University Press.

Pellegrino Aveni, V. (2007). Speak for your self: Second language use and self construction during study abroad. In S. Wilkinson (Ed.), *Insights from study abroad for language programs* (pp. 99–115). Boston, MA: Thomson Heinle.

Plonsky, L., & Oswald, F. L. (2014). How big is "Big"? Interpreting effect sizes in L2 research. *Language Learning*, 64(4), 878–912.

Tracy-Ventura, N., Dewaele, J.-M., Koylu, Z., & McManus, K. (2016). Personality changes after the "year abroad"? A mixed methods study. *Study Abroad Research in Second Language Acquisition and International Education*, 1(1), 107–127.

Whitworth, K. F. (2006). *Access to language learning during study abroad: The roles of identity and subject positioning*. (PhD), Pennsylvania State University.

10 Advising and supporting Anglophone sojourners
Key issues

There are numerous existing guides and discussions of good practice during study abroad (Beaven & Borghetti, 2015; Jackson, 2012, In press; Roberts, Byram, Barro, Jordan, & Street, 2001; Wilkinson, 2007). This brief concluding chapter does not replace these. We briefly draw a set of conclusions from the theoretical framework and empirical findings presented in earlier chapters, focusing on the particular circumstances of the Anglophone sojourner abroad. We believe these will be useful both for those advising Anglophone languages students undertaking residence abroad in multilingual environments, and for the students themselves, in order to progress toward what are usually ambitious goals of social and cultural engagement and L2 development.

The world is multilingual

Everywhere sojourners are likely to go, more than one language will be present, and people encountered will be plurilingual. Many of these people will know English and will be anxious to practise it. Anglophone students should not expect "immersion", either cultural or linguistic, and devices such as language pledges will offer only short-term protection, if any. Anglophone sojourners who are motivated to acquire L2s need to know that this is a choice, not a necessity, and that they will need to exercise active agency in order to achieve it. However, their English is a positive cultural asset too, which can open doors to local networks through teaching, through tutoring, through language tandems, and through the workplace. The desire of others to learn and practise English is reasonable, and LANGSNAP offers many examples of sojourners who successfully negotiated language exchanges, in many forms, using these both as immediate L2 learning opportunities and as entry points to L2 social networks.

The sojourner is plurilingual

Sojourners themselves are plurilingual, and they have complex emotional attachments and needs attaching to all of the languages they know. Continuing use of L1 is a normal part of the sojourn experience, and sojourners should not feel guilty about this; language pledges and so on can perform no more than a short-term, bootstrapping function. The internet offers direct access to home networks, and this can be an important means of reducing early homesickness and culture shock, and of providing ongoing emotional support, throughout the sojourn. Again, LANGSNAP offers positive examples of sojourners who made high L2 gains while staying in regular contact with family and friends at home and networking through English with Anglophone and international peers met abroad. However, unreflecting acceptance of such English-using networks as the principal/only social investment when abroad will clearly restrict L2 development. We have no examples in LANGSNAP of high gainers who did not have at least one intensive L2 network, or alternatively, many diverse L2 networks. We also see that high gainers become increasingly active as consumers of L2 resources online and start to participate in L2 virtual social networks, too.

Sojourner identity is many stranded

Whether at home or abroad, sojourners are emerging adults (Arnett, 2014), and "coming of age" will form an important part of their experience (Wolcott, 2013). In important respects, life insojourn will have continuity with life at home, involving, for example, much activity with a same-aged peer group in leisure time, and the emergence of romantic relationships. Compared with the value attached to peer group life, the placement and its associated activities may have only secondary importance.

In the right circumstances, this commitment to collective peer group living and leisure can lead to intensive local networking, as we have seen with successful flatshares and with engagement in activities such as sport or music. However, not all sojourners can find local flatmates, or show sporting or musical talent. In more general terms, the LANGSNAP evidence shows that high gainers are those who are most socially flexible, willing to network with age groups other than their own, willing to try new activities (e.g., to undertake service learning and volunteering), and well engaged with their placement. Again, sojourners need to manage their networking expectations and be willing to show such flexibility if they are to maximize L2 growth.

Sojourners must be problem-solvers

As emerging adults, sojourners are gradually tackling the challenges of independent living; once insojourn, they are confronted with a rush of practical problems all at once. Renting an apartment, registering for courses, opening bank accounts or getting a mobile phone will likely work differently in the host country and be particularly challenging in a new language, at a time when even making a phone call can seem very scary. However, sojourners can and do solve these problems, and in most cases they are excellent opportunities for growth, which once completed will likely have a positive influence on their self-confidence. The LANGSNAP evidence suggests not only that solving these problems can contribute to a sense of self-efficacy, but that this may then lead to greater willingness to tackle risk and more fundamental challenges as the sojourn progresses. For example, some high gain LANGSNAP participants were prepared to move house one or more times, until they found more inviting living arrangements.

Short-term and long-term ideal L2 selves

Almost universally, the LANGSNAP sojourners expressed similar short-term objectives for L2 development during the sojourn: to become orally fluent, and to acquire informal registers of language which they felt appropriate to their "emerging adult" life stage. For many, their student identity receded, and L2 literacy received little attention.

However, the sojourn experience had also reinforced participants' future aspirations to develop as plurilingual actors with mobile lifestyles and – possibly – international careers. For this type of future ideal self, "emerging adult" L2 proficiency will not necessarily be sufficient. Sojourners thus need to reflect more deeply on these longer-term ideal selves, and on how to exploit the many opportunities available insojourn to develop a more rounded L2 proficiency, including high levels of L2 literacy. There were examples of this among the LANGSNAP participants, but it is clear that many need additional encouragement to think longer term.

Intercultural learning

Again it is clear from the LANGSNAP evidence that the temporary nature of the sojourn, combined with the sojourners' emerging adult status, shields many sojourners from deep engagement in local society, so that many have not reflected deeply on cultural issues, and talked about cultural difference using a vocabulary drawn from stereotypes of everyday life. However, there were some encouraging examples of sojourners who had exploited their prior learning in the home university to develop a relativistic perspective on culture and to draw on theoretical resources to address difficult social issues such as racism. It is clearly challenging, but not impossible, for educators concerned with developing their students as "intercultural speakers" to make the sojourn a central learning opportunity. We believe that LARA-style training (Roberts et al., 2001) presojourn, plus encouragement and support for reflection both insojourn and especially afterwards, provide the necessary framework for this.

Engaging in the placement

Accounts in the literature regarding sojourners' engagement in the specific activities of their placement are variable (Alred & Byram, 2006; Ehrenreich, 2006; Murphy-Lejeune, 2002). Clearly, however, all placements offer distinctive challenges, both cultural and linguistic, and are important sites for learning of both types. LANGSNAP sojourners undertaking a university placement were faced with new registers related to university life, and a new pedagogic culture, as well as different expectations regarding prior content knowledge; some students remained resistant to unfamiliar teaching styles and assessment practices, throughout their entire stay. Teaching assistants encountered new speech styles related to pedagogy, as well as different classroom cultures; workplace interns were faced with the task of acquiring the relevant register and vocabulary for the area they were working in. Again, various forms of placement-specific preparation could reduce culture shock and facilitate social insertion. These could include not only familiarization with relevant linguistic registers, but also encouragement to adopt a relativistic cultural perspective and spirit of ethnographic enquiry when encountering new study/workplace norms.

Touristic travel

Some writers on the sojourn abroad have criticized sojourner in-country travel as conflicting with local engagement and networking in a particular locality (Adams, 2006). However, it is clear that for the sojourners themselves, regional travel is a central part of the overall experience. The LANGSNAP sojourners all engaged in some form of cultural or touristic excursions, often with fellow sojourners or visiting family, and spoke enthusiastically about these experiences and the encyclopedic cultural knowledge they had developed in this way. Yet it was clear that there were indeed tensions in many cases between extensive travel and local network development.

Educators therefore need to understand better sojourners' enthusiasm for travel, and how to maximize its contribution to intercultural learning. Again, reflection presojourn on the purposes of touristic travel, on different types of travel choice, and on how these contribute to or conflict with other goals of the sojourn, could help sojourners to manage this aspect of their stay abroad in a more strategic way.

Conclusion

This whole book should be read as strongly committed to the sojourner experience. The LANGSNAP evidence confirms its irreplaceable educational value and life-transforming character for participants. We have concentrated throughout on the Anglophone dilemma in a multilingual world, and we have shown how motivated Anglophones can navigate their way to plurilingual practice and advanced L2 competence in contemporary conditions. We hope that many more Anglophones will continue to have the opportunity to do so, and that the LANGSNAP project can help them and their mentors to be successful. We are developing a set of resources to support study abroad programme designers and leaders, drawing on the LANGSNAP experience, and these can be consulted at http://generic.wordpress.soton.ac.uk/langsnapguides/.

References

Adams, R. (2006). Language learning strategies in the study abroad context. In M. A. DuFon & E. Churchill (Eds.), *Language learners in study abroad contexts* (pp. 259–292). Clevedon: Multilingual Matters.

Alred, G., & Byram, M. (2006). British students in France: 10 years on. In M. Byram & A. Feng (Eds.), *Living and studying abroad: Research and practice* (pp. 210–231). Clevedon: Multilingual Matters.

Arnett, J. J. (2014). *Emerging adulthood: The winding road from the late teens through the twenties* (2nd ed.). Oxford: Oxford University Press.

Beaven, A. & Borghetti, C. (Eds.) (2015). *Intercultural education resources for Erasmus students and their teachers*. Koper: Annales University Press.

Ehrenreich, S. (2006). The assistant experience in retrospect and its educational and professional significance in teachers' biographies. In M. Byram & A. Feng (Eds.), *Living and studying abroad: Research and practice* (pp. 186–210). Clevedon: Multilingual Matters.

Jackson, J. (2012). Education abroad. In J. Jackson (Ed.), *The Routledge handbook of language and intercultural communication* (pp. 449–463). Abingdon/New York: Routledge.

Jackson, J. (In press). Training for study abroad. In Y. Y. Kim (Ed.), *The Wiley-Blackwell encyclopedia of intercultural communication*. Hoboken, NJ: Wiley-Blackwell.

Murphy-Lejeune, E. (2002). *Student mobility and narrative in Europe: The new strangers*. New York: Routledge.

Roberts, C., Byram, M., Barro, A., Jordan, S., & Street, B. (2001). *Language learners as ethnographers*. Clevedon: Multilingual Matters.

Wilkinson, S. (Ed.). (2007). *Insights from study abroad for language programs*. Boston, MA: Thomson Higher Education.

Wolcott, T. (2013). An American in Paris: Myth, desire, and subjectivity in one student's account of study abroad in France. In C. Kinginger (Ed.), *Social and cultural aspects of language learning in study abroad* (pp. 127–154). Amsterdam: John Benjamins.

Names index

Adams, R. 38, 41, 205, 252
Ågren, M. 76
Aguerre, S. 40–1
Ahrens, J. 2
Alarcón, I.V. 107
Allen, H.W. 36, 73
Alred, G. 39, 251
Arche, M. 59, 107
Armstrong, N. 20
Arnett, J.J. 38, 159, 250
Ascensión-Delaney, Y. 107

Back, M. 74
Baker-Smemoe, W. 42–3, 163, 247
Ballatore, M. 5
Bardel, C. 73, 78
Barkhuizen, G. 11, 35, 210
Barro, A. 6, 37, 249
Barron, A. 35
Bartning, I. 24, 72–3
Baschung, K. 66
Baumeister, R.F. 29
Bazergui, N. 68, 74–5, 127
Beaven, A. 249
Beeching, K. 20
Behrent, S. 9–10, 23–4
Belnap, R.K. 9, 42, 74, 134, 223
Benjamin, C. 18–19
Benson, P. 11, 35, 36, 210
Berthoud, A.-C. 20
Bhaskar, R. 30
Blackledge, A. 20
Blattner, G. 73
Bley-Vroman, R. 57
Block, D. 9, 11, 28–9, 30, 31, 33, 171
Blommaert, J. 4
Blum, S.D. 38
Board, K. 2
Bodycott, P. 11, 35, 210

Borghetti, C. 249
Bosker, H.R. 28, 68, 110
Bot, K. de 42
Bowden, H.W. 57
Bown, J. 9, 42, 137, 223
Bracke, A. 40–1
Breidbach, S. 2
British Academy 2, 3
Brown, J. 11, 35, 210
Brown, L. 22
Bulté, B. 26, 66
Busse, V. 3, 29, 196
Butler, J. 28
Butt, J. 18–19
Byram, M. 1, 5, 6, 10, 37, 39, 249, 251

Canagarajah, S. 2
Carey, A.G. 38
Carlo, C. 72
Carroll, J.B. 7, 73
Castañeda-Jímenez, G. 109
Chafer, T. 4, 43, 162
Chambers, F. 28
Chaudron, C. 57
Chevrot, J.-P. 9, 42, 163, 247
Chipere, N. 27
Cohen, A.D. 73
Coleman, J.A. 4, 5, 43, 73, 162
Collentine, J. 8, 77, 78, 107, 108
Comajoan Colomé, L. 117
Commission on the Abraham Lincoln Study Abroad Program 6
Comp, D. 6
Compernolle, R.A. van 19, 23, 73
Connor-Linton, J. 20
Cook, H.M. 22, 25
Cox, J.G. 76, 108
Creese, A. 20
Crystal, D. 20, 26

256 *Names index*

D'Amico, M.L. 107, 127
Daniels, H. 39, 40, 41
David, A. 77, 109
De Clercq, B. 26–7, 77
De Federico de la Rúa, A. 39
De Haan, P. 107
De Jong, N. 28, 68, 110
DeKeyser, R. 8, 24, 75–6, 78, 128, 129
DePaul, S.C. 6
Dervin, F. 1, 5, 10, 23, 28, 31, 190
Desmets, M. 66
De Swaan, A. 1, 4, 220
Deulofeu, J. 72
Dewaele, J.-M. 72, 73, 196, 225
Dewey, D.P. 8–9, 23, 24, 42–3, 61, 68, 74, 75, 134, 137, 223, 225
De Winter, U.J. 7
Dimova, S. 1, 20
Doble, G. 5, 7, 40, 73
Doerr, N.M. 19
Domínguez, L. 59, 107
Dörnyei, Z. 3, 29
DuFon, M.A. 22
Duperron, L. 76
Duran, P. 27
Dyson, P. 5, 73, 74

Education First 4
Eggett, D. 9, 42, 137, 223
Ehrenreich, S. 10, 39–40, 251
Ercolani, A.P. 64
Escobar, A.M. 42
European Commission 2
Evans, C. 5
Extra, G. 20

Fafulas, S. 108
Fagyal, Z. 42
Farrell Whitworth, K. 33
Ferencz, I. 5
Findlay, A. 2
Finn, K. 38, 159
Florij, A. 28
Foote, R. 107
Ford, P. 6
Forsberg Lundell, F. 73
Foster, P. 26, 67, 77
Frain, M. 6
Freed, B.F. 7–8, 8–9, 61, 68, 74–5, 76, 77, 106–7, 127, 128

Gadet, F. 20
Gallagher, J. 4
Gallego Balsà, L. 22, 220

Garcia, O. 2, 21
García-Amaya, L. 107, 108, 127
Gardner, D. 9, 42
Gardner-Chloros, P. 21
Garrett, P. 22, 220
Gasser, L. 42
Gautier, R. 9, 42, 163, 247
Geeslin, K.L. 107, 108
Ginther, A. 57
Godfrey, L. 26, 76, 77
Goldoni, F. 32, 33, 41
Granfeldt, J. 76–7
Granger, C. 72
Granger, S. 65
Grey, S. 76, 108
Grin, F. 20
Gudmestad, A. 107
Gudmundson, A. 78
Guijarro-Fuentes, P. 72, 107
Gunnarsson, C. 76–7
Guntermann, G. 76, 106, 108, 127, 129

Haberland, H. 1
Halter, R. 8–9, 61, 74
Hancock, V. 73
Härkonen, A. 31
Hasler-Barker, M. 108
Hawkins, E. 4
Hawkins, R. 18–19, 68, 74–5, 127
Healey, F.G. 5, 37
Henriksen, N. 108
Hernández, T.A. 106, 127, 225
Higgins, T.E. 29
Hilstrom, R. 74, 134, 223
Hoffa, W.W. 6
Holdsworth, C. 38
Holliday, A. 37
Holton, M. 38
Housen, A. 11, 25–6, 27, 66, 76
Howard, M. 8, 21–2, 73, 76, 78, 129, 211
Huensch, A. 110, 112
Huguet, Á. 20
Hülmbauer, C. 21
Hulstijn, J.H. 28
Hultgren, A.K. 1, 20

Ife, A. 77, 108–9, 129
Iino, M. 22, 220
Inagaki, S. 66, 76, 107
Irie, K. 29
Isabelli, C.A. 76, 108, 129
Isabelli-García, C. 9, 33, 42, 75, 108, 128
Iwasaki, N. 35
Iwashita, N. 57, 110

Jackson, J. 9, 37, 219, 247, 249
Jarvis, S. 67, 109
Jenkins, J. 2
Jensen, C. 1, 20
Johnston, B. 6
Jones, E. 30
Jones, G. 77
Jordan, S. 6, 37, 249

Kalocsai, K. 1, 23, 190
Kaltschuetz, D. 25
Kanwit, M. 108
Keller, J.M. 6
Kemp, J. 59
Kihlstedt, M. 27
Killam, J. 108
Kim, H.-Y. 66, 76, 107
Kim, J.O. 72
King, R. 2
Kinginger, C. 2, 3, 4, 7, 8, 9, 10, 19, 21, 22, 23, 25, 32, 33, 38, 40, 43, 57, 68, 73–4, 127, 205, 219, 229, 247
Kirkpatrick, A. 1
Klapper J. 8, 41, 76, 223, 225, 247
Klein, W. 24
Kolb, C. 2
Kormos, J. 27
Kovàcs, E. 23
Koylu, Z. 196, 225
Kramsch, C. 28, 29, 37
Kuiken, F. 11, 25, 27, 76–7
Kurata, N. 42

Labeau, E. 27
Lafford, B.A. 19, 74, 75, 105
Lakkaraju, K. 42
Lambert, C. 27
Langley, J. 59
Lanvers, U. 2
Lasagabaster, D. 20
Lawton, W. 30
Lazar, N. 75, 77, 107, 128
Lemée, I. 8, 21–2, 73, 211
Lennon, P. 27
Leonard, K.L. 107
Leone, L. 64
Lindkvist, C. 78
Llanes, À. 8, 25, 75–6, 128
Long, M.H. 24
Lonsmann, D. 1
Lord, G. 107, 108
Lörz, M. 196
Lozano, C. 60
Lüdi, G. 20

Ludwig, R. 20
Lv, J. 57
Lybeck, K. 42

McCarthy, P.M. 67
Macdonald, M.M. 30
Machart, R. 10
McManus, K. 27, 57, 64, 79, 88, 91, 110, 124, 165, 196, 225
MacWhinney, B. 58–9, 64, 67
Maeda, Y. 57
Magnan, S.S. 19, 74, 75
Maiworm, F. 1, 20
Malvern, D. 27, 67
Mar-Molinero, F.C. 20
Marsden, E. 7, 77, 109
Martínez-Gibson, E.A. 107
Martinsen, R.A. 42
Meara, P.M. 61, 74, 77, 97, 108–9, 125, 129
Meier, G. 39, 40, 41
Mellors-Bourne, R. 30
Mendikoetxea, A. 60
Mercer, S. 36
Merkx, G. 4
Merritt, M. 6
Messelink, A. 10
Milroy, L. 42, 139–40
Milton, J. 61, 77, 97, 125, 129
Mitchell, R. 6, 7, 59, 64, 79, 88, 91, 107, 110, 124, 165
Möhle, D. 76
Monto, M.A. 38
Montrul, S. 107
Mora, J.C. 68, 74, 75, 128
Mougeon, R. 73
Muller, N. 72
Murphy-Lejeune, E. 10, 11, 31–2, 33–4, 38, 39, 40–1, 43, 205, 219, 251
Myles, F. 6, 7, 59, 65, 107

Nadasdi, T. 73
Netz, N. 196
Nichols, A. 37
Nishida, C. 76, 108, 129
Norris, J.M. 11, 25, 57, 110
Norton, B. 28
Nott, D. 5

O'Connor DiVito, N. 90
O'Regan, J.P. 30
Ortega, L. 11, 25, 57, 110
Oswald, F.L. 79, 110, 223
Oudenhoven, J.P. van 64, 196

Paffey, D. 19
Paige, R.M. 73
Pallotti, G. 26
Papatsiba, V. 37, 38, 39, 41, 205, 219
Pascual y Cabo, D. 25
Patron, M.-C. 9
Pavlenko, A. 29, 247
Peckham, D.J. 23
Pellegrino Aveni, V. 11, 22, 32, 33, 247
Perdue, C. 24, 72
Pérez-Vidal, C. 8, 26, 107
Perpiñán, S. 107
Perugini, M. 64
Phipps, A. 37
Pinget, A.-F. 28, 68, 110
Plews, J. 11, 31, 34, 205
Plonsky, L. 79, 110, 223
Polanyi, L. 7–8, 32, 33
Preisler, B. 1
Prévost, P. 72
Prodeau, P. 72

Quast, H. 196
Quené, H. 28, 68, 110

Rabie, S. 57, 110
Rampton, B. 4
Raupach, M. 76
Rees, J. 8, 41, 76, 223, 225, 247
Regan, V. 8, 21–2, 24, 73, 211, 220
Rehner, K. 73
Richards, B. 27, 67
Ridder-Symoens, H. de 4
Rindler Schjerve, R. 20
Ring, S. 9, 42
Rivers, W.P. 2
Roberts, C. 6, 37, 249, 251
Robinson, J.P. 2
Rodríguez-Sabater, S. 107
Rothman, J. 25
Rowles, D. 5
Rowles, V. 5
Rowlett, P. 66
Rüegg, W. 4
Rumbley, L.E. 7
Ryan, S. 29

Salaberry, M.R. 107
Sanders, T. 28, 68, 110
Sankarayya, U. 5, 7, 40, 73
Sanz, C. 8, 76, 108
Sasaki, M. 68, 107, 128
Schauer, G.A. 8
Schlyter, S. 72
Schmitz, K. 72

Schoonen, R. 28
Segalowitz, N. 8–9, 28, 61, 68, 74, 75, 106–7, 127
Seidlhofer, B. 21
Selwyn, N. 38
Serafini, E.J. 76, 108
Serrano, R. 75–6, 77, 78, 128, 129
Sharifian, F. 1
Sherman, T. 23
Shiri, S. 22–3
Shively, R.L. 25, 73
Siegal, M. 22, 35
Skehan, P. 25, 28, 68, 110
Smithers, A. 5, 7, 40, 73
So, S. 75, 77, 107, 128
Steinel, M.P. 28
Stern, H.H. 5
Stevens, D. 37
Stewart, Melissa 32, 33
Stewart, Miranda 20
Stoessel, S. 42
Stolte, R. 3, 196
Street, B. 6, 37, 249
Swarup, S. 42

Taguchi, N. 10, 22, 35
Talburt, S. 32, 33
Tarone, E. 26, 76, 77
Tavakoli, P. 28, 68, 77, 110
Taylor, F. 29
Teichler, U. 1, 5
ten Thije, J.D. 10
Tidball, F. 77–8
Tinsley, T. 2
Tonkyn, A. 67
Toris, C.C.M. 107
Towell, R. 18–19, 68, 74–5, 127
Tracy-Ventura, N.K. 57, 59, 79, 107, 110, 112, 124, 126, 165, 196, 209, 225
Tragant, E. 75–6, 128
Treacy, C. 26, 76, 77
Treffers-Daller, J. 77–8
Trentman, E. 32–3, 41, 162, 205
Trévise, A. 72
Twombly, S. 32

UNESCO 1
Uscinski, I. 105

Valls-Ferrer, M. 68, 74, 75, 128
Van der Zee, K.I. 64, 196
Van Esch, K. 107
Van Mol, C. 31
Vedder, I. 11, 25, 76–7
Véronique, D. 72

Vetter, E. 20
Vives Boix, G. 77, 108–9

Wächter, B. 1, 20
Walters, J. 59
Weedon, C. 28, 29
Wei, L. 2, 21
Weyers, J.R. 107
Whitworth, K.F. 42, 225
Wigglesworth, G. 67
Wiklund, I. 42
Wilkinson, J. 37
Wilkinson, S. 19, 22, 33, 73, 249

Williams, L. 19, 23, 73
Williams, M. 3, 29, 196
Willis, F. 5, 7, 40, 73
Wit, H. de 4
Wolcott, T. 7, 38, 39, 250
Wolfe-Quintero, K. 26, 66, 67, 76, 91, 107, 121
Woodfield, S. 30

Yager, K. 76, 106, 127
Ya mur, K. 20
Yan, X. 57
Yang, J.-S. 8, 73, 74, 75, 109

Subject Index

accuracy, analysis of 27, 67, 84, 89, 107–8, 115, 117, 119
accuracy, definition of 25, 27
accuracy, L2 development 27, 75–6, 78, 84–91, 108, 115–21, 128, 129, 222
activity theory 36
advanced learner variety 24, 25, 37, 72–3, 74–5, 76, 78, 84
agency 30, 163, 171, 172, 187, 189, 190, 194–5, 222, 226, 232, 233, 234, 243, 244, 245, 249
American Council on the Teaching of Foreign Languages (ACTFL) 74, 106
Analysis of speech unit (ASU) 26, 67, 84, 89, 90, 108, 109, 111; ASU, definition of 67; Error-free ASUs 84–5, 98, 113, 115–17, 126, 128
Analysis of Variance (ANOVA) 110, 113, 121
Anglophone L2 learners/sojourners 1, 2, 3, 4–8, 9, 10–11, 18, 19, 20, 21–3, 25, 29, 31, 36, 39, 42, 44, 52, 105, 117, 144, 149, 150, 163, 189, 190, 194, 202, 205, 228, 233, 234, 235, 236, 239, 240, 243, 244, 245, 249–52
Arabic 2, 4, 20, 22, 23
at-home/SA L2 learning comparisons 7, 8, 75, 76, 77, 106–7, 107–8, 128, 129
attitudes *see* motivation
attrition 53, 113, 124, 128
autonomy *see* independence

Basque 20, 170, 178, 193

CAF framework 11, 25–6, 27, 57, 58, 66–8, 73, 76, 77, 79, 108, 110
Caisse d'allocation familiale (CAF) 145, 183, 185–6
case study 33, 42, 107, 108; *see also* LANGSNAP participants

Castilian 174, 178, 193, 229
Catalan 20, 22, 193
CHAT transcription system 58, 59, 64, 66
Chinese 4, 20, 55
Christmas 43, 148, 160, 162–3, 231, 237, 243, 245
CLAN 67, 96, 123
clause, definition of 66; error-free clauses 27, 67, 84, 85, 89–90, 109, 115–17, 119–20, 126, 128, 222, 224–7; ratio of clauses to T-units 26, 66, 77, 91–3, 121–3, 126; ratio of finite clauses to all clauses 66, 91, 94–6
codeswitching 20, 21
Cohen's *d* 79, 81–4, 86, 88, 90–3, 96–7, 110, 113–15, 118–21, 124, 126
colloquial language 19, 158, 211, 211
coming of age 31, 32, 36, 38, 40, 209–15, 219, 234, 236, 250
community 11, 139; classroom community 37; community of practice 39, 40–1; host/local community 9, 32, 230, 237–8
complexity, syntactic/structural 11, 25, 26, 60, 66, 72, 73; analysis of 26, 66, 91, 121; definition of 25, 26; L2 development of 75, 76–7, 78, 91–6, 108, 121–3, 129; *see also* L2 French development; L2 Spanish development
critical realism 30
Cronbach's alpha 64, 165
culture 5, 6, 11, 20, 32, 33, 34, 37, 40, 144, 159, 162, 179, 199–203, 219, 240, 251; academic/educational culture 7, 39, 40, 208, 251–2; cultural empathy 64, 196; cultural relativism 203, 251; culture shock/challenges 31, 33, 199, 233, 237, 243, 244, 250, 252

declarative knowledge 24, 129
dialect 19, 22, 212

domestic settings *see* living arrangements
Dutch 106, 107

Elicited imitation (EI) 57–8, 72, 79–80, 110–11, 127, 222, 223–4, 225, 226
emotional engagement/support 142, 146, 159, 162, 163, 194, 205, 228, 236, 247, 249, 250
Emotional stability 64, 196, 209
employability 30, 38
English: as hypercentral/global language 2, 20, 220, 244, 249; as lingua franca (*see* lingua franca usage); as medium of instruction 1, 6, 20, 232; use of English abroad 165, 167, 168, 169, 171, 173–4, 175–6, 182, 189–92
Erasmus scheme 2, 5, 24, 31, 39, 55, 179; Erasmus students 23, 41, 142, 146, 147, 153, 179–80, 188, 190, 205, 206, 216, 232, 233, 234, 238, 239, 240, 241
ethnicity/race 29, 204–5
ethnocentricity 33–4
ethnorelativism 33–4, 36
Eurocentres Vocabulary Size Test 77
European Economic Community 5
examinations 38, 152, 196, 204, 208, 238, 241, 242

Facebook *see* Online activity
family (of sojourner) 3, 20, 23, 36, 40, 43, 134, 139, 145, 148, 150, 161, 162–3, 170, 171, 189, 196, 202, 228, 231, 232, 235–6, 237, 240, 242, 245, 250; visits by sojourner's family 148, 150, 156, 161, 162–3, 189, 228, 231, 232, 237, 240–1, 243, 250; visits to family at home 43, 161, 162–3, 237
feature reassembly 25
Finnish 170
flexibility 31, 64, 196, 225, 238, 245, 247, 250
fluency 8, 27–8, 67–8, 105, 110, 211, 214, 220, 222, 225, 234; breakdown fluency 27, 68, 75, 107, 111; fluency, analysis/ measures of 67–8, 80, 107, 111, 113; fluency, definition of 25, 27–8; fluency, oral 27, 74, 80, 98, 106–7, 109, 111, 126, 127–8, 129, 206, 210, 219, 239, 242; fluency, written 27, 68, 80, 82–4, 107, 108, 113–15, 126, 128, 129; fluency development 24, 74–5, 78, 80–4, 98, 106–7, 111–15, 127–8; *see also* L2 French development; L2 Spanish development; repair fluency 27, 68, 75, 107, 111; speed fluency 27, 67, 75, 80–2, 107, 111–13; utterance fluency 27, 67, 75, 81, 107, 111–13
Foreign Service Institute Oral Interview 106
free time/leisure practices, general 11, 18, 20, 23, 38, 39, 41, 62, 134, 135–7, 140, 142, 145, 250; cultural activities 41, 157, 174, 237; festivals/demonstrations 156, 193, 203, 241; "going out"/casual meetings 41, 135, 145, 149, 151, 160, 163, 190, 228, 233–4, 235, 237, 238, 239, 240–1; home cooking, meals and entertaining 9, 41, 145, 146, 151, 157, 258, 177, 201, 233, 240–1; reading 145, 213, 231–2, 242; touristic travel 38, 41, 135, 146, 148, 149, 150, 156, 159–61, 162–3, 190, 231, 237, 241, 243–4, 245, 252; using media (films, TV) 41, 145, 146, 151, 179, 231, 233–4, 238
free time/leisure practices, organized 38, 41, 62, 63, 134, 135–6, 145, 250; craft 145, 155, 237; music 41, 142, 143, 154, 155, 157, 158–9, 171, 186; religious practice 145, 179; sport 39, 41, 135, 142, 143, 145, 149, 150, 154–5, 158, 171, 186, 228–30, 232–3, 237, 240; student associations 145, 153–4; voluntary work 41, 153–4, 228–30, 237, 250
Friedman test 79, 81, 82, 83, 84, 85, 86, 88, 89, 90, 91, 92, 96, 115, 118, 119, 124
friendship 23, 38, 39, 139, 197; Anglophone peer friends 33–4, 43, 134, 145, 148, 149, 150, 163, 173, 189–90, 231–2, 233–4, 235–6, 237, 239–40, 241, 242, 244; home friends 11, 23, 43, 161, 162–3, 189, 215–16, 231, 232–3, 240, 242, 244, 245; international peer friends 38, 43, 134, 142–3, 146–8, 149–50, 153, 163, 179–80, 215, 228, 230–1, 232, 233–4, 239, 240–1, 245; local friends (non-peers) 134, 157–9, 237, 240; local peer friends 32, 41, 43, 58, 134, 142, 143, 147, 150–6, 163, 172–3, 228, 231–2, 233–4, 235–6, 237, 238–9, 240, 241, 242–3; workplace colleagues 32, 144, 150, 157–8, 235–6, 237

Galician 20
gender 9, 19, 29, 31, 32–3, 36, 152, 159, 197–9, 205, 219; gendered subject positions 22, 32–3, 197–9

Subject Index

German 3, 4, 7, 8, 36, 39, 41, 53, 55, 74, 106, 170, 187, 192, 193, 214
goals/expectations of sojourners 30, 36, 142–4, 197, 206, 214, 251
goals of SA programmes 5–6
grammaticality judgement test 64, 108
grammaticalization 24

high gain sojourners 12, 41, 42–3, 163, 222, 225, 226–44, 245, 248, 250, 251
history of study abroad 4–7
home life *see* living arrangements
homestay *see* living arrangements
home university 1, 5, 6, 10, 38, 52, 55, 57, 114, 116, 120, 124, 167, 196, 209, 251; home university classes 55, 114, 115, 126, 192, 203, 205, 215, 216; home university preparation 142, 197, 205; home university project 167, 168, 170, 193, 205, 208, 213, 234, 237, 243, 246

identity 9, 28–36, 196–220, 250–1; ideal L2 self 3, 11, 29, 36, 210, 214–15, 217, 219, 220, 232, 239, 245, 247, 251; identity, British 202–3; identity, definitions of 28–9; identity, social construction of 29, 35, 210, 220; identity-related L2 proficiency 35, 210–14, 251; L2 identity 11, 23, 25, 35, 52, 58, 68, 73, 196–205, 209, 210–15, 219–20, 222, 238, 245; L2-related personal competence 36; sojourner/Erasmus identity 11, 22, 31–2, 33, 34, 35, 36, 68, 142, 203, 205–9, 226, 233; student identity 11, 36, 38, 159, 206–9, 215–16, 220, 250; workplace intern identity 206–7
ideology 11, 19, 34
idiomaticity 211–12, 214
immersion 8, 11, 19–20, 23, 43, 73, 75, 232, 249
independence 5, 30, 31, 36, 156, 157, 206, 209, 215
individual differences 8, 9
informal speech *see* register
intelligibility 210
interaction 9, 10, 19, 20, 21, 22, 23, 24, 25, 29, 32, 33, 34, 41, 42, 43, 65, 75, 137, 140, 165, 181, 199, 210–11, 216, 234, 235, 239, 242, 244
intercultural awareness/sensitivity 3, 4, 5–6, 7, 9, 30, 37, 43, 186, 219; presojourn intercultural training 37, 251–2

intercultural competence 11, 18, 33, 36, 37, 38
intercultural learning 1, 10, 31, 32, 33, 37, 38, 147, 205, 251–2
intercultural speaker/self 18, 34, 37, 219
International Baccalaureate 196
internet *see* online activity
interpersonal skills 30
IRIS repository, the 62, 63
"island" programmes 7, 39
isolation/loneliness 4, 154, 162, 236, 244
Italian 7, 55, 77, 152, 170, 192, 239, 241

Japanese 4, 8, 10, 22, 35, 42, 106, 170
Junior Year Abroad 6

L1 French speakers 55, 57, 65, 88, 90; comparison with L2 speakers 79, 81, 82, 83–4, 91–2, 92–3, 95–6, 97
L1 Spanish speakers 53, 55, 57, 65–6; comparison with L2 speakers 108, 110, 112, 113–14, 122–3, 124–5, 126, 129
L1 speaker/native speaker 19, 111, 187, 220; L1 speaker corpus/ corpora 61, 88, 90; L1 speaker judgements 27, 106; L1 speaker norms/usage 19, 27, 35, 37, 76, 88
L2 development 7, 8, 9, 10, 11, 25, 33, 52, 57, 72, 73, 134, 150, 222, 223, 225, 228, 241, 245, 247, 249, 250, 251; L2 development, opportunity for 3, 8, 43, 45, 78, 153, 171, 181, 183, 191, 193, 251; L2 development, timing 88–9; L2 development, ultimate achievement 8, 223; L2 development, variability in 7, 8, 25, 74, 76, 78, 81, 82, 85, 89, 90, 92, 95, 105, 110, 114, 116, 119, 120, 127, 223; *see also* L2 gain
L2 engagement 42, 43, 55, 61–2, 78, 165–71, 176, 222–3, 225, 226, 229, 232, 236, 239, 245
L2 French development 72–98, 127–9; accuracy, oral 75–6, 84–9, 98; accuracy, written 75, 89–91; discourse 72; fluency, oral 74–5, 80–2, 98; fluency, written 75, 82–4; formulaic language 73; grammatical gender 27, 76, 185; *Imparfait* (IMP) 27, 67, 76, 84, 85–7, 128–9; information structure 72; lexical diversity 96–7, 98; lexis 73, 77–8, 96–8; morphosyntax 72, 76, 79–80; *Passé composé* (PC) 67, 76, 84, 87–8, 128–9; proficiency 73, 74, 79–80, 98; receptive lexical knowledge 97–8; sociolinguistic

variation 73; sociopragmatics 73; subjunctive mood 64, 67, 76, 84, 88, 89, 90–1; syntactic complexity 75, 76–7, 91–6, 98; tense and aspect 25, 27, 65, 67, 76
L2 gain 223–6; high gain sojourners 222, 225–44, 245, 248, 250; L2 gain scores 222, 225–6
L2 input 8, 19, 24, 25, 232
L2 motivational self system 3, 29; ideal L2 self (*see* identity)
L2 proficiency 2, 3, 5, 7, 8, 11, 24, 25, 27, 35, 37, 42, 57, 72, 74, 77, 78, 79, 88, 105, 106, 109, 203, 214, 222, 251; identity-related L2 proficiency (*see* identity); insojourn L2 proficiency development 73, 74, 79, 98, 105, 106, 110–11, 126, 127, 225, 244, 248; measurement of L2 proficiency 42, 57–8, 74, 79, 106, 110; presojourn L2 proficiency 43, 129, 223, 225, 226, 230, 238
L2 Spanish, development 105–29; accuracy, oral 107–8, 115–19, 126; accuracy, written 107–8, 126; fluency, oral 106–7, 111–13, 126, 251; fluency, written 107, 113–15, 126; grammatical gender 25, 107, 108; imperfect (IMPF) 67, 108, 115, 117–19, 126, 128–9; lexical diversity 109, 123–3; lexis 108–9; number 108; preterit (PRET) 67, 108, 115, 117–19, 128–9; proficiency 106, 110–11, 126; pronoun system 25; receptive lexical knowledge 109, 125–6; *ser/estar* 107, 108; sociolinguistic variation 108; subjunctive mood 107, 108, 109, 213; syntactic complexity 108, 121–3; tense and aspect 25, 67, 107–8
L2 use 23–4, 165–94; bilingual/mixed language practices 165, 167, 175, 178, 182; L2 use measures 8–9, 61–2; relationship with L2 development 9, 222–47; use of French in France 165–7; use of other languages 165, 170–1, 192–4; use of Spanish in Mexico 165, 169–70; use of Spanish in Spain 165, 167–9
LANGSNAP instruments: argumentative essay 60–1, 65, 66, 67, 68, 80, 82–4, 89–91, 91–6, 113, 119–21, 121–4, 129; background questionnaire 53; Brothers Story 59; Cat Story 59; Elicited Imitation Test (French) 57–8, 79–80, 127, 222–5; Elicited Imitation Test (Spanish) 57–8, 110–11, 127, 222–5; *Gay Marriage* prompt 60–1, 83, 91, 93–5, 122–3; grammaticality judgment test 64; *Junk Food* prompt 60, 83, 91, 93–5, 122–3, 129; Language Engagement Questionnaire 55, 61–2, 165–71, 183, 222–5, 227, 228, 229, 230, 232, 233, 235, 236, 238, 239; *Marijuana* prompt 60, 83, 91, 93–5, 122–3; Multicultural Personality Questionnaire 55–7, 64, 196, 209, 225; oral interview (French/ Spanish) 58, 60, 64, 65, 66, 67, 68, 84, 88, 96, 123–5, 134, 142, 151, 159, 165, 171, 175, 190, 193, 197, 199, 203, 204, 208, 209, 214, 215, 216, 217, 219, 228, 234, 240, 244; oral picture-based narratives 59, 65–8, 80, 82–3, 84–8, 111–13, 115–19, 121, 123–4, 126, 128; participant observation 64–5; reflective interview 57, 64, 68, 197, 210; Sisters Story 59; Social Network Index (L1), (L2) 134, 139, 140–1, 222–9, 230, 232, 233, 235, 236, 238, 239; Social Networks Questionnaire 55, 62–3, 134, 137–9, 222, 228–9, 234, 235, 239, 240; Swansea Levels Test X-Lex 61, 97–8, 125–6
LANGSNAP participants 10, 18, 52–5, 69, 196; Alice 238–9; Caroline 235–6; case studies 69, 157, 161, 177, 222, 228–44; Heather 239–42; Kirsten 232–3; L1 French group 55; L1 Spanish group 55; L2 French group 53–5; L2 Spanish group 54–5; Lucy 236–8; Megan 242–4; Nadia 233–5; Rosie 230–2; Terence 228–30
LANGSNAP project: data collection schedule 55–6; learner corpus/digital repository 58, 65–6, 69; project aims 52; project overview 10–11
Language Contact Profile 8–9, 61, 74
language pledge 20, 23, 249
language variation 19, 20, 22, 77; age based variation 19, 211; class based variation 19, 20; regional variation 19, 20, 22, 174, 212, 220; sojourner attitudes toward variation 21–3, 193–4, 211–12, 220; *see also* sociolinguistic variation
LARA project 6, 37, 251
leisure practices *see* free time
length of stay 8, 109, 129, 244

264 Subject Index

lexical complexity 11, 26–7, 66–7, 78, 96–7, 98, 108–9, 123–5; lexical complexity measure *D* 27, 67, 96–7, 123–5; lexical density 26–7; lexical diversity 26–7, 66–7, 77–8, 96–7, 105, 109, 123–5, 129; lexical richness/sophistication 26–7, 78
lexis 8, 24, 60, 73, 105, 129; L2 development of 76, 77–8, 96–8, 123–7, 129, 212–13; receptive vocabulary knowledge 77, 97–8, 125–7; receptive vocabulary measures 61, 77
lingua franca usage 2, 20, 21, 23, 188, 245; English as lingua franca (ELF) 1, 2, 4, 6, 10, 21, 23, 165, 180, 187, 188, 189, 190, 232; French as lingua franca 23–4, 171, 179, 187–9, 232; Spanish as lingua franca 171, 179, 187–9, 231, 239, 240
listening comprehension 74, 210, 240–1
living arrangements: domestic practices/home life 134, 135, 136, 137, 146, 151, 171–5; homestay 8, 22, 40, 143, 144, 149, 150, 154, 228, 230, 242, 244; institutional accommodation 40–1, 149, 174–5, 236; living alone 40, 144, 149, 235, 237; relations with host family 22, 40, 156–7, 174, 228–30, 231, 242, 244; shared apartments 40–1, 144, 149, 150–2, 232, 233, 235, 238, 239, 244
local attachment/identification 202, 230, 238, 242, 243–4
low gain sojourners 41, 42–3

Mann-Whitney U test 79, 81, 82, 84, 91, 97
Mayan 171, 192, 193
mentors 20, 39, 68, 155, 158, 176, 182, 194, 232, 252
metalinguistic awareness 8
morphosyntax 7, 8, 24, 25, 76; *see also* L2 French development; L2 Spanish development
motivation 3, 4, 29, 30, 36, 42, 163, 172, 174, 193, 204, 211, 214, 236
multilingualism/plurilingualism 2, 3, 4, 11, 20, 21, 205, 218, 219, 220, 244, 249, 251; multilingual communities/environment 3, 11, 20, 37, 165, 171, 182, 244, 245, 247, 249, 252; multilingual subject, multilingual identity (*see* self, multilingual); plurilingual practices 21, 23, 44, 61, 139, 182, 194, 220, 242, 252

nationality 9, 29, 31, 33–4, 36, 197, 199–203, 219, 232, 240; co-national friendships 33, 39, 43, 197; national stereotypes 199, 201, 203
negotiation of difference/of identity 7, 40
negotiation of language use 24, 171, 239; at home 171–5; at leisure 192; through music 186; in private tutoring 183; in schools 175–9, 191; in service encounters 171, 183–6, 189, 190–2; through sports 186; in tandem language exchanges 182–3; at university 179–81; at the workplace 181
new strangers 31–2, 205, 219
Norwegian 106
Número de identidad de extranjero (NIE) 145, 183
NVivo 68

online activity 4, 11, 43, 45, 62, 63, 134, 135, 136, 137, 145, 146, 162, 163, 165, 166, 168, 169, 171, 183, 189, 216, 228, 231, 232, 235–6, 237, 239, 240, 242, 245, 250
Openmindedness 31, 64, 196, 248
Oral Proficiency Interview (OPI) 42, 74, 75, 106

Peace Corps 106, 108
personal development 5, 10, 11, 37, 38
personality 11, 55–7, 59, 64, 196, 209, 225
placement contexts: host school 5, 39, 135, 143, 146, 149, 150, 155–6, 170, 175–9, 184, 188, 193, 195, 201, 202, 204, 228, 236–7, 242–3, 245, 252; host university 22, 40, 41, 62, 93, 135–7, 140, 142, 143, 144, 147, 148, 152–3, 155, 161, 179, 183, 190, 193, 207, 208, 230, 233, 239, 240, 241, 242, 245, 251; host university classes 143, 152–3, 155, 167, 170, 172, 180, 182, 190, 192, 193, 206, 208, 214, 230, 232, 233–4, 238–9, 240, 242, 245; host workplace 135–7, 140, 142, 182, 245, 252
placement roles 8, 18, 31, 39; exchange student 1, 5, 10, 39, 41, 55, 109, 142–3, 144–8, 150, 151, 152, 157, 174, 183, 190, 206, 207–8, 213, 214, 226, 232, 233, 234, 238, 239, 241, 245; language assistant 4–5, 10, 20, 31, 39–40, 55, 135, 136, 142, 143, 144–8, 149, 150, 155, 175–8, 183, 188, 190, 198, 203–4, 207, 208, 213, 226, 228–9, 230, 236–8,

242; workplace intern 5, 10, 20, 40, 55, 135, 136, 141, 144, 145, 149–50, 158, 175, 181–2, 206–7, 208, 213, 226, 235–6, 237, 245, 252
Polish 20, 55, 170, 193, 219
politeness 7, 22, 25, 35, 200, 234
Portuguese 53, 55, 152, 170, 171, 192, 193
Praat 68
pragmatics/sociopragmatic competence 7, 8, 21, 24, 25, 35, 73, 105, 210
proceduralization 24

qualitative research methods: case study 33, 42, 107, 108, 225; conversational analysis 9, 10; interview 9, 42; learner diaries 42; observation 9, 42

reading 36, 41, 74, 167, 168, 169, 171, 213, 216, 231, 232, 244, 245
reference grammar 18, 19
reflection/reflective capacity 36, 37, 64, 68, 142, 180, 205, 214, 219, 247, 251, 252
register 19; formal *vs*. informal 19, 20, 35, 73, 211–12, 213–14, 220, 234, 251
repair 23–4, 28, 75, 107; *see also* fluency
resilience 31, 233, 238, 247
return to study 215–16
romantic partners 32, 33, 36, 38, 43, 139, 150, 152, 157, 159–62, 163, 189, 190, 198–9, 216, 219, 231–2, 234, 235–6, 240, 242–3, 244, 250
Russian 7, 170, 192

second language acquisition 2, 7–10, 24–5, 26, 52, 65; Generative theory 24–5; Interaction Hypothesis 24; language socialization 9, 10, 22, 25; learner corpus research 52, 60, 65; skill acquisition theory 24; The social turn 9
Self, the: actual self 29; ideal self 29, 232, 233, 239, 247; L2 self *see* identity; linguistic self concept 35–6; multilingual self 23, 24, 28, 64, 218, 219, 230, 232, 233, 236, 238, 239, 242, 247, 249; ought self 3, 29; private self 29, 35; public self 29, 35, 180
self-awareness 5, 28, 219
self-confidence *see* self-efficacy
self-development 206
self-discovery 31
self-efficacy 5, 30, 36, 64, 185, 186, 196, 209, 220, 234, 235, 238, 244, 250
self-reliance 5, 36

service encounters 8, 166, 167, 168, 171, 183–6, 189, 198, 206
sexual activity 38, 159, 197
sexual harassment 7–8, 32, 159, 198
Shapiro Wilk test 79
short-term study abroad 20, 105, 107, 108
Simulated Oral Proficiency Interview (SOPI) 106
Skype *see* online activity
social class 19, 29, 197, 203–4, 205; migratory elite 31, 197
Social initiative/adaptability 64, 196, 241, 245
social media *see* online activity
Social network analysis (SNA) 9, 41–3; Network Strength Scale 139; SA Social Interaction Questionnaire 42
Social Network Index (L1) (L2) 134, 139, 140, 222, 223, 225
social networks 11, 38, 41–3, 68, 239; density 42, 140, 163; dispersion/diversity 42, 163, 231, 247; durability/strength 42, 134, 137, 140, 141, 163; intensity/frequency 42, 134, 137–9, 163, 247; multiplexity 42, 140; and language change 42; and language development 42–3, 163, 222–5, 226–7, 232, 239, 244–5, 247–8; and language use 42–3, 134–7, 139–42, 150–6, 163, 171, 179, 186–7, 189–90, 194–5, 223, 229, 231–2, 233–4, 237, 239, 240–1; longitudinal network development 43, 134; size 42, 134–7, 140
social relations *see* friendship
sociocultural research *see* qualitative research methods
sociolinguistic competence 9
sociolinguistic variation 7, 8, 19, 20, 21, 42, 211; in L2 French development 35, 73, 210–12; in L2 Japanese 35; in L2 Spanish development 105, 108, 210–12
sociopragmatic competence *see* pragmatics
speech rate 68, 75, 80–2, 89, 107, 111–12, 127, 222, 223, 225
standard language 4, 18, 19, 20, 24, 174, 192, 220, 241
Statistical Package for the Social Sciences (SPSS) 68
Swedish 106

tandem exchanges 142, 147–8, 153, 171, 177, 182–3, 216, 249

266 Subject Index

target language 7, 10, 11, 18, 20, 21, 22, 23, 39, 64, 142, 171, 190, 196, 202, 210, 216, 220
teachers 39, 143, 146, 149, 157–8, 175, 176–8, 179, 182, 183, 191, 194, 202, 203, 204, 228, 230, 231–2, 236–8, 242–3
Test de français international 74
Three Word Association Test (A3VT) 109
"Top 5" contacts 63, 137–9, 140, 237, 240
translanguaging 2, 3, 20, 21, 43
transnational identity 36, 216–19
t-test 126
T-units 26, 66, 67, 76, 89, 109, 128; definition of T-unit 66; error-free T-units 67, 89–90, 107, 108, 119–21; mean length of T-unit 26, 76, 91, 92–4, 107, 121–3, 126, 128; ratio of T-units to clauses *see* clause

tutoring, private 157, 159, 183, 228, 237
type-token ratio (TTR) 67

valenciano 20, 170, 171, 178, 193, 194, 230
vernacular language *see* register
virtual context *see* Online activity
vocabulary *see* lexis
VocD 67, 96, 123

Welsh 170, 171
Wilcoxon Signed Rank test 79, 81, 82, 83, 85, 86, 88, 90, 91–2, 96, 97
world language system 1–2, 220; central languages 2; hypercentral/global language 2, 20, 220, 244, 249; peripheral languages 2; supercentral languages 2, 4, 8, 220

X-Lex test 61, 97–8, 125–6, 129